a Portuguesa de

s

Globalização e os fundamentos da cidadania

Grafia atualizada segundo o Acordo Ortográfico da Lín
1990, que entrou em vigor no Brasil em 2009.

Edição: Haroldo Ceravolo Sereza/ Joana Monteleone
Editora assistente: Danielly de Jesus Teles
Projeto gráfico, diagramação e capa: Jean Ricardo Frei
Assistente de produção: Emerson Dylan
Assistente acadêmica: Bruna Marques
Revisão: Alexandra Colontini
Imagens da capa: <*pixabay.com*>

CIP-BRASIL. CATALOGAÇÃO-NA-FONTE
SINDICATO NACIONAL DOS EDITORES DE LIVROS, RJ

G478

Globalização e os fundamentos da cidadania
Organização Murilo Gaspardo. - 1. ed.
São Paulo : Alameda, 2017.
P. : IL. ; 21 CM

Inclui bibliografia
ISBN: 978-85-7939-444-7

1. Direito público. I. GASPARDO, Murilo.

17-46561 CDU: 342

ALAMEDA CASA EDITORIAL
Rua 13 de Maio, 353 – Bela Vista
CEP 01327-000 – São Paulo, SP
Tel. (11) 3012-2403
www.alamedaeditorial.com.br

Introdução

Murilo Gaspardo

Desde 2013, o Departamento de Direito Público (DDPB) da Faculdade de Ciências Humanas e Sociais (FCHS) da Universidade Estadual Paulista "Júlio de Mesquita Filho" (UNESP) – Campus de Franca – SP realiza, anualmente, o "*Seminário de Direito do Estado*". O evento integra as atividades de pesquisa, estudos e divulgação da produção científica dos grupos de pesquisa "Governança global, direitos humanos e democracia", "Núcleo de estudos de Justiça Constitucional e democracia", e "Direito Regulatório" (certificados pelo CNPq), além do projeto de extensão "Núcleo de Cidadania Ativa da UNESP/Franca – SP" (reconhecido e financiado pela Pró-Reitoria de Extensão Universitária da UNESP).

A primeira edição do Seminário compreendeu a realização de 2 conferências seguidas de debates. A partir dessa experiência, traçamos alguns objetivos para o evento: (1) criar um espaço para debate anual da produção intelectual do próprio Departamento; (2) estruturar seus eixos temáticos de forma harmônica com a área de concentração e as linhas de pesquisa do Programa de Pós-graduação em Direito da FCHS/UNESP; (3) ampliar o diálogo com pesquisadores de outras instituições brasileiras por meio conferências e sessões de comunicações orais de trabalhos de pesquisa; (4) abordar temas academicamente relevantes; (5) participar do debate público sobre os problemas políticos e jurídicos contemporâneos; (6) buscar o reconhecimento e o apoio de agências de fomento à pesquisa; (7) a internacionalização.

A partir da segunda edição, passamos a incluir na programação a apresentação e o debate de comunicações orais de pesquisas científicas, com participação somente de alunos da própria FCHS, bem como a publicação de Anais reunindo o conjunto dos trabalhos apresentados em sua versão completa. A partir da terceira edição, começamos a receber pesquisadores da região de Franca – SP, sendo que na quarta foram apresentados mais de 100 trabalhos de autores de diversos estados brasileiros. Outro passo importante do IV Seminário, realizado em 2016, foi a internacionalização: além de renomados conferencistas brasileiros, contamos com as participações do professor e ativista no campo da democracia global Fernando Iglesias, da Argentina, e do professor e pesquisador Giovanni Allegretti, do Centro de Estudos Sociais (CES) da Universidade de Coimbra, Portugal – processo que teve continuidade em 2017, ocasião em que recebemos o Professor David Held, da Universidade de Durham, Reino Unido.

"Reforma Política nos 25 Anos da Constituição Federal de 1988", "Novas Perspectivas para a Democracia Brasileira" e "Teorias da Constituição e Novas Concepções de Cidadania" foram os temas das três primeiras edições do Seminário. Em 2016, o tema escolhido para o IV Seminário de Direito do Estado foi "Globalização e os Fundamentos da Cidadania".

Discutir os impactos da globalização sobre a compreensão e o exercício da cidadania é uma tarefa imprescindível tanto para acadêmicos que atuam no campo do Direito e das Ciências Sociais em geral, como para as lideranças políticas e a sociedade civil. Trata-se de questão extremamente relevante, quando se considera, por exemplo, que: decisões fundamentais são tomadas em arenas internacionais em relação às quais o controle da cidadania é frágil ou inexistente; diante da crise migratória, a compreensão dos direitos de cidadania restritos aos nacionais revela-se insuficiente; fatores de ordem global, como a crise econômica internacional e as mudanças climáticas, impõem severas limitações à capacidade de os Estados implementarem políticas públicas – indispensáveis para a concretização dos direitos de cidadania; o nacionalismo, a xenofobia e o autoritarismo avançam em todo o munto.

Vivemos, pois, no Brasil e no mundo, tempos de crise das instituições, de retrocessos nos direitos humanos e ameaça aos pilares da cidadania e da convivência democrática. O que a comunidade acadêmica tem a dizer sobre esse contexto? Seremos capazes de dialogar com movimentos sociais e lideranças políticas para ajudar a forjar alternativas aos tempos sombrios que atravessamos?

Esta obra coletiva, que resultou das atividades desenvolvidas durante o IV Seminário de Direito do Estado da UNESP/Campus de Franca – SP, aborda essas e outras questões em uma perspectiva multidisciplinar.

Este livro é composto por 13 Capítulos divididos em 3 blocos: no primeiro deles (Capítulos 1 a 4) encontramos as contribuições de autores convidados do exterior; no segundo (Capítulos 5 a 7) são abordados fundamentos teóricos e questões gerais sobre globalização e cidadania; já no terceiro (Capítulos 8 a 13), os trabalhos tratam de problemas mais específicos (como governança ambiental e cidadania) e da interface entre as dimensões global e nacional na compreensão do sentido, dos limites e das perspectivas para a cidadania.

No capítulo de abertura ("Broken Politics: from 9/11 to the present"), David Held trata dos sinais de colapso da ordem política liberal estabelecida após a Segunda Guerra Mundial, dos fatores que explicam a situação em que nos encontramos hoje e das tendências que podem ser identificadas.

Na sequência, Giovanni Allegretti aborda o tema "Incentivare la partecipazione cittadina in una epoca di populismi: alcuni esempi internazionali per pensare all'attivazione di circoli virtuosi". O autor problematiza a banalização da ideia de participação cidadã e o consequente esvaziamento de seu sentido e de sua força política, resultando em processos "pseudo-participativos". Por outro lado, destaca experiências fundadas na diversidade de formas participativas nas quais a participação é efetiva, e não apenas ritual e retórica, revelando potencial para revitalização da democracia.

Fernando Iglesias, por sua vez, trata de "Citizenship in the age of Globalization" a partir da discussão sobre dois projetos específicos de inovação institucional na esfera global, em relação aos quais também é politicamente engajado: a criação da Corte Penal Latino-americana e do Caribe contra o Crime Organizado (COPLA) e da Assembleia Parlamentar das Nações Unidas (UNPA). Para tanto, o autor retoma as origens do conceito de cidadania e cidadão, analisando sua transformação em face da globalização, o que exige que a democracia seja pensada para além da concepção e das instituições nacionais, de maneira que a grande questão política é "como construir uma ordem democrática global baseada na cidadania universal?". É a partir desses fundamentos que se desenvolvem as campanhas pela criação da COPLA e da UNPA: a primeira com o objetivo de enfrentar a criminalidade organizada, o que não tem ocorrido de forma satisfatória pela ação dos Estados; e a última com a finalidade de viabilizar a representação democrática em escala global.

Fechamos o primeiro bloco do livro com o artigo de Maria Hylma Alcaraz Salgado sobre "La garantía del contenido esencial de los derechos fundamentales". A autora discute o significado, o conteúdo essencial, a garantia e a função social dos direitos fundamentais, bem como a aplicação dos princípios da ponderação e da proporcionalidade.

No capítulo 5, iniciando as discussões dos autores brasileiros sobre os fundamentos teóricos a propósito da relação entre globalização e cidadania, Regina Laisner escreve sobre o tema "Diálogos teóricos dos modelos de 'globalização' da democracia: intersecções entre Ciência Política e Relações Internacionais". A autora traça um panorama sobre os quatro principais modelos normativos para a democracia transnacional: o liberal-internacionalista, o pluralista radical, o cosmopolita e o deliberativo. Para tanto, a autora tem como referência a Teoria Política, mas, ao mesmo tempo, procura aprofundar as perspectivas para a aplicação de tais modelos ao debate no campo das Relações Internacionais.

Em seguida, Caio Gracco Pinheiro Dias trata da relação entre "Direito Internacional e governança global". Inicialmente, o autor revisa o conceito de governança global para, em seguida, tratar do Direito Internacional como uma das instituições por meio das quais ela se opera. A partir dessas premissas, o autor analisa as alterações no sistema internacional de uma perspectiva histórica e teórica, desde os antecedentes da Organização das Nações Unidas até o contexto contemporâneo, bem como seus impactos para a governança global e para o Direito Internacional, culminando no que David Held, Thomas Hale e Kavin Young denomina de *gridlock*, na revalorização da soberania estatal e do nacionalismo, bem como na fragilização do sistema da ONU e do Direito Internacional em sua capacidade de garantir a ordem, paz e a segurança.

Ainda neste bloco, Marcela Benhossi e Daniel Campos de Carvalho exploram o "fortalecimento dos primados democráticos nas práticas e na retórica da governança internacional contemporânea", por meio da análise da cidadania no processo de integração da Europa e nas experiências sul-americanas (UNASUL e MERCOSUL).

Passando aos trabalhos que tratam de problemas mais específicos, no Capítulo 8, David Succi Júnior e Samuel Alves Soares discorrem sobre "A hibridização das Forças Armadas no Brasil: as missões policializadas e as debilidades democráticas e estratégicas".

Na sequência, temos dois capítulos voltados para a temática ambiental. Fernanda Mello Sant'Anna e Júlia Abdalla Lunardi discutem os impasses da governança ambiental no que se refere ao acesso e ao uso dos recursos naturais, especialmente a água e a energia, ambos fundamentais para a organização social e a qualidade de vida de todos. Além disso, tratam dos conflitos sociais envolvendo esses recursos e o papel do Estado, apresentando o "caso do nexo entre água e energia e suas implicações para os países e a sociedade em geral".

Já Maria Galleno de Souza Oliveira e José Carlos de Oliveira dissertam sobre "os desafios da construção de políticas de enfrentamento aos riscos de desastres: reflexões sobre a inclusão da participação efetiva dos afetados". Os autores problematizam a própria concepção de "desastres socioambientais", analisando suas implicações, classificação, as instâncias e os instrumentos por meio dos quais se opera sua governança, o quadro brasileiro, bem como os meios para seu enfrentamento, que devem incluir o protagonismo da população local na construção de políticas públicas.

Os capítulos 11 e 12 abordam questões pertinentes ao exercício da cidadania no âmbito brasileiro. Murilo Gaspardo e Liz Marina Tamião Santana discutem as condições histórico-sociais de exercício da cidadania no Brasil, sintetizadas pela ideia de cidadania bloqueada, que deve ser tomada como condicionante (não determinante) em quaisquer projetos de reforma institucional do sistema democrático. O trabalho tem como pressuposto a concepção de que a compreensão abrangente sobre os dilemas contemporâneos da cidadania deve considerar tanto os fatores globais como os nacionais e suas implicações recíprocas.

José Duarte Neto e Guilherme Pinho Ribeiro analisam a atuação das Comissões Parlamentares de Inquérito no Senado Federal na 52ª e na 53ª Legislaturas. Para tanto, tomam como referência a constatação segundo a qual a corrupção é uma das maiores dificuldades para o desenvolvimento sustentável e o exercício pleno da cidadania no mundo globalizado, bem como de que "a soberania do Estado ainda remanesce como trincheira factível para qualquer combate em âmbito global".

Fechamos o livro com artigo de Paulo César Corrêa Borges e Paulo César de Oliveira Borges sobre um projeto de extensão universitária no campo da cidadania: "Fundamentos da cidadania para professores e alunos fundamentais: a integração da Pós-graduação com a Graduação, na Política Nacional de Extensão Universitária". Trata-se da avaliação de uma experiência exitosa de "ampliação da sala de aula, para além dos muros da universidade, como espaço privilegiado de ensino e de pesquisa, indissociáveis da extensão".

É indispensável registrarmos que o processo de internacionalização do Seminário de Direito de Estado e a publicação desta obra contou com apoio decisivo da CAPES, instituição à qual agradecemos imensamente. Esperamos, com este livro, dar continuidade aos debates do IV Seminário de Direito do Estado sobre as relações entre a globalização e os fundamentos da cidadania.

Broken Politics: from 9/11 to the present[1]

David Held

The inauguration of President Trump, the separation of the UK from the European Union, the rise of the populist right across the US and Europe, and the political clamp down in Turkey imposed by President Erdogan, are among countless signs that the postwar liberal order, established after 1945, has begun to collapse. The UN and EU were created to contain the outward aggression and inward brutality of states and to establish an overarching framework of international and regional law that made individual states subject, in principle, to the standards and requirements of human rights, responsible sovereignty and non-intervention. For nearly 70 years, these institutions helped engender an open and relatively stable world order that allowed the world economy to flourish, lifting many countries out of poverty, changing the balance of world economic power and establishing a much more plural and multipolar global system.

Yet, it also unleashed an untrammelled globalization, new patterns of winners and losers, and new global challenges that in the case of climate change pose existential threats. How did this happen? What

1 This essay examines some of the themes explored more fully in my recent EBook, *Global Politics after 9/11*, published by Global Policy and Wiley.

are the underlying trends? And where does this leave us today? This essay reflects on these big questions. It begins by examining the legacy of 9/11, which punctured the US's sense of invulnerability, and unleashed ill-thought-out violence across many parts of the world. 9/11 led to several failed wars, enflaming an already disorganized Middle East and North Africa and intensified huge global problems such as the spread of terrorism and forced migration. The essay then moves to the consider globalization and its impact on governance at many levels before it traces out the political pathways ahead.

9/11 and its Aftermath

9/11 was both a crime against the United States and a crime against humanity. Terrorism fuses the roles of judge, jury and executioner in the merciless pursuit of self-proclaimed causes. Faced with 9/11, the US and its allies could have come together to defend what was under outrageous attack: citizens from across the world, democracy, justice, and the rule of law. But they did not. The war in Iraq in particular undermined international law, weakened international institutions, and, along with the wars in Afghanistan, Libya and Syria, eroded stability and peace throughout the Middle East and elsewhere.

The post 9/11 wars were led by people that had no understanding of the countries they were fighting in, no grasp of the culture or language, no sense of the politics and the peoples, no account of local interests and divisions, and no plan for once the fighting had stopped. These wars were led by men who, at best, were gripped by the belief they had the ability to reshape and control other countries in their own image. In going to war in Afghanistan against Al-Qaeda, in Iraq against Saddam Hussein, in Libya against Colonel Gaddafi, and in Syria against Bashar al-Assad, the US and its allies entered protracted conflicts, different as these have been, which disorganised states, created vacuums, and opened up the spaces for armed groups and fanatical extremists to thrive among the chaos. Despite each war failing, one after another, the US and its allies appear to have learnt few lessons, and entered each war as if nothing had been grasped about previous conflicts.

Of course, there was a great deal to deplore about the autocratic regimes in these countries and the systematic abuse of human rights that was all too typical in each one of them. This is well known and amply documented. But outrage against these regimes is not enough to create informed judgements about how to change such states and societies. The transformation of countries is a very complex and difficult process. War is a blunt and weak instrument to change regimes, and it rarely works. The exceptional conditions which shaped the Second World War and after, which allowed the allies to occupy Germany and Japan and begin a process of reform, enabled the long-term reconstruction of these states and their democratic transformation. In contemporary circumstances, where democratic societies are hesitant to commit troops and are highly sensitive to the loss of national lives, on the one hand, and where globalization links people across the world, highlighting the costs and sacrifices involved in engagements of all kinds, on the other, these conditions are simply absent.

The creation of democratic states is, moreover, a long and arduous historical process, fraught with risk and uncertainty. The history of the West alone highlights the difficulties of nation-building, and of cultural change. Democracy took over three hundred years to reach its modern form in Europe, and even then it was nearly derailed by the rise of fascism, Nazism and Stalinism in the mid-twentieth century. The shift in people's identities from subjects to citizens, with equal rights and obligations in a political community, and where victory or defeat at the polls are prospects that have to be accepted, rests on intricate cultural processes. Separating individual identity as a member of a group, tribe, ethnic unit, or religious order from the culture and demands of citizenship involves an arduous and historically difficult set of transformations. The values and requirements of citizenship in a democracy come to trump those of other forms of social and cultural identification, such that being a member of a tribe or ethnic group is secondary to the rule of law and constitutional demands. These delicate processes of change cannot be short-circuited if democratic public life is to develop and prosper. And, yet, this is exactly what the post-9/11 wars sought to do, and failed to do. The most elementary understanding of democratic history would have warned Western political leaders and foreign policy makers against taking such a stance.

Minimum wisdom has shaped the post-9/11 era with all the consequences we live with today. Broken states across the Middle East, mass migration from and through warzones, the constant threat of terrorism, the rise of xenophobia and nationalism, and the mounting socio-economic challenges facing Western states constitute the current period. The one thing that all this should not be considered is a surprise. These difficult and challenging problems were the inevitable result of misconceived wars, and they plot the complex ramifications that have followed. One of the latter has been damage to the idea of democracy. How could democracy be a universal political ideal if it was used as one of the principle justifications of the disastrous post 9/11 wars? How much damage was done to democracy by the violent efforts to depose the Middle East autocrats in the name of democracy, and by all the death and destruction that followed? Even if it is true, of course, that the actual motives for the post 9/11 wars were mixed, including the pursuit of terrorists in Afghanistan, oil in Iraq and Libya and domestic electoral advantage in Libya and Syria, the idea of democracy and the pursuit of human rights became embroiled in the war makers' rhetoric.

The short-lived Arab Spring

Some of the consequences of this can be traced throughout the Arab Spring. The uprisings that swept across the Middle East in 2011 promised a political transformation as significant as that of 1989—the velvet revolution that brought down the Soviet Union and its satellite states. The economic stagnation of the region, the failures of corrupt and repressive regimes, conjoined with a disenchanted youthful population wired together as never before, triggered a political struggle few anticipated. Yet, almost from the outset, there was a lack of a common vision for the transformation of the political regimes and the wider the Middle East. The initial peaceful demonstrations in Tunis and Cairo quickly gave way to a messy and uncertain pathway of transition. A few years on the contagious revolutionary fervour faded as successor regimes failed to deliver quick or lasting improvements in living standards, the quality of life and governance. Moreover, the brutal civil war in Syria, the radicalisation of militia groups in Libya, and discrediting of the Muslim Brotherhood as a governing alternative in Egypt all strengthened the forces resisting change throughout the region. The removal of Mohammed Morsi from the Egyptian Presidency in July 2013 and consequent reinstatement of military-led rule encapsulated the stunning reversion to the *status quo ante* in the Arab world's most populous nation.

In 1989 the movements of Central and Eastern Europe by and large shared an ambition to topple their governments and replace them with Western European forms of democracy, the entrenchment of human rights and the benefits of consumer-led economic growth. As the direction of travel was in western interests, governments in Europe and North America wholeheartedly welcomed them. By contrast, the signifier 'democracy' carried much more complex meaning in the Arab world in 2011. This was because the West had propped up most of the Arab autocrats, seemed to switch sides to support the peoples seeking change only in the cynical last minutes, led a war against terrorism largely in the Arab world, which was perceived by young Arabs across the Middle East as imperialism in yet another manifestation. Against this background, democracy appeared all too readily as a veil masking the shifting tide of western geopolitical interests, propping up authoritarian leaders in the name of 'stability,' commercial and oil concerns, and support for Israel's security.

The factors underpinning the weakening of the Arab Spring and its subsequent usurpation by anti-revolutionary forces from within and outside the Middle East were complex and various. But the tainting of democracy by the post 9/11 wars was certainly one of the disorganizing and disorienting forces of the movements for change. Who gets what, when and why are no longer questions confined to particular state silos, democratic or otherwise. The era we live in today is one of both colossal promise and uncertainty. Why? One of the primary reasons is globalization, which has unsettled established political relations, altered labour market conditions, created dense webs of global economic interconnectedness, shifted the costs and benefits of established social and economic policy, and formed new patterns of winners and losers.

Globalization and Global Governance

Globalization is not a new phenomenon; various forms of globalization have developed over time from the spread of world religions and the rise of empires to the rebuilding of the world economy after the Second World War. The extensity, density and velocity of global interconnections today, however, were given an enormous impetus by the digital revolution and the advent of satellite communication. The epiphenomenon of these global shifts is the instantaneous movement of information, which has made social media a feature of everyday life across the world. But deeper shifts have occurred in the very way the world economy is organized making possible 24 hour trading in world financial markets, the stretching of the economic division of labour across the world, and the rapid movements of goods and services. In short, we have entered a world of overlapping communities of fate, where the fate and fortunes of countries have become increasingly intertwined in all aspects of life, from the economy to security and the environment.

Globalization today creates a world of remarkable opportunity and risk. Opportunity because a global division of labour, world trade patterns, global communication infrastructures, a rule based institutional order and a growing sense that action is needed now on global challenges creates unparalleled prospects for prosperity, development and peaceful coexistence. Risk because never before have human communities been so densely connected allowing a crisis in one place, whether economic or security driven, to ricochet across the world in seconds. Hence, the era is one of significant promise and colossal challenges. At the same time, the knowledge humankind has developed is no longer just an elite privilege; diffused and available on the internet (accessible to over a third of the world's population), the cognitive resources of science and culture can be explored and exploited by a diversity of actors, with benign or regressive intent.

The global challenges we face today cross many sectors of human life. But by and large they are indicative of three core types of problems – those concerned with sharing our planet (climate change, biodiversity and ecosystem losses, water deficits), sustaining our life chances (poverty, conflict prevention, global infectious diseases) and managing our rulebooks (nuclear proliferation, toxic waste disposal, intellectual property rights, genetic research rules, trade rules, finance and tax rules). In our increasingly interconnected world, these global problems cannot be solved by any one nation-state acting alone. They call for collective and collaborative action – something that the nations of the world have not been good at, and which they need to be better at if these pressing issues are to be adequately tackled.

Until recently, the West has, by and large, determined the rules of the game on the global stage. During the last century, Western countries presided over a shift in world power – from control via territory to control via the creation of governance structures created in the post 1945 era. From the United Nations and the formation of the Bretton-Woods institutions to the Rio Declaration on the environment and the creation of the World Trade Organization, international agreements have invariably served to entrench a well-established international power structure. The division of the globe into powerful nation-states, with distinctive sets of geopolitical interests, and reflecting the international power structure as it was understood in 1945, is still embedded in the articles and statutes of leading intergovernmental organizations, such as the UN, the IMF and the World Bank. Voting rights are distributed largely in relation to individual financial contributions, and geo-economic strength is embedded and integrated into decision-making procedures.

The result has been susceptibility of the major international governmental organizations (IGOs) to the agendas of the most powerful states, partiality in the enforcement of their operations (or lack of them altogether), their continued dependency on financial support from a few major states, and weaknesses in the policing of global collective action problems. This was dominance based on a 'club' model of global governance and legitimacy. Policy at the international level was decided by a core set of powerful countries, above all the G1, G5 and G7, with the rest largely excluded from the decision-making process.

Shifting Centre of Economic Gravity

Today, however, that picture is changing. The trajectory of Western dominance has come to a clear halt with the shortcomings and failures of dominant elements of western economic and security policy over the last three decades. The West can no longer rule through power or example alone. At the same time, Asia is on the ascent. Over the last half-century, East and Southeast Asia has more than doubled its share of world GDP and increased *per capita* income at an average growth rate almost 2½ times that in the rest of the world. In the last two decades alone, emerging Asian economies have experienced an average growth rate of almost eight per cent – three times the rate in the rich world. In the 1980s, the Asian tigers – South Korea, Taiwan, Hong Kong, Singapore – put themselves on the global economic map; from the 1990s onwards, India and China, among others, began to grow at unprecedented speed until, of course, China became the largest economy in the world (measured by Purchasing Power Parity) and the second largest (in nominal terms). This trend was given an enormous impetus by the financial crisis of 2008, which for several years saw a collapse and subsequent stagnation of growth of much of the West, while the Asian economies continue to grow at a rapid pace. These developments have generated a significant shift in the centre of economic gravity toward the East. In the nineteenth century, the world's centre of economic gravity lay somewhere in the mid-Atlantic. It is now shifting rapidly eastwards, and by 2050 is predicted on current trends to fall between India and China.

The trajectory of change is towards a multipolar world, where the West no longer holds a premium on geopolitical or economic power. Moreover, different discourses and concepts of governance have emerged to challenge the old Western orthodoxy of multilateralism and the post-war order. At the same time, complex global processes, from the ecological to the financial, connect the fate of communities to each other across the world in new ways, requiring effective, accountable and inclusive problem-solving capacity. How this capacity can be ensured is an altogether different matter.

While large parts of the world were in ruins after the Second World War, the US and its allies were able to create a new institutional architecture to help produce a form of 'governed globalization'. The UN system, the Bretton Woods institutions, and many more agencies, despite being shaped by American interests above all, put in place a rule-based international system that was sufficiently peaceful, open, and liberal to allow the world economy to take off once again. What is striking about this system is that, over time, it allowed new entrants to the world economy, not just on liberal terms, but on their own. India and China, along with other BRICS countries, are often understood to have been successful because they adopted the liberal rule structures of the post-war international economy. The mantra of the so-called Washington Consensus was that market liberalization and global market integration are the key to prosperity, and many economists have understood India and China's success in these terms. But the truth is that they managed their entrance into the world economy, only liberalizing sectors once they were strong, only lowering tariffs selectively, keeping hold of core investment decisions and maintaining managed currencies.

Of course, the post-war liberal order was far from peaceful for everyone. The US and the Soviet Union fought proxy wars across the world for nearly 50 years, and sought to carve out their own distinctive spheres of political economic influence. Nonetheless, the post-war institutional structures kept the Great Powers talking to each other and, along with the threat of mutually-assured destruction (MAD), created the conditions for a deepening of interdependence between them and their allies. The nuclear stand-off of the Cold War paradoxically drew world powers closer together as a way to mitigate the threat and ensure that military posturing did not escalate into all-out nuclear confrontation. Thus, despite all its complexities and risks, the post-Second World War era of 'governed globalization' contributed to relative peace and prosperity around the world over several decades. While the economic record of the post-war varies by countries and region, many experienced significant growth, and living standards rose rapidly across several parts of the world.

Gridlock and Multilateral Politics

The post-war institutions created conditions under which a multitude of actors could benefit from forming corporations, investing abroad, developing global production chains, and engaging with a plethora of other social and economic processes associated with globalization. This is not to say that they were the only cause of the dynamic form of globalization experienced over the last few decades. Changes in the nature of global capitalism, including breakthroughs in transportation and information technology, are obviously critical drivers of interdependence. Nonetheless, all of these changes were allowed to thrive and develop because they took place in a relatively open, peaceful, liberal, institutionalized world order. By preventing World War Three and another Great Depression, the multilateral order arguably did just as much for interdependence as digital communication, satellite technology, and email.

These developments, however, have now progressed to the point where it has altered our ability to engage in further global cooperation. That is, economic and political shifts in large part attributable to the successes of the post-war rule-based order are now amongst the factors grinding that system into gridlock. As a result of the remarkable success of global cooperation in the post-war order, human interconnectedness weighs much more heavily on politics than it did in 1945, and the need for international cooperation is marked. Yet the "supply" side of the equation, institutionalized multilateral cooperation, is stalling. In areas such as nuclear proliferation, the explosion of small arms sales, terrorism, failed states, global economic imbalances, financial market instability, global poverty and inequality, biodiversity losses, water deficits and climate change, multilateral and transnational cooperation is now increasingly ineffective or threadbare. Gridlock is not unique to one issue domain, but appears to be becoming a general feature of global governance: cooperation seems to be increasingly difficult and deficient at precisely the time when it is extremely urgent.

There are four reasons for this blockage, or four pathways to gridlock as they are called: rising multipolarity, institutional inertia, harder problems, and institutional fragmentation. Each pathway can be thought of as a growing trend that embodies a specific mix of causal mechanisms. First, reaching agreement in complex international negotiations is hampered by the rise of new powers like India, China and Brazil, which means that a more diverse array of interests have to be hammered into agreement for any global deal to be made. On the one hand, multipolarity is a positive sign of development; on the other hand, it can easily bring both more voices and interests to the table that are hard to weave into coherent outcomes. Second, the institutions created 70 years ago have proven difficult to change as established interests cling to outmoded decision-making rules that fail to reflect current conditions. Third, the problems we are facing on a global scale have grown more complex, penetrating deep into domestic policies and are often extremely difficult to resolve. Fourth, in many areas international institutions have proliferated with overlapping and contradictory mandates, creating a confusing fragmentation of authority.

These trends combine in many sectors to make successful cooperation at the global level extremely difficult to achieve. The risks that follow from this are all too obvious. To manage the global economy, prevent runaway environmental destruction, reign in nuclear proliferation, or confront other global challenges, we must cooperate. But many of our tools for global policy making are breaking down or inadequate – chiefly, state-to-state negotiations over treaties and international institutions – at a time when our fate and fortunes are acutely interwoven. Signs of this today are everywhere: climate change is still threatening all life as we know it, conflicts such as Syria continue to run out of control, small arms sales proliferate despite all efforts to contain them, migration has increased rapidly and is destabilising many societies, and inequality threatens the fabric of social life across the world. While it is far from gloom and doom in all respects, these are dangerous trends stemming from governance structures that are no longer fit for purpose.

Politics at a Crossroads

We are at a crossroads. One road points to the inexorable rise of authoritarianism, while another opens up a more hopeful cosmopolitan future. The path to authoritarianism can be created by the dangerous drift in the world order, and a search for decisive solutions from 'strong man' leaders faced with a world that is seemingly out of control and where a retreat to the familiar (and away from the Other) offers a tempting way forward. We see such trends across many different kinds of countries, from Brexit Britain to Trump's America, Duarte's Philippines, Putin's Russia, Modi's India, and Erdogan's Turkey. Of course, we have been here before. The 1930s saw the rise of xenophobia and nationalism in the context of prolonged and protracted economic strife, the lingering impact of World War I, weak international institutions and a desperate search for scapegoats. The 2010s has notable parallels: the protracted fallout of the global financial crisis, ineffective regional and international institutions, and a growing xenophobic discourse that places virtually all blame for every problem on some form of Other.

But there are alternative routes. To begin with, we have the option of recalling where the pursuit of authoritarianism leads. The routes chosen in the 1930s all led to calamity and destruction, and the rediscovery in the 1940s onwards of the dangers of simply putting up the shutters, pursuing protectionism and denying the equal dignity of each and all. The architects of the post-war era, who put in place a re-invigorated law of war and the human rights regime, set down elements of a universal constitutional order in which the principles of the equal moral standing of each and every person, and the equal rights and duties of each and all, became the bedrock of peace and stability.

Moreover, a cosmopolitan model of politics and regulation can be found in some of the most important achievements of law and institution building in the twentieth century. These developments set down a conception of rightful authority tied to human rights and democratic values which can be entrenched in wide-ranging settings. In this perspective, political power is legitimate, if and only if, it is democratic and upholds human rights. In addition, the link between territory, sovereignty and rightful authority is, in principle, broken since rightful authority can be exercised in many spheres and at many levels, local, subnational, national and supranational. Accordingly, citizenship can be envisaged, as it is already in the European Union, as equal membership in the diverse, overlapping political communities which uphold common civic and political values and standards. Citizenship, thus conceived, is not built on an exclusive membership of a single community but on a set of principles and legal arrangements which link people together in the diverse communities which significantly affect them. Accordingly, patriotism would be misunderstood if it meant, as it all too often has done, 'my country right or wrong'. Rather, it comes to mean loyalty to the standards and values of rightful authority – to common civic and political principles, appropriately embedded.

Suitably developed, this conception of global politics envisages a multilayered and multilevel polity, from cities to global associations, bound by common framework of law, a framework of law anchored in democratic principles and human rights. The state does not wither away in this conception; rather, it becomes one element in the protection and maintenance of political authority, democracy and human rights in the dense web of global forces and processes that already shape our lives. Perhaps more importantly still, it points to a political order no longer exclusively anchored in *raison d'état* and hegemonic state projects but in principles of global cooperation and cosmopolitan association.

The European Union in Crisis

The European Union today articulates some of these complex and contradictory trends. At its core the EU can be characterized as a Kantian project: an attempt to create a peaceful union of European states from the wreckage of the Second World War and the orgy of violence that left Europe broken and exhausted, cooperating on all transregional issues. This ideal remains fundamental to the European project even though the reality is fraught with the compromises of geopolitics. The EU has been through turbulent cycles of deepening and broadening – first the core states, then Spain, Portugal, Greece, then, after the fall of the Berlin Wall, membership was extended to central and eastern European states. But behind all the turbulent transitions, European leaders like Chancellor Kohl were eager to move forward the European ideal through the policy and practice of extending and entrenching the Union as a multilevel polity combining elements of supranational, national, regional and local governance.

However, this ideal is increasingly compromised by a series of regional and global challenges. The lingering impact of the global financial crisis on European economic growth, the collapse of the Greek economy and its aftermath, the unsettling impact of mass migration across

Europe's southern and eastern borders, and terrorism which has struck in Paris, Nice and Brussels, are, among other problems, testing the governance capacities of the Union itself. The governance capacity of the Union has typically been well adapted to a world of rising prosperity, which could accommodate key interests and allow all boats to rise together. Moreover, the European Union was strongly bound together in the post-war years because of two crucial social and symbolic experiences. The first of these was the Second World War and its legacy. The second was the Cold War which gave Europe a marked sense of negative integration. But when the Cold War came to an end and the threat of the Soviet Union was over, the question arose: what would bind Europe in the future? In the 1990s and early 2000s, faced with mounting economic and social difficulties, the EU needed positive ideals and norms of integration, such as commitments to social justice, sustainability and well-being, which were too often either latent or absent. Perhaps the British decision to support Brexit is the most obvious expression of this set of profound weaknesses and difficulties.

Under these circumstances, identity and distributional struggles typically intensify; mutual gain gives way to zero-sum, and the social order risks fragmentation and sectional struggle. It is not a surprise, accordingly, that the rise of the far right is a sustained and troubling trend. From Nigel Farage and UKIP in the United Kingdom, to Le Pen and the National Front in France, to Golden Dawn in Greece, to Norbert Hofer in Austria, and to the Danish People's Party in Denmark, this trend is manifest across Europe. The retreat to nationalism and militant identity politics is counter to the process of national accommodation that has underpinned European peace since the end of the Second World War. It is as if all that was learnt in the wake of Second World War and the Holocaust and Gulag risks being undone. And yet, it would be false to assign all responsibility for the erosion of accommodation to right wing politics. Exclusionary politics can, and does, come from all sides of the political spectrum and has clear manifestations on the far-left in Britain, France and Germany to name a few.

A Future worth Struggling for

The years since 9/11 have cast a dark shadow over global politics in many respects. The wars and crises of this period have put at risk the wisdom and achievements of the architects of the post Second World War era: of the founders of the UN and EU, of those who established and advanced the human rights regime, of the many actors and agencies that have tried to mitigate climate change and other environmental threats, and of those who have struggled to address poverty and inequality across the world, among many other pressing issues. But while these wars and crises have put this all at risk, the achievements of the post-1945 era have not yet been undermined or damaged to the point of no return. The future is still in our hands. Our forebears created stepping stones to a universal constitutional order, and we can still walk across them and build on them further. This remains a future worth struggling for.

At the same time, we have to remember at all stages the lessons of the post-9/11 years, lessons which are as pragmatic as they are normative. The approach to politics and social transformation must, in all respects, be the opposite of the era of minimum wisdom, minimum understanding of history and development, and the shoot from the hip attempts to impose single models of government on different peoples and cultures. It is still important to be ambitious for change, yet it is equally important to modest in the means deployed. The use of force must always and everywhere be a last resort and can only be a means to protect people if embedded in a transformative plan that builds on the needs and aspirations of those who have been subjected to brutal regimes, and who will have to live with the consequences of intervention, soft or hard. We need to learn the languages of others, by not simply grasping their words, but by understanding the deep structure of meaning that is rooted in their traditions and ways of living. And we need to be informed by an understanding of what is possible; that is, by an understanding that culture changes according to its own rhythm and typically very slowly, and that people's identities are embedded in long traditions of cultural development and only shift with the passage of time.

The other side of the cosmopolitan commitment to the equal moral worth of every human being, and to the equal freedom of each and all, is an acceptance of the plurality of ways of living and a tolerance of this diversity in all its richness, with one qualification – that pluralism does not undermine the boundaries of moral and political equality. With this understanding, we can begin to move out of the dark shadow of 9/11 and its aftermath and seek to establish a global order that serves the many, and not the few. But it will not be easy. Every element of this project needs rearticulation, renewed defense and a new generation of activists and champions.

Incentivare la partecipazione cittadina in un'epoca di populismi: alcuni esempi internazionali per pensare all'attivazione di circoli virtuosi[1]

Giovanni Allegretti

Quando si parla di "partecipazione" dei cittadini, ci si riferisce a una vasta serie di significati e azioni così differenti che finiscono per contribuire a fare del termine una *buzzword*, ossia un concetto debole destituito di un suo pregnante e univoco significato. Se, come già riconosceva Kelsen negli anni '20 del '900, i rischi peggiori per la democrazia provengono dai suoi successi[2] (poiché è proprio il suo affermarsi come "parola d'ordine" universalmente condivisa a trasformarla in un'etichetta priva di senso), ai processi partecipativi – che della democrazia sono parte sovente non considerata maggioritaria – può

1 Questa riflessione deve molto alle discussioni collettive all'interno del progetto EMPATIA (Enabling Multichannel Participation Through ICT Adaptations) finanziato dal Programma di Ricerca e Innovazione Horizon 2020 con contratto No 687920. Ringrazio vivamente i colleghi Michelangelo, Arkaitz, Sofia, Carlo, Paolo, Luis, Ana Raquel, João, Andrè, Nelson e mio padre Umberto per i preziosi suggerimenti. Una versione ridotta e di taglio differente e' stata pubblicata nel 2016 sulla rivista italiana "Il Ponte", Special issue: "Populismo, democrazia, insorgenze. Forme contemporanee del politico", n. 8-9/2016, con il titolo "Invertendo una spirale al ribasso: quale ruolo per i percorsi partecipativi?", p. 79-94.

2 Cfr. la Prefazione a H. Kelsen, *Essenza e valore della democrazia*, in Kelsen (1995).

applicarsi una considerazione simile, ancorché il successo si relazioni più con la necessità di non escluderli dal livello discorsivo che non in funzione di specifici risultati concretamente rilevati da qualche parte del pianeta. In tal senso, i rischi dello svuotamento del concetto di "partecipazione" cominciano soprattutto quando essa viene invocata quasi come una *soluzione taumargica* all'insofferenza nei confronti diogni riduzione ritualistica della democrazia e come una *panacea* all'incompletezza della democrazia rappresentativa.

Volendo riassumere in macrocategorie i più frequenti significati correnti attribuiti al termine "partecipazione"[3] individuati alla voce "Democrazia Partecipativa" dell'ultima edizione della Enciclopedia del Diritto Italiana (che, per la prima volta, nel 2011, ha ritenuto indispensabile inserire analisi approfondite delle implicazioni di ambiti di azione come la "democrazia partecipativa" e la "democrazia deliberativa"[4]) po-

3 U. Allegretti (2011) individua significati legati a: a) la partecipazione dei cittadini alle elezioni; b) la candidatura o l'esercizio di cariche elettive; c) la collaborazione tra organi e istituzioni diverse nell'esercizio di funzioni pubbliche; d) l'azione dei partiti politici; e) la partecipazione dei cittadini agli organi e alle attività di democrazia diretta, tra cui le assemblee civiche e i vari tipi di referendum; f) l'azione dei gruppi di interesse, dei gruppi di pressione, dei sindacati dei lavoratori e dei datori di lavoro ; g) le molte forme di mobilitazione spontanea dei cittadini; h) il coagularsi di queste forme in "movimenti"; i) l'esercizio in autogestione da parte di cittadini singoli o più spesso associati, di attività di rilievo pubblico; l) l'intervento dei titolari di posizioni giuridiche protette – diritti soggettivi, interessi legittimi individuali o collettivi - nei procedimenti che li riguardano, che danno luogo a "partecipazione procedimentale" ; m) l'inserimento di rappresentanti di gruppi sociali o di categorie e di esperti entro organi pubblici, inclusi quelli della comitologia propria dell'Unione Europea, che concretizzano forme normalmente chiamate di "partecipazione organica"; n) varie forme di consultazione, occasionali o abituali, spesso selettive, di rappresentanze sociali e di esperti da parte delle istituzioni; o) i procedimenti di concertazione tra istituzioni e rappresentanze sociali, in primo luogo i sindacati ; p) le attività svolte in regime di sussidiarietà sociale.

4 Vedi U. Allegretti (2011) e R. Bifulco (2011).

tremmo dire che, al di là dei molti usi che restano del tutto interni alla sfera della rappresentanza politica, ve ne sono una serie che fotografano modalità di autorganizzazione sociale dei cittadini (interne a quelle che Ibarra, 2007, ha definito forme di "partecipazione per irruzione"). Altre accezioni del termine si riferiscono, invece, a processi "su invito" (*id.*) in cui le istituzioni si aprono a proporre – o a "concedere" - spazi più o meno strutturati e formalizzati di coinvolgimento degli abitanti nel lavoro quotidiano o nella programmazione strategica delle istituzioni. Queste ultime ipotesi, sovente limitate all'ambito locale (che, in ogni caso, resta spesso lo spazio privilegiato dove prendono forme le maggiori e più genuine innovazioni partecipative[5]), sono quelle che maggiormente ci interessano nel seguito di questa riflessione, che vorrebbe contribuire a capire in che misura l'apertura delle istituzioni alla partecipazione diretta degli abitanti (in forme non convenzionali, o almeno diverse dai tradizionali istituti della democrazia diretta proceduralizzata, come quelli rappresentati dai referendum o dai percorsi dettagliatamente normati per la presentazione dei iniziative di legge di iniziativa popolare) può contribuire ad arginare alcune derive della politica in direzioni demagogico-populiste, o può finire per divenire parte di queste ultime.

Misurare l'intensità della partecipazione

Fin da quando, alla fine degli anni '60, Sherry Arnstein cercò di riassumere e raffigurare schematicamente, in una 'Scala della Partecipazione Civica" (1969), le "complicate interazioni sociali che si formano tra comunità ed amministrazioni nei processi di uso e trasformazione del territorio" (Garau, 2013), si è consolidata la coscienza diffusa che il coinvolgimento degli abitanti di un territorio nella costruzione delle politiche e dei progetti pubblici, ossia la relazione tra spazi di democrazia partecipativa e istituzioni della democrazia rappresentativa, abbia molti gradi di intensità differenti. Questi possono includere visioni

5 Vedi Smith (2009) e Fung e Wright (2002).

blandemente partecipative come vere e proprie forme di "non-partecipazione" che utilizzano, però, la presenza dei cittadini per legittimarsi e cercare di legittimare le decisioni assunte dai tradizionali decisori pubblici.

La scala immaginata dalla sociologa statunitense, i cui pioli corrispondono all' *estensione del potere dei cittadini* nell'ambito delle relazioni con le loro istituzioni rappresentative, fotografa, quindi, sia veri e propri processi partecipativi (rispettosi dell'autonomia e dell'autorganizzazione sociale) sia varie mistificazioni che corrispondono ad una negazione dell'essenza della partecipazione (che la Arnstein classifica in due principali categorie: la manipolazione e la terapia[6]), sia – infine - percorsi partecipativi che non vanno oltre il "tokenism"[7] e che includono la mera informazione, la consultazione e diverse strategie per contenere i conflitti.[8]

6 La Manipolazione è presentata come una strategia che porta gli attori istituzionali (powerholders) a ricorrere ad informazioni parziali che convincano la comunità di una particolare proposta presentata in fase preliminare (e magari la convincano a votarla come la migliore in uno spazio che simula un certo grado di libera partecipazione. L'attività di trattamento e sostegno terapeutico è, invece, una "terapia correttiva" (Garau, 2013, p. 48) portata avanti da personale competente e accettata come partecipazione dalla stessa comunità, che - paragonando l'inadeguatezza e la debolezza sociale a una malattia mentale – simula di sanari i mali riscontrati, senza però rimuovere le ragioni che li hanno prodotti: ossia cerca di rimuoverre appena ostacoli sul cammino del processo decisionale, nell'interesse degli stessi decisori tradizionali.

7 Per "tokenism" si intende di solito una forma superficiale di discriminazione positiva, fatta di cambiamenti o di concessioni di natura solo simbolica, Molto usato dal movimento dei diritti civili afroamericano statunitense durante gli anni '50 e '60, il vocabolo si riferisce originariamente alla pratica di produrre vari tipi di moneta che non hanno in sè valore (come i soldi del Monopoli, le collanine dei villaggi turistici, etc.) ma "lo acquistano solo nei contesti in cui sono usati" (Gangemi, 2010, p. 13).

8 Vale la pena sottolineare che l'informazione è vista dalla Arnstein come il primo passo per entrare nel campo della partecipazione nella misura in cui permnette ai cittadini di conoscere i propri diritti; la consultazione è è vista come forma di "ascolto selettivo" (Sintomer e Allegretti,2009) che usa i cittadini principalmente

Ovviamente, questo punto di coagulazione del dibattito ha aperto molti filoni differenti di analisi del tema, la cui difformità principale risiede nel punto di vista, che può interessarsi dell'emancipazione e dell'acquisizione di potere degli attori sociali (lo stesso punto di vista scelto dalla Arnstein) piuttosto che della trasformazione del ruolo degli attori istituzionali, o – ancora - degli effetti concreti di modifica delle politiche e dei progetti a partire da diverse modalità di interazione tra gli attori, per capire se esistono differenti tipologie di relazioni tra "società politica" e "società civile" (per esempio in termini di co-gestione) capaci di massimizzare i benefici delle politiche per un territorio e la società in esso insediata.

Chi, come l'associazione Internazionale IAP2[9], ha cercato di riadattare e attualizzare la "scala" di Arnstein in termini di "dover essere", con l'obiettivo di definire modi corretti e costruttivi di forgiare percorsi realmente partecipativi, si è trovato davanti alla necessità di offrire definizioni sintetiche e chiare, che contengano implicitamente – "ad excludendum" – una coscienza di ciò che non può considerarsi a buon diritto partecipazione (nella misura in cui non offre nè voce nè voto ai cittadini in relazione alle decisioni istituzionali). Così, lo "Spettro della parteci-

---

come "informatori privilegiati" ma non offre loro lo spazio per avere voce e voto; mentre la "pacificazione" (integrando limitate rappresentanze cittadine in organismi pubblici, ancorchè in minoranza numerica e in forme di coinvolgimento intermittenti e non continuative, con poca centralità soprattutto nella fase di implementazione delle decisioni) aiuta a formare gruppi eterogenei, garanti anche degli interessi popolari nei processi decisionali.

9 La IAP2 (la cui costola italiana AIP2 si è costituita il 4 ottobre 2011 a Firenze) ha per obiettivo – come risulta chiaro dalla sua carta dei valori e dal suo codice etico – la promozione e il miglioramento delle pratiche di partecipazione pubblica e di democrazia deliberativa attraverso il contributo di soggetti individuali, collettivi e istituzionali in relazione a questioni di interesse pubblico ai diversi livelli (locale, regionale, nazionale). Le attività dell'associazione e le sue finalità sono ispirate a principi di pari opportunità tra uomini e donne e rispettose dei diritti inviolabili della persona. Vedi http://aip2italia.org.

pazione" consolidato nel 2007 dalla International Association for Public Particpation (IAP2) riarticola la sua visione dei percorsi partecipativi in una sequenza progressiva di cinque gradi di intensità nel coinvolgimento dei cittadini in vari momenti di un percorso di assunzione delle scelte di pubblico interesse (informare, consultare, coinvolgere, collaborare, attribuire potere e capacità di decisione[10]), messi in relazione diretta con le "promesse" che ne definiscono l'essenza all'interno del discorso politico che utilizza tali terminologie.[11] L'accento posto sulle "promesse" non è casuale, nella misura in cui – il più delle volte - la lettura proposta della democrazia partecipativa è quella di un poderoso ed efficace complemento delle istituzioni rappresentative votato a permettere il compimento di

---

10 In tale spettro, "informare" è identificato con il "fornire al pubblico informazioni equilibrate e obiettive per aiutarlo a capire il problema, le alternative, le opportunità e/o le soluzioni"; "consultare" significa "ottenere un feedback pubblico su analisi, alternative e/o decisioni"; "coinvolgere" implicherebbe "lavorare direttamente con i cittadini durante tutto il processo per assicurare che le loro preoccupazioni e aspirazioni siano costantemente comprese e prese in carico"; "collaborare" con i cittadini dovrebbe avvenire "in ogni aspetto della decisione, compreso lo sviluppo di alternative e l'identificazione della soluzione preferita" mentre "attribuire potere e capacità di decisione" implicherebbe "collocare il processo decisionale definitivo nelle mani dei cittadini" (IAP2, 2007).

11 Le promesse implicite di ognuno dei 5 livelli sarebbero le seguenti: "vi terremo informati" corrisponde al livello partecipativo del mero "informare"; "vi terremo informati, ascoltaremo e riconosceremo le vostre preoccupazioni e aspirazioni, e vi forniremo un feedback su come gli input forniti dai cittadini hanno influenzato la decisione" corrisponde al "consultare"; "Lavoreremo con voi per assicurare che le vostre preoccupazioni e le vostre aspirazioni si riflettano direttamente nelle alternative sviluppate e vi fornimo un feedback su come gli input forniti dai cittadini hanno influenzato la decisione" è la promessa che corrisponde al livello partecipativo del "coinvolgere"; il "collaborare" implica la promessa di "lavorare insieme con voi per formulare soluzioni e incorporare i vostri consigli e le raccomandazioni nelle decisioni, nella misura massima possibile", mentre "attribuire potere e capacità di decisione" corrisponde alla promessa "metteremo in pratica ciò che voi avrete deciso" (IAP2, 2007).

quelle "promesse non mantenute" della democrazia che Bobbio (2005) ha presentato come un aspetto centrale di un regime di governo costantemente incompiuto e in permanente evoluzione.[12] L'aspetto interessante di un tale lavoro di attenta e calibrata definizione, che – pur conscio delle sue indispensabili semplificazioni – punta al "cuore" dei problemi nodali del tema a cui si riferisce, riguarda la ricerca di una "traduzione culturale" di una questione complessa che possa parlare a tutti i cittadini, a prescindere dal loro livello di formazione e del loro interesse per la politica, o almeno per quel mondo istituzionale che da molti viene identificato *tout court* con il termine "politica", lasciando ai margini tutto ciò che si riferisce alla militanza civico-associativa e all'impegno profuso dai cittadini nella salvaguardia e nel miglioramento dei territori dove vivono e della loro qualità di vita quotidiana.

Purtroppo, la chiarezza che le "scale" e gli "spettri" che cercano di misurare l'intensità dei percorsi partecipativi istituzionali pongono nel loro centro è sovente temuta e, quindi, messa ai margini dalle istituzioni, al momento di impegnarsi in processi di dialogo sociale. La chiarezza di principi e obiettivi, infatti, costituisce uno scomodo compagno di viaggio, mentre l'ambiguità concettuale – che non impegna le istituzioni in un vero nuovo "patto sociale" con i cittadini di cui esse debbano pagare le conseguenze in caso di violazione – è molto più facile da gestire e reinterpretare secondo l'utilità o le congiunture del momento. Pertanto, non è una sorpresa che risulti assai difficile incontrare quadri normativi in

12 Per Bobbio, le sei principali «promesse non mantenute» della democrazia sono: 1) che l'individuo sovrano è spodestato dalla società pluralista e dalle sue forme di associazionismo organizzato; 2) la centralità della rivincita degli interessi di parte su quelli politici; 3) la persistenza delle oligarchie;4) lo spazio limitato in cui esercitare il diritto di partecipare alle decisioni che li riguardano; 5) il potere invisibile (o "cripto governo") di forze politiche eversive che agiscono nell'ombra e hanno contatti coi servizi segreti o che per lo meno non sono ostacolati da questi ultimi; 6) il cittadino non educato tende ad essere vittima dell'apatia politica, del disinteresse, e si fa corresponsabile di comportamenti come il voto di scambio, l'astensionismo, il nepotismo e la difesa di privilegi clientelari.

cui gli spazi di democrazia partecipativa non appaiano come una mera "subordinata" delle istituzioni rappresentative, invece che un loro complemento di pari dignità. O dove - perlomeno – vi sia una traduzione – in termini di doveri istituzionali – dei principi di responsabilità che dovrebbero illuminare il nuovo "contratto sociale" di chi si impegna ad aprire procedure e arene di vero dialogo sociale.

Un caso di normazione avanzata è sicuramente quello della Regione Toscana che, nella sua scala di competenza, si è data nel 2007 una legge di inquadramento della partecipazione dei cittadini alle decisioni pubbliche, che è stata costruita attraverso quasi due anni di dibattiti in pubblico e con l'utilizzo di diverse metodologie partecipative che hanno facilitato la stesura di un testo condiviso. Tale genesi spiega perchè la legge regionale toscana 69/2007 – il cui incipit sottolineava che la partecipazione dei cittadini alla costruzione delle politiche è "un diritto" che necessita di essere reso esigibile attraverso azioni concrete[13] - risulti così differente da altre normative[14] concepite attraverso un più tradizionale percorso di scrittura ad opera di soli esperti (Sgueo,

13 L'art. 1 della Legge 69/2007 recitava: 1. "La partecipazione alla elaborazione e alla formazione delle politiche regionali e locali è un diritto; lapresente legge promuove forme e strumenti di partecipazione democratica che rendano effettivo questo diritto".

14 Vedi, per esempio, la La legge regionale n. 3/2010 dell'Emilia Romagna, il cui articolo 1 è formulato in termini di conquista progressiva, e dando fin dalle prime righe, una centralità simbolica alla rappresentanza: "La democrazia rappresentativa è un ideale fondativo degli Stati moderni ed è riconosciuta come una condizione essenziale per affermare il diritto di partecipazione dei cittadini dal Trattato dell'Unione europea, dalla Carta dei diritti fondamentali dell'Unione europea, dalla Costituzione italiana e dallo Statuto regionale. Lo sviluppo della democrazia partecipativa è coerente con gli ideali fondativi della Repubblica, promuove una maggiore ed effettiva inclusione dei cittadini e delle loro organizzazioni nei processi decisionali di competenza delle istituzioni elettive, rafforza la democrazia".

2010).[15] Non stupisce, pertanto, che nella legislazione toscana – che dichiara di voler promuovere la partecipazione come modalità ordinaria di governo – si trovi in posizione centrale l'affermazione di un "dovere di risposta" che le istituzioni si devono assumere davanti ai risultati prodotti dai percorsi partecipativi che hanno incentivato.[16] Tale obbligo risulta non solo la condizione minima necessaria per non frustrare chi ha dedicato tempo e risorse intellettuali e emozionali a discutere in pubblico di temi di interesse comune, ma anche una indispensabile forma di "riconoscimento" dell'impegno di ogni singolo cittadino o cittadina da parte delle istituzioni, indipendentemente dalla convergenza di opinioni che si sia manifestata durante il percorso di dialogo sociale e fatto salvo il diritto dei rappresentanti istituzionali di assumere "in piena autonomia" decisioni difformi da quelle emerse durante il processo partecipativo, purchè assumendosene la responsabilità e motivandone le ragioni. Un simile obbligo, già reso patente nella legislazione francese sul Dibattito Pubblico rafforzata nel 2002 e a cui la Toscana si è ispirata

---

15 Umberto Allegretti ha ben descritto, in numerosi suoi lavori (vedi Allegretti U., 2006) lo spirito intriso di scetticismo con cui soprattutto i giuristi si approssimano ai temi della partecipazione come ad una prassi dell'azione politica a cui perciò non tendono a riconoscere dignità di oggetto si studio e approfondimento, non stupendosi – pertanto – che l'attenzione ai percorsi partecipativi venga soprattutto da discipline più antropocentriche come l'antropoliga e la sociologia, o da settori delle scienze umane e politiche che hanno perduto la certezza del loro statuto disciplinare e cercano nuove strade per ridefinirsi, come l'urbanistica.

16 Vedi l'art. 10 comma 3 della Legge 69/2007 che recita (riguardo al Dibattito Pubblico sulle grandi opere infrastrutturali): "Entro tre mesi dalla pubblicazione del rapporto, il soggetto proponente dichiara pubblicamente se intende: a) rinunciare al progetto o presentarne uno alternativo;b) proporre modifi che al progetto, indicando quelle che intende realizzare; c) continuare a sostenere il medesimo progetto sul quale si è svolto il dibattito pubblico, argomentando motivatamente le ragioni di tale scelta". Nessun punto simile (e nessun termine come argomentare, spiegare, dichiarare) è presente nella Legge 3/2010 della Emilia Romagna, che pur si è spesso riferita al processo di stesura dell'omologa normativa toscana.

(Revel *et alii*, 2007), costituisce un elemento centrale della *responsiveness*, da intendersi come precondizione per ogni processo partecipativo, sia nella sua dimensione di impegno a identificare catene di responsabilità chiare (in grado di opporsi ai tradizionali difetti della burocrazia deresponsabilizzata e spersonalizzata), sia nella dimensione temporale resa visibile dalla traduzione francese del termine (*reactivitè*), ossia nel suo impegno a tradurre gli esiti dei percorsi partecipativi in risultati concreti sul territorio in tempi celeri, che risultino realisti in termini di fattibilità ma al contempo tollerabili in relazione alla pazienza degli abitanti che hanno investito energie nel percorso di dialogo sociale. L'obbligo di rispondere, e di farlo in lassi di tempo accettabili, non andrebbe concepito in termini di dialogo uno-a-uno tra istituzione e singolo cittadino (come tradizionalmente avviene nelle maggioranza delle osservazioni ai piani regolatori, o nella "partecipazione procedimentale" che soddisfa diritti soggettivi e interessi legittimi individuali di una persona o di un gruppo nei procedimenti che li riguardano), ma come una componente centrale di quel principio di *"pubblicità"* (ossia di visibilità pubblica) che dovrebbe rappresentare la differenza tra la "buona" e la "cattiva politica".

Abitare in una casa di vetro

Come scriveva Norberto Bobbio (2011) quando difendeva la definizione di democrazia come "potere in pubblico" (1999), i nostri sistemi di potere oggi non sono comprensibili senza "ammettere che al di sotto del governo visibile c'è un governo che agisce nella penombra... e ancor più in fondo un governo che agisce nella più assoluta oscurità... un potere invisibile che agisce accanto a quello dello Stato, insieme dentro e contro, sotto certi aspetti concorrente sotto altri connivente, che si vale del segreto non proprio per abbatterlo ma neppure per servirlo", o meglio "se ne vale principalmente per aggirare o addirittura violare impunemente le leggi"; e una democrazia piena si ha solo se minimizza la capacità delle forme di potere occulto di "sottrarre le proprie azioni al controllo democratico (...per) controllare lo Stato senza essere a sua volta controllato" (*id*). Se immaginiamo l'idea di "potere in pubblico" come quell'insieme "di espedienti istituzionali che costringono i governanti a prendere le loro decisioni alla luce del sole e permettono ai governati di «vedere» come e dove la prendono" (Bobbio, 1999, p. 338), dobbiamo riconoscere che nel passaggio concettuale dalla democrazia diretta della "agorà ateniese, l'adunanza all'aria aperta dove si riuniscono i cittadini ad ascolta gli oratori e quindi ad esprimere la loro opinione alzando la mano" alla "democrazia rappresentativa (dalla democrazia degli antichi a quella dei moderni) scompare la piazza ma non l'esigenza della «visibilità» del potere, che viene soddisfatta in altro modo, con la pubblicità delle sedute del parlamento, con la formazione di una pubblica opinione attraverso l'esercizio della libertà di stampa, con la sollecitazione rivolta ai leader politici a fare le loro dichiarazioni attraverso il mezzo della comunicazione di massa".[17] Ma cosa succede se questi espedienti, che il primo grande storico del governo rappresentativo (François Guizot, purtroppo poco tradotto in italiano) aveva immaginato come strumenti per sottoporre "i poteri all'obbligo di cercare la giustizia e la ragione sotto gli occhi di tutti, allo scopo che ogni cittadino sia convinto che questa ricerca è stata fatta in buona fede" (2009), vengono gradualmente meno, come va accadendo sempre più in istanze politiche ed economico-finanziarie le cui decisioni sono coperte da omissis o prese in spazi intrasparenti e

---

17 Come osserva Bobbio, la democrazia si potrebbe ridefinire idealmente "come quella forma di governo in cui anche le ultime fortezze del potere invisibile sono state espugnate e il potere, come la natura, non ha più segreti per l'uomo". Secondo lo stesso autore "Appartiene all'essenza stessa del potere di occultarsi. Ma ciò non toglie che la diversa estensione delle due sfere, rispettivamente del potere visibile e del potere invisibile, sia uno dei criteri che permetta una netta distinzione fra governo democratico e autocratico (...) Anche il monarca assoluto, l'autocrate, il dittatore moderno, si presenta in pubblico, perché ha bisogno di mostrare i segni visibili della propria potenza. Ma il pubblico cui si presenta è una folla anonima, indistinta, chiamata ad ascoltare e ad acclamare, non a esprimere un'opinione ma a compiere un atto di fede. A questa visibilità puramente esteriore del signore della vita e della morte dei propri sudditi deve fare riscontro l'opacità delle decisioni dalle quali la loro vita e morte dipendono (1999).

inaccessibili? Se è indubbio che loro sparizione farebbe vacillare la stessa democrazia rappresentativa, che "può svolgersi solo nella sfera della pubblicità" dato che "non c'è nessuna rappresentanza che si svolga in segreto e a quattr'occhi" perchè "rappresentare significa rendere visibile [...] un essere invisibile per mezzo di un essere che è presente pubblicamente" (Bobbio, 1999, p. 339), la riduzione progressiva della sfera della pubblicità nell'operato istituzionale rappresenta un'approssimazione pericolosa alle forme autocratiche del potere.[18] Se, pertanto, vogliamo immaginare gli strumenti della democrazia partecipativa come contributi a restaurare i valori centrali della democrazia *tout court* ed "estendere l'area del potere visibile rispetto a quella del potere invisibile" (*id.*), è indispensabile che il principio di pubblicità diventi il loro perno nodale, e sia applicato a tutto: alle regole e ai procedimenti, ai dibattiti, al modo in cui sono tratte (e, successivamente, trattate) le conclusioni per trasformarle in politiche, piani, strategie e progetti.

Anche sotto il profilo della maturazione del comportamento dei cittadini, agire in uno spazio aperto e trasparente porta vantaggi. Soprattutto nella misura in cui obbliga ad assumersi responsabilità rispetto alle proprie scelte, ad ascoltare gli altri (e non solo a parlare), a spiegare i benefici collettivi di proposte che partono da interessi individuali o di piccoli gruppi, e a dover spiegare il perchè di ciò che si propone e a prendere in considerazione modifiche emerse dal parere degli altri. Ciò può spiegare perchè - sovente - in numerosi percorsi partecipativi la rappresentanza della piramide sociale risulta incompleta, non essendo assenti solo i gruppi sociali più vulnerabili, ma anche gli scaloni più

18 Come ha icasticamente osservato Bobbio "Il potere ha una tendenza irresistibile a nascondersi. Elias Canetti ha scritto in forma lapidaria: 'Il segreto sta nel nucleo più interno del potere'. Si capisce anche perché: chi esercita il potere è tanto più sicuro di ottenere gli effetti desiderati quanto più si rende invisibile a coloro sui quali intende dominare. Uno dei temi principali della trattatistica politica dei secoli in cui prevalgono forme di governo autocratiche è quello degli *arcana imperii*" (1999, p. 339).

alti, specialmente quelli legati al mondo dell'impresa e delle professioni. Questa assenza è tanto più evidente laddove esistano altri canali "concorrenti" di dialogo uno-a-uno con l'amministrazione pubblica (per esempio, incontri riservati tra sindaco e imprenditori o appuntamenti personali concessi ai cittadini), che non obbligano a negoziare in spazi aperti dove mettere in discussione pubblica interessi, guadagni e compensazioni che il territorio si attende ogni qualvolta è oggetto di trasformazioni. Il filosofo politico Jon Elster (2005) ha parlato di a questo proposito della "forza civilizzatrice dell'ipocrisia", da leggersi come capitale positivo in una democrazia che – in uno spazio pubblico regolato – permette di smorzare i toni e generare dialogo al di là dei pregiudizi di partenza.

Come dimostrano molte esperienze di partecipazione svolte in paesi del Sud, in contesti urbani informali il cui impegno civico si modella – in genere – sui *desiderata* di *ras* o trafficanti locali di sostanze stupefacenti, gli spazi pubblici di partecipazione hanno anche un valore *liberatorio* per le persone, nella misura in cui trovarsi insieme a discutere dei propri interessi – tanto più se con l'appoggio di facilitatori esperti ed eticamente corretti – può aiutare ad affrancare dalla dipendenza da figure carismatiche o autoritarie (Forester e Weiser, 1996) che hanno di solito la forza di soggiogare o plagiare gli altri per realizzare le loro convenienze. Come dettomi in un'intervista da un cittadino molto coinvolto in un bilancio partecipativo brasiliano "sentirsi stupidi in uno spazio pubblico è un insegnamento che non si dimentica: quando capisci che avevi un'occasione, che la hai persa per seguire qualcun altro che faceva solo i suoi interessi, e vedi che altri hanno saputo cogliere quella stessa opportunità per migliorare la loro vita, subisci un trauma che ti aiuta a non sbagliare più in futuro, e a fare massa critica con altri ex-stupidi come te per alterare il tuo comportamento futuro...".[19]

---

19 Intervista a E.Z. nel quartiere Cristal di Porto Alegre, realizzata il 9 maggio 1999 nell'ambito della tesi di dottorato "*Verso una colloquialità tra città informale e città formale: ipotesi di lettura di una esperienza esemplare*", discussa il 3 aprile 2000

In tale prospettiva, si capisce perchè la letteratura consideri in genere più "poveri" (in termini interazionali) tutti quei percorsi sedicenti partecipativi che, in realtà, sommano in un momento pubblico preferenze raccolte in spazi che non godono della caratteristica della pubblicità, come accade a molti percorsi di votazione pubblica via internet dove ogni momento importante (specialmente proposte e votazioni) si svolge *online*, spesso in assenza di arene di dialogo e argomentazione dove si possano spiegare e dibattere adesioni, contrarietà e controproposte. Ovviamente esiste sempre la possibilità di introdurre microregole che aiutino a privilegiare la capacità costruttiva in relazione all'espressione di mere posizioni oppositive. Per esempio, a Feltre (dove l'amministrazione ha cercato di eliminare spazi di dialogo sociale concorrenti per eviatre che si svuotino di pubblico a vicenda e ognuno scelga quelli che gli convengono di più per garantire poco pubblicità alle sue negoziazioni con i poteri pubblici), i vari laboratori partecipativi che decidono delle politiche comunali insieme ai cittadini[20], hanno una regola fissa che permette di presentare critiche sulle politiche pubbliche solo se contestualmente un cittadino presenta proposte costruttive per migliorare la qualità della vita. L'idea, emulata dal 2015 nel Forum dei Servizi della città brasiliana di Canoas, ha teso a mutare completamente il clima dei percorsi partecipativi, dando loro una prevalenza costruttiva e orientata alla soluzione di problemi, ma soprattutto evitando che l'esistenza di una tipologia quasi unica di spazio partecipativo lo trasformi in un "lamentatoio" senza costrutto.

Si potrebbe asserire che sulla questione della previsione di spazi "pubblici e regolati" che facilitino l'incontro e il confronto di argomentazioni si costruisce una "linea abissale" del pensiero (Santos, 2007), un vero discriminante che separa le pratiche e le teorie partecipative *sostanziali*, da quelle il cui richiamo al coinvolgimento dei cittadini e delle cit-

---

presso la Università degli Studi di Firenze, Facoltà di Architettura, Dipartimento di urbanistica.

20 Cfr. http://partecipo.comune.feltre.bl.it.

tadine nelle decisioni è meramente *rituale* o *retorico*. Una delle ragioni sta nel fatto che la necessità del potere di sottrarsi agli sguardi del pubblico rivela un "disprezzo del popolo, considerato incapace di capire i supremi interessi dello stato (che sarebbero, a giudizio dei potenti, i suoi primi interessi) e facile preda dei demagoghi". Può la "*demofobia*" (che è al contempo paura e disprezzo del popolo[21]) essere una componente accettabile della democrazia partecipativa come lo è stata a lungo e in molti luoghi della democrazia *tout court*? La risposta sembra, ovviamente, negativa. A lungo, le limitazioni censitarie all'orizzonte del suffragio universale sono state tra i metodi più diffusi per rivelare la "paura delle classi dominanti di fronte all'eventualità di uno stabile ingresso nell'arena politica di quelle classi pericolose che per la prima volta si erano affacciate da protagoniste sul palcoscenico della storia europea all'epoca della Rivoluzione (Francese)" (Costantini, 2012, p. 8), almeno fino a quando alcuni esponenti più accorti della borghesia liberale occidentale non si accorsero " delle potenzialità di controllo sociale insite nel suffragio universale e nelle istituzioni democratiche rappresentative" (*id.*). Da allora, e tanto più con lo sviluppo novecentesco dei mezzi di comunicazione di massa, gli strumenti al servizio della demofobia (storicamente dimostratasi una componente non incompatibile con i regimi democratici rappresentativi, dalla Rivoluzione Americana in poi) sono andati moltiplicandosi, per arrivare oggi a sofisticati dispositivi tesi a garantire la "governabilità", che di fatto attenuano la forza della rappresentanza e cercano di espellere dall'arena della competizione democratica sopratutto le frange ideologiche più estreme e meno "malleabili" dell'arco costituzionale. Un preclaro esempio di queste distorsioni lo abbiamo in Italia, dove il sistema elettorale abbonda da decenni di soglie, correzioni a tentativi di uso del sistema maggioritario, premi di maggioranza ecc. L'interessante è osservare come questi strumenti hanno finito per espandere la sfiducia e la paura dal "volgo" allo stesso funzionamento del sistema rappresentativo, come

21 Cfr. Bearzot, C.; Canfora, L.: Pombeni, P. (2012) e Pellizzetti (2014).

ben sintetizzato da Gustavo Zagrebelsky (2015) in una sua celebre invettiva contro la "governabilità", dove sottolinea come, quando usata "per indicare unilateralmente il bisogno di efficaci strumenti di governo attribuendola "alla macchina di governo, allora la domanda che sorge, non maliziosa ma realistica, è: governabile, sì, ma da chi? Docile, sì, ma nei confronti di chi?". In tale visione, occorrerebbe restaurare la possibilit à che la governabilità, "come forza che legittima l'azione del governo" dipenda essenzialmente "dalla libera partecipazione politica e dal coinvolgimento attivo dei cittadini, dal confronto e dalla discussione su cui si forma l' humus delle decisioni politiche", e per far questo bisogna evitare che il disincanto che genera "rinuncia volontaria all'esercizio del primo e basilare diritto democratico" sia continuamente alimentato non già solo dal "sentimento antipolitico e antiparlamentare che è sempre presente in ogni società (...) alimentato dall'incredibile diffusione della corruzione pubblica" ma anche dalla "frustrazione interiorizzata che (...) deriva da una convinzione assai più profonda e difficilmente scalzabile, ossia che i governanti non siano solo " tutti uguali perché tutti disonesti, ma (...) l'uno uguale all'altro nell'inutilità e nell'inconcludenza" (*id.*). In un panorama in cui alla politica sono demandate sempre meno decisioni, imposte da istituzioni di secondo e terzo grado la cui sorgente democratica è così lontana dai cittadini da non essere più percepibile neppure come *la delega di una delega* (ma piuttosto come un abuso di potere e una espropriazione della stessa democrazia), l'inaridimento delle sorgenti sociali della governabilità fa passare la stessa "da problema di democrazia (a) questione di ingegneria costituzionale al servizio dell'efficienza dei mercati, i quali hanno bisogno di costituzioni reattive alla loro continua instabilità, di decisioni pronte, assolute e cieche, cioè di interventi esecutivi". Ancora una volta, si propaganda una vuota e artificiale idea di "vita costituzionale buona" che mira a "nuove e interessate allocazioni di potere (Zagrebelsky, 2015). Un simile quadro, in cui la percezione del deficit democratico si trova paradossalmente aggravata anche da una maggiore coscienza diffusa dei diritti che l'evolversi dell'educazione, lo sviluppo dei nuovi media e, per alcuni decenni, dello stato sociale ha permesso, soprattutto alle nuove generazioni (Norris, 2011), richiede gli sforzi tipici di un'*era della sfiducia*, ossia la apertura di spazi di *controdemocrazia* (Rosanvallon, 2012) in grado di restaurarne i valori centrali e di conferirle *alta intensità* (Santos, 2003). L'uso degli strumenti di democrazia partecipativa, diffusamente visto come un'argine all'ulteriore crisi e come un movimento controcorrente per la sua regressione, trova il suo spazio fulcrale in questo quadro. Ma, purtroppo, ne subisce anche i contraccolpi, per lo più sotto forma di *colpi di coda* di istituzioni rappresentative che si percepiscono come moribonde, e si trasformano in parassiti che cercano di succhiare la linfa vitale dai processi partecipativi, nella speranza di "dominarne la bestia ribelle che è in loro" e di "addomesticare" o "cooptare" i percorsi partecipativi (Allegretti 2014; Dias, 2013) in modo da riprendersi alcuni margini di discrezionalità decisionale che avevano loro affidato (temporaneamente), quando avevano accettato di aggrapparsi ad essi nella speranza di esserne rivitalizzati. La tendenza a voler mettere la museruola e il guinzaglio ai percorsi partecipativi li può rendere dei veri e propri "boomerang politici", perchè – invece di farli percepire come reintegrazioni della qualità democratica perduta dalle istituzioni – li fa sentire come la *longa manus* della partiticocrazia sulle altre sfere della politica (nel senso più ampio delle strategie di governo ma anche di pedagogia e di impegno civico legate alla *polis*). Un esempio classico lo si può trovare nelle derive di alcuni bilanci partecipativi (o BP), quei percorsi (formalmente ispirati dall'esperienza radicale della Porto Alegre degli anni '90, ma ormai diffusi in quasi 3000 città del pianeta con modelli molto diversi[22]) che puntano a coinvolgere gli abitanti di un territorio nelle decisioni su una fetta dei bilanci pubblici e nella stesura di una parte dei documenti economico-finanziari, in genere a scala municipale. In genere si tratta di esperienze che coinvolgono "universalmente" nelle decisioni tutti gli abitanti e gli utilizzatori di uno specifico territorio (so-

22 Vedi Sintomer *et alii* (2014).

prattutto i residenti, ma anche chi vi studia o lavora, e in alcuni casi anche i turisti o gli emigrati in altri paesi che da lì provengono), con meccanismi del tipo "una testa, un voto". Ma vi sono esperienze che hanno tentato di imprigionare il meccanismo in concezioni meramente consultive (configuratisi come spazi di "scelta selettiva" in cui un governo sceglie quali opzioni di investimenti realizzare nelle lunghe liste di sogni presentate dai cittadini) o di costringerli entro limiti legalisti legati a una visione ristretta di comunità, che impedisce ai minorenni e ai non residenti di votare la lista delle priorità su cui investire, o limita la possibilità di indicare gerarchie di investimenti da compiere al solo associazionismo organizzato (e registrato in appositi albi). Queste ultime esperienze – come dimostra il caso del Portogallo[23] - hanno di solito fallito, venendo percepite come trappole politiche o stanchi rituali partecipativi dominati dalle istituzioni. I percorsi di maggiore successo restano, per contro, quelli che hanno osato riflettere la complessità della compagine sociale offrendo agli abitanti, intesi come produttori di territorio e cultura (indipendentemente dal loro *status* formale), spazi di co-decisione che si "affidano" alle capacità degli abitanti[24] non solo sulle politiche e i progetti di interesse pubbliche, ma anche sulle stesse regole da usare per rendere il percorso participativo uno spazio di autonomia sociale orientato a promuovere la giustizia distributiva e la salvaguardia e valorrizazione dei beni comuni,

---

23 Cfr. Alves e Allegretti, 2012 e Allegretti e Dias 2015. In Portogallo, fino al 2013, il tasso di mortalità delle oltre 100 esperienze di Bilancio partecipativo sviluppatesi a partire dal 2002 è stato del 77% (con punte dell'85% nei casi di processi sperimentati a livello circoscrizionale e non di un intero municipio). Il 90% di queste esperienze interrotte è stato di processi consultivi (ossia che non prevedevano la deliberazione da parte dei cittadini sulla gerarchia delle proposte prioritarie da mettere a bilancio), e il 98% sono state sospese dalla stessa amministraziuone che le ha avviate.

24 Il termine ricalca la definizione data dalla ex-PB Unit inglese, che aveva definito il BP come uno spazio in cui i governi "affidano ai cittadini la decisione su una parte o il totale degli investimenti rispetto ad un bilanciodi loro interesse" (vedi http://www.pbpartners.org.uk/category/resources).

e non – invece – a potenziare l'aspetto competitivo, o la lotta tra le lobby e i gruppi organizzati per destinare la maggior parte degli investimenti pubblici ai loro luoghi di vita o ai settori tematici di loro interesse. Il caso del Bilancio Partecipativo di New York, che dal 2011 ha mietuto successi crescenti e i cui promotori hanno ricevuto decine di riconoscimenti internazionali – è una metafora importante di tale legame tra successo e apertura di credito alle capacità di elaborazione creativa dei cittadini: esso, infatti, opera su una parte delle risorse a disposizione dei consiglieri comunali eletti – chiamata "fondi discrezionali" - di solito usate per coltivarsi l'elettorato attraverso distribuzione di risorse "a pioggia", e pertanto il percorso partecipativo si propne esplicitamente come "freno" alle derive clienteliste ed autoreferenziali della democrazia rappresentativa.

Tiepida si è anche dimostrata l'accoglienza di bilanci partecipativi che permettono ai cittadini di esprimere una scelta nell'ambito di una lista di opzioni bloccate (come nel caso della seconda edizione del BP elettronico della metropoli brasiliana di Belo Horizonte, o del primo anno del BP del comune portoghese di Vila Franca de Xira, subito modificato per non rischiare il fallimento) o di congegni organizzativi tesi a ridurre l'incidenza ripetuta dei percorsi participativi sull'operato delle istituzioni e sul loro funzionamento tecnico-amministrativo. Per esempio, i bilanci partecipativi che hanno "biennalizzato il loro ciclo"[25] – con la dichiarata motivazione di voler adattarsi alle lentezze della burocrazia nel produrre effetti concreti sul territorio per le proposte approvate partecipativamente – alla fine sono percepiti come dei "riformatori deboli", perché rinunciano a usare il processo partecipativo come opportunità per sfidare l'inerzia

25 Biennalizzare il ciclo significa che –nonostante il processo di bilancio sia annuale – il ciclo di partecipazione si realizza un anno su due, e viene seguito nell'anno successivo da un ciclo di realizzazione meticolosa delle proposte co-decise nell'anno prima. Lo sopo dichiarato di tale biennalizzazione è evitare che le lentezze burocratiche frustrino le aspettative degli abitanti, e attendere per una nno la messa in opera dei progetti codecisi con la popolazione prima di riaprire un ciclo di consultazioni su nuovi progetti.

della compagine amministrativa e riorganizzarla ai fini di una migliore produttività. Tali limitazioni di sovranità dei percorsi partecipativi non sono sempre necessariamente conseguenti alla sola volontà delle istituzioni. Infatti, in molti casi (come ha ben mostrato Ganuza e Nez, 2012) il boicottaggio delle forme di partecipazione universalista parte dal cuore sociale di un sistema concertativo, ossia dall'associazionismo organizzato che teme di perdere i suoi privilegi di negoziazione con le istituzioni in tradizionali tavoli di concertazione, a vantaggio di cittadini comuni non necessariamente dediti all'impegno e alla militanza organizzata.

Merita, infine sottolineare, che sono moltissimi i casi in cui la democrazia rappresentativa, pur fingendo di volersi aprire all'accoglimento di pratiche partecipative strutturanti, cerca di neutralizzarne gli effetti creando artificiosi anticorpi nelle regole dei procedimenti. I casi recenti più eclatanti sono certo quelli della legge elettorale della Provincia canadese della British Columbia (Fung, Warren e Gabriel, 2011), affossata dalle regole del referendum che doveva confermare la proposta elaborata attraverso una giuria cittadina, e quello della nuova Costituzione Islandese (Allegretti, Corsi, Allegretti, 2016; Gylfason, 2013), redatta da 25 cittadini attraverso un percorso partecipativo di oltre due anni, ma affondata dal Parlamento grazie al farraginoso meccanismo del doppio passaggio parlamentare previsto per la sua ratifica. Frequenti sono anche le pratiche "tutelate", dove l'ingegneria organizzativa della partecipazione è usata da una istituzione contro un'altra ed assume caratteristiche di paternalismo benevolo. È il caso di vari casi di consigli di comunità venezuelani che – pur essendo pratiche locali di grande interesse potenziale (Allegretti, 2006) – hanno finito per essere utilizzate dalla Presidenza della Repubblica (grazie al fondo speciale lì creato per sostenerli) come strumento di indebolimento del peso delle istituzioni locali in mano alle opposizioni o a correligionari del partito al governo riottosi o poco docili nei loro comportamenti verso i livelli amministrativi superiori.

Tutti questi esempi – specie quando mostrano la tiepida attrittività di rituali pseudopartecipativi che scambiano la "buona governance" a cui vorrebbero appartenere per un malinteso principio di rafforzato controllo e limitazione delle competenze e delle prerogative dei meccanismi partecipativi - suggeriscono quattro riflessioni principali da tenere in conto quando si vuole realmente dare alle pratiche partecipative il senso di *rivitalizzatori* della democrazia. Esse sono:

1) che la democrazia partecipativa, per riuscire a ricostruire fiducia nelle istituzioni, necessita di essere lasciata libera di sviluppare il suo potenziale pedagogico/emancipatorio per le persone, esprimendo lo spirito di rivoluzione sopito che cova sotto il riformismo delle ingegnerie istituzionali: quel non sapere esattamente "verso dove si andrà", liberando energie creative e e passioni, ma con la certezza che si sta costruendo forte capitale umano e relazionale;

2) che esiste una crescente "intolleranza dei cittadini verso l'irrilevanza delle pratiche partecipative" (Santos, 2014) che non accetta che siano ridotte a mere sperimentazioni prive di effetti e di reale e convinto supporto politico, come dei giusti tempi (e della giusta durata) della loro messa in opera. In tale prospettiva, la reale partecipazione degli abitanti nei percorsi partecipativi va vista come una variabile dipendente e ipersensibile dei loro effetti, e gli stessi cicli di funzionamento dei dispositivi per il dialogo sociale sono "tecnologie sociali" che vanno costantemente (e incrementalmente) ripensate e migliorate in funzione dei loro risultati (i cicli di realizzazione delle concrete promesse) e della crescita/trasformazione progressiva dei loro variegati pubblici;

3) che risulta indispensabile porre impegno nel tenere costantemente in conto le percezioni generate nei cittadini dai percorsi partecipativi (così come dalle metodologie e dai linguaggi usati) per reinvertarli costantemente o aiutarli a spiegare meglio i loro obiettivi. È, infatti, logico che neppure le buone intenzioni del personale tecnico-politico sono sufficienti a garantire che un processo sia capace di ricostruire fiducia

mutua tra istituzioni e cittadini e attrarre participanti motivati e attivi – soprattutto in ambiti territoriali segnati da tensioni e conflitti e dove si rilevino forti connotati di sfiducia nelle istituzioni, problemi di corruzione o tessuti sociali portatori di rivendicazioni radicali (Allegretti, 2014). In tale prospettiva, la valutazione dei processi partecipi deve essere componente centrale dell'adozione degli stessi, come ha ben dimostrato la Legge Toscana sulla Partecipazione, che (sia nella versione del 2007 che nella rinnovata formulazione del 2013) ha incluso una "clausola di dissolvenza", ossia la previsione di una decadenza della legge alla fine di un predefinito ciclo temporale, finito il quale sarà necessario valutarne il funzionamento e riconfermarne (o reindirizzarne) i contenuti e le forme.

4) che è importante che gli spazi di democrazia partecipativa non siano "mimetici" rispetto a quelli della rappresentenza, e non adottino le stesse regole. Infatti, per raggiungere la necessaria complementarietà tra le due è indispensabile rafforzare le peculiarità, e rendere visibili e valorizzare le differenze. Per esempio, laddove sia necessario ricorrere a spazi di "rappresentanza" in specifiche fasi di un percorso di dialogo sociale (come accade in molti bilanci partecipativi, quando richiedono di approfondire temi o proposte che non sarebbe facile trattare con numeri molto elevati di partecipanti), è importante immaginare la nomina di portavoce o delegati popolari con vincoli imperativi di mandato, revocabili in caso di mancato compimento dei compiti loro attribuiti, e sollecitati (in termini di accountability) a rispondere delle loro azioni davanti alle comunità di origine con maggiore frequenza di quanto non accada nei mandati elettorali, per esempio con cadenza annuale.

Con tali premesse, si comprende perchè la maggior parte dei percorsi partecipativi siano stati oggi concepiti per svolgersi alla scala locale (ossia in quegli ambiti considerati, a torto, meno strategici e quindi più adatti alla sperimentazione) che alcune culture definiscono come "piccola democrazia" (come rivela il termine finlandese "*pieni demokratia*"), immaginandola come lo spazio privilegiato per praticare approcci di partecipazione "di prossimità" o "di quartiere" (definiti "*democratie de proximité*" in Francia, "*neighbourhood democracy*" nel Regno Unito, "*wijkaanpak*"nei Paesi Bassi, o "*bürgernahe Verwaltung*" in Germania - letteralmente "l'amministrazione vicina al cittadino").

Quando la partecipazione vuole ravvivare la democrazia: alcuni ambiti di azione nodali

La questione della scala (esiste una scala obbligata in cui la democrazia partecipativa funziona meglio? O addiritura una scala unica a cui essa è ammissibile?) è andata soggetta, negli ultimi anni, a revisioni sempre più radicali, dimostrando che la scala non struttura barriere assolute, ma semmai ostacoli che vanno messi in relazione con temi, obiettivi e capacità di sviluppare percorsi pedagogici a servizio della crescita di ambizioni della partecipazione. Lo dimostrano i processi partecipativi di taglio strategico-valoriale che hanno accompagnato la riforma costituzionale irlandese del 2012-2014 (Wall, 2013; McGee, 2015) o quella islandese del 2009-2012 (Ólafsson, 2014), dimostrando come il trasformarsi delle procedure verso un aumento della partecipazione incide anche su un mutamento non secondario dei contenuti previsti, specie in direzione di una previsione di maggior coinvolgimento futuro degli abitanti nelle politiche. E lo dimostra anche una serie di sperimentazioni regionali di giurie dei cittadini o altri percorsi partecipativi in province o regioni di grande dimensioni come il Kerala Indiano (Isaac e Franke, 2002), il Rio Grande do Sul Brasiliano, il British Columbia canadese, il Poitou Charentes francese (Sintomer e Talpin, 2011) o le regioni italiane del Lazio (Allegretti, 2011) e della Toscana (Allegretti e Casillo, 2015; Bortolotti e Corsi, 2012). E lo mostra il processo di costruzione di un Bilancio Partecipativo a scala nazionale (il primo al mondo) avviato dal Ministero della Modernizzazione Amministrativa e dalla Presidenza del Consiglio Portoghese all'inizio del 2016 per tradurre in un esperimento--pilota la promessa fatta dal Partito Socialista durante la campagna elettorale, e assunta poi dall'intera maggioranza progressista che supporta il nuovo governo.

In questa prospettiva, diventa centrale soprattutto occuparsi di principi che – frattalmente, alle varie scale a cui le esperienze di democrazia partecipativa prendono forma – possono risultare centrali nell'ottimizzare il loro ruolo di "riconnettori democratici" per ristabilire relazioni di fiducia tra cittadini e istituzioni. Avendo in precedenza sottolineato alcuni elementi di necessaria differenziazione che i percorsi partecipativi devono mantenere al fine di valorizzare la loro *alterità ontologica* rispetto alla democrazia rappresentativa, vale la pena qui concentrarsi su alcuni *elementi condivisi* che necessita massimizzare perchè i cittadini e le cittadine coinvolte nei percorsi partecipativi sentano l'appartenenza di questi alla democrazia *tout court*, e possano immaginarli come una guida nell'auspicato percorso di reintensificazione democratica. A tal fine, dopo aver già esposto l'importanza del dare centralità al principio di "pubblicità" delle arene di dialogo sociale, può essere utile riprendere alcuni punti del decalogo di dieci capisaldi della democrazia con cui il costituzionalista Gustavo Zagrebelsky (2007)[26] ha cercato di fotografare i contenuti minimi necessari dell'ethos democratico. Ne evidenzierei sette:

1) Se la democrazia deve "credere in se stessa e non lasciar correre sulle questioni di principio" (come quelle che riguardano il rispetto dell'uguale dignità di tutti gli esseri umani, dei diritti che ne conseguono, dell'uguale partecipazione alla vita politica e delle procedure relative), per il resto essa deve riconoscere di essere "relativistica nel senso preciso della parola, cioè nel senso che i fini e i valori sono da considerare relativi a coloro che li propugnano e, nella loro varietà, tutti ugualmente legittimi". Per Zagrebelsky, se "il relativismo dell'insieme è condizione necessaria della democrazia" (giacché consente a tutti di far valere i

26 Il decalogo è stato rinvigorito durante la Lezione Magistrale di Gustavo Zagrebelsky per l'apertura della prima edizione della "sua" Biennale Democrazia di Torino, tenuta il 23 aprile 2009 al Teatro Carignano.

propri valori mentre il dogma pare incompatibile, e più adeguato alle autocrazie), essa deve evitare di nutrire i suoi nemici, ossia gli atteggiamenti di nichilismo o scetticismo diffusi nella società che la minacciano nella misura in cui chi non ha fede in nulla, non ha motivi per difendere una forma di governo rispetto a un'altra, tanto più una forma di governo come la democrazia che presuppone l'aspirazione dei singoli a promuovere e affermare le proprie posizioni e convinzioni. In tale prospettiva, la partecipazione (in quanto componente del vivere democratico) non può non iniziare come una aspirazione a una migliore e più intensa democrazia, ma necessita anche di sollecitare i più scettici, motivandoli con obiettivi concreti che (almeno inizialmente) possano attrarli, anche solo perchè reappresentano la possibilità di raggiungere convenienze individuali o di gruppo. L'offerta di spazi collettivi in cui riflettere e discutere è – come abbiamo visto – un anticorpo (e un valore aggiunto) necessario contro la degenerazione individualista, ma un certo equilibrio tra individuo e collettività è indispensabile in un'epoca dove pochi credono nella mediazione dei corpi intermedi del tessuto sociale. Non è un caso che nelle costituzioni della Bolivia e dell'Ecuador la democrazia partecipativa (legata a termini come civismo e cittadinanza) sia raffigurata come un modello differente dalla "democrazia comunitaria", che dialoga maggiormente con forme di partecipazione legate ad una appartenenza originaria (per esempio di tipo etnico-culturale) che non può essere scelta e comporta difficoltà ad essere rigettata senza compromettere la stessa identità della persona. In tale ottica, la democrazia partecipativa deve cercare un punto di equilibrio tra individui e gruppo, rigettando chi mette lo "strabordare dell'invidualismo" in relazione diretta con la democrazia, come se ne fosse un corollario precipuo o un "privilegio negativo" perchè l'ethos relativistico può coesistere con qualunque altro regime politico, e – anzi (come dimostra bene il caso della Cina) – in un regime autoritario può facilmente sfociare nel "più cinico opportunismo individualistico"

(Zagrebelsky, 2007).[27] L'importante, nella partecipazione, non sarebbe allora "comprimere l'individualismo" (in forma artificiale o di effimero radicamento, come avverrebbe in un regime autocratico), ma creare spazi che offrano opportunita per metterlo in costruzione e canalizzarlo. Similmente, possiamo applicare una tale prospettiva anche ai conflitti – che della differenza tra visioni e interessi sono la manifestazione più visibile. Infatti, un percorso partecipativo che li salta, li rimuove, li soffoca o li nasconde, invece che esplicitarli e cercare di farli convergere verso un punto comune, sarà destinato a vederli riemergere ed esplodere intorno e fuori di sè in altri momenti.

2) "La democrazia è fondata sugli individui, non sulla massa", e favorire la massificazione e la spersonalizzazione dei membri di una società significa – come già mostrato dalle lungimiranti analisi di Tocqueville sull'America del primo Ottocento - aprire la strada alla tirannide (della maggioranza). Ortega y Gasset (1979) scriveva che una democrazia senza qualità individuali apre la strada ai demagoghi, mentre i regimi totalitari, a loro volta, hanno bisogno, di *uomini-massa*, invece che di *uomini--individui*. Se i percorsi di democrazia partecipativa vogliono contribuire a preservare democrazie ormai stanche dalla degenerazione demagogica non potranno non combattere la passiva adesione alle mode e curare al massimo grado l'originalità di ciascuno dei suoi membri, concepita "non come stramberia, amore estetizzante della stravaganza ma, etimologicamente, come seria capacità di dare inizio, origine a un progetto, a un rinnovamento che produce vita nuova e combatte la passiva e animalesca ripetitività" (Zagrebelsky, 2007). Ovvero, la democrazia partecipativa deve essere un contributo per affrontare la preoccupazione sul procedere delle nostre società verso l'omologazione (che riguarda molti livelli dell'esistenza, dai consumi opportunamente detti "di massa" alla

27 In tale visione, per Zagrebelsky, "la critica alla democrazia per i suoi caratteri relativistici, non è una critica a una forma degenerata di democrazia ma è, *tout court*, il rigetto della democrazia".

formazione delle identità culturali e alla formazione dei pregiudizi) e per aiutarla a mantenersi come un "regime non pianificato" e "non de-terministico, cioè determinato da una necessità che sta fuori, o alle spalle degli esseri umani, come la legge della storia o una ideologia qualsiasi che si impossessa degli uomini e li trasforma in suoi automi" (*ibidem*). Tale ambizione, coime dimostrano molti processi partecipativi concreti, richiede – da parte dei promotori – una certa dose di coraggio, per provocare e sfidare constantemente i partecipanti con proposte che alzino il tiro sulla qualità dei risultati prodotti. Per esempio, nel Bilancio Partecipativo di Porto Alegre (come ben mostra Fedozzi, 2000) l'amministrazione municipale ha dovuto lottare strenuamente per far accettare principi di sostenibilità dello sviluppo, regole capaci di promuovere azioni affermative per i più deboli e modalità di pianificazione dei quartieri popolari, che sembravano andare contro la visione mimetica di un immaginario appiattito sui modelli visuali massificati prodotti dalla televisione. Necessita quindi adottare coraggio per affrontare i "miti" proposti spesso dalla maggioranza dei partecipanti, per cercare di far comprendere e gradualmente affermare progettazioni originali frutto di una riscoperta capacità creativa pianificatrice dissepolta con filologica pazienza sotto una coltre di pregiudizi e "immagini facili".

3) Se la democrazia non può non essere pensata in stretta relazione con il principio di uguaglianza (specialmente uguaglianza di opportunità) e in opposizione al privilegio[28], ogni processo partecipativo dovrà avere sommamente a cuore la promozione della "isonomia", pro-

28 Come ben sintetizza Zagrebelsky (2007), "Il privilegio ha (...) conseguenze nefaste nello spirito pubblico. Una società che si divide per privilegi dispone i suoi membri come su una scala: chi sta su e chi sta giù; chi sta su guarda dall'alto al basso chi sta giù. Ciò avvelena i rapporti, generando disprezzo sociale da parte dei primi nei confronti dei secondi. In questi ultimi, poi, produce arrivismo e genera una rincorsa insensata, tanto più accanita e spietata quanto più vuota di contenuto".

prio per contrastare la deriva attuale di molte democrazie moderne che tendono a rafforzare la polarizzazione sociale e una progressiva differenziazione – *de facto,* ma in alcuni casi anche *de iure*– di specifici gruppi di cittadini davanti alla legge. Parlare di "isonomia" serve a chiarire che l'uguaglianza non deve aver nulla a vedere con l'omologazione o la massificazione sociale e culturale, ricordata al punto precedente, ma con la esistenza di leggi valide per tutti, di *regole fredde* che non solo consentano a tutti di portare nella partecipazione sentimenti caldi (affinchè l'arena che viene costruendosi sia uno spazio di passione politica e di com-passione umana, oltre che un tavolo di negoziazione di interessi) ma che permettano che "le identità particolari siano ininfluenti rispetto alla pari partecipazione alla vita sociale" (ancorchè possano pesare poi sui contenuti trattati in ogni percorso di dialogo sociale), garantendo spazi "potenzialmente multi-identitari" (Zagrebelsky, 2007). Ciò risulta indispensabile in un'ottica convinta che la "democrazia non può accontentarsi della tolleranza", e che è l'assolutismo "che quando si ammorbidisce può parlare il linguaggio della tolleranza. Non la democrazia, alla quale si addice invece il linguaggio dei diritti di cittadinanza, ugualmente riconosciuti a tutti" (*id.*). A volte si tratta di piccole norme condivise per il funzionamento degli incontri pubblici (come quelle che regolano il tempo di parola di ogni partecipante, il modo di prendere le iscrizioni a parlare, i divieti di interventi multipli, l'etica del rispetto, le modalità di costruzione dell'ordine del giorno, il sorteggio dell'ordine degli interventi o dell'ordine di apparizione delle proposte su una scheda di voto, e simili) o per la gestione degli spazi *on-line* (regole di rispetto nelle chat, gestione dell'anonimato di chi interviene, randomizzazione delle proposte per sceglierne l'ordine ad ogni diversa visualizzazione, etc.). In ogni caso, non si tratta di questioni ininfluenti, specialmente quando aiutano i cittadini non solo a sentirsi uguali tra di loro, ma anche ad avere gli stessi "diritti" (per lo meno dentro lo spazio partecipativo) delle loro controparti politiche. E quando aiutano a capire che ai corpi intermedi organizzati della società non è dato godere di speciali privilegi per il loro ruolo di "rappresentanza sociale" ma semmai è richiesto di agire da motivatori ed attrattori di un percorso dove ogni partecipante si può sentire uguale agli altri. In realtà, nello stabilimento delle regole dei percorsi partecipativi è importante che valga un altro dei pilastri dell'etos democratico che Zagrebelsky ha richiamato nel suo testo del 2007, ovvero "la diffidenza verso le decisioni irrimediabili". Infatti, per quanto è importante che in ogni ciclo partecipativo le regole siano chiare e rispettate da tutti, da un ciclo all'altro è non solo possibile, ma forse indispensabile, valutare come hanno funzionato e poterle modificare. Il che richiede statuti normativi abbastanza flessibili da non restare imbrigliati (da un ciclo all'altro) nella perpetuazione continua del passato.

4) In tale ottica, vale la pena sottolineare che la partecipazione dovrebbe potenziare *l'atteggiamento sperimentale* che è componente centrale della democrazia, la quale "è orientata da principi, ma deve imparare quotidianamente anche dalle conseguenze delle proprie azioni". Porre attenzione alle conseguenze dell'agire significa non solo investire e dare continuamente il giusto spazio alla valutazione (possibilmente collettiva e plurale) dei percorsi partecipativi e dei loro effetti sul territorio, l'amministrazione e la società – il che non avviene spessissimo nei percorsi partecipativi reali – ma anche comunicare e dibattere queste valutazioni in modo da prendere le migliori misure possibili per migliorare in futuro la *performance* del dispositivo partecipativo e ottimizzare il suo contributo alla rivitalizzazione della democrazia. Il mantenimento di questo spirito sperimentale – sempre pronto a innovare e aggiungere componenti creative a quanto già messo alla prova in passato – può costituire un utile strumento per contrastare la vocazione populista, che spesso si fa visibile nell'intenzione di trasformare immediatamente ed imperiosamente in leggi la cosiddetta volontà popolare.

5) Se "la democrazia è *la forma di vita comune di esseri umani solidali tra loro (...) e l'emarginazione sociale è contro la democrazia*" perchè

esprime l'idea di virtù repubblicana di Montesquieu, *quell'amore per la cosa pubblica* che presuppone *disponibilità* a mettere in comune qualcosa di sé, anzi il meglio di sé: tempo, capacità, risorse materiali"[29] è indubbio che ogni processo partecipativo dovrà riuscire a stimolare atteggiamenti altruistici e non potrà ridursi a sommare preferenze individuali senza farsi carico di stimolare dibattiti sui beni comuni e gli interessi collettivi. Se – come rivendicato da Santos (2007) – un processo partecipativo ha anche il ruolo di appoggiare la democrazia nel farsi "ecologia di saperi", aprire spazio alle "assenze" dei tradizionali modi di fare politica e società, e valorizzare "epistemologie altre" (*id.*) da quelle che forgiano i modi correnti di leggere il mondo, nessuno potrà "essere lasciato indietro, abbandonato a se stesso e alle difficoltà della sua vita particolare" (Zagrebelski, 2007) e al cinismo del darwinismo applicato alla vita sociale richiamato già oltre un secolo fa da Herbert Spencer (Toscano, 1980). Questa è, forse, la sfida più difficile da affrontare, specialmente per quei percorsi che utilizzano le nuove tecnologie come fonte di riduzione dei costi e richiamo per un'ampia fetta di cittadini inizialmente poco impegnati civicamente. Ed è tanto più difficile per i percorsi partecipativi che si propongono di non centrarsi su corpi intermedi già sensibili ma di attrarre individui spesso scettici su ogni ruolo di rappresentanza e di *advocacy* dei più deboli. In tale ottica, è oggi indispensabile pensare a progetti ibridi (dove l'online cede il passo in alcune fasi a recuperare vecchi modi di incontrarsi faccia-a-faccia, anche con l'uso di momenti festivi e conviviali) e multicanale, che mettano in campo metodi diversi per raccogliere idee e preferenze, si propongano metodi differenziati di *outreach* (ossia di raggiungere i cittadini là dove vivono) e azioni affermative per coinvolgere *i sommersi* e non solo i salvati, per usare il linguaggio di Primo Levi. Quello dell'inclusione è un cammino difficile e lento. Tra gli oltre 3.000 Bilanci Participativi oggi esistenti al mondo, solo pochi hanno tentato di

---

29 Faccio qui riferimento al discorso di Zagrebelski che ha aperto la Biennale Democrazia (2009, già citato).

introdurre criteri sociali per raggiungere effetti di giustizia distributiva (Marquetti *et alii*, 2007), e non tantissimi hanno creato linee speciali di azione basate sulla discriminazione positiva per includere direttamente "i più poveri tra i poveri". In ogni caso, si sono sempre dovuti scontrare sia con chi pensa che la partecipazione dovrebbe solo limitarsi a premiare chi meglio si impegna ed organizza (con una visione meramente competitivo-liberista della stessa) sia con chi pensa che sia meglio che diseredati siano inclusi soprattutto per via indiretta, attraverso la mediazione di professionisti sensibili e riflessivi che Goodman e la generazione dei grandi processi partecipativi americani degli anni '70 definivano come urbanisti, sociologi o antropologi *di parte* (Forester, 1988). Oggi, sembra essersi raggiunta la consapevolezza che solo il coinvolgimento diretto dei più deboli in percorsi davvero inclusivi può contribuire alla democrazia, e per questo sono necessarie molte attenzioni ed accorgimenti in ogni istante, a partire dalla gradulaità con cui i processi partecipativi evolvono (perchè nessuno li rigetti come stanchi e ripetivi rituali burocratizzati) fino a quella che Zagrebelsky (2007) definisce la "cura delle parole in quanto numero e in quanto qualità". Perchè per restituire alla democrazia la sua essenza di convivenza basata sul dialogo, il mezzo che permette il dialogo non può essere ingannatore, ma le parole dovranno essere "precise, specifiche, dirette; basso tenore emotivo, poche metafore; lasciar parlar le cose attraverso le parole, non far crescere parole con e su altre parole; no al profluvio che logora e confonde" (*id.*). Oggi viviamo sempre una tensione tra chi ritiene che la politica debba abbassare i suoi linguaggi al livello della strada, e chi ritiene che la pedagogia civica dei processi partecipativi debba ambire a complessificare il linguaggio, insegnando ai cittadini ad usare il linguaggio delle leggi e delle tecno-burocrazie, perchè tanto è quello che poi regola gli atti amministrativi. Forse, la soluzione sta nel mezzo, nell'incontrarsi a metà strada di attori che fanno sforzi per adattarsi e comprendersi mutualmente. Nel processo partecipativo che, nel 2014, ha accompagnato il Piano Metropolitano di Sviluppo di Belo Horizonte (in Brasile) il team di facilitatori comprendeva un gruppo di teatro di strada che realizzava delle piccole commedie storpiando gli astrusi termini tecnici del linguaggio pianificatorio, fino a renderli familiari e amati dai cittadini partecipanti. Un buon esempio di come l'arte (come insegnano le tecniche di *facilitazione visuale*[30]) può aiutare a rendere la realtà e l'impegno civico-politico più comprensibili e attraenti per tutti.

6) Se "la democrazia è discussione, ragionare insieme" o "per ricorrere a un'espressione socratica, filologia e non misologia" (Zagrebelsky, 2007), ogni processo partecipativo dovrà porsi come attivatore e ricettore dello "spirito del dialogo", sapendo che "chi odia i discorsi e il confronto delle idee, alla persuasione preferisce la sopraffazione". Dovrà quindi mantenersi, in ogni fase, una forma di governo "*discutidora*" (come la chiamava con sprezzo il reazionario di ottocentesco Juan Donoso Cortés, 1972) e non cedere alla tentazione di concedersi fasi dove trionfa l'atteggiamento tecnoburocratico o l'insofferenza della politica per il dibattito democratico prende il sopravvento ed espropria i cittadini della loro capacità decisionale per affermare i suoi tempi e la sua superiorità di visione. Di fatto, è provato anche uno solo di questi tentativi di cambiar registro da parte delle istituzioni che interagiscono in un percorso partecipativo, viene vissuta come una insopportabile "ri-espropriazione" dello spazio originariamente concesso alla società in nome della "governabilità" o di ritmi decisionali che il cittadino vive come proiezioni della "casta" e atti di eterodirezione. In tale ottica, un lento ma virtuoso percorso di ricostruzione della fiducia si può trasformare in pochi istanti in un boomerang politico, per un gesto di impazienza o una parola sbagliata che (agli occhi dell'ipersensibilità che segna tutti coloro che si trovavano colti in un precario e difficile sforzo per accettare di credere all'esistenza di una "buona politica') vanifica ogni promessa di ascolto e rivela la totale falla-

---

30 Cfr. http://graphicfacilitation.blogs.com o http://visualfacilitators.com/en

città di un "patto" che era stato accolto con buona (ancorchè guardinga) disposizione nonostante lo scetticismo iniziale...

7) Per preservare l'integrità del ragionare, la democrazia necessita innanzitutto di rispettare - come osserva Zagrebelsky - "la verità dei fatti, che è la base di ogni azione orientata a intendersi onestamente" e rigettare le tentazioni di disprezzare i fatti, travisarli appositamente o addirittura creali o ricrearli *ad hoc* come accade in molte dittature ideologiche orwelliane centrate "sulla propaganda e il bombardamento dei cervelli" e che "trattano i fatti come opinioni e instaurano un relativismo nichilistico applicato non alle opinioni ma ai fatti" mettendo "la verità (...) sullo stesso piano della menzogna, il giusto su quello dell'ingiusto, il bene su quello del male". Fuggire questa tentazione non è facile, neppure nel semplice atto dell'autorappresentazione. Basta vedere quanti processi partecipativi (come il Bilancio Partecipativo di Lisbona) vendono informazioni ritoccate sul numero di partecipanti che li hanno sostenuti, per autorappresentarsi come dei successi piuttosto che affrontare una coraggiosa autocritica sui perchè di una mancanza di affezione dei cittadini in relazione ad essi. Eppure è ineludibile, per una democrazia partecipativa che voglia contribuire a rinvigorire la democrazia *tout court*, aderire all'imperativo socratico di "né intestardirsi né lasciar correre" e – ancor più – di apprezzare come la virtù massima di chi ama il dialogo il rallegrarsi di essere scoperto in errore. Un percorso partecipativo serio necessita quindi di elaborare la capacità di mantenere sempre vivo lo "spirito del dialogo", e di spingere i suoi partecipanti a non considerare una sconfitta, o - peggio ancora - un'umiliazione, l'essere colti in errore, vedendola invece come una opportunità per migliorare attraverso la conoscenza di cose nuove e punti di vista diversi. Per coltivare questa virtù, il processo partecipativo dovrà promuovere il pluralismo come strumento di conoscenza, creando percorsi gnoseologici e epistemologici basati sull'idea arendtiana che «nessuno, da solo e senza compagni, può comprendere adeguatamente e nella sua piena realtà tutto ciò che è obiettivo, in quanto gli si mostra e

gli si rivela sempre in un'unica prospettiva, conforme e intrinseca alla sua posizione nel mondo. Se egli vuole vedere ed esperire il mondo così com'è 'realmente', può farlo solo considerandolo una cosa che è comune a molti, che sta tra loro, che li separa e unisce, che si mostra a ognuno in modo diverso, e dunque diviene comprensibile solo se molti ne parlano insieme e si scambiano e confrontano le loro opinioni e prospettive. Soltanto nella libertà di dialogare il mondo appare quello di cui si parla, nella sua obiettività visibile da ogni lato» (Arendt, 2006, pag. 40). Se, ancora una volta, ciò che è centrale è contribuire la pluralità di prospettive su uno stesso fatto, una stessa esigenza o una stessa politica, un percorso partecipativo dovrà non limitarsi a confrontare opinioni su ciò che si deve fare (sul futuro), ma anche su come tale azione va connessa al passato e alle carenze o ai cambiamenti che hanno reso necessario superarlo. Non è un caso che oggi molte amministrazioni locali ed organizzazioni sociali (a partire da Porto Alegre) vadano investendo sulla creazione di Osservatori delle politiche pubbliche, visti non solo come spazi di controllo sociale dell'azione istituzionale, ma anchge come restauratori della verità dei fatti e della grandezza dei numeri diffusi. In tal senso, queste strutture (attraverso la loro composizione mista che associa attori istituzionali, sociali e del mondo della ricerca) ambiscono a rompere i monopoli della produzione di dati (che genera dubbi sulla natura interessata degli stessi) proprio restaurando un "filtro" e un controllo multiplo tra il momento della produzione delle conoscenze su un territorio e il suo governo e il momento della diffusione delle stesse, per evitare che le informazioni messe in circolo siano più strumenti di propaganda che di conoscenza. Tali osservazioni possono anche configurarsi come consigli scientifici, ossia come spazi in grado di aiutare a formulare "buone domande" capaci di aiutare a prendere buone decisioni ed evitare che gli esiti dei percorsi di interazione tra istituzioni e cittadini producano risultati perversi sulla base di posizioni demagogico/populiste come nell'epico dialogo tra Pilato e i cittadini per la scelta della liberazione di Gesù o Barabba (Zagrebelsky, 1995) o nel percorso decisionale sedicente partecipativo che, nel 1446, alterò completamente il progetto pre-barocco di Filippo Brunelleschi per la chiesa di Santo Spirito, banalizzando molte delle straordinarie peculiarità immaginate dal grande architetto prima della sua morte precoce.

Una conclusione aperta

Non vi è dubbio che - mentre i regimi formalmente riconosciuti come democratici si espandono per il pianeta - la democrazia passa per una crisi di attendibilità, che include una crescente percezione di legittimità ridotta delle sue istituzioni. In tale frangente, la reazione più comune del potere è quella di accentuare i suoi modi di occultarsi. Ma, come ha scritto Bobbio (1999), "gran parte della storia del pensiero politico può essere interpretata come un continuo tentativo da parte dei sudditi di strappare i veli o le visiere o le maschere dietro cui si nascondono i detentori del potere, di estendere l'area del potere visibile rispetto a quella del potere invisibile". Cosi, in questa visione di carattere agonistico (Mouffe, 2013), si avverte, senza dubbio, da parte di sempre più ampie componenti della cittadinanza, la crescente rivendicazione di un "diritto" a partecipare in forma più permanente alle decisioni, al di là degli stretti spazi e delle intermittenti occasioni che i rituali elettorali della democrazia rappresentativa lasciano a percorsi decisionali inclusivi di tipo collaborativo.

Le esperienze concrete di apertura delle istituzioni pubbliche alla partecipazione, di certo, non sono sufficienti a rispondere da sole a questo desiderio di coinvolgimento diretto, ma è indubbio che, nell'ultimo decennio, vi è stata una crescita (in numero, qualità e entusiasmo dei partecipanti) dei percorsi partecipativi "su invito"- specialmente in ambito locale - su cui vale la pena riflettere e appuntare una maggiore attenzione. Se prendiamo un paese come il Portogallo, con altissimi tassi di astensionismo elettorale, e guardiamo ad alcuni processi consolidati, come il Bilancio Partecipativo di Cascais (città di 200.000 abitanti a guida conservatrice), ci rendiamo conto che la partecipazione in questo processo ha "doppiato" addirittura i voti che hanno eletto il sindaco nelle ultime elezioni, e quest'ultimo lo ha assunto come un mantra, orgogliosamente, nei suoi discorsi pubblici, aumentando gradualmente il peso del percorso partecipativo nel quadro delle decisioni generali.[31] Le ragioni stanno nelle caratteristiche di un percorso trasparente, che produce effetti in tempi brevi, che lascia con coraggio spazio crescente ai cittadini per scegliere, dettagliare e monitorare i progetti e che sa crescere e trasformarsi creativamente di anno in anno con i suoi partecipanti, prestando attenzione ai loro palpiti e desideri di cambiamento costante, proprio di chi – crescendo con la democrazia – diventa ogni anno non solo più esigente e critico, ma anche più costruttivo ed entusiasta.

Certo, non è questo lo standard della maggior parte dei processi partecipativi nel pianeta. Come ben ricorda Fung (2011), la maggioranza dei percorsi partecipativi istituzionalizzati è ancora di tipo "deontologico" (ossia si accontenta di mettere in campo più spazi di dialogo sociale perché considera questo un 'fine" buono in sé), mentre sono molte meno le pratiche "consequenzialiste" in cui la partecipazione è vista come un "mezzo" per raggiungere altri obiettivi specifici (di inclusione sociale, giustizia redistributiva, trasparenza, lotta alla corruzione o quali essi siano) e il successo della sperimentazione è giudicato in funzione dell'impatto che essa ha sul territorio e sulla società in funzione della coerenza di strumenti messi in campo per ottenere risultati in campi ben chiari (e da subito chiariti come orizzonti di senso dei processi) della trasformazione socio-economica, culturale, istituzionale e/o territoriale.

Spesso, come si è visto, i percorsi partecipativi imbastiti con la missione (esplicita o implicita) di ricostruire il dialogo interrotto tra cittadini e

---

31 I Votanti del BP nel 2015 sono stati oltre 55.900 (una crescita del 71% rispetto al 2011, anno di inizio della sperimentazione) mentre nel 2013 il Sindaco è stato eletto con poco più di 28.000 voti. In parallelo, i fondi destinati alle priorità decise dai cittadini sono passati da 1,4 a oltre 4 milioni di Euro in 5 anni. Vedi http://www.cascais.pt/camara-residentes/destaque/op-cascais-2015--votacao-recorde-de-55919-votos-parabens-todos e http://www.cm-cascais.pt/orcamento-participativo-2015.

istituzioni rappresentative non riescono nell'obiettivo, perché sono "addomesticati", o incompleti nell'acquisire il coraggio di mettere realmente il cittadino nel centro della decisione, o semplicemente perché sono "mimetici" rispetto alle forme della democrazia rappresentativa o subordinati dentro un orizzonte di significati che dà priorità agli approcci tecno-burocratici e proceduralisti. Per esempio, non osano mettere in campo forme di *contro--expertise* (Revel *et alii*, 2007) in grado di valorizzare il "sapere politico" e i "saperi esperti" della cittadinanza, ma si limitano ad aprire spazi ai "saperi d'uso" dei cittadini (Sintomer, 2010), senza rendersi conto che la sfiducia nella politica coinvolge direttamente il mondo della conoscenza tecnica che la supporta (considerato gregario e cooptato alle ragioni della politica partitica o agli interessi del mercato) e che necessita "sfidarlo" apertamente per riconquistarsi la fiducia degli abitanti.

In tale quadro, non si mette in dubbio la stretta connessione che esiste - e deve esistere - tra democrazia rappresentativa e i percorsi partecipativi al fine di attivare "circoli virtuosi" (Ganuza e Francès, 2012) di rivitalizzazione della democrazia, ma è necessario comprendere che, per realizzare la sua promessa di complementarietà con la rappresentanza, la partecipazione necessita di valorizzare le sue componenti di alterità e unicità, e veder riconosciuta l'autonomia sociale (in termini di capacità di azione, di margini di manovra decisionale e di specificità epistemologiche) rispetto alle istituzioni. Altrimenti, la sua ontologia subordinata non sarà percepita come sufficientemente forte e attrattiva da meritare che i cittadini investano il loro poco tempo libero, le loro conoscenze, le loro passioni e i loro entusiasmi in attività di importanza civica che, per di più, comportano la necessità di accettare sforzi per cambiare linguaggi, superare la tendenza alla mera critica per acquisire doti e volontà propositive, e mettere in discussione se stessi e le proprie convinzioni davanti agli altri. Perché non va sottostimato che confrontarsi sulle idee comporta un passo avanti convinto e coraggioso nella concezione del rapporto tra minoranze e maggioranze, specie in un panorama politico che ci ha abituato alla *dittatura delle maggioranze* e a cui la democrazia partecipativa dovrebbe poter apportare una riflessione sulla costruzione graduale e rispettosa delle convergenze (piuttosto che del consenso), invece di scimmiottarne la pura ricerca di facile governabilità. Come ha scritto Zagrebelsky (2007), sarebbe necessario giungere a comprendere insieme che "la ragione d'essere e di operare delle minoranze è la sfida alla bontà della deliberazione presa, nell'aspettativa di prenderne un'altra diversa. Per questo, ogni deliberazione in cui una maggioranza sopravanza numericamente una minoranza non è una vittoria della prima e una sconfitta della seconda. È invece una provvisoria prevalenza che assegna un duplice onere: alla maggioranza di dimostrare poi, nel tempo a venire, la validità della sua decisione; alla minoranza, di insistere per far valere ragioni migliori. Ond'è che nessuna votazione, in democrazia (salvo quelle riguardanti le regole costitutive o costituzionali della democrazia stessa) chiude definitivamente una partita. Entrambe attendono e, al tempo stesso, precostituiscono il terreno per la sfida di ritorno tra le buone ragioni che possano essere accampate".

In tale prospettiva, è chiara la necessità di costruire spazi partecipativi che rappresentino prima di tutto un nuovo principio etico-politico (Baierle, 1992), capaci di costruire pedagogia civica e di spiegare l'essenza della democrazia, prima ancora di contribuire alla trasformazione delle politiche pubbliche e del governo del territorio, o – ancora meglio – di farlo contestualmente, attraverso *l'apprender facendo*. Sarebbe interessante, in contesti di processi partecipativi che abbiano le caratteristiche che abbiamo cercato di evidenziare in questo articolo, capire quali elementi costitutivi avrebbe la sua *folksonomia*[32], ossia quali parole chiave

32 Il neologismo, derivato dal termine inglese *folksonomy* (che unisce i termini "folk" e "tassonomia"), "indica l'operazione di categorizzare informazioni compiuta dagli utenti mediante l'utilizzo di parole chiave (o tag) scelte liberamente"; e nel web 2.0 rappresenta, pertanto, "la metodologia utilizzata da gruppi di persone che collaborano spontaneamente per organizzare in categorie le informazioni disponibili attraverso internet" (cfr. https://pt.wikipedia.org/wiki/Folksonomia, consultata il 22 dicembre 2015).

comporrebbero la tassonomia creata dagli abitanti in base ai loro criteri individuali. Servirebbe, infatti, a riflettere in maniera più definita i valori centrali riconosciuti ai percorsi di dialogo sociale secondo il modello concettuale della popolazione che essi riescono (o meno) a mobilizzare.

A questo punto ci si potrebbe domandare: perché – se "alla sinistra si attribuisce la dimensione dell'orizzontalità come risoluzione dell'esistenza nell'orizzonte storico-temporale" (Veneziani, in Carnevali, 2013) e l'anelito all'egualitarismo "inteso (...) non come l'utopia di una società in cui tutti sono uguali in tutto ma come tendenza, da un lato, a esaltare più ciò che rende gli uomini eguali che ciò che li rende diseguali, dall'altro, in sede pratica, a favorire le politiche che mirano a rendere più eguali i diseguali" (Bobbio, 1999) – molta sinistra, in vari paesi, è ancora tiepida, quando non del tutto scettica, rispetto alla necessità di impegnarsi in seri processi partecipativi?

La risposta più facile è che la possibilità di esercitare da soli il potere discrezionale che è loro concesso dalla rappresentanza, resta una forte tentazione trasversale per coloro che ascendono a cariche pubbliche, indipendentemente dalla collocazione ideologica; e se lo è per molte persone, lo è - a maggior ragione - per le strutture-partito che temono ogni concorrente che possa minacciare la loro centralità nel sistema. Naturalmente, si tratta di un'equivocata visione del termine potere, che confonde la sua componente di "autorevolezza" con l'esercizio della autorità, o non riesce a comprendere la realtà attuale, dove l'acquisizione di autorevolezza conquistata per via ignora dialogica può costituire una premessa indispensabile per i cittadini per non nutrire rigetto nei confronti di chi ha incarichi di governo. Ma gli abiti interpretativi sono difficile da superare, come mostrano molto bene vari amministratori che, pur impegnati in avanzati percorsi partecipativi, continuano a designarsi con il termine di "decisori politici" così vanificando parte del lavoro fatto per mostrare ai loro concittadini la centralità attribuitagli all'interno delle scelte per il territorio. In tale prospettiva, una seconda spiegazione di questa – per altri versi, incomprensibile – disattenzione (o incredulità) delle forze di sinistra rispetto all'importanza dei percorsi partecipativi per la gestione delle nostre democrazie, viene, di certo, da una sorta di "pigrizia" nell'affrontare gli sforzi che una "buona partecipazione" richiede a chi la vuole praticare con serietà. Sforzi che non risiedono solo nel seguire alcuni di quei precetti che abbiamo cercato di visualizzare nella seconda parte di questo articolo, ma anche nella necessità di accettare che – come hanno ben colto Revelli (2009) e Serra (2013) - la "chiave, pesante come una croce, maledetta come un dovere, che la sinistra si porta in spalla, è la complessità. È la cognizione che la realtà è una cosa complicata, che la sua lettura è una cosa complicata, e che il primo inganno da disinnescare, se si vuole provare a essere una comunità cosciente, è appunto la semplificazione in quanto tale: non solo e non tanto perché è strumento di propaganda, quanto perché in sé, nella politica come nella vita, la semplificazione è menzogna" (Serra, 2009). I percorsi partecipativi potrebbero, forse, essere gli spazi privilegiati per riscoprire questo un ruolo della politica come spazio per spiegare e capire insieme la complessità, abbandonando – da un lato – il facile "sloganismo" (più proprio dei populismi che della democrazia), e – dall'altro – quel linguaggio "spesso criptico, spesso respingente, e nei casi peggiori altezzoso e inconcludente in pari misura" che genera "le accuse di 'snobismo' e di 'antipatia' che oggi grandinano su molta sinistra e sugli intellettuali di ogni calibro" (*ibidem*).

Il superamento di queste due ragioni, che bloccano dal comprendere l'importanza che una seria sperimentazione di spazi di democrazia partecipativa avrebbe per la democrazia (e per una sinistra che voglia essere attenta a ravvivarla e ad aumentarne il grado di intensità), non potrà che essere congiunto e contestuale. E richiede di accettare la dimensione ibrida della partecipazione, quel suo essere al contempo riformismo (nella lentezza e gradualità delle trasformazioni, nella costruzione consensuale delle regole) ma anche rivoluzione (nella centralità dell'orizzonte utopico, nella solidità e radicalità dei principi che supportano la trasformazione, nell'incertezza di quale saranno gli sbocchi finali di un percorso di mutamento istituzionale *non addomesticato e non domabile*, che si costruisce in parallelo alla maturazione degli attori). Richiede di accettare una visione del riformismo come "politica delle compatibilità (...) che non esclude affatto un principio di radicalità" intesa come "strumento che serve a perseguire due obiettivi: a individuare con nettezza i problemi, e a suscitare identità" (Berselli, 2008). In una tale ottica, chi concepisce la sinistra come "quella vasta area della politica e del pensiero che pretende di organizzare il cambiamento della società, prima interpretandolo e poi orientandolo", e la cui funzione principe è proprio "progettare il cambiamento" (Serra, 2013), non può facilmente giustificare il disinteresse per ciò che sta accadendo nel mondo delle pratiche partecipative, e per essere parte attiva di queste sperimentazioni.

Riferimenti bibliografici

Allegretti, G. (2003). *L'insegnamento di Porto Alegre. Autoprogettualità come paradigma urbano*. Firenze: Alinea.

Allegretti, G. (2000) *Verso una colloquialità tra città informale e città formale: ipotesi di lettura di una esperienza esemplare*, discussa il 3 aprile 2000 presso la Università degli Studi di Firenze, Facoltà di Architettura, Dipartimento di Urbanistica.

Allegretti, U. (2006), Basi giuridiche della democrazia partecipativa in Italia: alcuni orientamenti. *Democrazia e Diritto*, Roma, n. 3, p. 151-66

Allegretti, U. (2008). Democrazia partecipativa e processi di democratizzazione. *Democrazia e diritto*, n. 2, 2008.

Allegretti, U. (2010). *Democrazia partecipativa. Esperienze e prospettive in Italia e in Europa*. Firenze: Firenze University, 2010.

Allegretti, U. (2011). Democrazia partecipativa. *Enciclopedia del diritto. Annali IV*, p. 295 ss.

Allegretti, U.; Corsi, C.; Allegretti, G. (2016). Constituent Process and Constituent Assembly: the making of constitutions through the larger involvement of citizens. *Forum di Quaderni Costituzionali - Rassegna*, Jul. 2016, 1-25.

Arnstein, S. R. (1969). A ladder of citizen participation, *Journal of the American Institute of Planners* 35(4), p.216-224.

Arnstein, S. R. (1975). A working model for public participation, *Public Administration Review*, 35(1), 70-73.

Berselli, E. (2008). Per un populismo della sinistra, *La Repubblica*, 25 ottobre 2008.

Bifulco, R. (2011), Democrazia deliberativa, *Enciclopedia del diritto. Annali IV*, p.271 ss.

Bobbio, L. (a cura di, 2004). *A più voci. Amministrazioni pubbliche, imprese, associazioni e cittadini nei processi decisionali inclusivi*. Napoli: Scientifiche Italiane.

Bobbio, N. (1999). *Teoria generale della politica*. Torino: Einaudi, 1999.

Bobbio, N. (2005). *Il futuro della democrazia*. Torino: Einaudi (prima edizione, 1984).

Bobbio, N. (2011). *Democrazia e segreto*. Torino: Einaudi (a cura di M. Revelli).

Carnevali, E. (2013), "Che cos'è sinistra?". *Micromega online*, 17 luglio 2013, scaricabile da: http://temi.repubblica.it/micromega-online/che-cose-sinistra/?printpage=undefined.

Dahl, R .A. (2005). *La democrazia e i suoi critici*. Milano: Ed. Riuniti.

Donoso Corté, J. (1972). *Saggio sul cattolicesimo, il liberalismo e il socialismo*. Milano: Rusconi (edizione originale, 1850).

Elster, J. (2005). *Argomentare e negoziare*. Milano: Bruno Mondadori.

Gangemi, G. (20110). L'E-democracy come risvolto tecnologico della partecipazione, in De Pietro L. (a cura di), *L'evoluzione dei modelli e delle tecnologie per la partecipazione. L'esperienza del Consiglio regionale del Veneto*. Venezia: Marsilio.

Garau C. (2013). *Processi di Piano e Partecipazione*. Napoli: Gangemi.

Guizot, F. (2009). *Historia de los orígenes del gobierno representativo en Europa*. Oviedo: KRK.

Habermas, J. (1984). *Storia e critica dell'opinione pubblica*. Bari: Laterza.

http://cidadaosporcoimbra.pt/

IAP2 (2007). *Spectrum of public Participation, scaricabile da*: http://c.ymcdn.com/sites/www.iap2.org/resource/resmgr/imported/IAP2%20Spectrum_vertical.pdf.

Kelsen, H. (1995). *La democrazia*. Bologna: il Mulino.

Manin, B. (1996). *Principes du gouvernement représentatif*. Paris: Flammarion.

Ortega y Gasset, J. (1979). *La ribellione delle masse. Scritti politici*. Torino: UTET.

Regione Emilia Romagna (2010), *LEGGE REGIONALE* 09 febbraio *2010, n. 3*, Norme per la definizione, riordino e promozione delle procedure di consultazione e partecipazione alla elaborazione delle politiche regionali e locali, in *BOLLETTINO UFFICIALE* n. 18 del 9 febbraio 2010.

Regione Toscana (2007), *LEGGE REGIONALE 27* dicembre 2007, n. 69, Norme sulla promozione della partecipazione alla elaborazione delle politiche regionali e locali, in *BOLLETTINO UFFICIALE*, n. 1 del 3 gennaio 2008.

Revel, M. *et allii* (a cura di, 2007), *Le débat public: une experience française de démoratie participative*. Paris: La Découverte.

Revelli, M. (2009). *Sinistra destra. L'identità smarrita*. Milano: Laterza.

Rosanvallon, P. (2008). *La légitimité démocratique. Impartialité, réflexivité, proximité*. Paris: Seuil, 2008.

Santos, B. De Sousa (2007). Beyond Abyssal Thinking. From Global Lines to Ecologies of Knowledges, *Review*, XXX, 1, p. 45-89.

Santos, B. de Sousa (2009). Os Desafios da Democracia Participativa" In *Actas do III Encontro nacional sobre orçamento participativo*, Lisboa/S. bras de Alportel: Associação.

Serra, M. (2013). Progressisti, smettete di rimpiangere il passato, *La Repubblica*, 16 luglio 2016, http://www.repubblica.it/la-repubblica--delle-idee/societa/2013/07/16/news/progressisti_smettete_di_rimpiangere_il_passato-63089995/?ref=search

Sgueo, G. (2010), "Democrazia di Prossimità e Legislazione Regionale. Le Leggi N. 69 del 2007 della Regione Toscana e N. 3 del 2010 della Regione Emilia Romagna", in *Scientia Iuris*, Londrina, v. 14, nov. 2010, pp. 193-219.

Sintomer, Y. (2009). *Il potere al popolo. Giurie cittadine, sorteggio e democrazia partecipativa.* Bari: Dedalo.

Sintomer, Y. (2011). Délibération et participation: affinité élective ou concepts en tension?, *Participations*, n. 1, 2011, pp. 239 ss.

Sintomer, Y.; Allegretti, G. (2009), *I bilanci partecipativi in Europa. Nuove esperienze democratiche nel vecchio continente.* Roma: Ediesse.

Tocqueville, A. De (2006). *La democrazia in America* (1835-1840), a cura di C. Vivanti, trad. di A. Vivanti Salmon, Einaudi, Torino 2006, soprattutto libro II, parte IV, capitolo vu. La citazione del testo è a p. 780.

Wilcox, D. (s.d.). *The Guide to effective Participation*: http://www.partnerships.org.uk/guide/index.htm.

Zagrebelsky, G. (1995). *«Crucifige!» e la democrazia.* Torino: Einaudi.

Zagrebelsky, G. (2015). *Moscacieca.* Milano: Laterza.

Zagrebelsky,G. (2007). *Imparare democrazia.* Einaudi: Torino 2007, p.15-38.

A case for COPLA and UNPA – Citizenship in the age of Globalization: Citizenship and institutional innovation in the global sphere: the proposals for the creation of a Latin American and Caribbean Criminal Court Against Organized Crime (COPLA) and a United Nations Parliamentary Assembly (UNPA)

Fernando Iglesias

From the *urbi* to the *orbi*

"Citizen" and "citizenship", what meaningful words! They both come from "city", that is to say, from proto-modern burgs, those primitive European cities that, at the dawn of Modern Times, rescued the best Athenian traditions and gave birth to Modern Democracy. Burgs, the cities of that age, constituted the initial expression of a multi-cultural/multi-ethnical/multi-religious cosmopolite society that gradually overcame the aristocratic-classist-confessional-elitist character of ancient times and feudal states. Burgs built a public common space and established participative mechanisms of negotiation and decision-making. Burgs were the place where interracial-intersexual-intercultural- cross-breeding processes occurred. Burgs meant the most concrete negation of "the idiocy of rural life" and "reactionary barbarism hostile to strangers", according to well-known Marx's statements. Burgs inaugurated a world were Knowledge, Information, Diversity, Communication, Innovation and Subjectivity were destined to become decisive, in a "world that was not necessarily defined by its own reproduction and where innovation had citizen rights"[1].

Across centuries, things have changed dramatically. At present, the impact of global phenomena is visible all along the social sphere. Beyond individual desires and collective projects, the citizens of this early-global world are submitted to worldwide processes that, directly and indirectly, affect all the aspects of human life. "Perhaps you are not interested in Globalization, but Globalization is interested in you" paraphrasing Trotsky's statement on war.

Due to globalization, the distinction between the First and the Third world vacillates. Due to global migrations, the poor periphery of the globe arrives directly at the suburbs of central cities, causing a commotion in the job market and challenging national conceptions of security, cultural identity, and citizenship. On the other hand, the extension of economic benefits to every inhabitant of Earth -no-matter-where-he-lives- under the only condition of being capable of interacting in global processes constitutes a de-territorializing mutation. Globalization is, in many aspects, convergence: living within an emergent global framework means that territorial barriers seem to be there, but they are not there anymore.

Due to globalization, the Third and the First world do still exist but they get mixed in a less territorial way, meanwhile national loyalties get brooked. Why should American enterprises pay higher taxes for improving the skills of American workers, when Mexican immigrants can do the job or it can be outsourced to China? Why should American corporations contribute to the education of the American youth when highly qualified workers can be found anywhere in the world? Why should corporations finance long-term investments in education and infrastructure in a country where they don't know for how long they will be in? Why should they be interested in collaborating with workers and institutions of a given country when "outside" global corporations can

1 Todorov, Tzvetan. *Deberes y Delicias*. Madrid: Fondo de Cultura Económica, 2003.

enter the national market and abandon it as soon as a negative trend appears in the horizon? Why should national élites pay for well-skilled/educated/healthy citizens if they are not available anymore because they get sent off to war in order to defend 'national' interests? Why, if students and workers can emigrate to another point of the global market looking for better salaries and opportunities?

The model of national taxation, which has been the base of modern taxation for centuries, has exploded in a spatial, a temporal and a social way. As Globalization becomes the norm, spatial mobility determines individual survival in lower classes and self-realization in middle/upper classes. It changes the coordinates with respect to the past, when most human beings spent all their lives working for survival chained to land -during the agrarian age- and tied to factories and offices where their mother-tongue language was spoken -during the industrial one. Post-industrial computerized networks wherein terminals and connective nodes are globally distributed destroy the spatial slavery that confined workers to immobile means of production and deprived them of the access to a free-market of jobs. The battle against global Berlin Walls therefore takes a central place in the democratic vindication of the citizens of the world.

When the social gap grows between individuals who are strongly fixed to territory and those who can travel and communicate all over the globe, a global Apartheid limits the spatial mobility of the vast majority of human beings, trying to crystallize the inherited privileges of first-world national citizens. Whereas in developed countries high-qualified workers increase their mobility and transnational migration is an accepted strategy for individual development; a global Apartheid tries to keep the barriers between world citizens of first category and those of third category. This contemptible form of manipulation of territorial frontiers, which get porous for products but impenetrable for human beings, reminds the regulation of mobility and residence that was characteristic of totalitarian regimes. Consequently, since the fall of the Berlin Wall, the

Republican right of national citizens to move freely claims for a worldwide extension of support. Equal access to territories and universal rights of residents become a basic vindication of human rights in the global age.

A second westphalia on the making

National citizenship became possible only after the acceptance of the secular character of the State and the relegation of religion from the public to the private sphere. The Peace of Westphalia (1648) was the founding episode of a new period of Modernity in which Nation-States became the center of the social universe, overcoming religious and feudal contexts. Belonging, community, solidarity and common fate, which depended on religious connotations, waxed to territorial secular categories. A veil of ignorance fell over the religious ascription of each member of the national community and progressively covered ethnical and gender definitions, political opinions and every other form of discrimination among national citizens. Yet, belongings and rights acquired a national status and were fixed to territorial. Human rights were understood and applied in a national way and provided by national institutions.

After the second Thirty Year War (1914-1944), the Universal Declaration of Human Rights (1948), the First People's World Constitutional Convention (UN, 1950) convened by United Nations, and the creation of the European Community of Carbon and Steal (1951) meant consistent advances towards surpassing national contexts and the proclamation of the sovereignty of individuals over States. In a way, they all pre-announced a second Westphalia in the making, and constituted promising developments bound to overcome the nation-centered framework established at the original Westphalia (1648). Yet, a planetary democratic order was not established during the past century. Far from it. The Korean War and the new division of the world in West and East wasted every continuation of those efforts and left the work unfinished. The supra-national character of the Democracy and the Republic, the universal dimension of modern citizenry and the benefits of the trans-

-nationalization of economy were then restricted to European limits, and all over the world national states conserved their role as the central actors in the global arena. Thus, the second Westphalia constituted a failure. It is still an unfinished continuation of the first one.

Nowadays, at the beginning of the XXI Century, modern citizenship and rights must be still unchained from the heavy burden of nations. In order to do so, Democracy must be distinguished from national conceptions and institutions by some kind of a Second Westphalia. The settlement of religious ascription to the private sphere, which was the basic achievement of the First Westphalia, must still be completed by the relegation of national belonging to a private option and the abolition of national origins as discriminatory sources of rights among human beings. This discard of the territorial conditioning of citizenry gets a *sine-qua-non* condition for the settlement of non-rhetorical Human Rights equally valid for each world citizen. As techno-economic globalization becomes a universal paradigm, National citizenship and universal Human Rights get intrinsically incompatible, and the idea of Human Rights and World Citizenship become the two faces of a single coin.

Beyond new Berlin walls and raising national-populism, a second Westphalia is still in the making: for good or bad, a global techno-economy is opening its road to the future. The idea of a national common destiny, which was constitutive of the previous political order, becomes an old-fashioned myth when global forces divide national citizens in global winners and national losers. In addition, prescriptive/collective/national communities of identity and belonging are gradually replaced by individual/free/transversal/de-attached groups defined by a-territorial factors. These communities of interests, which are being globally interconnected through the Internet, are just a little part of a more generalized and vast phenomenon.

Today, the contradictions between universal rights and national citizenship have become evident. Within national societies that pretend to be founded on Democracy and Equality, migrants are blocked at frontiers or lose most of their rights by crossing national borders. Meanwhile national citizenry continues to be exalted, global migrants depend on a humiliating system of authorizations and stamps on passports that constitutes the soft version of Lager procedures. Even in the case of a successful integration, the first generations of migrants had no political rights, and in the frequent disputes between migrants and natives, national institutions grant all the rights to the powerful ones and obligations upon the weak ones.

However, in a post-traditional/post-totalitarian society marked by the experiences of the 20th Century, the meanings of the words "national belonging" are being inverted. The same countries that refuse Mexicans emigrants, depend increasingly on Hispanics for the recruiting of their national armies. Through the refusal to wear military uniforms and to die on behalf of national states, modern individuals reject the previously common idea that "citizens belong to nations" and start to consider that nations must belong to their citizens. The same definition of "territorial belonging" becomes obsolete: Who could rationally say that New York is still a city that "belongs" to the United States, as well as London to the United Kingdom or Barcelona to Spain...?

An explosive mix fuels a clock-bomb placed in the core of "national societies" (whatever this expression still means). Indeed, the term can hardly conserve its original significance when a minority of national citizens who are connected to global fluxes get gradually richer, while most people are employed in local jobs with low salaries or become excluded by unemployment. When members of a "national community" are no longer tied to a common future and a national citizenship is unable to guarantee a decent job, the basic deal that had allowed individual and social progress during National Modernity, is corroded. Then, related notions of national belonging and community become abstract even if people vote for leaders who vindicate them. The national-industrial alliance between citizens and warriors symbolized by the tractor-driver Stajanov and the Unknown Soldier becomes obsolete. Workers and soldiers, the emblematic heroes of national-industrial times, are now over as social models within a globalized framework.

The case for a universal citizenship

"September 11th" (2001) showed the failure of the most powerful national state in History in protecting its citizens lives even in its financial and military centers: Wall Street and the Pentagon. From its very beginning, the 21st Century annunciated that national states tend to fail. Now, it becomes evident that if their leaders bet on Nineteenth-century autarchic paradigms, the process accelerates. Beyond the huge differences that separate Uganda and the United States, both nations are decreasingly unable to determine a progressive context; a lesson -may be- that it will be reinforced by the results of the Brexit and the Trump administrations' "achievements". Within this framework, the fixation of Democracy to spatial dimensions turned into the key of the hegemony of Capitalism over Democracy. Neo-Liberalism and neo-Conservatism are the two complementary aspects of the imbalance between a global economy and a national/inter-national political structure. The pro-globalist market fundamentalism is complementary – and not a contradictory- to the anti-globalist nationalistic fundamentalism.

Beyond national populist theories and practices, History shows that universalizing and de-territorializing techno-economic processes cannot be eternally kept separated from political aspects. As soon as de--territorialization, de-attachment and de-centralization become the rule in modern societies, the walls start to claim that no human being is illegal and the expression "*sans-papier*" turns into nonsense. An increasing number of world citizens do not feel that they need a certificate of existence given by States. Rather, they begin to claim for the common possession of the planet and for a full and free mobility on its surface. The common possession of national public goods and the free mobility of people across the national territory are two elementary citizen rights without which modern Nation-States would have not been possible. In the shift from National Modernities to a genuine World-Modernity, their extension to the global scale -which was claimed by Immanuel Kant at the dawn of political Modernity- became a part of a necessary political program. Utopia? Probably. As big as the fall of the Iron Curtain and the Berlin Wall that divided the world by 1988.

Since powerful global economic agents overcome weak national political institutions, the world society is consequently conceived as an enormous global market, consumption takes the place of citizenry, life and world become merchandisable and human relationships are driven by an economic logic. A winner-takes-all world society gets a-territorially divided in global-winners and global-losers and a one-dimensional conception of human civilization proclaims "TINA!" (There Is No Alternative). The unbalance between Democracy and Capitalism, States and Markets, Provisions and Entitlements, Citizens and Managers, Political Equality and Economic Freedom, social organizations and Corporations, Solidarity and Competitiveness, Social Justice and Efficiency, are the most visible manifestation of the global polarities that rule the new scenario. They combat each other all over a worldwide arena enlarged by global processes. The struggle for hegemony between Economy and Politics becomes the core of the worlds social affairs.

This is not news. Totalitarianism and wild Capitalism were the basic answers that human civilization tested during the early 20th Century. They can shortly be described as 1) hegemony of Politics over civil society, economic system and individuals (totalitarianism) and 2) hegemony of capitalistic economy over democratic policy and society (wild capitalism). Over the ruins left by the wars and atrocities originated by their failures, an intrinsically unstable balance between economic and political principles came into play. This solution, which allowed a sustainable overcoming of both communism and wild capitalism, was initially established by the American New Deal and European social democracies. It also meant the constitution of unified national democracies in which Left and Right, Liberalism and Social democracy, conservatism and progressivism were combined. This was the base and core of prosperity and democratization for decades. Now, the time for the extension of this process to the global scale has come.

The contradiction between Human Rights and Citizen Rights (meaning universal rights versus national rights) was perfectly functional in the age of National Modernities. But within a global context, it has become an unacceptable source of discrimination. Fortunately, throughout the increment of global fluxes of migrants, investments, resources and intangible productive factors, global connectivity tends to destroy the feasibility of a previous universe where Human Rights were "internally" equal but "externally" unequal by definition. On the other hand, the character of rising nationalistic populist forces demonstrates that protectionism, xenophobia and territorial walls are inseparable of authoritarian projects.

There is no chance for national democracies to survive alone within a global context. As connective processes increase the possibilities of relevant human and societal connection, Democracy must move toward a larger scale or risk a collapse. The option is between moving forward from the initial "democracy of cities" to the extended "democracy of nations", to the democratic European continental unity, to a global democratic order, or increasing the risk of collapse of national democracies. Democracy is forced to emigrate and evolve or die. In times of the Greeks, Thucydides fixed three limitations to citizenship: "Women, slaves and foreigners are not citizens", he affirmed. From then to now, at least since the emancipation of slaves and the recognition of equal rights for women, only the territorial limitation (foreigners, strangers) remains active and must be removed by a real Democracy of Moderns.

Today, the relevant political question for the coming global world revolves around how to build a democratic global order based on a universal citizenship. All the traditional tensions that characterized the dawn of Nation-States and the building of national democracies resuscitate from the dark grave where they had been confined by the rhetoric of national unity. Restricted "Democracy" or Universal Suffrage? Enlightened Despotism or Democratic Representation? State Sovereignty or Individual Autonomy? Oligarchic Powers or Majority Principle plus full respect of the Rights of Minorities? Territorial Representation (based upon one state-one vote) or Democratic Representation (based upon one person-one vote)? Votes and power just for owners and Citizens of first category or universal equality beyond social and territorial ascription? Centrality of Executives or centrality of Parliaments? Judgement and punishment in the hands of Executives or independent judicial power? Participation or Exclusion? State or Republic? Dark secrecy or transparent debate? Accountability to territorial powers or accountability to citizens? Paternal hereditary privileges or fraternal human rights? Citizen rights given by "Land and Blood" or Universal Citizenship? Democracy "only when people are prepared" or Democracy as a process in which democratic capacities are built through the exercise of political rights? Common belonging and identity as *a priori* conditions of unity or as a predictable result of a democratic process developed within a liberal context? Extension or Restriction of the political unity? All these oppositions were gradually resolved in favor of the most democratic alternative during National Modernities. Nonetheless, they are just being elevated to the global scale where the decisive processes already occur. Perhaps Marx's statement which affirms that men only face the problems they are ready to solve, could be a base for rational optimism.

Let's see its physical base. Soon after the European states renounced their absolute national sovereignty following the Second World War, the establishment of the European Court of Human Rights was a first step in the devolution of sovereignty from States to citizens. By 1950, this supra-national court was created to protect Human Rights of European citizens even against their own governments. Predictably, the best results of the principle of individual sovereignty was obtained in this context, which suggests that if national citizens cannot request the protection of supra-national institutions every human right becomes a national privilege or an empty abstraction. However, what are the public goods that a global democratic architecture is supposed to defend and provide? Which are the supra-national phenomena, the unresolved crises raised by global processes, that the current national-international order is unable to regulate and solve? And which are the existing initiatives in order to build new institutions able to cope with the main challenges posed by globalization? Let's have a look at the campaign for the creation of a United Nations Parliamentary Assembly (UNPA) and a Latin American and Caribbean Criminal Court Against Organized Crime (COPLA).

Global crises require global solutions, not just international ones

Even if many organizations have reached global capabilities (such as the United States, the United Nations, the North Atlantic Trade Organization, the International Monetary Fund etc.), not one of them is globally democratic-representative. Even in the case of inter-national institutions as the General Assembly of the UN, the mechanism works as follows: people vote for an elector who votes a national candidate to the national government, who assumes the Presidency of a country and chooses a Minister of Foreign Affairs, who assumes office and chooses a representative to the United Nations. At least four steps (Elector/President/Minister/Delegate to the UN General Assembly –UNGA-) separate the representative from the citizens. In addition, only the political party who wins the election has a voice and a vote in international affairs, whereas the rest of the national political sphere is not represented at all. This, only in the lucky situation that the national power is elected through democratic methods, which is not the case in 49 of the 189 members of the UNGA. The consequence is that the representative of national citizens at the inter-national system represents the interests of a national government and not the interest of the citizens of the world.

This institutional distance applied to the global scale transforms the United Nations into a Matrioska game. You open the first Matrioska doll hoping to find a global democratic order and you just find inter--national institutions. You open the second Matrioska doll hoping to find an international order and you just find inter-governmental institutions. You open the third Matrioska doll hoping to find, at least, an inter-governmental order and you just find the delegate of an executive power that does not represent the minorities of his/her country nor its parliamentarian powers. At the end of the UN Matrioska game, you open the last doll and find a bald old man, wearing a grey suit with a briefcase full of instructions from the government that has elected him. Then, you see the bald old man making decisions on behalf of humanity and future generations. Despite the parliamentarian appearance of the UNGA all the UN inter-national/inter-governmental game is developed inside the field of executive powers, in perfect contrast with the recommendations of liberal and democratic authors who identified in Parliament the very core of Democracy.

Through "institutional distance" applied to the global scale -from local to national to regional to international to global- every sight of Democracy and accountability vanishes all along the process, meanwhile the opacity of the system is hidden behind the abstract rhetoric of "Global Governance". However, the democratic deficit of inter-national order cannot be abolished by a "democratic" Global Governance but for a real Global Democracy. Only democratically legitimated institutions could be able to make the proclaimed principles of the Universal Declaration of Human Rights real and concrete. Only democratic legitimated institutions could respect the essence of the UN Charter, which starts by "We, the people..." and not by "We, the nations..." Only democratically representative global institutions -like a World Parliament- could bring a genuine democratic global order.

Every concrete possibility of applying democratic solutions to economic, ecological and demographic crises, every rational attempt of peacefully solve the troubles caused by global terrorism, criminal mafia networks and military powers depends now on the application of democratic representation at a global scale. Yet, some objections must be considered:

1. The applying of the principle "one man- one vote" to the world would concentrate about one-third of the global political power in the hands of the inhabitants of just two nations, China and India.

2. It would imply such an outstanding redistribution of power that the little minority that inhabits in the First-World but concentrate most of global richness and power would object and oppose the entire process.

Are these objections insurmountable or can they be managed by applying, at the global level, the experience developed through the Democracy of cities, the Democracy of nations and the European Union? Nobody knows. But everybody can see the results of the lack of Democracy at the global scale; starting by the emergence of global crises (such as climate change, financial instability, international terrorism, worldwide migrations, nuclear proliferation, and so on) and the increasing lack of control of all them by national states. This is the hidden cause of the rise of national-populist forces all over the First World: all these crises are unified by these factors: 1) they all have causes that overcome the national framework, 2) they all cannot be solved by the intervention of a single national state or a group of national states, 3) they all require the intervention of a new kind of institution able to synthesize and conciliate the enormous diversity of the emerging global society, and new kinds of institutions for which the interests of all human beings are predominant.

Globalization means, unavoidably, the source of global crises that cannot be solved at the national level neither by international institutions within which national interests are predominant over global ones. If the emerging global society is not able to deliver such institutions, the predictable scenario will be determined by increasing chaotic trends and paranoid nationalistic reactions. The only rational way of avoiding a global collapse which dimensions could overcome the damages caused by the previous one is the building of a democratic global order. Progressively, of course, but as soon as possible. And the creation of an embryo of a world parliament looks as the first relevant step towards it. This is what the campaign for the United Nations Parliamentary Assembly (UNPA) is about.

UNPA – The embryo of a world parliament?

The history of the campaign and its amazing results are available at its website (http://en.unpacampaign.org/). Now, let me just underline the fundamental elements of the UNPA strategy. First, it is developed inside the UN framework but with no respect to the undemocratic rules fixed by the Charter, such as the UN Security Council (UNSC) veto rule. Indeed, a UNPA could be created through a decision of the UNGA under Article 22 of the UN Charter, according to which the UNGA "may establish such subsidiary organs as it deems necessary for the performance of its functions". The UNPA should be established as a consultative agency of the UN General Assembly (UNGA), ignoring the opinion of UNSC members and only depending on the majority of the UNGA members, most of them: developing nations who are presumably interested in a fairer distribution of power at the global level. Second, the UNPA campaign strategy does not ultimately rest on executive national powers but on the active participation of different sectors of the global civil society such as parliamentarians, academics, non-governmental organizations, individual activists, etc. Third, it does not propose a *ex nihilo* birth of a world parliament, but a progressive development of it, and its capabilities and powers; following all the existing experiences of parliamentarian building -both at national and the regional levels.

A United Nations Parliamentary Assembly created as a consultative agency of the United Nations General Assembly by its sovereign resolution would be able to advice and issue resolutions regarding global crises. Its directives could then be considered by the United Nations General Assembly and the governments represented in it as feasible strategies in favor of the control of global crises and the regulation of big global processes. It could also deal with the reform, modernization and democratization of the United Nations itself, an outstanding UN debt since its inception. Through the democratization of the United Nations, the UNPA could also become the embryo of a real World Parliament with full legislative powers strictly limited to global issues.

But, why not let the campaign speak for itself? According to its website:

1. A UNPA was first suggested in 1948. After the Cold War, support was voiced, inter alia, by the Liberal International (1992 and 2005), the Foreign Affairs Committee of the Canadian House of Commons (1993 and 2007), the InterAction Council (1994), the European Parliament (1994 and 2011), the Commission on Global Governance (1995), the World Commission on Culture and Development (1995), the Socialist International (2003), a majority of Swiss parliamentarians (2005), the World Federation of United Nations Associations (2006), the Pan-African Parliament (2007 and 2016), the Green World Congress (2008 and 2012), the Argentine Senate and Chamber of Deputies (2008/09), the Latin-American Parliament (2008), the Parliamentary Assembly of the Council of Europe (2009), in the report of the World Economic Forum's Global Redesign Initiative (2010), the Parliament of Mercosur (2011), and the East African Legislative Assembly (2013).

2. In 2007, the Campaign for a UNPA was launched with the support of former UN Secretary-General Boutros Boutros-Ghali to coordinate and strengthen pro-UNPA efforts internationally. Now, the creation of a UN Parliamentary Assembly is supported by a broad range of individuals and institutions from more than 150 countries. In particular, 625 current and 858 former members of parliament across principal party lines have endorsed the campaign to date. The sitting MPs represent an estimated 119 million people. Supporters include six current UN Special Rapporteurs elected by the Human Rights Council. Under the auspices of the campaign's host organization several studies were carried out to examine various aspects of the proposal. They also include current and former heads of state, foreign ministers, Nobel laureates, and over 400 professors, including from world-leading universities. Institutions that

have expressed support include numerous civil society organizations, parliaments, international parliamentary assemblies and party networks. For instance, the Pan-African Parliament, the European Parliament, and the Latin-American Parliament have adopted resolutions – as have the Socialist International, the Liberal International, or the Green World Congress.

3. The General Assembly would instigate the preparatory process and finally adopt the UNPA's Statutes. Limited only by the scope of its own powers, the assembly would be able to vest the UNPA with distinct rights and functions. Alternatively, the UNPA could be created through a new international treaty. This treaty would consist of the UNPA's Statutes and would be negotiated by a group of like-minded governments. To enter into force, the treaty would have to be ratified by a certain number of countries as stipulated in the Statutes. Rights and functions vis-à-vis the UN would have to be confirmed by a cooperation agreement adopted by the UN General Assembly. Again, the UNPA's rights could not exceed those of the General Assembly.

4. A United Nations Parliamentary Assembly (UNPA) for the first time would give popularly elected representatives a formal role in global affairs. As an additional body, the assembly will directly represent the world's citizens and not governments. Initially, states could choose whether their UNPA members would come from national parliaments, reflecting their political spectrum and gender equality, or whether they would be directly elected. Eventually, the goal is to have all members directly elected. Starting as a largely consultative body, the rights and powers of the UNPA could be expanded over time as its democratic legitimacy increases. The assembly will act as an independent watchdog in the UN system and as a democratic reflection of the diversity of world public opinion. In the long run, once its members are all democratically elected, the assembly could be developed into a world parliament which – under certain conditions and in conjunction with the UN General Assembly – may be able to adopt universally binding regulations. In short, the UN

should evolve from what many believe to be a generally ineffectual "talk--shop" into a viable democratic and legislative body.

5. On behalf of the British Broadcasting Corporation BBC, in 2004/05 the research institute GlobeScan conducted representative surveys in 18 countries representing 61% of the world population. In one of the questions concerning reforms of the United Nations, participants were asked about their opinion on "creating a new UN Parliament, made up of representatives directly elected by citizens, having powers equal to the current UN General Assembly that is controlled by national governments." On average, 63% supported the reform proposal, while only 20% rejected it. For the first time, this survey provides empirical evidence that the world's citizens overwhelmingly support the establishment of a directly elected world parliament.

As the former UN Secretary-General Boutros Boutros-Ghali stated at the launch of the UNPA campaign, "we need to promote the democratization of globalization before globalization destroys the foundations of national and international democracy. The establishment of a Parliamentary Assembly at the UN has become an indispensable step to achieve democratic control of globalization". Yet the building of a global democratic order does not mean the creation of a world state, or a centralized executive govern. It invokes the gradual construction of a federal network of political and juridical institutions able to cope with supra-national affairs and crises at each level. In this sense -and by following the subsidiary principle which establishes that each issue must be solved at the minimal possible level- the progressive creation of a world parliament should be complemented by new institutions at the regional scale. And the campaign for the creation of a Latin American and Caribbean Criminal Court against Organized Crime (COPLA) is a good example of that.

A regional court against organized crime

Criminal organizations related to drugs, arms and human trafficking, money laundering and other transnational crimes have become the greatest security threat in the Latin American and Caribbean region. For a variety of reasons, their activities have eluded effective control and jurisdiction of national institutions and current regional cooperation mechanisms. That is why, nowadays, Latin America is not only the most socially unequal region in the world but has also became the region with highest levels of criminal violence on the planet.

According to the United Nations Office on Drugs and Crime (UNODC), from a total of 157,000 violent crimes committed in 2013, Latin America is responsible for 36%, which makes them the most violent region in the world. Worst, organized crime accounts for 30% of violent deaths in the region (compared to 1% for other regions such as Europe, Asia and Oceania) and only 24% of reported homicides result in conviction (half the global average). Unfortunately, these statistics have not improved in recent years. Currently, nine of the 20 most violent countries of the world are a part of Latin America and the Caribbean.

But official data tends to underestimate the actual level of violence. Impunity, corruption and social inequality are key by-products of this grave situation. Current developments in Mexico, the spread of *maras* (young gangs) in Central America, the fact that governments and vast political sectors are being co-opted by organized crime, alongside the rise of criminal violence, arms and drug trafficking, and people forced into sexual and labor slavery, are all regional problems with a tremendous negative impact on the lives of Latin American citizens. Criminal groups associated with drugs, arms and human trafficking, money laundering and other transnational crimes have reached a regional dimension and have therefore escaped the control of national institutions. This the worrying scenario in which COPLA is proposed.

According to their promoters, the Latin American and Caribbean Criminal Court against Transnational Organized Crime (COPLA), based on the UN Palermo Convention against organized crime, is expected to be effective in the prosecution of key figures of organized crime, the confiscation of assets and the subsequent dismantling of criminal organizations. The COPLA acronym stands for Corte Penal Latinoamericana y del Caribe Contra el Crimen Transnacional Organizado (in English: Latin American and Caribbean Criminal Court against Transnational Organized Crime). Its creation is being proposed through a campaign spearheaded by Democracia Global, an Argentine NGO that convoked and included LA citizens and civil society organizations in the process, and hope to summon all Latin American and Caribbean governments who want to combat organized crime from a regional perspective and through international cooperation. The COPLA is proposed to be based on the United Nations Convention against Transnational Organized Crime (Palermo Convention) and its related protocols. As almost all Latin-American governs have signed them, as well as the Rome Statute of the International Criminal Court, the juridical base for the creation of a regional court in order to combat them already exist.

COPLA would be established as an independent body (not an organ of existing regional institutions) by means of an international treaty. The Court would be complementary to national criminal systems but it would also have the power of initiative to start its own investigations. It would work as a Court of last resort to intervene in those cases where states are not capable or not willing to take action. It would aim mainly at prosecuting the leaders of criminal organizations and confiscating their resources.

As an intergovernmental agency, in addition to its judicial functions, the COPLA should be mandated to coordinate security policies among state parties, foster cooperation among police forces and intelligence agencies in the region, articulate/harmonize/improve national legislation, protect witnesses and other meaningful factors in the fight against organized crime. Other long term goals of the establishment of the COPLA include institutional strengthening, transparency and reinforcement of rule of law through civil society accountability mechanisms, as well as economic improvement, by providing a better environment to attract foreign investment and lowering the current costs of corruption.

The amazing results of the COPLA campaign could be tracked at http://www.coalicioncopla.org/. They include the start of a coalition composed by NGOs such as the World Federalist Movement (international), INCIDE social (México), AVINA (Swiss), Libera (Italy), Cattedra Altiero Spinelli (Argentina), Planetafilia (Mexico), No Peace Without Justice (international), Comisión por la Carta Democratica Interamericana (Dominicana), Interamerican Institute for Democracy (Estados Unidos), World Federalist Movement-Canadá (Canadá), etc. Many intellectuals, political leaders and figures are already signatories of the petition (http://www.coalicioncopla.org/adhesion/), such as Mario Vargas Llosa, Anthony Giddens, David Held, Fernando Savater, Keith Best, Daniele Archibugi, Lucio Levi, Tonio Dell'Olio and Santiago Kovadloff, among many others. Being based on Buenos Aires, the impact on the Argentine political mainframe was high: the COPLA campaign obtained two unanimous resolutions of support by the two chambers of the National Congress, as well as a positive resolution by the Mercosur Parliament. Also the Argentine minister of Justice and Human Rights, Germán Garavano; the minister of Security, Patricia Bullrich; the director of the Anticorruption office, Laura Alonso; the Senate speaker, Federico Pinedo; and the national vice-president, Gabriela Michetti, have endorsed the petition for its creation and participated on concrete activities destined to raise awareness about the issue of organized crime and the COPLA proposal.

Coming years will be decisive for the UNPA and COPLA initiatives, but the tremendous impact of both campaigns at the supranational political level -despite the ridiculous amount of money that supported these efforts- is a good indicator of the sensitivity of the global public opinion on the necessity of being as innovative in politics as we human beings use to be in technology and economy.

Conclusions

As every transitional tool, national states were as progressive in their origins as reactionary and destructive in their latest hours. Stajanov –the Soviet hero of the industrial working class- and the Unknown Soldier -the hero of an industrial death- were the demi-gods that presided National Modernities. The metal arch that dominates the entrance to Auschwitz claiming that "Arbeit Macht Frei" is the wedding ring that consecrated their alliance. Industrial "Arbeit Macht Frei" is the perfect complement of national "Deutschland-über-alles". Oppression in life, and death in war are the two poisoned fruits that the false universality of National Modernities still offers to the citizens of the world. Not just by chance, the combat against oppression in life by labor and imposed death by war were the goals of the trade-unions and the Red Cross, the two first NGOs created by the world society. These are not just abstract words when a climate of frustration reigns all over the planetary surface.

The shift of citizenship from the *urbi to the orbi* is the crucial goal to be achieved by democratic forces during this century. A cosmopolitan democracy supposes that belonging and identity cannot be imposed prescriptively from top to bottom through invasive nationalistic propaganda promoted by public schools and financed with the scarce resources that states should apply to guarantee basic human needs. On the contrary, Democracy implies the full respect of autonomous-changeable-free--individual decision on the terms of personal identity and belonging. This is the exact meaning of the pawed term "Individuation" which does not signify "atomization" or "isolation" but dissolution of coercive belonging, identity and lifestyle. As Beck asserts, "individualization means, in a first instance, disembedding, and, in a second one, embedding to a new form of life... that substitute the previous ones, in which individuals must product and combine by themselves their own biographies".

Were children educated in individual identity and autonomy, in the development of a planetary conscience on our common trouble and destine, in the sense of belonging to the human race and on the consequent derived duties; were teachers and professors to spend in promoting these principles the same energy and time they use for describing national epopees, exalting national heroes, installing zombie categories within in-mature children's brains, all the banalities on the national character of human beings would probably disappear in the lifetime of one or two generations. Meaningfully, the same nationalistic ideologists who support the idea that nationalism is a constitutive part of the human nature are also the first in opposing the eradication of national catechisms in schools.

Nowadays, the existence and survival of human beings is menaced by the zombie categories derived from past times and lodged in the brain of the living... borrowing from them names, battle cries and costumes to present the new scene of world history in this time-honored disguise and this borrowed language, as Marx wrote once[2]. As children are not obligated to wear veils, adore crucifixes or pray to gods anymore, the day in which they will be no longer forced to sing national anthems, celebrate national festivities and apply more energy in the study of local tyrants than in the whole history of Chinese and Greek civilizations, will be –perhaps- the start of a Second-Westphalian order and the birth of a better and more peaceful world.

National Modernities were nothing but a suspension bridge between the democracy of the cities and the democracy of the world, between the *urbi* and the *orbi* and between ancient feudal particularism and Democratic-Republican universalism. Nothing about the current situation can be understood without considering the ambiguous character of nations, which reminds Janus, the Roman god who had two faces in order to simultaneously look to the past and the future. As well as industrialism was only a transitional phase from agrarian times to the civilization of knowledge, information, diversity, communication, innovation and emotion, Nation-States are a necessary but provisory step

2 Karl Marx, The 18° Brumario of Luis Bonaparte.

from ancient monarchic-ecclesiastic régimes to the planetary application of liberal-democratic-republican principles and institutions. Yet, along a dialectic parabola, Nation-States and the inter-national order have become the new ancient régime, whose dominion must be overcome in order to open the road towards a more democratic, equal, peaceful, humane and fair universe.

Globalization is the fact that defines our age. And more than globalization, the asymmetries and asynchronies of its different aspects. Human life gets problematic in a world in which technology and the economy move at global level and live in the XXI century, while policy continues to work with methods and rhythms of institutions created mostly during the XIX century. This dissonance, this asynchrony between policy development and techno – economy, has had and continues to have countless negative consequences that impact heavily on the lives of all inhabitants of the planet.

At the beginning of the XXI century, willing or unwilling, we humans are inhabitants of a global village put in a small planet that increasingly resembles a drifting spaceship. Yet we cannot consider ourselves world citizens because we have no rights as such, but as citizens of a particular country, and there are no regional and global institutions that guarantee them. It was Kant who made the distinction between perfect and imperfect rights, understanding the latter as rights for which there are specific institutions responsible for enforcing them. So it is today with human rights, raised in a revolutionary and innovative way in various declarations in the era of liberal and democratic revolutions (and later in the Human Rights Declaration of the United Nations (1948)) but which in practice have been limited to national rights granted by national institutions and on which the world citizens do not possess accountability, much less the right to participate in global decisions that concern us all.

National states are useless in order to regulate phenomena and processes that have become global. We watch politicians run after them from behind, armed with the few powers that national states still maintain, and we see the citizens of each country invaded by disappointment and disbelief about the ability of the political class to solve them. The result is the current rise of first-world nationalist populism, which could lead to the troubling situation in which the next UN Security Council could be composed by delegates appointed by Donald Trump, Marine Le Pen, Vladimir Putin, the Chinese Communist party and the fraction of the UK Conservative Party who is responsible for the Brexit.

The international scenario starts to resemble the one which led the world to great tragedies a century ago. The world is beginning to experience, as such, the same problems, and face the same alternatives, which the European people had to choose from almost 100 years ago: a new understanding of the relationship between territorial states and regional-global phenomena, or conflict.

Citizens of the world, reduced to mere inhabitants, live today in a global social space with little political control, almost no civic participation rights, and in which we attend, acquiescent, to processes over which we have almost no possibilities for action. The two largest institutional innovations which occurred after the last major disaster caused by extreme nationalism -the United Nations and the European Union- are in crisis and at risk of a collapse of unimaginable consequences. Its utility in the past is undeniable, but they are also outdated and in need of reform and democratization.

The two projects introduced by this paper, the creation of a Latin American and Caribbean Criminal Court Against Transnational Organized Crime (COPLA) and a United Nations Parliamentary Assembly (UNPA), are –in my opinion- the most concrete attempts to overcome the mere management of regional and global issues through existing national and international organizations. Both of them are strategies of the institutional innovation that is inherent to modern politics since its origin. The creation of the COPLA and the UNPA would empower citizens around the world, transforming regional and global citizenship in a way that Human Rights may no longer be abstract expressions, declarations of principles and dead letter.

La garantía del contenido esencial de los derechos fundamentales

María Hylma Alcaraz Salgado

Introducción

La referencia constitucional a la protección del contenido esencial de los derechos fundamentales aparece, por primera vez, en la Constitución alemana de 1949, seguida por otras Constituciones como la española, la portuguesa, entre otras. En la actualidad es cada vez más frecuente la inclusión de un precepto normativo en los sistemas jurídico-constitucionales que establezca la obligación de proteger el núcleo esencial de los derechos fundamentales.

Los estudios contemporáneos sobre los sistemas constitucionales ponen de manifiesto las nuevas orientaciones para la comprensión de los derechos fundamentales. Los derechos fundamentales, que tradicionalmente eran comprendidos como derechos de la persona, tienen su significado ampliado para incluir también los derechos de ciudadanía. En el marco de la teoría general de los derechos fundamentales, referidos derechos constituyen un conjunto de normas que contienen valores jurídicos vitales para el grupo social y que son garantizados por el ordenamiento jurídico constitucional.

Los derechos fundamentales no son todos del mismo tipo, y tampoco todas las personas son titulares de éstos derechos. Las diferentes clases de derechos fundamentales es consecuencia de los diversos intereses protegidos por las normas constitucionales. La diversidad de derechos fundamentales y de titulares pone de manifiesto el problema de la comprensión de sus contenidos, especialmente cuando surgen situaciones de aparente colisión entre los intereses jurídicamente protegidos por las normas jurídicas. La regulación y la interpretación de los conflictos de esta naturaleza están necesariamente vinculadas a la comprensión unitaria del sistema jurídico constitucional. Los derechos fundamentales describen valores que son asegurados por la Constitución. Como consecuencia, los valores protegidos deben ser analizados dentro de un orden jerárquico que establece cuáles son los bienes e intereses jurídicos de "mayor peso". La relevancia de un derecho fundamental en detrimento de otro no puede resultar del arbitrio, sino que debe ser la consecuencia de un juicio de ponderación y de proporcionalidad por medio de los cuales las restricciones impuestas al ejercicio de un derecho fundamental estarán jurídicamente justificadas. Entre tanto, la imposición de límites al ejercicio de los derechos fundamentales no puede, bajo ninguna circunstancia, modificar su núcleo esencial. La garantía del contenido esencial de los derechos fundamentales es también la garantía del equilibrio de las relaciones jurídicas y sociales.

El significado de los derechos fundamentales

La expresión *derechos fundamentales* es utilizada en las ciencias sociales de forma análoga, pero con variantes que hacen con que la expresión pueda aparecer unas veces como sinónimo de derechos humanos y otras veces como equivalente a las libertades públicas, sin contar los demás usos que pueden ser registrados en la literatura científica.

Desde un punto de vista formal, la noción acerca de los derechos fundamentales contiene las siguientes propiedades: a) el *carácter univer-*

sal de la imputación de éstos derechos; b) la *subjetividad* de la imputación de tales derechos.

La *universalidad* es un atributo que identifica la *cantidad* de los derechos fundamentales. Referidos derechos tienen su alcance normativo incidente dentro de un conjunto que abarca a *todos* en igualdad de condiciones.

Considerando su carácter universal, los derechos humanos corresponden a intereses generales de todos. Estos intereses coinciden "con las libertades y con otras necesidades fundamentales de cuya garantía depende la vida, la supervivencia, la igualdad y la dignidad de los seres humanos."[1] Teniendo en cuenta el valor reconocido a referidos intereses, ellos se encuentran bajo la protección del Derecho, es decir, son *intereses jurídicamente protegidos.*

El atributo de la universalidad debe ser comprendido en relación directa con la *cualidad* de los sujetos sobre los que inciden estos derechos. Como consecuencia, la *universalidad* de los derechos fundamentales es relativa. De hecho, "no todos los derechos fundamentales corresponden a todos los seres humanos y no todos los seres humanos son titulares de los mismos derechos fundamentales."[2]

Los derechos fundamentales pueden ser entendidos como "un conjunto de normas y posiciones adscritas a una disposición de derecho fundamental. Las disposiciones de derecho fundamental son las proposiciones de la Constitución que establecen los derechos fundamentales".[3] El concepto de derecho fundamental presenta una estrecha conexión con el concepto de norma de derecho fundamental porque es la norma válida que

---

1 FERRAJOLI, Luigi. *Principia iuris: teoría del derecho y de la democracia.* Traducción de Perfecto Andrés Ibánez, Carlos Bayón, Marina Gascón, Luis Pietro Sanchís y Alfonso Ruíz Miguel. Editorial Trotta, Madrid, 2011, libro 1, p. 690.

2 *Idem*, p. 686.

3 BERNAL PULIDO, Carlos. Estudio introductorio. In: ALEXY, Robert. *Teoría de los derechos fundamentales.* 2ª edición. Centro de Estudios Políticos y Constitucionales, 2007, p. XXIX.

reconoce a alguien un derecho fundamental. De esta relación se concluye que la norma de derecho fundamental enuncia un derecho subjetivo.[4]

El contenido esencial de los derechos fundamentales

Las proposiciones de la Constitución que establecen los derechos fundamentales son normas jurídicas. La norma jurídica contiene la previsión hipotética de una conducta, o realidad social, que se refleja en un juicio de valor y se expresa en lenguaje. La comprensión de los supuestos contenidos en las normas constitucionales es, de esta manera, el resultado de la interpretación de los signos que representan el objeto jurídicamente protegido.

Las normas constitucionales que definen una posición adscrita a una disposición de derecho fundamental conllevan a un análisis sintáctico, semántico y pragmático de sus signos.

Considerando los mandatos constitucionales cuyas prescripciones declaran un derecho fundamental, el punto de partida para la traducción de su significado es la determinación del sentido que se debe dar al término *derecho fundamental.* Como vimos anteriormente, el signo *"derecho fundamental"* no contiene un significado único. Por esta razón, el sentido que puede atribuirse a éste término depende de los contextos y circunstancias en los que los usuarios utilizan tal signo.

El derecho fundamental es un signo que representa las necesidades y libertades fundamentales del hombre sin las cuales no se puede vivir en condiciones que respeten la dignidad que es inherente a la persona humana. El mantenimiento de la vida es, pues, el núcleo esencial simbolizado por intermedio del signo *"derecho fundamental"*.

Entre tanto, el mantenimiento de la vida en las sociedades contemporáneas globalizadas exige la satisfacción de varias necesidades, todas ellas fundamentales para la supervivencia en este entorno. La pre-

4 ALEXY, Robert. *Teoría de los derechos fundamentales.* 2ª edición. Centro de Estudios Políticos y Constitucionales, 2007, p. 31.

servación de la dignidad de la persona - en espacio global y en el tiempo actual - no está vinculada apenas a las necesidades vitales, sino que también a la satisfacción de necesidades sociales y políticas. Por tanto, los derechos que deben ser reconocidos para la protección de la dignidad humana se amplían en razón directa de la complejidad de las estructuras sociales.

Formalmente, los derechos fundamentales se caracterizan por la universalidad y por la subjetividad de su imputación. Es decir, el reconocimiento jurídico de los derechos fundamentales se expresa en la norma jurídica, la cual contiene un enunciado prescriptivo cuyos destinatarios son todas las personas a quiénes se garantiza, subjetivamente, la protección de las necesidades fundamentales.

Pero, la enunciación formal de los derechos fundamentales no dice cuáles son éstos derechos y tampoco cuáles son los sujetos titulares de los mismos. Por eso, la catalogación de los derechos y la indicación de sus titulares dependen de cada Ordenamiento jurídico en particular.

El conocimiento de las características ontológicas de los derechos fundamentales permite determinar a qué clase pertenecen y a quiénes se puede atribuir la titularidad y su ejercicio, ya que no todos los derechos fundamentales pertenecen a todas las personas. Es decir, el contenido esencial del derecho fundamental es un importante vector hermenéutico.

En este sentido Martínez-Pujalte señala: "Cuando se presenta ante el operador jurídico un problema relacionado con un derecho fundamental, la primera tarea que debe abordarse es la determinación del contenido esencial del derecho."[5]

La determinación del contenido esencial del derecho, o el contenido constitucionalmente declarado, es lo que permite saber si un derecho fundamental ha sido violado. Por otra parte, el contenido esencial

5 MARTÍNEZ-PUJALTE, Antonio Luis. DE DOMINGO, Tomás. *Los derechos fundamentales en el sistema constitucional: teoría general e implicaciones prácticas.* Comares, Granada, 2011, p. 58.

del derecho es su núcleo rígido que no puede ser alterado, con lo cual no puede ser restringido por el legislador.

El contenido esencial de los derechos fundamentales constituye un límite absoluto a la actuación de los poderes públicos. "Esta infranqueabilidad de los derechos fundamentales para los poderes públicos... es una consecuencia de su posición central en el sistema constitucional,...que sitúa la dignidad de la persona y los derechos inherentes a ella como fundamento del entero sistema constitucional."[6]

Y, ¿cuál es el contenido esencial de un derecho fundamental?

De conformidad con lo que ha sido afirmado antes, los derechos fundamentales son los derechos necesarios al desarrollo de la personalidad y de la vida. Por esta razón, éstos derechos deben materializar los intereses fundamentales del hombre, es decir, el objeto de referidos derechos es un bien, que por su relevancia, debe ser jurídicamente protegido. Por tanto, cada derecho fundamental contiene *en si* la representación de un interese como la vida, la propiedad, la integridad física, la libertad, la igualdad, entre otros. De esta manera, el contenido esencial de un derecho es el bien jurídicamente protegido por la norma constitucional.

La tarea del intérprete, al establecer el sentido y alcance de un derecho fundamental, es delimitar el objeto del derecho, o determinar su núcleo esencial. Para llevar a cabo esta tarea el intérprete debe considerar el conjunto de las disposiciones constitucionales, además de considerar los fines perseguidos por la Constitución.

La garantía del contenido esencial de los derechos fundamentales

La determinación del contenido esencial de los derechos fundamentales está directamente vinculada al conjunto de la Constitución. Del mismo modo, la garantía del contenido esencial de los derechos fundamentales se sostiene en el Ordenamiento jurídico-constitucional.

6 *Idem.*

Dentro del sistema constitucional los derechos fundamentales contienen los valores supremos consagrados por la sociedad, y a la par garantizan la libertad.[7] Los derechos fundamentales son elementos constitutivos del conjunto constitucional y deben ser comprendidos en conexión con todo el sistema constitucional. Por conformar un sistema unitario, la Constitución abarca el conjunto de prescripciones que establecen el sentido de los derechos fundamentales, así como imponen sus límites. La comprensión sistémica de la Constitución es el punto de partida para la determinación del contenido esencial de los derechos fundamentales y, también, la referencia para garantizar su núcleo esencial.

El análisis conjunto de las disposiciones constitucionales pone de manifiesto que los valores jurídicos de la Ley Fundamental están relacionados unos con los otros, aunque no siempre resulte clara la relación inmanente de las normas constitucionales. El aparente antagonismo entre los valores jurídicos contenidos en las normas constitucionales resulta de la protección extendida a los bienes vitales tanto del individuo cuanto de la colectividad.

La función social de los derechos fundamentales

En la teoría clásica, los derechos fundamentales suelen ser asociados a los derechos individuales de libertad, lo que corresponde a una visión liberal e individualista de éste grupo de derechos. Desde esta perspectiva, los derechos fundamentales son valores supremos *de la persona*. Entre tanto, los derechos fundamentales no se refieren sólo a los derechos *de la persona*, sino que involucran también los *derechos del ciuda-*

---

7 Häberle señala que los derechos fundamentales son expresión de un ordenamiento de libertad ya realizado y, simultáneamente, son presupuesto para que este ordenamiento se constituya de nuevo una y otra vez a través de la actuación en libertad de todos. HÄBERLE, Peter. *La garantía del contenido esencial de los derechos fundamentales en la Ley Fundamental de Bonn: una contribución a la concepción institucional de los derechos fundamentales y a la teoría de la reserva de ley.* Traducción: Joaquín Brage Camazo. Dykinson-constitucional, Madrid, 2003, p. 7.

dano. La garantía del contenido esencial de los derechos fundamentales pone de manifiesto la tensión dialéctica entre los intereses protegidos por el ordenamiento jurídico-constitucional.

La idea de que los derechos fundamentales se refieren al conjunto de valores jurídicos consagrados por la Constitución, para la protección y garantía de los bienes vitales de la persona y de la comunidad, impone la indicación de la función ejercida por los derechos fundamentales dentro del sistema constitucional. Vinculados a las tesis sobre la garantía esencial de los derechos fundamentales surgen los teóricos que sostienen que referidos derechos cumplen una función social.

De conformidad con Häberle, el concepto de función social soluciona dos problemas: "la determinación de los límites (inmanentes) de los derechos subjetivos..., y la vinculación material del legislador en el ámbito de los derechos fundamentales".[8] Esto quiere decir que los derechos fundamentales limitan la actividad del legislador porque le impide corromper el núcleo esencial de referidos derechos, como también limitan el ejercicio individual de un derecho cuando se confrontan valores igualmente importantes. El concepto de función social pone de manifiesto la relación jerárquica que suponen los derechos fundamentales.

El concepto de función social es importante porque transforma la comprensión de los derechos fundamentales. De derechos exclusivamente individuales pasan a ser interpretados como "sustrato social", es decir, la base sobre la cual se armonizan las relaciones sociales. En este sentido son ilustrativas las palabra de Häberle: "La libertad y la función social no pueden contraponerse alternativamente una a la otra. La libertad de los derechos fundamentales debe poseer carácter 'social', en cuanto que debe ser actualizada en la vida social todos los días y a cada hora. En otro caso, se queda mera libertad formal."[9]

8 *Idem*, p. 12

9 *Idem*, p. 14

El principio de ponderación y el principio de proporcionalidad

Hay diferentes clases de derechos fundamentales y distintos titulares. Los derechos fundamentales, según pertenezcan a una u otra categoría, tiene por finalidad protegerá un determinado bien. Ocurre que los intereses protegidos pueden entrar en colisión. Esto no quiere decir que las normas que los reconocen estén en una relación antinómica, sino que los contenidos de tales normas pueden estar en conflicto entre sí, por ejemplo, al confrontar un interés individual con un interés colectivo.

La consecuencia de tal colisión de intereses es la restricción de un derecho fundamental. Pero, el contenido esencial de un derecho no puede ser modificado, ni tampoco limitado. La solución hermenéutica, en estos casos, es dada por los principios de ponderación y proporcionalidad.

Como vimos, los derechos fundamentales conforman un sistema unitario y son elementos constitutivos del orden constitucional. Dentro del sistema jurídico constitucional los derechos fundamentales deben mantener una relación de equilibrio, de la cual se deduce que la determinación del sentido de un derecho fundamental y la delimitación de su alcance dependen de un juicio de ponderación. El principio de ponderación supone el establecimiento de un orden jerárquico de valores, que constituye un sistema de referencia para decidir los conflictos que puedan surgir de la confrontación entre los bienes jurídico-constitucionales.[10]

El principio de proporcionalidad es, según Alexy[11], un juicio de ponderación por intermedio del cual se impone una limitación *justificada* a un derecho fundamental.

Si el resultado de la aplicación de los mandatos constitucionales, cuyo contenido resguarda un derecho fundamental, es una incompatibi-

10 Häberle desarrolla un importante análisis del principio de ponderación en la obra citada en este estudio.

11 ALEXY, Robert. Obra citada, p. 324.

lidad debe ser utilizado el principio de proporcionalidad para determinar la relación de precedencia entre las normas.

En caso de verificarse la colisión de preceptos constitucionales el principio de proporcionalidad "exige examinar la colisión a la luz de los juicios, máximas o principios... de adecuación, necesidad y proporcionalidad."[12]

Por intermedio de principio de adecuación el intérprete verifica si un determinado bien está contemplado en una norma constitucional; una vez constate que este bien está jurídicamente protegido, analiza la adecuación de la medida adoptada para tornar efectiva la norma constitucional. Si los medios utilizados para alcanzar los fines pretendidos por las normas constitucionales no son adecuados, el resultado de su aplicación (y la posible limitación de un derecho) no está justificado.

La utilización del principio de necesidad conlleva al planteamiento de la intensidad de las medidas restrictivas adoptadas. Es decir, si hay la necesidad de limitar un derecho fundamental, la cuestión es saber si es absolutamente necesaria la restricción o es posible encontrar otras soluciones que no lesionen el derecho.

El principio de proporcionalidad, en sentido estricto, es una valoración de la relación coste/beneficio obtenida como resultado de la restricción de un derecho fundamental. Si la limitación de un derecho produce menos sacrificios del derecho fundamental, entonces el principio de proporcionalidad cumple su función.

Los elementos que componen el principio de proporcionalidad *lato sensu* constituyen el denominado *test de proporcionalidad*, el cual permite saber si la limitación de un derecho fundamental está justificada y es, por tanto, lícita. Como ejemplo de la aplicación del test de propor-

---

12 DE DOMINGO, Tomás. *La teoría de la justicia del neoconstitucionalismo: los derechos fundamentales como núcleo del bien común*. In: MARTÍNEZ-PUJALTE, Antonio Luis. DE DOMINGO, Tomás, obra citada, p. 15.

cionalidad está la STF 136/1999[13] cuya fundamentación utiliza los juicios de adecuación, necesidad y proporcionalidad para solucionar la cuestión *sub judice.*

La utilización del principio de proporcionalidad no deja de ser la aplicación de un juicio de equidad. Considerando la función estructural de los derechos fundamentales en el sistema constitucional, las colisiones que pueden resultar de la aplicación de las normas deben ser reparadas, o aminoradas, para garantizar el contenido esencial de los derechos fundamentales y la efectividad del propio sistema.

Conclusiones

En este brevísimo ensayo sobre la garantía del contenido esencial de los derechos fundamentales apenas ha sido posible presentar los contornos generales del tema. En realidad, el estudio del contenido esencial de los derechos fundamentales contiene gran complejidad y requiere un análisis más profundizado. Sin embargo, el planteamiento del problema es importante porque pone de relieve las nuevas orientaciones de la teoría general del Derecho.

La comprensión de los derechos fundamentales está vinculada a las condiciones de espacio y tiempo. En lo largo recorrido histórico, los derechos fundamentales han sido concebidos de diferentes maneras: como derechos individuales, naturales, sociales, políticos... La evolución del concepto de derecho fundamental es también fruto de las transformaciones ocurridas en las estructuras sociales. En consecuencia de las modificaciones del espacio, el concepto de derecho fundamental se ajusta para cumplir una nueva función social. Entre tanto, el elemento permanente de los derechos fundamentales es el valor que debe ser protegido y garantizado por el sistema jurídico.

---

13 ESPAÑA. Tribunal Constitucional (Pleno). Sentencia 136/1999, de 20 de junio de 1999. *Boletín Oficial del Estado,* nº 197, de 18 de agosto de 1999.

Los valores vitales para la preservación de la dignidad humana y para la garantía de la ciudadanía están contenidos en los derechos fundamentales, los cuales enmarcan los límites de los poderes públicos y de los particulares.

En la práctica, la cuestión no es en absoluto sencilla. Los conflictos de intereses son constantes y la solución para las controversias impone un ejercicio de ponderación, lo que nos remite a las antiguas lecciones aristotélicas de equidad. Los contenidos constitucionalmente declarados deben medirse con la *regla lesbia*, la cual permite el ajuste del derecho a cada situación en concreto, desde que el ajuste no viole la esencia del derecho.

Referencias bibliográficas

FERRAJOLI, Luigi. *Principia iuris: teoría del derecho y de la democracia.* Traducción de Perfecto Andrés Ibánez, Carlos Bayón, Marina Gascón, Luis Pietro Sanchís y Alfonso Ruíz Miguel. Editorial Trotta, Madrid, 2011, libro 1.

BERNAL PULIDO, Carlos. Estudio introductorio. In: ALEXY, Robert. *Teoría de los derechos fundamentales.* 2ª edición. Centro de Estudios Políticos y Constitucionales, 2007.

ALEXY, Robert. *Teoría de los derechos fundamentales.* 2ª edición. Centro de Estudios Políticos y Constitucionales, 2007.

MARTÍNEZ-PUJALTE, Antonio Luis. DE DOMINGO, Tomás. *Los derechos fundamentales en el sistema constitucional: teoría general e implicaciones prácticas.* Comares, Granada, 2011.

HÄBERLE, Peter. *La garantía del contenido esencial de los derechos fundamentales en la Ley Fundamental de Bonn: una contribución a la concepción institucional de los derechos fundamentales y a la teoría de la reserva de ley.* Traducción: Joaquín Brage Camazo. Dykinson-constitucional, Madrid, 2003.

Diálogos teóricos dos modelos de "globalização" da democracia: intersecções entre Ciência Política e Relações Internacionais

Regina Laisner

Introdução

A democracia tradicionalmente foi compreendida como uma questão nacional, tendo a figura do Estado como seu principal agente e referência em termos de suas principais categorias de análise e interpretações. A necessidade da revisão desta perspectiva tem se colocado cada vez de forma mais intensa exigindo um novo formato de cidadania que reavalia a ordem internacional de Westfalia de "nacionalização da democracia" e as possibilidades de constituição de sua respectiva "globalização". Este é o tema a que se dedica este capítulo, considerando-se que esta exigência começou a ser respondida, consubstanciando a democracia, além das fronteiras, interesse sistemático dos estudiosos, muito recentemente e, ainda hoje, se restringe a poucos estudos e comumente referentes à literatura internacional.[1]

No que se refere às duas principais áreas dedicadas ao tema, no campo da Ciência Política o debate acerca da democracia recorrentemente se restringe à lógica estadocêntrica, ignorando-se traços e impactos da

1 Consultar sobre esta literatura: McGrew, 1999; Held & McGrew, 2003; Habermas, 2006; Held & Patomäki, 2006; Held, 2009; Held, 2010; Rovisco & Nowicka, 2011.

democracia, do ponto de vista transnacional, e no campo das Relações Internacionais, a reflexão, em geral, não é feita com profundidade adequada, tomando-se a democracia como um conceito de sentido quase único e relacionado ao modelo liberal do *main stream* da área, eximindo-se de um debate mais aprimorado e mais polifônico acerca de seus contornos, também no que se relaciona a seus aspectos transfronteiriços.

Dentro da literatura crescente no campo das Relações Internacionais sobre o tema da democracia transnacional, MacGrew (2003) em trabalho de referência de organização do debate, reconheceu quatro modelos normativos: o liberal-internacionalista, o pluralista radical, o cosmopolita e o deliberativo. Estes modelos trazem novos aspectos acerca da democracia em termos de sua "globalização" que serão aqui destacados, mas, estabelecem também, vínculos significativos com aspectos já tradicionalmente apresentados na teoria política contemporânea sobre democracia, que ajudam a entender melhor a sua própria estruturação e respectivos fundamentos que aí repousam. É envolto nestas questões que este texto se dedica a apresentar estes modelos propostos pelo autor, ainda hoje pertinentes, a partir do exercício de cruzamento das fronteiras da Teoria Política e da Teoria de Relações Internacionais. Seu propósito é especificar as matrizes dos modelos de democracia transnacional, tendo por base a Teoria Política, de maneira, não a diminuir a relevância do debate nas Relações Internacionais e seus aspectos de inovação e originalidade, mas justamente para aprofundá-lo e fortalecê-lo.

O modelo liberal-internacionalista

Em um contexto de *interdependência complexa*, como salientam os internacionalistas liberais Keohane e Nye (1999), os processos transnacionais mudaram o caráter do sistema internacional: o avanço das comunicações, a intensificação das transações financeiras, o volume do comércio, a atuação das empresas multinacionais, a influência recíproca de movimentos culturais e religiosos etc. foram cada vez mais forjando esta *interdependência* entre os países, assim como de novos atores "não estatais" desempenhando papéis às vezes mais relevantes que os próprios Estados no cenário mundial. (Keohane & Nye, 1999, p. 307).

Neste cenário, para esta perspectiva de cunho liberal, defende-se que há uma emergente ordem mundial pós-Vestfália em que os Estados nacionais se tornam cada vez mais interdependentes, recorrendo a mecanismos de cooperação internacional para a solução de seus problemas, sobretudo, nos momentos de reordenamento internacional depois das duas grandes guerras no século XX, quando mais esta perspectiva ganha força.

Deste ponto de vista a ordem mundial passa a ser vista, tal como salienta Gómez (2000, p. 76), como uma "poliarquia descentralizada e pluralista", ou seja, as decisões acerca do sistema internacional passam a ser executadas por vários atores, em que o Estado certamente continua como ator relevante, mas agora compartilha autoridade e legitimidade com outros, tais como agências internacionais, corporações transnacionais não governamentais, grupos internacionais de pressão, etc. Ocorre uma proliferação de instituições, regimes internacionais e redes de "geogovernança", a exemplo da criação da Liga das Nações e do Sistema das Nações Unidas.

Esta constatação nos leva a compreender que se constituem, a partir de então, outros centros de poder que não somente os Estados no processo de competição instaurado sob a democracia no sistema internacional, em uma clara revisão do modelo liberal clássico acerca da democracia. Neste modelo, a democracia é vista, sob parâmetros elitistas, como modelo de decisão com bases nacionais – como um método de competição pelo governo, ou como diria Schumpeter, seu grande ideólogo, "um arranjo institucional para se chegar a decisões políticas, no qual os indivíduos adquirem o poder de decidir utilizando para isso uma luta competitiva pelo voto do povo" (Schumpeter, 1943, p. 269). Nesta acepção procedimental da democracia se estabelece uma preocupação com as regras da tomada de decisão no jogo em que ela passa a ser identificada como um método de competição para a constituição de governos. Nela ficará a cargo das elites eleitas todas as atribuições do governo, capazes de gerar a racionalidade política necessária para a condução dos negócios públicos. Já para o pluralismo e, em um claro deslocamento do espectro de visão do Estado para a sociedade civil, há a defesa de que existem outros centros de poder, que não somente o Estado, no processo de competição instaurado sob a democracia, mas ainda vista, basicamente, como método de conquista de governos.

Deste modo, o desenvolvimento deste modelo de cunho competitivo-procedimental, mas agora pluralista, de democracia em nível internacional, o liberal-internacionalismo, tem como base o modelo de democracia proposto, fundamentalmente, por Robert Dahl que inaugurou um marco influente na discussão da democracia na Teoria Política, de caráter reformista.

Retomando um de seus mais importantes textos, "Poliarquia", escrito originalmente em 1971, Robert Dahl, ao se interessar sobre as condições sociais necessárias para a realização dos ideais democráticos em sociedades industriais complexas, identifica a competição entre grupos de interesse como uma condição crucial para a democracia. Deste modo, "ao chegar a decisões, o governo deve dar igual peso ao bem e aos interesses de todas as pessoas ligadas por tais decisões" (Dahl, 1997, p. 78). Nesta perspectiva, a igualdade intrínseca além de se mostrar um princípio moral razoável à fundamentação do governo de um Estado democrático representativo, tende a romper com o argumento da tutela política no qual se inscreve a ideia de que as pessoas comuns não têm competência para governar (Laisner, 2009).

De acordo com este autor, o que define a democracia são fundamentalmente duas dimensões: a competição e a participação – a primeira diz respeito à institucionalização das regras e a segunda, a processos através dos quais os segmentos sociais vão sendo institucionalizados, ou seja, passam a usufruir efetivamente das normas, a partir da inclusão das organizações políticas (partidos, associações, sindicatos, etc.) no mercado eleitoral. São estas duas dimensões que definem o grau de democratização de cada país. Portanto, em Dahl, a democracia como fruto da competição e da participação, se estabelece a partir de um equilíbrio de forças – equilíbrio de atores políticos inseridos em uma relação estratégica (Limongi, 1997).

O autor argumenta que devem existir certas características da organização social capazes de tornar as poliarquias democráticas factíveis (Dahl,1989). Na sua visão, as principais características da organização social dos países que se encaixariam na definição de poliarquia são: altos níveis de renda; expansão constante de renda; altos índices de urbanização; pequena população rural; alta percentagem de indivíduos detentores do grau universitário; economia orientada predominantemente para o mercado; indicadores de bem-estar geral, tais como alta expectativa de vida e baixos índices de mortalidade infantil (Dahl, 1989). Uma sociedade que dispõe de tais características, poderia ser definida então, como uma sociedade na qual o poder e influência estariam bem distribuídos.

No entanto, Dahl não trata dos mecanismos societários de participação capazes de dar cabo às carências estruturais de uma sociedade para atingir as condições que lhe parecem favoráveis ao surgimento e à consolidação da poliarquia, uma vez que seu objetivo *é discutir o procedimentalismo como método de constituição de governos e não como prática social* (Avritzer, 1996).

O mesmo ocorre no modelo liberal-internacionalista, inspirado na perspectiva dahlsiana, que privilegia a dimensão jurídico-institucional na forma de defesa de uma gradual reforma das estruturas de governança global para resolver problemas que são considerados de cunho estritamente políticos. A política aqui também é compreendida de forma restrita, mas em nível internacional agora, separada de outras esferas e reduzida a ela a extensão da democracia. Nesta direção, o conjunto de reformas institucionais tem como objetivo fortalecer as instituições que garantiriam direitos e deveres em nível internacional, tornando o sistema de governança global mais representativo a exemplo do Sistema de Nações Unidas, tal como aponta Gómez (2000, p. 77). Ademais, propõe-se a transposição do modelo de democracia doméstico para o nível global de maneira bastante simplória, poder-se-ia dizer, como se isso não representasse um enorme desafio, considerando-se já as dificuldades da institucionalização da representação em nível nacional. São largamente conhecidas as limitações no que diz respeito a esta ferramenta no caso de países subdesenvolvidos e muito mais no que diz respeito a casos como o da Organização das Nações Unidas (ONU), que deixam muito a desejar na equanimidade da representação, ainda que sob regras formais rígidas, mas que sucumbem, muitas vezes, diante de negociações de interesses que extrapolam o campo da política, pensada de maneira restrita.

Com o passar do tempo, no entanto, o entendimento dos limites do procedimentalismo democrático, apesar da sua hegemonia como forma de se pensar a democracia em nível nacional, começou a representar o questionamento de tal perspectiva a partir de visões analíticas contra-hegemônicas em que, cada vez mais, a democracia passou a ser pensada como uma gramática de organização da sociedade e da relação entre o Estado e a sociedade civil, em uma perspectiva ampliada da política e, consequentemente, da participação política. Nestes termos, abriu-se espaço para discutir o procedimentalismo como prática social e não apenas como método de constituição de governos. Tratam-se de propostas de alargamento da democracia, inclusive de seus tradicionais mecanismos de incorporação da sociedade civil que, historicamente limitou-se aos princípios da representação no Parlamento. Mecanismos estes que foram se mostrando insuficientes para a implantação das promessas da democracia procedimental, como seus próprios defensores, o reconheceram (a exemplo de BOBBIO, 2002) e que levaram à radicalização do debate acerca da democracia em nível doméstico, assim como em nível global.

O modelo pluralista radical

O radicalismo democrático com relação à ordem mundial se manifesta a partir de, pelo menos, duas visões principais, segundo Gómez (2000): uma de origem marxista baseada nos princípios da economia política e outra de origem comunitarista.

No que corresponde à perspectiva marxista, sabemos que Marx não teve uma contribuição significativa no que se refere à construção de uma teoria de relações internacionais e que não se dedicou tanto às discussões do desenvolvimento do capitalismo em nível internacional. Sua referência na construção da crítica ao sistema capitalista foi basicamente construída sob o olhar do nacional. Entretanto, não lhe escapou o aspecto da globalização do capital como necessidade básica para o futuro do próprio capitalismo. Já no Manifesto Comunista de 1848 afirmava:

> A necessidade de um mercado em constante expansão compele a burguesia a avançar por todo o globo terrestre. Ela precisa fixar-se em toda a parte, criar vínculos em toda a parte. A burguesia, pela exploração do mercado mundial, conferiu uma forma cosmopolita à produção e ao consumo de todos os países. (Marx, 1998, p. 09)

Assim, mesmo que diretamente não tenha oferecido grandes contribuições às teorias de Relações Internacionais, Marx pôde oferecer uma visão adequada e, de certa forma inaugural, acerca dos processos de internacionalização do capital e, consequentemente, da globalização como fenômeno mais amplo. Ademais, e principalmente, o fez sob uma perspectiva baseada nos princípios do materialismo histórico-dialético que permitiram uma perspectiva ao longo do tempo e crítica, extremamente relevante para a observação deste processo até os dias de hoje – aspecto muitas vezes desconsiderado em várias das leituras existentes acerca da globalização.

No que se refere especificamente ao olhar das Relações Internacionais podemos considerar, seguramente, a Teoria Crítica como uma perspectiva que se desenvolve tendo por base a perspectiva de Marx, recorrendo a várias de suas ideias e de seus sucessores. A inspiração em Antonio Gramsci neste aspecto é de se destacar.

Ao retomar os escritos de Marx defendendo uma visão mais fiel a eles, em contraposição ao marxismo em voga em sua época, Gramsci revigora o olhar sobre a indissolubilidade das questões materiais e simbólicas a partir do conceito de bloco histórico que a presume.[2] Deste modo, em clara crítica às visões economicistas simplificadoras do pensamento de Marx, Gramsci supõe que, para haver transformações em qualquer sociedade, é necessário que elas ocorram em seu conjunto, e não a partir da sua base material, considerando, portanto, que as questões simbólicas não são mero reflexo dessa base, mas sim constitutivas da mesma.

Assim, em Gramsci, a transformação social não se restringe ao mero assalto ao poder, e é pensada enquanto um processo. E para dar conta da forma como vê este processo de transformação social, ele se utiliza do conceito de hegemonia. O conceito de hegemonia em Gramsci se refere a um modo específico de construção ou exercício do poder em uma determinada sociedade. Específico porque implica em um modo de poder distinto da dominação, embora o termo hegemonia seja utilizado por muitos autores sem esta distinção. A dominação é baseada predominantemente na força e na coerção. A hegemonia, diferentemente, supõe como recurso predominante do poder o consentimento ativo dos que estão sob este poder e uma direção, ao invés da dominação, por parte daqueles que estão à frente dele (Gramsci, 1978).

---

2 A ideia de bloco histórico formulada por ele supõe uma indissolubilidade entre as forças materiais e os elementos culturais, estabelecendo uma equivalência entre eles e tornando qualquer ideia de determinação desnecessária. "(...) recordar a frequente afirmação de Marx sobre a 'solidez das crenças populares' como elemento necessário de uma determinada situação. Ele diz mais ou menos isto: 'quando esta maneira de conceber tiver a força das crenças populares', etc. outra afirmação de Marx é a de que uma persuasão popular tem, na maioria dos casos, a mesma energia de uma força material (ou algo semelhante), o que é muito significativo. A análise destas afirmações, creio, conduz ao fortalecimento da concepção de 'bloco histórico', no qual, justamente, as forças materiais são o conteúdo e as ideologias são a forma - sendo que a distinção entre forma e conteúdo é puramente didática, já que as forças materiais não seriam historicamente concebíveis sem forma e as ideologias seriam fantasias individuais sem as forças materiais." (Gramsci, 1978, p. 63)

O tema da hegemonia é central à Teoria Crítica nas Relações Internacionais e mais detidamente sistematizada por Cox. Este autor tem o cuidado de enfatizar a distinção das definições convencionais do conceito com o de supremacia ou de domínio, tal como enfatizado acima por Gramsci. Deste modo, na perspectiva deste pensador das Relações Internacionais, este processo envolve a institucionalização e a construção da legitimidade das classes dirigentes nas mais importantes esferas da política mundial, assim como o seria em escala nacional, donde se aplica mais comumente o pensamento de Gramsci, por sua vinculação mais direta à Teoria Política. A tese de Cox, não fugindo muito do modelo gramsciano, é de que para mudar a ordem mundial, construindo-se a hegemonia em larga escala, faz-se necessária a construção de novos blocos históricos dentro das fronteiras nacionais (Cox, 2007).

Para deixar mais clara esta proposição do que seriam estes novos blocos históricos, Cox propõe aplicar um modelo tripartite de esferas ou níveis de atividade que caracterizam as relações internacionais para a compreensão da política mundial: a dimensão vertical das relações internacionais, a relação entre Estado e sociedade civil e a dinâmica do processo produtivo (Nogueira e Messari, 2005, p. 142). De acordo com este autor, é preciso tomar estas três dimensões, em conjunto, para a construção da hegemonia em nível global, refletindo uma clara preocupação com a ordem vigente e sua necessária transformação – desigual no mundo da produção (em uma clara recuperação dos princípios marxistas de crítica à sociedade capitalista e dos seus efeitos mais avassaladores do capitalismo globalizado), desigual na relação entre Estados e sociedade civil (onde os próprios Estados acabam desempenhando um papel fundamentalmente "disciplinador" na mundialização do capital, com consequente enfraquecimento da sociedade civil) e desigual também no que se refere às conexões interestatais nas relações internacionais, em um cenário vertical em que alguns Estados certamente são mais influentes nas decisões internacionais do que outros, exercendo controle sobre as instituições formais e mesmo sobre as redes informais de governança global.

A transformação, nesta perspectiva, opera de forma menos idealista e mais refinada, em que os vários aspectos da construção da hegemonia são apontados em um claro movimento de resistência aos avanços da globalização construído nos três níveis: desde a luta na dimensão da produção, à democratização do Estado e da sociedade civil, assim como nos momentos de organização de instituições que possam "horizontalizar" as relações internacionais. Torna-se necessário, nesta visão, desencadear um processo de democratização que atinja todos estes níveis, do mais local ao mais global, lançando-se as bases para uma democracia substantiva em todos eles.

Este processo ainda tem como unidade básica de referência o Estado, lugar privilegiado de consolidação de conflitos e de interesses de uma classe sobre a outra. Porém, o Estado ao qual se refere, que é a unidade básica das Relações Internacionais, não se restringe ao aparelho burocrático-militar. Trata-se aqui do Estado ampliado, nas suas interconexões com as demais esferas já apontadas. São os Estados que, de certo modo, assumem uma vocação hegemônica, como aqueles que passaram por revoluções socioeconômicas completas (França e Inglaterra, por exemplo) e que têm capacidade de exportar os valores de suas transformações para demais partes do Sistema Internacional. (Cox, 2007).

E assim, uma hegemonia mundial representaria a expansão de uma hegemonia nacional estabelecida por determinada classe social como dirigente para o exterior, no caso da transformação que se espera, por parte da classe trabalhadora, tal como Gramsci já havia teorizado. Um processo que deve ser criado no contexto nacional, em uma revolução local, e não dentro das Organizações Internacionais, uma vez que essas instituições expressam as normas de uma hegemonia mundial, facilitando a expansão econômica das classes dominantes. Além disso, estas organizações têm um forte apelo ideológico que orienta, em boa medida, a ação dos Estados, legitimando certas instituições a práticas que favorecem os países dominantes, além de cooptar talentos.

A segunda vertente do radicalismo democrático de cunho global apresentada se baseia na organização de princípios comunitaristas "em uma combinação de formas de democracia direta e de autogoverno com novas estruturas de governança funcional global" (Gómez, 2000, p. 79).

O comunitarismo surge nos anos 1980 como um debate interno ao próprio liberalismo, constituindo uma das correntes que essencialmente contesta as limitações da teoria e da prática liberal. Ao contrário do que a nomenclatura possa indicar, a preocupação não é tão grande com a configuração de comunidades, mas sim com relação à configuração do sujeito liberal e com a forma em que são distribuídos os recursos sociais em uma sociedade justa.

Neste aspecto, entra em um debate com a perspectiva defendida por John Rawls (1997) acerca das definições de justiça sob os auspícios do liberalismo. Para Ralws os princípios de justiça podem ser fundados a partir de um consenso original entre os indivíduos como "um conjunto de princípios para escolher entre as várias formas de ordenação social que determinam essa divisão de vantagens e para selar um acordo sobre as partes distributivas adequadas" (Rawls, 1997, p. 5). São estes princípios que estabelecem uma espécie de contrato social – "uma carta fundamental de uma associação humana" (Rawls, 1997, p. 5) criada em uma espécie de consenso original. Este consenso original deve ser estabelecido com relação à estrutura básica da sociedade, pois é ela que estabelece o consenso necessário para que a justiça se faça presente nas demais instâncias da sociedade: "Para nós o objeto primário da justiça é a estrutura básica da sociedade, ou mais exatamente, a maneira pela qual as instituições sociais mais importantes distribuem direitos e deveres fundamentais e determinam a divisão de vantagens provenientes da cooperação social." (Rawls, 1997, p. 8). Esta estrutura básica se define, portanto, pelas principais instituições de uma determinada sociedade, quais sejam, as normas que regulam o acesso ao poder político, os direitos civis e políticos, o sistema de acesso ocupacional, sobretudo a educação e o sistema tributário, que regula a distribuição de renda, e o sistema de transferências. A justiça, por esta perspectiva, está nos procedimentos, portanto, e não nos resultados da distribuição – se os arranjos institucionais estabelecidos são justos os seus resultados também o serão. (Laisner, 2004, p. 341)

Já para os comunitaristas, embora a ideia de comunidade como coletivo responsável pela criação de valores seja relevante, o foco do debate é muito mais saber se é possível defender uma visão de justiça universalista referida a um ideal de liberdade que seja pautado muito mais nas normas partilhadas pela comunidade, do que na experiência individual.

Uma importante referência para se entender melhor esta perspectiva na Teoria Política são os trabalhos de Michael Walzer. Inicialmente, o argumento central deste autor, é a ideia de que uma vez que os indivíduos são sujeitos de cultura como membros de uma comunidade, eles são capazes de escolher princípios, entres eles o da justiça. Mas diferentemente de Ralws e seus sucessores, em "Esferas da Justiça: uma defesa da igualdade e da liberdade", Walzer (2003) propõe uma teoria pluralista da justiça, segundo a qual não existem princípios universais de justiça distributiva, uma vez que em cada lugar haverá mecanismos distintos de distribuição dos bens que são produzidos pelas distintas comunidades sociais. Daí os princípios de justiça serem em si mesmos plurais, uma vez que bens sociais distintos devem ser distribuídos também de formas distintas e não em um critério de distribuição que é prévio aos significados desses bens. É nessa direção que define o conceito de "igualdade complexa", central a este trabalho e que se refere à ausência de dominação na distribuição dos bens sociais.

A ideia é desenvolver mecanismos de constituição de "boas comunidades", guiadas, em diferentes níveis, até o global, pelo exercício da igualdade, por meio de autoridades que sejam responsáveis perante estas comunidades e seus respectivos cidadãos.

> Trata-se então de uma visão em que as comunidades de autogoverno de origens diversas, superpostas e espacialmente diferen-

> ciadas, se multiplicam como lugares de exercício de poder que recusam toda estrutura centralizada ou soberana de autoridade. Os agentes dessa mudança radical nas relações de poder global seriam os movimentos sociais críticos existentes (ambientalistas, de mulheres e pela paz), que desafiam tanto os Estados e as agências internacionais quanto as definições convencionais da política (Gómez, 2000, p. 80)

Em geral, na perspectiva do radicalismo democrático, tanto na visão do marxismo como na sua versão comunitarista, há uma defesa clara de mecanismos de democracia direta e participativa como forma de aprofundar a proposta de democracia anteriormente apresentada no modelo liberal-internacionalista, única e exclusivamente pautada pela ideia de representação, a partir do controle direto dos cidadãos da vida política no plano internacional. Este modelo, quando comparado à Teoria Política e suas matrizes, atualiza o modelo de democracia participativa que se constrói no contexto dos anos 1960, quando a palavra "participação" torna-se parte do vocabulário político popular a partir de vários movimentos estudantis, e que se difunde entre os trabalhadores naquela mesma década e na seguinte, em consequência de sua crescente insatisfação. Nesse mesmo período, os governos nacionais começaram a incorporar, em seus discursos, a questão da participação popular e alguns até a encaminhar políticas neste sentido, a exemplo da França, da Grã-bretanha e dos Estados Unidos. Os sentidos desta participação variavam desde sua origem referida à pólis grega, à participação restrita ao processo eleitoral, tal como na perspectiva procedimental/competitiva de democracia já apontada, aos novos conteúdos e sentidos que vêm adquirindo, ainda hoje, múltiplos e contraditórios.

Pateman (1992), tradicionalmente uma referência na discussão da perspectiva *participativa* da democracia, defende que Rousseau pode ser considerado o teórico por excelência da participação. Segundo ela, toda a teoria política deste autor apóia-se na participação individual de cada cidadão no processo político de tomada de decisões, e, em sua teoria,

Rousseau postula que a participação não é só um complemento que dá sustentação aos arranjos institucionais, "ela também provoca um efeito psicológico sobre os que participam, assegurando uma inter-relação contínua entre o funcionamento das instituições e as qualidades e atitudes psicológicas dos indivíduos que interagem dentro delas" (Pateman, 1992, p. 35), em um aspecto educativo e articulador dos indivíduos.

Como Pateman, os defensores desta perspectiva apresentam suas teses como um contraponto à perspectiva representativa que é predominante na definição dos contornos da democracia, tendo em vista a defesa da participação, da cooperação e da solidariedade como fundamentos de um projeto comum de sociedade. Isto exige, nesta visão, um acordo entre os indivíduos que inclui sentimentos comuns de reconhecimento e consideração do outro, contrariamente à lógica da competição da democracia representativa. Neste processo, a participação assume papel central – uma dimensão pedagógica na construção de uma democracia mais ampla. Uma dimensão no sentido de desenvolver capacidades de modo que os indivíduos privados se tornem cidadãos e os seus interesses se refaçam em direção ao bem-comum.

A despeito das questões e dúvidas levantadas acerca da democracia participativa, este clima de ativismo político com ênfase na participação e o reestabelecimento de experiências participativas que se desenvolveram gradualmente nos anos 1970 despertaram um renovado interesse nas possibilidades de formas consensuais de autogoverno.

E este interesse é retomado agora em nível internacional no modelo radical de democracia em nível global. Neste nível, a proposta é a criação de múltiplos espaços de pertencimento dos cidadãos (locais, nacionais, globais) de modo a estabelecer novas estruturas de organização social participativas que permitam a participação em escalas cada vez mais amplas.

Entretanto, se os problemas acerca desta perspectiva já são comuns numa escala geograficamente menos extensa, o que dizer acerca de sua ampliação? Em termos cosmopolitas, poder-se-ia encaminhar-se uma resposta?

O modelo cosmopolita

Podemos considerar que o cosmopolitismo tem uma larga história de interpretação e tem em Kant seu principal representante moderno, cuja proposta de "paz perpétua" se baseia em princípios universalistas. Para ele, os homens enquanto seres racionais têm sua conduta guiada por imperativos categóricos, que constituem uma espécie de base para todas as ações. A moral, para ele, assume a forma de um imperativo categórico e, deste modo todos os homens agem de acordo com ela. Partindo da ideia de que a moral é uma norma universal, elaborada pelos próprios homens, seres racionais, Kant chega à conclusão de que, as leis que regem a conduta humana fazem com que a humanidade seja um fim em si mesma. Desta forma, a dignidade dos homens estaria em agir segundo as normas feitas por eles mesmos de acordo com a moral (Andrade, 2004). Tal como destaca Santos (2007, p. 02):

> Esse sistema ético permite pensarmos a humanidade simultaneamente, enquanto um indivíduo que oferece a si mesmo a lei pela qual regula suas ações e enquanto coletivo de indivíduos que se orientam pelos mesmos princípios e que, deste modo, abrem caminho para concretização de uma comunidade ética universal.

A perspectiva é recolocar no centro da reflexão a reafirmação de princípios éticos comuns a toda humanidade de modo a superar divisões e conflitos, recuperando a capacidade de pensar a evolução moral da humanidade na constituição de uma comunidade ampla e autônoma, uma comunidade cosmopolita, baseada nos princípios da paz. Em "A Paz Perpétua", sua obra seminal, afirma:

> E, não obstante, a razão, desde o trono do máximo poder legislativo moral, condena a guerra como uma vida jurídica e converte,

> em troca, em um dever imediato o estado de paz, que não pode estabelecer-se ou garantirse, certamente, sem um pacto entre os povos: há de existir, portanto, uma federação de tipo especial à que se possa chamar federação da paz (foedus pacificum), que se distinguiria do pacto de paz (pactum pacis), já que este buscaria acabar com uma guerra e a outra buscaria terminar com todas as guerras para sempre. (Kant, 2006, p. 75/76)

Nesta mesma obra, Kant abordou três formas de direito sobre os Estados para a garantia da paz duradoura: o direito das gentes dos Estados, nas suas relações recíprocas, que determina o que é justo segundo unidades do poder e não segundo leis exteriores que limitam a liberdade das pessoas; o direito político exercido pelo povo no Estado, e o direito cosmopolita, aquele que permite condições de hospitalidade universal, na medida em que, conforme o autor, todo o estrangeiro que se comportar amistosamente não deve ser tratado com hostilidades devido à sua vinda em território de outrem, caso contrário, isso implicaria em um retorno ao estado de natureza hobbesiano, fato que contradiz a implantação da paz. Segundo o próprio autor:

> O direito de hospitalidade, não obstante, ou seja, a faculdade dos extrangeiros recém-chegados não se extende mais além das condições de possibilidade para tentar um comércio com os antigos habitantes. Desta maneira, podem estabelecer relações pacíficas partes lonjanas do mundo, relações que se converterão finalmente em legais e públicas, podendo, assim, aproximar o gênero humano a uma constituição cosmopolita. (Kant, 2006, p. 80)

O estabelecimento de um constituição cosmopolita, completaria junto com o direito das gentes (relações dos Estados entre si e seus povos) e o direito estatal o que Kant chama de direito público da humanidade como um ordenamento jurídico universal, para todos os cidadãos, como pertencentes não mais ao Estado A ou B, mas sim ao mundo.

Deste modo, os argumentos de Kant revelam a possibilidade de uma comunidade humana, com direito universal baseada na lógica da paz. Um processo que não pode ser construído e mantido sem um contrato dos povos. Tal contrato, continua Kant, seria feito por meio de avanço frente ao mero tratado de paz. "Há de existir, portanto, uma federação de tipo especial à que se possa chamar 'federação da paz' (*Friedensbund, foedus pacificum*), que se distinguiria do pacto de paz (*pactum pacis*) já que este buscaria acabar com uma guerra e a outra buscaria terminar com todas as guerras para sempre" (Kant, 2006, p. 43).

Os princípios e pressupostos de uma comunidade cosmopolita em Kant certamente influenciam o modelo cosmopolita de democracia, na medida em que vê nas virtudes da democracia um potencial em termos de sua constituição. Não da democracia nas bases atuais do liberalismo, mas da democracia como algo efetivo e amplo, não a algumas nações específicas, mas ao conjunto delas, de forma articulada. E no âmbito deste modelo, David Held é seguramente um dos principais representantes da proposta.[3]Seu objetivo fundamental é a reflexão acerca da construção de uma organização política no qual os cidadãos, de qualquer parte do mundo, possam ter voz e representação política nos assuntos internacionais.

Tal perspectiva se vincula claramente à crítica dos autores da Teoria Crítica das Relações Internacionais que apontam para as limitações dos Estados Nacionais quanto à incorporação de seus cidadãos. Ao invés de realizar suas promessas de representação e emancipação, na prática, estes Estados tornaram-se barreira neste sentido, uma vez que suas estruturas se apresentam como insuficientes para a realização desta tarefa e, ademais, incapazes na resolução de conflitos e promoção da solidariedade entre diferentes comunidades.

3 Patomäki afirma em entrevista a David Held, acerca de sua colaboração na configuração da perspectiva cosmopolita: "This theory was first outlined in your essay 'Democracy, the Nation-state and the Global System' (Held, 1991) and developed further in the book *Democracy and the Global Order* (Held, 1995). These have been extremely important openings" (Held & Patomäki, 2006, p. 116).

Mas, nem por isso, para Held, trata-se de negar o papel do Estado na construção da democracia cosmopolita.

> Cosmopolitanism is concerned to disclose the ethical, cultural and legal basis of political order in a world where political communities and states matter, but not only and exclusively. In circumstances where the trajectories of each and every country are tightly entwined, the partiality of 'reasons of state' needs to be recognized. While states are hugely important vehicles to aid the delivery of effective public recognition, equal liberty and social justice, they should not be thought of as ontologically privileged. They can be judged by how far they deliver these public goods and how far they fail; for the history of states is marked, of course, not just by phases of bad leadership and corruption but also by the most brutal episodes. A cosmopolitanism relevant to our global age must take this as a starting point, and build an ethically sound and politically robust conception of the proper basis of political community, and of the relations among communities (Held, 2011, p. 163).

Para ele, portanto, o problema não está no Estado em si como agente promotor de políticas. O problema parece estar "[...] na incapacidade de pensar a política para além do Estado, ou melhor, na insistência em pensar a política como um domínio exclusivo e excludente de uma comunidade circunscrita a um determinado espaço territorial" (Nogueira e Messari, 2005, p. 154), como afirmam seus comentadores.

Ao mesmo tempo, por força da ambivalência dos processos globalizantes, a soberania estatal e a territorialidade perdem força pelo incremento, a aceleração e ao aprofundamento das interconexões regionais e globais. Isso, para Held e demais defensores da democracia cosmopolita, gera um potencial transformador na medida em que ocorre um fenômeno de extensão e aprofundamento da democracia através

> [...] das nações, regiões e redes globais. É nessa direção que um modelo cosmopolita (e não internacional) de democracia se consagra, procurando especificar princípios e bases institucionais para a expansão de uma governança democrática nos, entre e através dos Estados, de modo a desenvolver "capacidade de administração e recursos políticos independentes no plano regional e global" (Held, 1996 *apud* Gómez, 2000, p. 82).

Mas para que esta potencialidade seja de fato aproveitada faz-se necessário novos arranjos institucionais para que a atividade política possa ser exercida de forma mais democrática na nova ordem. Uma ordem que impacta cidadãos de todo o mundo, articuladamente, mas cujo manejo permanece na mão ou do Estado ou de demais agentes não qualificados para tal decisão, desde uma perspectiva democrática. Assim, o que Held e demais defensores desta perpectiva propõem é a criação de um novo nível de governança, o global. Um nível que incorporaria uma escala mundial mas, ao mesmo tempo, caracterizado por uma perspectiva multinível, que para além do local e do nacional, incorporasse outros níveis como o regional, por exemplo. Níveis que, como afirma Held, estariam vinculados a múltiplos pertencimentos e múltiplas lealdades: local, nacional, regional e global, com respectivos direitos e deveres, que deveriam sobrepor-se (Held, 1997).

Desse modo, o pensamento cosmopolita se vincula à matriz kantiana quanto à possibilidade de alcançar, teleologimente, uma ordem política baseada, em última instância, na própria humanidade. Nela estaria o potencial, através dos princípios éticos da autonomia e do diálogo, as posibilidades efetivas da construção da democracia, em nível mundial. A esta altura, faz-se notar como estes princípios levam a aproximar esta tradição à perspectiva da democracia deliberativa na Teoria política, cuja matriz se finca nos mesmos princípios, fundamentalmente baseados nas proposições habermasianas que nos são caras, ainda que com distinções, para melhor compreender a proposta aqui apresentada do modelo cosmopolita de democracia.

O modelo deliberativo

A democracia deliberativa se refere à ideia de que a forma legítima de elaboração das leis e regras de funcionamento da democracia surge da deliberação pública dos cidadãos. Como medida normativa da legitimidade, a democracia deliberativa evoca ideais de legislação racional, políticas participativas e autogoverno civil. Cohen (1999) define a democracia deliberativa como uma associação na qual as relações são governadas pela deliberação pública de seus membros, e propõe uma abordagem do valor de uma associação que trata a própria democracia como um ideal político fundamental, e não simplesmente como um ideal derivado, que pode ser explicado em termos de valores de justiça ou igualdade de respeito. Em geral, esta visão é especialmente associada aos escritos de Jurgen Habermas (Elster, 1999).

Para Habermas, as comunicações que os sujeitos estabelecem entre si, mediadas por atos de fala, dizem respeito sempre a três mundos: o mundo objetivo das coisas, o mundo social das normas e instituições e o mundo subjetivo. As relações com esses três mundos estão presentes, ainda que não na mesma medida, em todas as interações sociais. A racionalidade própria do sistema capitalista, mediada pela lógica da utilidade e valor das coisas, e sustentada pela lógica do conhecimento científico, em geral, dá o tom da maior parte das interações sociais. Deste modo, com a institucionalização formal do meio monetário na emergência do capitalismo, a ação orientada para o sucesso, guiada por cálculos individualistas de utilidade, perde-se a conexão com a ação orientada para o entendimento mútuo (Habermas, 1987a).

A perspectiva habermasiana se constrói em referência a uma determinada forma de interação discursiva que seja capaz de romper com esta racionalidade instrumental. Esta interação deve ser levada a termo por agentes comunicativamente competentes, conhecedores das regras recíprocas de conduta, na perspectiva da teoria da ação comunicativa. Nas palavras de Habermas: "la acción comunicativa se basa en un proceso cooperativo de interpretación en que los participantes se refieren simultáneamente a algo en el mundo objetivo, en el mundo social y en el mundo subjetivo aun cuando en su manifestación subrayen temáticamente uno de estos tres componentes" (Habermas, 1987a, p. 171).

Em síntese, podemos dizer que, para Habermas, a *ação comunicativa* surge como uma interação dos sujeitos capazes de falar e agir, a partir de relações que se estabelecem para alcançar uma compreensão sobre a situação em que ocorre a interação, para tornar possível, em seguida, a elaboração de planos de ação com vistas a coordenar suas ações a partir do *entendimento.*

> El concepto de entendimiento (Verständigung) remite a un acuerdo racionalmente motivado alcanzado entre los participantes, que se mide por pretensiones de validez susceptibles de crítica. Las pretensiones de validez (verdad preposicional, rectitud normativa y veracidade expresiva) caracterizan diversas categorías de un saber que se encarna em manifestaciones o emisiones simbólicas (Habermas, 1987b, p.110).

O entendimento resultante deste tipo de ação, em tese, seria capaz de submeter tradições, normas e autoridades a processos comunicativos de questionamento e julgamento discursivo, levando à substituição de um consenso baseado na convenção por outro, pós-convencional e ancorado em processos abertos de comunicação.

Nisso consistiria o potencial emancipatório da ação comunicativa: na possibilidade real de uma distribuição igualitária de oportunidades de intervenção na interação pelos seus participantes. O consenso, para ser legítimo, precisa ser o resultado de um processo no qual todos os participantes da interação tenham condições de expressar seus pontos de vista de forma não coagida e sustentar, perante outros, suas opiniões e interesses.

A esfera pública passa, assim, a indicar a dimensão da sociedade onde este intercâmbio discursivo torna-se possível, não exatamente um cenário de interesses ou campo de enfrentamento entre Estado e sociedade, mas uma prática de discurso crítico racional dos assuntos públicos, tal como aponta Calhoun (1992) em sua interpretação da obra de Habermas.

Assim como Habermas, Hannah Arendt assinala os procedimentos dialogais, como a ação compartilhada e a convivência de uma pluralidade dos interesses, como traços fundamentais do espaço público, que se define como o lugar ou o momento no qual os homens podem, através da fala, compartilhar interpretações a respeito do mundo em que vivem (Telles, 1990). O reconhecimento público, a legitimação da diferença, da alteridade, aparecem, nestes autores, como procedimentos que delineiam a emergência deste espaço público de debate e deliberação, cenário no qual os conflitos de interesses são administrados com base em normas pactuadas e públicas e não confinados ao terreno do privado ou submetidos ao interesse do mais forte.

Hannah Arendt não acredita nos consensos perenes e estáveis, mas aposta justamente na possibilidade de reinvenção, sempre continuada, de acordos provisórios e retomáveis. Mais do que o consenso, ela enfatiza a explicitação das diferenças, ainda que irredutíveis. O reconhecimento de sujeitos, de falas, de argumentos e de interesses diferentes, sua pertinência e relevância para a construção de um mundo comum, como "artefato humano" (Laisner, 1999) onde seja possível e plausível viver, é parte significativa da sua contribuição específica para a construção de um conceito atual de espaço público.

Para Arendt, a política não é o campo da verdade, não é o campo do conhecimento; é sim o campo da contingência e exige formulações que não têm a escora da verdade, mas que podem ser aceitas em nome de uma prudência, de um discernimento compartilhado. A política, ela diz, se refere à construção de um mundo comum que é plural. A legitimidade de uma proposição, em Hannah Arendt, tem uma ancoragem intersubjetiva, na medida em que é pela aceitação do outro que ela se realiza. Não se trata de estabelecer ou procurar o consenso, mas tomar como possível o entendimento que é fruto da comunicação entre homens diferentes, expressa nas diferentes falas presentes na esfera pública. Não é a unicidade que está em jogo, mas sim a possibilidade de vivenciar a experiência de estar junto sem que isto afete a pluralidade envolvida. Por meio da fala, ela nos diz, os homens agem politicamente, na medida em que eles trocam posições acerca do certo e do errado, do justo e do injusto. Porque não há regras gerais passíveis de serem aplicadas aos casos particulares, o juízo político, para ser afirmado, precisa ser compartilhado no espaço público. (Arendt, 1995; Arendt, 1973).

Nesse ponto, parece importante enfatizar que, ao pressupormos a possibilidade de construção conjunta e compartilhada da coisa pública, com base nos processos comunicativos na esfera pública, não se está, de forma alguma, pressupondo que os indivíduos abram mão, *a priori*, de seus interesses privados. Pelo contrário, trata-se de, debatendo e negociando com outros interesses divergentes e por vezes antagônicos, tentar afirmar seus interesses como direitos legítimos. Isto representa um processo muito mais rico e complexo do que o simples abandono – ademais, irrealista – da perspectiva de realização dos interesses particulares.

No espaço público, os indivíduos e os grupos estão sim buscando realizar os seus interesses. Sua realização, no entanto, tem como parâmetro a legitimidade das reivindicações concorrentes, ou seja, há o reconhecimento não apenas do conflito, mas da sua legitimidade, na medida em que o outro é visto como um sujeito igualmente portador de direitos. A noção de bem comum pode ser, dessa forma, desnaturalizada na medida em que seu conteúdo é objeto de discussão. Esta é a ideia. Ainda assim, se reconhece que a concepção da esfera pública, enquanto um procedimento, que toma como ponto de partida a suposição da igualdade, assentada no reconhecimento das diferenças, mesmo a partir das experiências nacionais, enfrenta, evidentemente, dificuldades imensas de serem superadas. E muito mais quando pensamos na proposta de extensão deste modelo para o nível mundial. Mas é possível afirmar que a dimensão dessas dificuldades indica, ao mesmo tempo, a medida da importância que essa questão assume para o debate sobre a construção da democracia no sistema internacional.

Considerações Finais

Em um contexto cada vez mais intenso de interconexões regionais e globais o debate acerca da construção da democracia tem exigido a incorporação dos impactos transformadores deste processo na edificação da cidadania contemporânea. Uma nova formatação que reavalia a "nacionalização da democracia" e as possibilidades da constituição de sua respectiva "globalização". Ao mesmo tempo, há uma forte sensação de que os mecanismos construídos sob esta nova formatação e seus respectivos organismos, desde o Fundo Monetário Internacional à Organização das Nações Unidas, entre outros, não têm dado conta de dirimir os desafios desta globalização, pelo menos não em uma perspectiva democrática. Neste sentido é que se coloca Keohane:

> To be effective in the twenty first century, modern democracy requires international institutions. In addition, to be consistent with democratic values these institutions must be accountable to domestic civil society. Combining global governance with effective democratic accountability will be a major challenge for scholars and policy makers alike in the years ahead (Keohane, 1998, p. 87).

Esta proposição de Keohane nos chama a atenção para a necessidade de um sério e profundo exame dos sentidos da democracia na contemporaneidade e, ademais, no que nos corresponde, enquanto teóricos, de como a teoria pode nos auxiliar a pensar seus caminhos e descaminhos. Desde os modelos de democracia global apresentados por MacGrew (2003), tentamos, neste capítulo, apresentar as contribuições das Teorias de Relações Internacionais, a partir da identificação e análise das matrizes e fundamentos vindos da Teoria Política, com vistas a contribuir para este debate, à luz da interseção das duas áreas.

Na busca de uma ordem mundial mais democrática o modelo cosmopolita termina combinando aspectos fundamentais, tanto do liberalismo-internacionalista, como do radicalismo, a partir de ideias tais como salienta Gómes (2000, p. 83): centralidade do autogoverno, da democracia direta e participativa, de um lado, ênfase na abordagem constitucional-legal e primazia do poder político na condução da governança global atrelado ao processo democrático de tomada de decisão, de outro, e ademais a própria democratização das relações econômicas globais e das formas de governança. Neste sentido, esta visão, em articulação às demais aqui apresentadas, fortalecem e aprofundam o debate acerca da democracia. Mas é importante salientar que no debate entre céticos e transformacionistas dentro das Relações Internacionais, estes modelos, de maneira geral, têm como pré-requisitos e, em oposição ao ceticismo dos realistas, o reconhecimento do desejo e a perspectiva da possibilidade da democratização da ordem mundial, ainda que reconhecendo suas dificuldades e mesmo sendo ora mais reformistas, ora mais radicais. Este é o principal requisito de análise deste trabalho e que se articula com o objetivo da contribuição a que se dedica a apresentar: o desejo da construção da democracia e estímulo ao seu debate, tendo como ponto de partida a teoria, para justamente incentivar a sua prática, inclusive e porque não dizer, principalmente, em nível internacional.

Referências Bibliográficas

ANDRADE, Regis de Castro. Kant: a liberdade, o indivíduo e a república. In: WEFFORT, Francisco (Org.). *Os clássicos da política*. Rio de Janeiro: Ed. Ática, Vol. 2 2004.

ARENDT, Hannah. *A condição humana*. Trad. Roberto Raposo, 7ª ed. Rio de Janeiro: Forense Universitária, 1995.

ARENDT, Hannah. *Crises da República*. São Paulo: Perspectiva, 1973.

AVRITZER, L. *A moralidade da democracia*: ensaios em teoria habermasiana e teoria democrática. São Paulo: Perspectiva; Belo Horizonte: Ed. UFMG, 1996.

BOBBIO, N. *O futuro da democracia*: uma defesa das regras do jogo. Rio Janeiro: Paz e Terra, 2002.

CALHOUN, C. (ed.) *Habermas and the Public Sphere.* Cambridge: MIT Press, 1992.

COHEN, J. Deliberation and democratic legitimacy. In: BOHMAN, J.; REHG, W. (Ed.). *Deliberative democracy*: essays on reason and politics. Cambridge: MIT Press, 1999. p.67-91.

COX, R. W. Gramsci, Hegemonia e relações internacionais: um ensaio sobre o método. In: Stephen, Gill (Org.), *Gramsci, materialismo histórico e relações internacionais.* Rio de Janeiro: Editora da UFRJ, 2007.

DAHL, R. *Poliarquia.* São Paulo: Edusp, 1997.

DAHL, R. *Preface to democratic theory.* New Haven: Yale University Press, 1989.

ELSTER, J. The market and the forum: three varieties of political theory. In: BOHMAN, J.; REHG, W. (Ed.). *Deliberative democracy*: essays on reason and politics. Cambridge: MIT Press, 1999, p.3-33.

GÓMEZ, J. M. *Política e democracia em tempos de globalização*, Rio de Janeiro: LPP – Laboratório de Políticas Públicas, 2000.

GRAMSCI, A. *Concepção Dialética da História.* Trad. de Carlos Nelson Coutinho. 3ª ed. Rio de Janeiro: Civilização Brasileira. 1978.

HABERMAS, J. *Teoría de la acción comunicativa.* Volumen 2: Crítica de la razón funcionalista. Taurus: Madrid, 1987a.

HABERMAS, J. 1987b. "Teoría de la acción comunicativa. Volumen 1: Racionalidad de la acción y racionalización social". Taurus: Madrid, 1987b.

HABERMAS, J. *El occidente escindido:* pequeños escritos políticos X. Traducción: José Luis López de Lizaga. Madrid: Editorial Trotta, 2006.

HELD, D. "Cosmopolitanism, democracy and the global order". IN: ROVISCO, Maria & NOWICKA (ed.). *The Ashgate research companion to cosmopolitanism*, Ashgate Publishing Limited and Ashgate Publishing Company, Farnham& Burlington, 2011.

HELD, D. *Cosmopolitanism*: ideals and realities. Cambridge: Polity Press and Blackwell Publishing Ltd, 2010.

HELD, D.Globalization and Cosmopolitan Democracy. *Peace Review*, v. 9, n. 3, p. 309-314, September 1997.

HELD, D. Restructuring Global Governance: Cosmopolitanism, Democracy and the Global Order. *Millennium*: Journal of International Studies Vol.37 No.3, 2009, pp. 535–547.

HELD, D. & PATOMÄKI, H. Problems of Global Democracy: A Dialogue. *Theory*, Culture & Society (SAGE, London, Thousand Oaks and New Delhi), Vol. 23(5): 115–133, 2006.

HELD, D. & McGREW, A. *The Global Transformation Reader*: na introduction to the globalization debate. 2ª edition, Cambridge: Polity Press and Blackwell Publishing Ltd, 2003.

HELD, D. *Models Of Democracy*. Stanford: Stanford University Press, 1996. In: GÓMES, J. M. *"Política e democracia em tempos de globalização"*, Rio de Janeiro: LPP – Laboratório de Políticas Públicas, 2000.

KANT, Immanuel. *Para a Paz Perpétua*. Tradução /Bárbara Kristensen.– Rianxo : Instituto Galego de Estudos de Segurança Internacional e da Paz, 2006. – (Ensaios sobre Paz e Conflitos; Vol. V).

KEOHANE, R. 'International Institutions: Can Interdependence Work?', *Foreign Policy* , 1998, Spring, p. 82-96.

KEOHANE, R. & NYE, J. "Realism and complex interdependence". In: VIOTTI, Paul; KAUPPI, M. *International relations theory*. Boston: Allyn and Bacon, 1999.

LAISNER, Regina Cláudia. A Participação em questão: ponto ou contraponto da representação na teoria democrática? *Estudos de Sociologia* (São Paulo), v. 14, p. 17-35, 2009.

LAISNER, Regina Cláudia. Democracia e justiça: em busca de uma nova relação em Ralws. *Leviathan* (São Paulo), São Paulo, v. 1, n.1, p. 329-349, 2004.

LIMONGI, F. Prefácio. In: DAHL, R. *Poliarquia*. São Paulo: Edusp, 1997.

MARX, K. Manifesto do Partido Comunista/ Karl Marx e Friedrich Engels: prólogo de José Paulo Neto. São Paulo: Cortez, 1998.

McGREW, A. Democratising Global Governance Democratic Theory and Democracy beyond Borders. *Theoria*: A Journal of Social and Political Theory, Nº. 94, Governance and Globalisation, December 1999, pp. 1-29

McGREW, A. Models of Transnacional democracy. In: HELD, David & McGREW, A. *The Global Transformation Reader*: na introduction to the globalization debate. 2ª edition, Cambridge: Polity Press and Blackwell Publishing Ltd, 2003.

NOGUEIRA, J. P.; MESSARI, N. *Teoria das Relações Internacionais: correntes e debates*. Rio de Janeiro: Elsevier, 2005.

PATEMAN, C. *Participação e teoria democrática*. Rio de Janeiro: Paz e Terra, 1992.

RAWLS, J. *Uma Teoria da Justiça*. São Paulo. Martins Fontes, 1997.

ROVISCO, M. & NOWICKA, M. *The Ashgate Research Companion to Cosmopolitanism*. Farham, England & Burlington, USA: Ashgate Publishing Limited, 2011.

SANTOS, Robinson dos. Educação moral e civilização cosmopolita: atualidade da filosofia prática de Kant. *Revista Iberoamericana de Educación*. Vol. 41, 2007.

SCHUMPETER, J. *Capitalism, socialism and democracy*. Londres: Allen & Unwin, 1943.

TELLES, V. S. Espaço público e espaço privado na constituição do social: notas sobre o pensamento de Hannah Arendt. *Tempo Social*, v. 2, n. 1, 1990.

WALZER, M. *Esferas da Justiça:* uma defesa da igualdade e da liberdade. São Paulo: Martins Fontes, 2003.

Governança global e Direito internacional

Caio Gracco Pinheiro Dias

Governança

As ações humanas, quer isoladas, quer em conjunto, quando direcionadas a bens percebidos como escassos, podem provocar impactos para os interesses, desejos e necessidades de outros seres humanos; quanto mais próxima a convivência, maior é a possibilidade desses impactos acontecerem e serem relevantes, influenciando, com isso, a tomada de decisões e o comportamento dos seres humanos impactados. A situação resultante da interação desses comportamentos imbricados pode levar a uma existência mais segura e confortável ou, por outro lado, a uma situação insegura e desagradável para os seres humanos. A reflexão sobre os efeitos dessa interação, se orientada pelo objetivo de criar condições para uma existência mais segura e confortável, conduz à identificação dos comportamentos que são compatíveis com esse fim, bem como dos que não são. A maneira como as sociedades humanas convencem e/ou coagem seus integrantes a praticar aquelas e a evitar estas, buscando com isso a construção de uma situação desejável de convivência entre eles, é o que se entende, neste texto, por *governança.*[1]

Governança, nesse sentido, implica que um ou mais integrantes de uma dada sociedade pratiquem ações destinadas a criar e manter um padrão de condutas que seja conducente aos fins que aquela sociedade se atribui e isso aponta para uma íntima conexão com o conceito de *ordem*, como definido por Hedley Bull (2002, p. 3–4, 51). Porém, como sugere Bull, a ordem numa sociedade pode surgir de modos que independam de ações destinadas a criá-la e mantê-la[2], como, por exemplo, pelo condicionamento dos integrantes da sociedade, que "agiriam de forma coerente com os objetivos sociais elementares simplesmente por força de um reflexo condicionado" (Bull, 2002, p. 52)[3]; no mesmo sentido, Rosenau afirma

1 Segue-se aqui a definição proposta por James Rosenau, assim explicada: "governance is here conceived at a very abstract level as spheres of authority (SOAs) at all levels of human activity - from the household to the demanding public to the international organization - that amount to systems of rule in which goals are pursued through the exercise of control." (Rosenau, 1997, p. 145)

2 Na análise que faz do conceito de ordem na vida social, Bull identifica um papel central para as regras (*rules*), que servem para dar clareza de quais comportamentos são compatíveis – e quais não são – com os valores e objetivos de uma dada sociedade (Bull, 2002, p. 52); contudo, como concebe regras como meros construtos mentais que somente desempenham um papel na vida em sociedade na medida em que sejam eficazes, *i.e.*, observadas pelos atores sociais em alguma medida (Bull, 2002, p. 53), o foco da análise de Bull centra-se nas funções que precisam ser desempenhadas por alguém para que as regras sejam socialmente eficazes: criação, comunicação, aplicação, interpretação, imposição, legitimação, modificação e proteção das regras (Bull, 2002, p. 54). Essas funções, que, em seu conjunto, abarcam o significado da expressão *regulação*, podem ser entendidas, no pensamento de Bull, como uma enumeração das ações que, em conjunto, caracterizam a *governança* no sentido adotado neste texto.

3 Neste texto, salvo quando a referência for à edição traduzida para o português da obra citada, todas as traduções são do autor.

que nem todos os arranjos societais de que consiste a ordem[4] derivam de um esforço consciente da parte daqueles que os sustentam, usando o mecanismo de fixação de preços num mercado como exemplo de uma "agregação auto regulatória que ajuda a criar ordem" (Rosenau, 1992, p. 5). Tanto na hipótese de uma sociedade de indivíduos condicionados a agir de acordo com um certo padrão, quanto na resultante ordenada de atores egoístas buscando maximizar seus ganhos em negociações com outros atores egoístas, é possível identificar uma ordem, mas nenhum dos dois exemplos aponta para o que se denomina governança, que pressupõe uma atividade conscientemente orientada para a criação e manutenção de ordem (Rosenau, 1992, p. 5–6), ou, dito de outra forma, uma *regulação* destinada a dirigir os comportamentos dos indivíduos de forma que sejam compatíveis com objetivos partilhados (Rosenau, 1995, p. 14–15), algo inexistente nos dois exemplos.

Essas atividades, nas sociedades humanas, são tipicamente a atribuição de pessoas a quem tenha sido formalmente atribuída autoridade jurídica ou política para fazê-lo – seja pelo ordenamento jurídico, por tradição, pela predominância física, por um critério dinástico ou por qualquer outra justificação aceita pelo grupo; nesses casos, praticar tais atividades é *governar*. Empregar a palavra governança para se referir a tais atividades ressalta o fato de que, conquanto elas sejam por definição o âmbito de atuação do governo, elas ultrapassam o campo da autoridade formalmente estabelecida; governança é, pois, um gênero do qual governo é uma espécie.

Não espanta, assim, que no campo da análise das relações internacionais a discussão e a reflexão teóricas sobre governança tenham ganhado corpo (cf. Finkelstein, 1995, p. 368). De fato, quando se investiga a forma como os Estados, convivendo num sistema anárquico, definem, equacionam e, por vezes, solucionam os problemas que transcendem

4 Rosenau se refere especificamente à ordem global, mas o raciocínio pode, penso, ser ampliado para todas as outras manifestações do fenômeno.

suas fronteiras, a primeira dificuldade conceitual costuma derivar do fato de que a vida em sociedades organizadas na forma de Estados nos acostumou – ou adestrou – a tomar governo por sinônimo de governança. Diante da ausência de uma autoridade política e jurídica formal no plano internacional, a inexistência de um governo mundial tende a ser tomada por ausência de governança, donde a equivalência entre anarquia e desordem, típica da perspectiva hobbesiana sobre relações internacionais (Bull, 2002, p. 23–24). No final da década de 1970, Hedley Bull enfrentou essa questão argumentando que a melhor analogia para a convivência entre os Estados não é o estado de natureza descrito por Hobbes, mas o de Locke (Bull, 2002, p. 46–47), donde o título de sua obra mais famosa: "A Sociedade Anárquica", na qual anarquia é sinônimo de ausência de governo, e não de desordem, porquanto a análise da história das relações entre os Estados revela padrões que só se podem explicar a partir de valores e objetivos compartilhados para cuja consecução os Estados cooperam por meio de instituições como a balança de poder, a guerra e o direito internacional.

Nos anos 1990, a aceleração do processo de globalização econômica, que, juntamente com o término da guerra fria, trouxe a questão econômica para o centro das atenções da política internacional, pondo em xeque a centralidade dos problemas de segurança estratégico-militar que prevaleceu no pós-guerra e, ao mesmo tempo, colocou em questão a predominância do Estado como ator nas relações internacionais, estimulou uma nova onda de estudos sobre o tema da governança no plano internacional, ou, como se costuma denominá-la, governança global.[5] Se, antes,

5 Um ponto focal desses estudos é o periódico *Global Governance: A Review of Multilateralism and International Organizations*, cuja primeira edição foi publicada em 1995. Inicialmente quadrimestral, a revista se tornou trimestral em 1998 e está hoje no volume 23. Uma mirada sobre os temas de alguns dos artigos de sua edição inaugural – democracia global (Boutros-Ghali, 1995), deslocados e refugiados (Deng, 1995), instabilidade política em países do terceiro mundo (Ayoob, 1995) e operações de paz da Organização das Nações Unidas (Barnett, 1995) – mostra que,

para Bull, o objetivo fora demonstrar, em plena Guerra Fria, a limitação da leitura *realista* das relações internacionais, por não dar o devido valor à ideia de sociedade internacional, o estudo do tema da governança assumia naquele momento uma importância primeiramente prática: tratava-se de desenvolver e esclarecer as bases teóricas que permitissem compreender o funcionamento dos sistemas de governança em nível global "em um contexto onde as ações dos Estados, suas soberanias e governos, não são precondições para a forma como os eventos se desenrolam" (Rosenau, 1992, p. 29). Assim, se para Bull o importante era demonstrar a viabilidade da regulação das relações internacionais com base não na força, mas em valores e regras, mesmo dada a estrutura anárquica do sistema internacional, nos anos 1990 a questão era compreender como se dá essa regulação, quem são seus atores e como aprimorá-la[6]; que essa regulação que chamamos governança global independa de um governo também global já não era mais considerado tão problemático quanto duas décadas antes, donde se pode concluir que, para os estudiosos do tema, o postulado central d'"A Sociedade Anárquica" era dado como evidente.[7]

---

em grande medida, os temas centrais da agenda internacional atual não são diferentes dos de 22 anos atrás, pois nos vemos hoje discutindo a democratização das instituições globais, a crise causada pelo grande número de refugiados gerados por instabilidades políticas e conflitos armados em países do então chamado terceiro mundo e o seu impacto no avanço da xenofobia nos países desenvolvidos, bem como o papel – e a responsabilidade – da ONU diante dos conflitos que motivam esse enorme deslocamento humanos.

6 Segundo David Kennedy, essas perguntas ainda estão, em grande medida, sem resposta. Escrevendo em 2009, ele afirmava que "estamos apenas começando a decifrar o mistério da governança global. O simples mapear os modos do poder global e identificar os canais e alavancas de influência permanece um enorme desafio sociológico" (Kennedy, 2009, p. 39)

7 Toma relevo nessa época, para além da elucidação dos mecanismos em si da governança global, a questão do papel que nela têm indivíduos e organizações não-governamentais, *i.e.*, a chamada *sociedade civil*. A Comissão sobre Governança Global, um grupo de 28 notáveis, sem vinculação direta com a Organização das

Para Bull, é possível falar em sociedade na anarquia na medida em que se identifique uma ordem nas relações entre indivíduos, *i.e.*, na medida em que seus comportamentos se adequem a um padrão que permita a consecução de valores e objetivos comuns. Nas relações internacionais, essa ordem, como visto, não é um resultado automático, mas o produto da cooperação mais ou menos consciente dos Estados na operação do que ele denomina *instituições da sociedade internacional*[8] (Bull, 2002, p. 68–71), sendo isso o que permite a existência de ordem e, consequentemente, sociedade, mesmo inexistindo um poder a que estejam os Estados subordinados política ou juridicamente; na ausência desse poder comum, de um governo global, é a cooperação dos Estados no funcionamento das instituições internacionais que limita os impulsos egoístas e desagregadores dos Estados, permitindo, ainda que nem sempre, a prevalência dos objetivos comuns sobre os interesses imediatos e individuais dos Estados.[9]

Nações Unidas, mas por esta apoiada, em seu relatório apresentado em 1995, expressamente incluiu a sociedade civil no conceito de governança, nos seguintes termos: "Governança é a soma dos vários modos pelos quais indivíduos e instituições, públicas e privadas, gerenciam suas relações. (...) Inclui instituições formais e regimes encarregados de assegurar conformidade, assim como arranjos informais que pessoas e instituições ou concordaram, ou percebem atender a seus interesses" (Carlsson *et al.*, 1995, cap. 1). Embora reconheça a importância da questão, que inclusive será abordada mais adiante, o conceito de governança com o qual este texto trabalha não inclui, necessariamente, a participação de atores não-estatais.

8 "Instituição não denota necessariamente uma organização ou estrutura administrativa, mas, ao invés, um conjunto de hábitos e práticas moldados para a consecução de fins comuns" (Bull, 2002, p. 71)

9 "Essas instituições servem para simbolizar a existência de uma sociedade internacional que é mais do que a soma de seus membros, para dar substância e permanência para sua colaboração na execução das funções políticas da sociedade internacional e para *moderar sua tendência de perder de vista os interesses comuns*" (Bull, 2002, p. 71 - grifei)

Direito Internacional

Dentre essas instituições, encontramos o direito internacional, que Bull define como "um conjunto de regras que vincula os Estados e outros atores na política mundial em suas relações mútuas e que se considera como tendo status jurídico" (2002, p. 122). Por conjunto de regras, Bull entende "proposições imperativas gerais que são ligadas logicamente umas às outras de tal forma que integram uma estrutura comum" (Bull, 2002, p. 123); essas regras "existem" num plano exclusivamente normativo, sendo o teste de validade de uma norma a verificação de sua compatibilidade com condições estabelecidas em outra norma. Contudo, na medida em que influenciam os comportamentos de seus destinatários, regras têm um impacto concreto, ainda que as condutas finais dos atores não sejam produto, exclusivamente, do que elas prescrevem (Bull, 2002, p. 123). Nesse sentido, o direito pode ser considerado como um processo social, que se distingue dos demais porque as decisões que produz são modeladas necessariamente em função de regras previamente estabelecidas por consenso (Bull, 2002, p. 123-124). O conjunto composto por essas regras, por sua vez, é entendido pelas pessoas que operam o direito internacional como tendo natureza jurídica, para além das normas morais e de etiqueta, ainda que os teóricos e filósofos do direito discordem sobre essa natureza ou os critérios para identificá-la, sendo essa crença na juridicidade das regras internacionais o que permite o aparecimento de um conjunto de práticas internacionais que desempenha um papel importante no funcionamento da sociedade internacional (Bull, 2002, p. 130).[10]

10 Para Bull, essa crença está ligada ao "acidente histórico" de a sociedade internacional moderna ter se "desenvolvido a partir de um sistema unitário anterior, a Cristandade Ocidental, e nesse sistema as noções de direito - cristalizadas no direito romano, no direito divino, no direito canônico e no direito natural - eram preeminentes" (Bull, 2002, p. 137). Atribuir às regras internacionais uma natureza jurídica, assim, implica diferenciá-las de regras meramente morais e

Para Bull, o papel desempenhado pelo direito internacional na manutenção da ordem internacional é triplo. Em primeiro lugar, serve para proclamar o "princípio fundamental ou constitucional da política mundial na presente era (...) o princípio de que os seres humanos e o território estão divididos em estados, cada qual com sua própria esfera de autoridade, mas unidos por um conjunto comum de regras" (Bull, 2002, p. 134-135). Em segundo lugar, é tarefa do direito internacional enunciar as regras fundamentais de coexistência entre estados e outros atores no plano internacional, regras referentes à limitação de violência, aos acordos celebrados entre eles e à soberania (Bull, 2002, p. 135). Por fim, o direito internacional ajuda a "estimular a conformidade com as regras da sociedade internacional" (Bull, 2002, p. 135), não tanto na forma de imposição de limites aos Estados – *que dificilmente conseguem prevalecer quando em conflito com os interesses vitais destes* –, mas por meio de uma estrutura de acordos e compromissos pela qual os Estados podem "tornar públicas suas intenções sobre uma dada matéria; tranquilizar-se mutuamente sobre suas políticas em relação a tal matéria; especificar precisamente qual é a natureza do compromisso, seus limites e condições; e dar solenidade ao compromisso de forma a criar uma expectativa de permanência" (Bull, 2002, p. 135).[11]

O direito internacional, assim, cumpre um papel – *ainda que seja de difícil mensuração* – na manutenção da ordem internacional. Nesse sentido, é possível entender o direito internacional como um instrumento de governança internacional; é mesmo possível afirmar que, tanto para Bull quanto para Rosenau, esse papel é central, já que ambos conce-

reforçar a sensação – e expectativa – de obrigatoriedade delas decorrente (Bull, 2002, p. 137).

11 Em sentido semelhante, Malcolm Shaw escreve que o direito internacional é "uma cultura no sentido mais amplo, na medida em que constitui um método para comunicar demandas, contra-demandas, expectativas e previsões, assim como provê uma infraestrutura para avaliar e determinar a prioridade de tais demandas" (Shaw, 2003, p. 63)

bem governança, em alguma medida, como *regulação* (Bull, 2002, p. 54; Rosenau, 1995, p. 14–15). O que chamamos de governança, na medida em que se refere a comandos ou diretivas, resulta em expectativas sobre o comportamento dos demais integrantes do grupo que são formalizadas na forma de regras, as quais encontram no direito internacional um campo de práticas que reforça sua eficácia.

O direito internacional, contudo, por surgir no âmbito da convivência entre unidades políticas independentes, não sujeitas formalmente a quaisquer outras autoridades, tem características que o distinguem do direito como o conhecemos no âmbito interno dos Estados, a mais marcante sendo talvez o fato de que tem de operar, na quase totalidade das vezes, na ausência de coerção institucionalizada; nele, a *vis directiva* da persuasão e do convencimento é mais importante do que a *vis coactiva* da imposição pela força (Bobbio, 2004, p. 37). Sua denominação "direito", porém, o aproxima semanticamente do direito estatal, o que gera incompreensões e mal-entendidos. Em primeiro lugar, porque torna usual o uso do direito interno como critério de aferição do valor e da eficácia do direito internacional, levando a um juízo geralmente negativo acerca do direito internacional, posto que seja verdade que, como disse Louis Henkin, "quase todos os Estados observam quase todos os princípios do direito internacional e quase todas as suas obrigações quase sempre" (Henkin, 1979, p. 47).[12] Em segundo lugar porque funda a crença de que um reforço institucional que

12 A dualidade entre direito interno e direito internacional, embora parta de diferenças bastante evidentes entre os meios sociais em que se desenvolve a regulação das relações entre pessoas sujeitas a um estado soberano e a regulação das relações entre estados soberanos, tende a superestimar as "deficiências" do direito internacional e a subestimar as do direito interno. Em específico, sobre a percepção de inutilidade do direito internacional, sua incapacidade de se impor sobre o poder militar e econômico das grandes potências, os estudos críticos e, mais recentemente, as pesquisas empíricas sobre o direito têm evidenciado que essa é uma característica também de muitas áreas do direito estatal, que foi durante muito tempo posta fora de foco por uma teoria excessivamente formalista, cada vez mais divorciada da realidade que deveria compreender e descrever.

dote o direito internacional dos "dentes" que lhe faltam é a chave para o incremento de sua capacidade de cumprir as funções para as quais se destina. A redução do jurídico ao coercitivo é, assim, duplamente perniciosa: como critério de avaliação e como vetor da ação destinada a aprimorar o funcionamento do direito internacional e, por conseguinte, a governança global.

Esses dois problemas são indícios de uma tendência à sobrevalorização de modelos verticalizados de organização jurídica ou, dito de outra forma, de "distribuição de autoridade (que se distingue de poder) entre diferentes instituições jurídicas e entidades políticas separadas" (Falk, 1959, p. 295), modelos nos quais se estabelece uma hierarquia entre centros dotados de graus diversos de autoridade normativa. Por contraste, a organização jurídica das relações internacionais, formalmente, é predominantemente horizontal, os Estados sendo centros de igual autoridade normativa, e o direito internacional reconhece e sanciona essa horizontalidade por meio dos princípios de igualdade soberana e de não intervenção. Num mundo em cada vez mais acelerada transformação, no qual a capacidade do sistema internacional de dar conta dos desafios que se colocam para a humanidade nos campos da segurança, da proteção ambiental e do desenvolvimento humano tem se revelado cada vez mais insuficiente, dada a crescente dificuldade em se construir consensos que permitam a cooperação entre Estados[13], essa tendência pode e tem levado a diagnósticos e à politicas inadequadas, quando não contraproducentes.

Richard Falk, em seu clássico artigo de 1959 sobre as concepções vertical e horizontal de ordem jurídica, buscava ressaltar, contra a opi-

13 Essa crescente incapacidade de construção de consensos foi denominada por David Held – de forma particularmente feliz – *gridlock*, um fenômeno que se manifesta em praticamente todos os temas da agenda internacional e que resulta num vácuo de governança, deixando desatendidas necessidades cruciais para a vida no planeta, mas que, ironicamente, é o resultado do próprio sucesso das iniciativas regulatórias e das instituições multilaterais do Pós-Segunda Guerra em reforçar a interdependência entre os Estados (Hale; Held; Young, 2013)

nião de muitos à época[14], a importância de se buscar o entendimento das formas horizontais de ordenação internacional, entendidas pelo autor como "padrões recíprocos de afirmação e deferência que produzem um aspecto de estabilidade que com frequência é suficiente para ser classificado como direito" (Falk, 1959, p. 297). Queria, com isso, refutar a tese segundo a qual o direito internacional, na ausência de instituições verticais efetivas, não passaria de uma "infrutífera formulação de aspirações compartilhadas" (Falk, 1959, p. 297, citando Corbett), e defender a juridicidade e eficácia do direito internacional concebido como uma ordem jurídica de caráter horizontal. Para fazê-lo, escolhe um tema específico – *a delimitação da jurisdição de um Estado vis-à-vis as dos demais Estados* – e demonstra como essa delimitação, que previne a ocorrência de muitos conflitos de competência (ou jurisdição) entre os Estados, ocorre em grande medida pela autocontenção dos Estados, e não por força de uma regra clara aplicada por órgãos centralizados com autoridade para determinar aos Estados que se comportem desta ou daquela maneira.[15] Essa abordagem que rejeita a desconfiança em relação aos mecanismos horizontais de ordenação de condutas no plano internacional, penso, pode e deve ser levada em conta quando se consideram problemas outros que não apenas a delimitação da competência jurisdicional do Estado.

---

14 Simbolizada, no artigo, pela obra do canadense naturalizado norte-americano Percy Ellwood Corbett (1892-1983), para quem "o progresso em direção à maior clareza e efetividade da ordem jurídica internacional dependerá menos da formulação e reformulação de princípios gerais, ou da codificação, e mais de arranjos para a administração supranacional de interesses comuns específicos" (Corbett, P.E. Law and Society in the Relations of States. New York: Harcourt Brace and Company, 1951, p. 68-69, *apud*. Falk, 1959, p. 297)

15 "[O] impacto proibitivo do direito internacional sobre a discricionariedade do Estado em delimitar sua competência jurídica é marginal. Limitações efetivas derivam do que poderia ser utilmente descrito como o impacto *permissivo* do direito internacional; essa é outra forma de conceber a influência de sistemas ordenadores horizontais sobre o exercício da discricionariedade estatal" (Falk, 1959, p. 311)

A distinção entre duas concepções de ordem jurídica, uma vertical e outra horizontal, está situada no cerne do debate normativo sobre a organização das relações internacionais para o enfrentamento dos desafios globais contemporâneos. Nesse ponto, antes de mais nada, há que se constatar que, no que toca aos problemas que a humanidade como um todo, ainda que não de forma homogênea, enfrenta, o contexto presente é desconhecido na história humana. O desenvolvimento tecnológico posterior à Revolução Industrial, mas principalmente depois do término da Segunda Guerra Mundial, deu à ação humana um alcance e uma inédita capacidade disruptiva e destrutiva. Nossa expansão geográfica e exploração dos recursos do meio ambiente tem levado à/criado o risco de extinção de inúmeras espécies animais e vegetais, com consequências imprevisíveis para o equilíbrio ecológico do planeta; a atividade humana altera a configuração dos espaços onde se dá, gerando mudanças climáticas locais, ao mesmo tempo em que seus subprodutos, seja na forma de poluição, seja na do lixo gerado pelo – *cada vez mais rápido* – descarte dos produtos consumidos, são provavelmente causadores de mudanças nos padrões climáticos globais. O desenvolvimento dos meios de transporte barateou o custo de fretes, permitindo uma intensa circulação de cargas e pessoas, mas criando com isso o risco de difusão de riscos sanitários e epidemias em escala global. A tecnologia de telecomunicação avançou a ponto de conectar o mundo inteiro numa grande rede de troca de informações, mas colocou em xeque – *mate, talvez* – as possibilidades de preservação de um espaço de privacidade individual, ao mesmo tempo que cria um território onde atividades criminosas podem vicejar. Por fim, mas não menos importante, a tecnologia bélica chegou a um grau de destrutividade que faz com que um eventual conflito militar entre as grandes potências crie risco para a continuidade da vida humana no planeta, ou ao menos para a continuidade da civilização como a conhecemos; os armamentos também se tornaram mais acessíveis a grupos que não concentram o poder econômico e humano que tem o Estado, *privatizando* o uso da força, tornando, com isso, mais fragmentárias e difíceis de prevenir as ameaças para a segurança de populações civis que sejam o alvo da ação desses grupos. Os avanços tecnológicos colocam em questão até mesmo a continuidade da evolução genética da espécie humana (cf., p.ex., Stock, 2008, negando que a evolução humana tenha cessado) e abrem a perspectiva de influirmos conscientemente nesse processo. Se, como espécie, pretendemos sobreviver e prosperar, precisamos regular nossa atuação no que ela impacta sobre o planeta e sobre as atividades/interesses dos demais seres humanos. Precisamos, pois, de *governança.*

As alterações no sistema internacional e o seu impacto para a governança global e para o Direito Internacional

Essa necessidade se traduziu em políticas concretas no plano internacional pela primeira vez na segunda metade do Séc. XIX, quando os impactos da revolução industrial se fizeram sentir no custo econômico e humano que que as guerras – *e a preparação para elas* – impõem aos Estados. Ao movimento humanitário, que clamava por tratamento mais humano para os envolvidos em conflitos armados, conjuga-se o interesse estatal em reduzir os custos de defesa, criando o momento para a realização de conferências internacionais das quais resultaram tratados internacionais estabelecendo proteções para feridos em campanha[16], limitando

16 A Conferência de Genebra de 1864, reunindo doze estados, da qual resultou a Convenção de Genebra para a Melhoria da Condição de Feridos e Doentes nas Forças Armadas em Campanha, foi a primeira nesse sentido. Suas disposições foram revistas em outra Conferência em Genebra em 1906, e numa terceira em 1929, quando foi também adotada a Convenção relativa ao Tratamento dos Prisioneiros de Guerra. Em 1949, nova Conferência em Genebra revisou os textos dessas duas convenções, adotando outras duas: uma sobre Feridos, Doentes e Náufragos das Forças Armadas no Mar, e outra sobre Proteção de Civis em Tempo de Guerra. Finalmente, em 1977, dois Protocolos Adicionais às Convenções de 1949 foram adotados, atualizando seus termos e estabelecendo limites para a conduta de combatentes em conflitos de caráter não-internacional, que se tornaram mais frequentes que os conflitos de caráter clássico, interestatal, no pós-II Guerra (cf. Holsti, 1996, cap. 2). O conjunto das normas originadas

meios e métodos de guerra[17] e estabelecendo mecanismos para solução pacífica de controvérsias, de forma a tentar limitar o uso da força militar.[18] A devastação causada pela I Guerra Mundial dá o impulso definitivo para esse processo, levando ao estabelecimento da Liga das Nações – *e seu mecanismo de segurança coletiva*[19] – e da Corte Permanente de Justiça

---

desses acordos, que forma parte do Direito Internacional Humanitário, costuma ser denominado *Direito de Genebra.*

17 A s Conferências de Paz da Haia de 1899 e 1907 resultaram em diversos Tratados e Declarações relativos à proibição de uso de certos armamentos e táticas de combate, como, p.ex., munições explosivas, gases venenosos e asfixiantes e bombardeios aéreos. Um Protocolo negociado em Genebra em 1925 buscou o banimento das armas químicas e biológicas, resultando na posterior adoção da Convenção sobre a Proibição do Desenvolvimento, Produção e Estocagem de Armas Bacteriológicas (Biológicas) ou Tóxicas e sobre sua Destruição (1972) e da Convenção sobre a Proibição do Desenvolvimento, Produção, Armazenagem e Utilização de Armas Químicas e sobre sua Destruição (1993). O conjunto das normas desses acordos, que também integra o Direito Internacional Humanitário, é comumente referido como *Direito da Haia.*

18 O primeiro desses tratados foi a Convenção sobre a Resolução Pacífica de Controvérsias Internacionais, um dos textos adotados na I Conferência de Paz da Haia (1899), tendo sido revisada na II Conferência de Paz (1907), passando a estabelecer a Corte Permanente de Arbitragem Internacional. Nesta Conferência, foi ainda adotada a Convenção sobre a Limitação do Uso da Força para a Cobrança de Dívidas Contratuais.

19 O Pacto da Liga das Nações (1919) estabeleceu o primeiro sistema de segurança coletiva global: previu expressamente a obrigatoriedade do recurso a meios pacíficos de solução de conflitos, e tornou ilegal a guerra quando uma das partes oferecesse ou aceitasse uma solução para a disputa proposta por meios pacíficos, cabendo ao Conselho da Liga a determinação de um Estado que violasse essa *moratória* da guerra; caso o Conselho fizesse essa determinação, seria acionado o dever de todos os membros da Liga de declarar guerra ao Estado agressor, aliando-se ao Estado agredido para defendê-lo. Em 1928, essa obrigação de somente recorrer à guerra de forma subsidiária seria ampliada pelo Pacto Briand-Kellogg, pelo qual as partes contratantes renunciaram mutuamente à guerra como instrumento de política externa.

Internacional.[20] Analisando a maneira como os Estados se articularam para enfrentar o problema comum da segurança num sistema anárquico, fica evidente a opção pelo modelo verticalizado, com a intenção de dotar o direito internacional de características análogas ao direito interno como estratégia de governança (Torelly, 2016, p. 22). É o início do esforço de sistematização e de codificação do direito internacional consuetudinário, bem como da criação de organizações internacionais modernas e de tribunais internacionais permanentes. É também um período de total predominância do Estado soberano como protagonista da governança global, pouco ou nenhum espaço sobrando para a atuação decisiva de particulares ou coletividades não-estatais[21], donde a relevância central das regras de reconhecimento da estatalidade, cruciais para determinar o acesso ao processo decisório do direito internacional (Torelly, 2016, p. 22-23). Contudo, a estratégia de verticalização da ordem jurídica internacional se desenrolou com total respeito à soberania estatal, resultando num sistema de governança incapaz de controlar os impulsos desagregadores dos Estados quando os impactos da crise de 1929 levaram a um acirramento de tensões que eclodiu na II Guerra Mundial.[22]

---

20 O tratado contendo o Estatuto da Corte Permanente de Justiça Internacional foi adotado em Genebra, em 13 de dezembro de 1920, entrando em vigor em setembro do ano seguinte. A Corte teve sua primeira sessão em 30 de janeiro de 1922.

21 É de se notar que o reconhecimento generalizado da personalidade jurídica de direito internacional das organizações intergovernamentais só se deu após a II Guerra Mundial, com o Parecer Consultivo da Corte Internacional de Justiça no Caso das Reparações (*Reparation for injuries suffered in the service of the United Nations, Advisory Opinion: I.C.J. Reports 1949, p. 174*).

22 Amado Luiz Cervo assim descreve os fatores que levaram à crise dos anos 1930 e, ao final, à II Guerra Mundial: " crise produziu antes de tudo efeitos nacionais. O período de sua origem situa-se entre 1929 e 1932. Desde aí, todos os dados se tornam negativos. Os eventos americanos propagaram-se pela Europa, com ruínas materiais: queda dos preços, da produção industrial, do comércio internacional, das reservas monetárias e do emprego. (...) O capitalismo desmoronou: individualismo, livre iniciativa e mercado cedem o passo ao nacionalismo eco-

Findo o conflito, que rearranjou a distribuição de poder no sistema internacional, desalojando as potências europeias do centro do sistema e substituindo-as pelas duas superpotências, Estados Unidos e União Soviética, o problema da guerra continuou central e, ainda, agravado pelo desenvolvimento das armas nucleares. A catástrofe humanitária da guerra, por outro lado, e as raízes econômicas do conflito na crise pós-1929, levaram ao reconhecimento formal do vínculo entre paz, direitos humanos e comércio, que está na base da concepção da Organização das Nações Unidas, organização que ocupou o *locus* central na governança global do Pós-II Guerra – *ainda que menor, na prática, do que fora imaginado, por conta da paralisação do Conselho de Segurança após a Guerra da Coréia.*

A crítica de Edward H. Carr aos artífices da Liga das Nações, em quem identificava um "desejo de evitar o concreto em favor das generalizações abstratas", (Carr, 2001, p. 42), parece ter sido levada em conta pelos "construtores da Paz Vindoura" a quem dedicou sua obra mais célebre. A ênfase no direito internacional foi atenuada, retomando a política o papel central; a Organização foi dotada de órgãos mais especializados, dedicados a questões específicas que, nos termos da Carta, tivessem um impacto na paz e na segurança internacionais[23]; a tomada de decisão sobre as ques-

---

nômico, ao protecionismo alfandegário e à autarcia política. Pelo lado político, assistiu-se à descrença nas instituições do Estado liberal, ao acirramento das lutas partidárias e doutrinárias, à busca de alternativas radicais, ao crescimento de egoísmos nacionais. (...) A crise não adveio do craque da bolsa de 1929 (...). A crise veio dos fatores de agravamento anteriormente referidos e afetou as relações internacionais de duas formas: pela indiferença e hostilidade diante da cooperação e pela prática generalizada de adotar soluções nacionais para problemas internacionais" (Cervo, 2007, p. 145).

23 Donde a divisão da ONU em três Conselhos: o de Segurança, encarregado de agir quando uma ruptura da paz e da segurança tenha ocorrido ou seja iminente, cujas decisões obrigariam todos os membros da Organização; o de Tutela, encarregado principalmente de supervisionar o progressivo desenvolvimento dos territórios submetidos a Mandato da Liga das Nações em direção ao autogoverno ou independência; e o Econômico e Social, fórum de discussões e estudos

tões centrais de segurança internacional passou a distinguir as grandes Potências dos Estados menores, tendo aquelas, no Conselho de Segurança, assento permanente e direito de veto sobre eventuais decisões que considerem contrárias a seus interesses, revelando uma ênfase maior no equilíbrio de poder do que na representação proporcional (Torelly, 2016, p. 25).

Dois fatores, contudo, impediram esse sistema de governança centrado na ONU de funcionar como imaginado: o primeiro, que não deixava de ser previsível nos momentos finais da guerra, era o acirramento das relações entre EUA e URSS; ambos membros permanentes do Conselho de Segurança, a hostilidade mútua das políticas externas de ambos fechou as portas para a sua atuação conjunta no Conselho, paralisando-o pelo uso do veto.

O segundo fator foi o expressivo crescimento no número de membros da Organização, via de regra oriundos de antigas colônias europeias na Ásia e África. Por um lado, esse ingresso de novos membros tornou, em números absolutos, muito pequena a representação das grandes potências; por outro, esses novos Estados começam a se articular de forma independente ao eixo tradicional – *Leste-Oeste* – que dividia a política mundial até o momento, inserindo outras coordenadas no debate político: o conflito *Norte-Sul*, entre países desenvolvidos e países subde-

---

sobre temas da agenda internacional de natureza econômica, social, cultural, educacional, sanitária, com o poder de formular *recomendações* relativas a tais assuntos, assim como em relação com a promoção e proteção de direitos humanos e liberdades fundamentais para todos, sob o qual se aninhou a vasta rede de *agências especializadas* da ONU, cada uma delas uma organização intergovernamental com atuação setorial específica. Como se vê, o primeiro Conselho lida com a paz na sua acepção negativa (cf. Bobbio, 2003, p. 143), buscando garantir a *ausência de guerra ou sua cessação*. Os outros dois, com a paz na sua acepção positiva, ou "paz de satisfação" (Bobbio, 2003, p. 156), na medida em que, buscando a emancipação de todos os povos do domínio colonial e a melhoria de condições de vida por meio do desenvolvimento econômico e do respeito aos direitos fundamentais, buscariam garantir "a falta de conflitos de tal gravidade que sua solução só possa ser confiada à força" (Bobbio, 2003, p. 156) senvolvidos[24]; a percepção de interesses comuns entre eles, distintos dos que opunham EUA e seus aliados a URSS e seus aliados, motivou que formassem um grupo de interesse dentro da ONU que foi chamado de Bloco dos Não-Alinhados. Como são numerosos, sua atuação coordenada com outros blocos de países com interesses semelhantes[25] acabou por capturar, em certa medida, o funcionamento de órgãos da ONU como a Assembleia Geral e o Conselho Econômico e Social – *nos quais as grandes potências não têm poder de veto* – e, com isso, influenciar em suas decisões e na formação de suas agendas de trabalho; isso trouxe para o primeiro plano do temário da governança do período os assuntos da descolonização e do desenvolvimento econômico. Contudo, na medida em que diminuiu o controle das grandes potências sobre esses fóruns, fez com que estas passassem a focar a sua atuação – *e contribuições pecuniárias* – em órgãos onde têm um efetivo controle: o registro da participação dos EUA na ONU é um exemplo particularmente eloquente dessa ten-

24 Terminologia que, recentemente, foi revista pela ONU, passando a dividir o mundo em Economias Desenvolvidas e Economias em Desenvolvimento, com uma terceira categoria incluindo os países com Economia em Transição, *i.e.*, no processo de passagem de uma economia planificada para uma economia de mercado. Dentro dos grandes grupos também se identificam subgrupos, como o das Economias Mais Desenvolvidas, no primeiro, e os Países Menos Desenvolvidos, no segundo.

25 O discurso anti-hegemônico e anti-imperialista dos Não-Alinhados, contudo, fazia com que frequentemente suas posições, ao denunciar e se opor ao que percebiam como exploração dos países capitalistas, fossem coincidentes com as posições defendidas pela União Soviética e os demais países comunistas. Daí que o governo dos EUA identificasse, nas votações desses países na Assembleia Geral, uma tendência maior de alinhamento com a URSS do que com os Estados Unidos, atribuída em parte à "cultura política da ONU, que frequentemente enxerga o mundo por categorias quase-marxistas", algo que o governo dos EUA considerava "prejudicial não apenas aos Estados Unidos, mas a todas as democracias industrializadas" (UNITED STATES OF AMERICA. DEPARTMENT OF STATE. BUREAU OF INTERNATIONAL ORGANIZATION AFFAIRS, 1984, p. 10)

dência[26], assim como a sua reação – *em grande parte devida à oposição no Congresso à destinação de recursos do orçamento federal para a ONU, percebida como hostil aos interesses dos EUA* – de deixar de pagar integralmente o valor definido para o Orçamento Regular Anual da ONU, preferindo aplicar recursos por contribuições voluntárias para os vários fundos da Organização, cuja destinação pode ser controlada pelo doador, e para aquelas missões de paz com as quais concorda.

---

26 A dificuldade em controlar os resultados de votações na Assembleia Geral das Nações Unidas, em especial em questões centrais para a política externa dos Estados Unidos, fica evidente quando se consultam os Relatórios sobre as Práticas de Voto nas Nações Unidas que, por lei, o Departamento de Estado dos EUA deve apresentar anualmente ao Congresso. No relatório mais recente, relativo à 70ª Assembleia Geral, de 2015, a média de votos coincidentes com os EUA nos 79 casos submetidos a votação plenária foi de 43,2%, inferior à média do ano anterior, de 44.6%; nas 13 questões consideradas importantes (*key votes*), em 7 das quais os EUA ficaram vencidos, a média foi de 61% de votos coincidentes, mas nas 18 votações relativas a Israel a coincidência de votos com os EUA foi de apenas 4% (UNITED STATES OF AMERICA. DEPARTMENT OF STATE. BUREAU OF INTERNATIONAL ORGANIZATION AFFAIRS, 2016, p. 29, 48 e 69). O relatório referente à 55ª Assembleia Geral, de 2000, registra 43% de votos concordantes em votações plenárias – *registrando uma queda sensível em comparação com os dados da 50ª Assembleia Geral, de 1995, quando a média foi de 50,6% de votos coincidentes* - e 47,9% de votos coincidentes nas 11 *key votes*, em 6 das quais os EUA ficaram vencidos (UNITED STATES OF AMERICA. DEPARTMENT OF STATE. BUREAU OF INTERNATIONAL ORGANIZATION AFFAIRS, 2000, p. 39 e 84). O primeiro relatório elaborado pelo Departamento de Estado, referente à 38ª Assembleia Geral, de 1983, não registra uma média global de votos coincidentes, mas divide os países por regiões geográficas, registrando médias de 18,6% na região da África, 14,2% na Europa Oriental, 26,8% nas Américas, 53,8% na Europa Ocidental, 21,5% na Ásia e Pacífico e 93,3% com Israel, listado como "*sem afiliação*" (UNITED STATES OF AMERICA. DEPARTMENT OF STATE. BUREAU OF INTERNATIONAL ORGANIZATION AFFAIRS, 1984), indicando que, nos anos 80, a divergência das votações na Assembleia Geral com a política externa dos EUA era mais acentuada do que atualmente.

Esses dois eventos, ao polarizar o debate sobre as relações internacionais e diminuir a legitimidade da ONU como fórum de negociação e deliberação democrática sobre normas internacionais, podem explicar o fato de que, nesse período, como afirma Marcelo Torelly, tenha florescido a abordagem funcionalista do direito internacional, a qual, em contraste com o período do entre guerras, não buscava a "construção de uma ordem universal neutra", mas via na coincidência das prescrições das normas jurídicas internacionais com valores daqueles que têm poder para tomar decisões em casos concretos o critério ultimo de validade do direito internacional (cf. Torelly, 2016, p. 26–28). A divisão do mundo em dois campos de poder equivalente que esposam valores conflitantes faz com que a governança global deixe de se focar no todo para se concentrar em problemas específicos, submetidos a agências especializadas, no âmbito das quais transcorre um processo de tomada de decisão do qual o direito é antes um produto do que um critério orientador, processo no qual a ênfase no aspecto técnico das questões discutidas é uma estratégia para manter afastada a disputa política global e permitir a *gestão* de problemas concretos (Torelly, 2016, p. 28).

O resultado desse processo é um direito internacional que se mostra cada vez mais fragmentado ou, conforme a interpretação teórica que se dê ao fenômeno, dividido em regimes auto continentes (Torelly, 2016, p. 29–32). Exemplo de até onde chega esse processo de diferenciação pode ser encontrado no fato de que mesmo os processos de produção normativa podem variar de regime para regime, conforme o assunto em torno do qual se estruture o regime e a racionalidade própria do discurso que nele se desenvolve: compare-se, por exemplo, o Direito Internacional dos Direitos Humanos, no qual, num mal disfarçado retorno ao jusnaturalismo, invoca-se com frequência normas internacionais que valem mesmo contra a vontade dos Estados – *o chamado* jus cogens, *definido no art. 53 da Convenção de Viena sobre Direito dos Tratados (1969)* –, com o Direito Internacional do Meio Ambiente, no qual, para suplantar a reticência dos Estados em aceitar obrigações exigíveis e sancionáveis de preservação ambiental, é necessário lançar mão de uma "não-norma" ou "quase-norma", uma norma da qual não deriva obrigação, mas que, nem por isso, deixa de ser jurídica: o *soft law* (cf. Nasser, 2005; cf. tb. Shaw, 2003, p. 110–112). Cada regime, à sua maneira e de forma coerente com a racionalidade que prevalece em cada um, soluciona de maneira absolutamente diversa o problema da dificuldade de obtenção do consenso dos Estados que, no direito internacional, é condição de validade das normas internacionais; em ambos, contudo, o que esses novos processos de formação normativa revelam, ao se afastar do consentimento estatal, é a predominância do processo de tomada de decisão e das forças políticas que o moldam sobre as normas internacionais que o deveriam orientar; mais, como em alguns regimes essas forças políticas conseguem uma melhor coordenação do que em outros, o desenvolvimento e a consolidação desses regimes não ocorre num mesmo ritmo.

O final da Guerra Fria, entretanto, com a derrubada do Muro de Berlim e o esfacelamento da União das Repúblicas Socialistas Soviéticas, altera profundamente esse quadro. A derrocada do regime comunista na União Soviética e do controle que exercia sobre seus satélites na Europa Oriental, evidenciada em primeiro lugar na indecisa reação quanto à travessia de refugiados do lado oriental para o lado ocidental da Alemanha – *que culmina na noite de 9 de novembro de 1989 com a demolição do Muro de Berlim* – e, em segundo lugar, pela queda do regime comunista na Tchecoslováquia, na esteira da Revolução de Veludo de novembro-dezembro de 1989, completa-se com a fragmentação da União, em dezembro de 1991. A desorganização causada por esse processo, a ascensão de grupos políticos com plataformas de liberalização econômica e o desprestígio generalizado das ideias comunistas afasta o risco de uma guerra entre as superpotências e cria as condições para a hegemonia do pensamento liberal. Essa vitória do liberalismo se completa quando, em muitos países do chamado Terceiro Mundo, diante da percepção do fracasso, em termos de desenvolvimento econômico, de políticas econômicas nacionalistas, as teses do livre mercado e do livre comércio passam a integrar as plataformas políticas dos grupos que assumem o governo desses países e começam a implantar reformas econômicas orientadas pelos ditames do chamado *Consenso de Washington*. É um momento em que aparenta haver um consenso global sobre os valores que devem orientar a regulação da atividade econômica, inclusive no plano internacional e, até por isso, de enfraquecimento da posição dos países em desenvolvimento em negociações internacionais. No campo do Comércio Internacional, esses consenso e enfraquecimento explicam, em parte, o destravamento de negociações internacionais e a posição vantajosa que os países desenvolvidos obtiveram nessas negociações.[27]

No campo da governança global, esse primeiro momento traz a esperança de um incremento na cooperação entre os Estados, com um maior papel podendo ser desempenhado pelas Nações Unidas no campo da segurança. O primeiro teste, a reação coordenada à agressão iraquiana ao Kuwait, resulta na primeira operação no âmbito do Cap. VII da Carta a envolver o uso de forças militares contra um Estado membro desde a Guerra da Coreia em 1950, já que, até aquele momento, o exercício do poder de veto sempre impediram esse tipo de intervenção coletiva; enfraquecida, preocupada com os problemas internos que acabariam levando à sua desagregação menos de um ano após os primeiros tiros serem disparados no Golfo Pérsico, a URSS não teve como se opor à decisão de autorizar o uso da força contra o Iraque pela Resolução 678/1990 (S/RES/678).[28]

---

27 Um exemplo particularmente importante está na Rodada Uruguai, cujo encerramento em 1994 representou uma vitória para as economias desenvolvidas e a aceitação pelas economias em desenvolvimento de um sistema bem menos fav orável a elas (cf. Holanda Filho, 1998, p. 70)

28 A posição da URSS foi fortemente criticada por seus aliados no Oriente Médio, que apontavam nela um sinal de fraqueza e decadência (Fuller, 1991, p. 65). Outro membro permanente que poderia ter se oposto à Resolução, vetando-a, era a China, mas esta optou pela abstenção, em troca do que obteve a suspensão das sanções que sofria desde o massacre ocorrido na Praça da Paz Celestial em 1989 (Kristof, 1991).

Esse período inicial de otimismo não teve longa duração. Já em 1991, o rastilho da desagregação dos regimes comunistas faz aflorar as tensões entre os grupos étnicos que compunham a então Iugoslávia, eclodindo em 1991, com a declaração de independência da Eslovênia em abril, uma guerra civil que se arrastou por quase 10 anos e trouxe de volta à Europa cenas de atrocidades e crimes de guerra que se julgavam ter ficado para sempre no passado. Em 1994, no ápice da guerra civil iniciada em 1990 entre as duas principais etnias, Hutu e Tutsi, que compõem a população Ruanda, três meses de matança generalizada levaram ao extermínio de cerca de dois terços da população Tutsi e à criação de um fluxo de milhões de refugiados de ambas as etnias que desestabilizou a região. Esses dois eventos foram testes à capacidade de intervenção da ONU para a manutenção da paz e da segurança internacionais, e o resultado foi desastroso. Em Ruanda, a Missão das Nações Unidas de Assistência para Ruanda (UNAMIR) mostrou-se incapaz de agir para evitar o genocídio, inclusive por decisão do Departamento de Operações de Paz da ONU, e perdeu boa parte de seu efetivo quando, já iniciados os massacres, a Bélgica retirou suas tropas da Missão após a morte de 10 de seus soldados (Carlsson; Han; Kupolati, 1999). Na Iugoslávia, em especial na Bósnia-Herzegovina, como admitido em relatório elaborado por determinação da Assembleia Geral da ONU, erros de julgamento e incapacidade de tomar decisões[29] contribuíram para o fracasso na missão

29 O relatório, elaborado pelo então Secretário-Geral, Kofi Annan, é explícito ao reconhecer os erros da Organização na proteção de civis em Srebrenica: "A experiência das Nações Unidas na Bósnia foi uma das mais difíceis e dolorosas em nossa história. É com o mais profundo arrependimento e remorso que nós revisamos nossas próprias ações e decisões em face do ataque a Srebrenica. Por erros, decisões erradas e incapacidade de reconhecer o escopo do mal que confrontávamos, falhamos em fazer nossa parte para salvar o povo de Srebrenica da campanha sérvia de extermínio. Ninguém lamenta mais que nós as oportunidades perdidas para obter paz e justiça. Ninguém lamenta mais que nós o fracasso da comunidade internacional em tomar ação decisiva para pôr fim ao sofrimento e encerrar uma guerra que produziu tantas vítimas. Srebrenica simbolizou uma verdade que as

de proteger os civis bósnios alvos de ataques de milícias sérvias, algo que viria a se repetir, como reconhece o próprio Secretário-Geral em seu relatório, na crise do Kosovo, em 1999 (Annan, 1999, parag. 502).

Essa dificuldade e, por vezes, incapacidade de agir coletivamente de forma efetiva se manifesta também em outras áreas. No campo do comércio internacional, após o triunfo histórico de Marraquexe, que resultou na criação da Organização Mundial do Comércio, os Estados membros se mostraram incapazes de avançar na criação e aperfeiçoamento das regras da OMC. A Rodada Doha, a primeira após a Rodada Uruguai (1986-1994), iniciou em 2001 e já se arrasta há quase 16 anos sem perspectiva de conclusão. O interesse de muitos Estados na edição de novas regras, contudo, fez com que redirecionassem seus esforços para o campo regional, buscando o estabelecimento de acordos comerciais bilaterais e regionais, em cujo bojo se editam normas compatíveis com as já previstas nos acordos da OMC – *regras OMC-in* –, normas que vão além daquelas previstas nestes acordos – *regras OMC-plus* – e normas que regulam temas não cobertos pela OMC – *regras OMC-extra* (Thorstensen; Ferraz, 2014, p. 6). A multiplicação de acordos comerciais bilaterais, regionais e multilaterais cria problemas para as grandes empresas globais, cuja atividade produtiva globalizada tem de ser compatibilizada com marcos jurídicos nem sempre harmônicos[30], mas a multilateralização dessas regras, que poderia harmonizar esses regimes, tem-se revelado ainda impossível.

Nações Unidas e o mundo só entenderam tarde demais: que a guerra na Bósnia era tanto uma causa moral quanto um conflito armado. A tragédia de Srebrenica irá assombrar nossa história para sempre" (Annan, 1999, parag. 503).

30 Essa teia de regimes normativos foi denominada *tigela de espaguete* (*spaghetti bowl*) por Jagdish Bhagwati (cf. Baldwin, 2006, p. 1)

Gridlock e o Direito Internacional

Essa dificuldade de cooperação,[31] não podia deixar de ser, afeta a possibilidade de os mecanismos de governança global darem conta de suas funções. Em questões cruciais, como a segurança internacional, a preservação ambiental e a proteção de direitos humanos, essa dificuldade pode custar vidas e riqueza.

Na sua investigação sobre as razões dessa dificuldade, Thomas Hale, David Held e Kevin Young apontam para o notável sucesso da ordem internacional do Pós-II Guerra na institucionalização das relações entre os Estados, que criou:

> (...) condições nas quais atores podiam se beneficiar criando empresas multinacionais, investindo no exterior, desenvolvendo tecnologias para cadeias globais de produção e outras atividades associadas com a globalização. Essas escolhas, combinadas com a lógica expansionista do capitalismo e a com a inovação em tecnologia de base, mudou a natureza da economia mundial, radicalmente incrementando a dependência de povos e países de todos os cantos do mundo. Essa interdependência, por seu turno, criou a demanda por mais institucionalização, que os Estados providenciaram, buscando os benefícios da cooperação, começando o ciclo novamente. Por todo o período do Pós-Guerra, passando pelo fim da Guerra Fria e indo além, o mundo desfrutou de um período de interdependência auto reforçada. (Hale; Held; Young, 2013, p. 26)

A globalização da economia criou oportunidades de desenvolvimento que vários países aproveitaram, tornando o mundo crescentemente mais multipolar, pois aumentou o número de Estados que precisam consentir para que haja cooperação, ao passo que reduz a capacidade dos Estados mais poderosos de impor sua vontade (Hale; Held; Young, 2013,

---

31 Para outros exemplos desse *gridlock* na cooperação internacional, cf. Hale, Held e Young (2013).

p. 31). Ao mesmo tempo, ampliou também a pauta de problemas locais que passaram a ter uma dimensão internacional, estendendo o alcance temático da governança global e, pelas diferentes características de cada país, reforçando a multipolarização, já que mesmo médias e pequenas potências, em certos assuntos, poderiam ter algo a oferecer que interessasse aos grandes (Hale; Held; Young, 2013, p. 33) e que não seria entregue sem contrapartidas.

Nesse contexto de crescente multipolaridade, três outros fatores contribuem para o problema, levando ao impedimento da cooperação internacional: a inércia institucional que impede a atualização das estruturas criadas no Pós-II Guerra para melhor refletirem a distribuição de poder no sistema internacional atual, ampliando o "hiato de governança" entre a ordem multilateral existente e os bens públicos necessários; a maior abrangência e complexidade, em comparação com 1945, dos problemas atuais, que estabelecem uma conexão entre fatores localizados em diferentes Estados, e cujo enfrentamento conjunto demanda uma articulação de políticas mais amplas e profundas, que, justamente por isso, torna-se mais difícil de se obter; finalmente, a diversidade e multiplicidade de organismos e instituições internacionais criados desde 1945, como visto na seção anterior, caracteriza um sistema de governança fragmentado no qual a ação coletiva é mais difícil (Hale; Held; Young, 2013, p. 41–42, 44 e 46).

A isso se soma um fator novo, originado no interior dos Estados: a rejeição do *ethos* internacionalista e cosmopolita, a súbita revalorização da soberania estatal e do nacionalismo nas economias desenvolvidas. Isso se explica, entre outros fatores, porque o processo de globalização é percebido como tendo imposto um alto custo para uma parcela de sua população, que experimenta uma crescente insegurança pela falta de emprego, quer por causa da transferência de postos de trabalho para países em desenvolvimento – *a China, em particular*[32] – quer pelo influxo de imigrantes, voluntários ou refugiados, que são percebidos como competidores pelos empregos cada vez mais escassos, insegurança essa que se vê agravada pela fragilização da rede de proteção social pelas políticas de austeridade adotadas por muitos países na esteira da crise econômica de 2008. Esse sentimento anti-internacionalista acaba sendo apropriado por grupos políticos dentro desses Estados, muitos deles populistas, levando a governos hostis às demandas globais, que percebem como injustificadamente limitadoras de sua soberania, o que, por sua vez, reforça o *gridlock*, levando mesmo a retrocessos no que toca à cooperação, como no recente plebiscito que decidiu pela saída do Reino Unido da União Europeia.

Esse discurso seria facilmente denunciável em suas contradições e falhas lógicas, mas ele ganha credibilidade por se amparar num fenômeno que caracteriza tanto a política doméstica quanto a internacional nos últimos 30 anos: a apropriação por organismos especializados, de natureza técnico-executiva, da capacidade decisória que tradicionalmente foi dos parlamentos eleitos pelo povo para representá-lo[33], fenômeno que, no plano internacional, com o avanço da globalização, é agravado pela verticalização dos processos de tomada de decisão, que deslocam a competência decisória que antes se situava no interior do Estado para organismos supra ou transnacionais, que têm uma menor sensibilidade às demandas locais (Torelly, 2016, p. 29). Esse rearranjo tecnocrático dos processos políticos cujo produto irá afetar, por vezes de maneira desastrosa, a vida de grandes grupos de pessoas no interior dos Estados, justifica-se no fim de isolar questões especificas – *como a política comer-*

---

32 Muito embora o deslocamento de processos fabris para países em desenvolvimento seja menos responsável pela eliminação de postos de trabalho nas economias centrais do que os ganhos de produtividade trazidos pela evolução tecnológica (cf. Irwin, 2016, p. 88–89).

33 Exemplo representativo dessa tendência é a discussão sobre a autonomia dos Bancos Centrais na definição da política monetária de um Estado, limitando-se a influência do Governo ou do Parlamento nessa decisão.

cial, p.ex. – do risco de contaminação por embates políticos em outros campos (Torelly, 2016, p. 28), mas, ao alijar as populações diretamente afetadas por essas decisões do processo deliberativo, mina a legitimidade dessas instituições, em especial em momentos como o atual, em que os resultados práticos desse arranjo são percebidos como insatisfatórios.

Além disso, após vinte e cinco anos de hegemonia liberal nas relações internacionais, período em que o princípio de não-intervenção foi frequentemente deixado de lado para a promoção ou garantia de valores que, nas palavras de Hedley Bull, não seriam os da sociedade internacional, o resultado parece ser uma diminuição da capacidade do direito internacional de cumprir suas funções como instituição de manutenção da ordem internacional. Desde a introdução da proteção aos direitos humanos, em 1944, como um dos princípios constitucionais da ordem do Pós-II Guerra, inseriu-se um elemento de tensão na estrutura do direito internacional clássico, pois é impossível a perfeita compatibilização das regras de respeito à soberania e de jurisdição exclusiva do Estado sobre os assuntos domésticos com a afirmação de direitos de que os indivíduos seriam titulares independentemente de atribuição do Estado onde estejam, direitos esses que serviriam de limite para o que o Estado possa fazer ou deixar de fazer em relação aos indivíduos sob sua jurisdição. Mas com o término da Guerra Fria, assistiu-se a uma erosão do princípio da soberania, principalmente a partir do conceito de intervenção humanitária, argumento que ganhou curso nos meios diplomáticos como forma de justificar o uso unilateral da força armada em situações nas quais o Conselho de Segurança não tivesse aprovado uma ação coletiva. O primeiro grande exemplo do uso prático dessa doutrina foi dado durante a crise humanitária em Kosovo, quando a promessa de exercício do poder de veto pela Rússia (INDEPENDENT INTERNATIONAL COMMISSION ON KOSSOVO, 2000, p. 4) – *que superara o momento crítico de desorganização e buscava reocupar um lugar de protagonismo no cenário internacional, saindo em defesa de um aliado histórico* –, fez com que a decisão de intervir fosse tomada pela Organização do Tratado do

Atlântico Norte (OTAN) à revelia do Conselho de Segurança; um uso de força militar claramente unilateral e em contradição com o art. 2(4) da Carta da ONU, mas "legítimo" aos olhos do intervencionismo liberal dos anos 1990.[34]

Esse padrão intervencionista se manteve e se agravou nos anos seguintes, com resultados desastrosos do ponto de vista da segurança e estabilidade de certas regiões do mundo, como o Oriente Médio, onde foi particularmente aplicado. A invasão do Iraque pelos EUA em 2003, com o pretexto declarado de combater a Al-Qaeda – *que não tinha atividades em território iraquiano antes da invasão* –, destruir armas de destruição em massa – *que depois se confirmou não* existirem – e libertar o povo iraquiano do jugo de um ditador sanguinário, resultou na destruição das estruturas de governo daquele País e, dado o completo fracasso no projeto americano de "construção de Estado", na criação de um vácuo de

---

34 No Relatório sobre Kosovo, a Comissão Independente chefiada por Richard Goldstone concluiu: "[A] diplomacia falhou em produzir esses resultados [proteção dos kosovares de origem albanesa e a autonomia da província] de forma consistente. Essa situação leva à conclusão geral de que a campanha da OTAN foi ilegal, mas legítima. Tal conclusão está ligada à ideia controversa de que um "direito" de intervenção humanitária não é consistente com a Carta da ONU se concebida como um texto normativo, mas que ele pode, dependendo do contexto, refletir o espirito da Carta no que se refere à proteção geral de populações contra perseguição em larga escala. Uma intervenção humanitária, pois, pode ser legitimamente autorizada pela ONU, mas será frequentemente questionada juridicamente do ponto de vista das obrigações decorrentes da Carta no que se refere à soberania dos Estados" (INDEPENDENT INTERNATIONAL COMMISSION ON KOSSOVO, 2000, p. 186 – grifei). Deve-se criticar a indevida confusão que a Comissão faz entre o uso da força unilateral e o uso da força por decisão do Conselho de Segurança, agindo com base no Cap. VII da Carta. Ainda que se possa questionar se uma decisão do Conselho de autorizar uma intervenção militar por questões humanitárias é compatível com o respeito à soberania estatal, o que houve no caso do Kosovo foi uma decisão *sem qualquer autorização* do Conselho, tomada unilateralmente por uma aliança militar sem qualquer fundamento na Carta.

poder que deu espaço para o crescimento de organizações paramilitares, a maior e mais perigosa das quais é o *Daesh*, também conhecido como Estado Islâmico. É fato que, assim como no caso do Kosovo, o uso da força contra o Iraque não fora autorizado pelo Conselho de Segurança, mas o fato da "Coalizão dos Dispostos" que participou da invasão incluir parte relevante das potências ocidentais, bem como o fato consumado da subsequente ocupação do território iraquiano ter sido reconhecido pelo Conselho de Segurança[35], são indícios de um enfraquecimento da regra de proibição do uso unilateral de força. Esses sinais certamente foram percebidos por muitas nações, em especial por Irã e Coreia do Norte, que, temendo serem os próximos a sofrerem intervenção externa, retomaram seus planos de desenvolvimento de armas nucleares.

Mas é na esteira da chamada Primavera Árabe que os exemplos mais recentes desse intervencionismo liberal se fizeram sentir de forma mais trágica. Embora a Tunísia, onde o movimento teve origem em 2010, tenha conseguido fazer a transição para um regime democrático, tendo realizado eleições parlamentares em 2011 e presidenciais em 2014, o mesmo não se verificou nos outros cinco Estados onde o movimento teve mais tração: Egito, Líbia, Iêmen, Síria e Bahrain. Em dois deles, Síria e Líbia, a reação obstinada dos governos agravou o dilema da força estatal – *pelo qual um Estado fraco ou enfraquecido, para recuperar sua força, adota medidas de força que terminam por enfraquecê-lo ainda mais e minar sua legitimidade* (Holsti, 1996, p. 116 ss.) – a tal ponto que as estruturas governamentais ruíram: na Líbia, a desorganização do governo levou à morte brutal de Muammar Gaddafi e a um estado de permanente guerra civil que se mantém até este momento; na Síria, Bashar Al-Assad somente conseguiu se manter no poder por força de apoios externos, principalmente do Irã e, de forma mais explícita, da Rússia, mas ao custo da destruição generalizada da infraestrutura de seu país e de um êxodo de refugiados que reduziu a população em 25% no curso de cinco anos.

35 Resolução 1483, aprovada em 22 de maio de 2003 (S/RES/1483)

Diante da violência com que se desenrolaram as crises nos dois países, a ONU foi instada a agir e o fez, primeiramente, no caso da Líbia: o Conselho de Segurança aprovou uma operação militar para impedir que o governo de Gaddafi atacasse sua própria população civil, impondo uma área de exclusão aérea sobre o país e autorizando "todos os meios necessários" para a proteção de civis e de áreas habitadas por civis, exceto a ocupação da Líbia por forças estrangeiras[36]. Na implementação da Resolução, contudo, a coalizão liderada pelos Estados Unidos, Reino Unido e França flagrantemente ultrapassou os limites de seu mandato, inclusive com o uso de forças especiais em solo e o disparo de mísseis contra alvos militares em solo. Os ataques tornaram insustentável a conservação do regime, que caiu deixando em seu lugar um vazio de poder cuja resultante ainda não pode ser identificada, mas cujos resultados do ponto de vista da piora das condições de vida no país podem ser estimados a partir das levas de refugiados que buscam chegar de barco à Itália e à Europa.

O exemplo do abuso em relação aos limites da autorização para intervenção na Líbia influenciou negativamente as possibilidades de o Conselho de Segurança autorizar uma missão semelhante em relação à Síria. Isso levou à situação atual, uma guerra civil na qual é extremamente difícil identificar quem são os combatentes e quais são as linhas de conflito e de aliança, com a tensa circunstância de as forças americanas estarem, ao menos nominalmente, atuando em conjunto com forças rebeldes e, por isso, em potencial conflito com as forças armadas russas, que atuam ao lado das tropas governistas. No caso da Síria, mas já no caso da Líbia, o direito internacional mostrava sua incapacidade de servir como instrumento para a manutenção da ordem, enfraquecido pela crescente desconsideração de seus princípios pelos países envolvidos nesses conflitos.

O resultado, que não deve espantar, é que, ao decidir como se comportar num mundo em que os padrões de conduta expressos nas

---

36 Resolução 1973, aprovada em 17 de março de 2011 (S/RES/1973)

normas internacionais já não são observados, os Estados deixem de depositar confiança nessas mesmas normas e passem a fazer suas estimativas acerca do comportamento dos demais sem levá-las em consideração. Mais: a aproximação das normas internacionais do que se percebe como sendo valores liberais fragiliza o direito internacional, pois mina nos Estados a confiança de que esse mecanismo não se voltará contra eles, especialmente quando se trata de Estados que identificam em sua posição geopolítica uma exposição em relação aos interesses dos EUA; a identificação do direito com a pauta política hegemônica norte-americana. Essa falta de confiança no direito internacional e nas instituições internacionais é outro fator a incrementar a dificuldade de cooperação no plano internacional.

Retomando o paradoxo apontado por Hale, Held e Young, o caminho perseguido pela governança global do Pós-II Guerra até hoje foi bem-sucedido, mas nos levou a um beco sem saída. Retraçar o caminho dependerá de um debate sobre como recuperar a confiança dos Estados e de suas populações no direito internacional e no sistema de governança global, abalado pelos anos de hegemonia liberal e pela falta de atenção com os prejudicados pela globalização. Sem confiança não há cooperação e sem cooperação não há governança. E sem governança estamos todos em perigo.

Referências

ANNAN, K. *Report of the Secretary-General pursuant to General Assembly resolution 53/35: The fall of Srebrenica*. New York: [s.n.]. Disponível em: <http://www.un.org/en/ga/search/view_doc.asp?symbol=A/54/549>.

AYOOB, M. The New-Old Disorder in the Third World. *Global Governance*, v. 1, n. 1, p. 59–77, 1995.

BALDWIN, R. E. *Multilateralising regionalism: Spaghetti Bowls as Building Blocs on the Path to Global Free Trade*: NBER Working

Paper. Cambridge, MA: [s.n.]. Disponível em: <http://www.nber.org/papers/w12545.pdf>.

BARNETT, M. The New United Nations Politics of Peace: From Juridical Sovereignty to Empirical Sovereignty. *Global Governance*, v. 1, n. 1, p. 79–97, 1995.

BOBBIO, N. A ideia da paz e o pacifismo. In: BOBBIO, N. (Ed.). *O problema da guerra e as vias da paz*. São Paulo: Editora UNESP, 2003. p. 137–163.

BOBBIO, N. Presente e Futuro dos Direitos do Homem. In: BOBBIO, N. (Ed.). *A Era dos Direitos*. 2. ed. São Paulo: Elsevier, 2004. p. 25–45.

BOUTROS-GHALI, B. Democracy: A Newly Recognized Imperative. *Global Governance*, v. 1, n. 1, p. 3–11, 1995.

BULL, H. *The Anarchical Society: A Study of Order in World Politics*. 3. ed. Hampshire: Palgrave, 2002.

CARLSSON, I. *et al. Our Global Neighborhood: The Report of the Commission on Global Governance*. Oxford, England: Oxford University Press, 1995.

CARLSSON, I.; HAN, S.-J.; KUPOLATI, R. M. *Report of the Independent Inquiry into the Actions of the United Nations during the 1994 Genocide in Rwanda*. New York: [s.n.]. Disponível em: <http://www.un.org/en/ga/search/view_doc.asp?symbol=S/1999/1257>.

CARR, E. H. *Vinte anos de crise - 1919 - 1939 - uma introdução ao estudo das relações internacionais*. Tradução Luiz Alberto Figueiredo Machado. 2. ed. Brasília: Editora Universidade de Brasília; Imprensa Oficial do Estado de São Paulo, 2001.

CERVO, A. L. A Instabilidade Internacional (1919-1939). In: SARAIVA, J. F. S. (Ed.). *História das Relações Internacionais Contemporâneas - Da Sociedade Internacional do Séc. XIX à Era da Globalização*. 2. ed. São Paulo: Saraiva, 2007. p. 131–167.

DENG, F. M. Dealing with the Displaced: A Challenge to the International Community. *Global Governance*, v. 1, n. 1, p. 45–57, 1995.

FALK, R. A. International Jurisdiction: Horizontal and Vertical Conceptions of Legal Order. *Temple Law Quarterly*, v. 32, n. 3, p. 295–320, 1959.

FINKELSTEIN, L. S. What is Global Governance? *Global Governance*, v. 1, n. 3, p. 367–372, 1995.

FULLER, G. E. Moscow and the Gulf War. *Foreign Affairs*, v. 70, n. 3, p. 57–76, 1991.

HALE, T.; HELD, D.; YOUNG, K. *Gridlock: Why Global Cooperation is Failing When We Need It Most*. Cambridge: Polity Press, 2013.

HENKIN, L. *How Nations Behave*. New York: Columbia University Press, 1979.

HOLANDA FILHO, S. B. DE. Livre Comércio versus Protecionismo: uma antiga controvérsia e suas novas feições. *Estudos Econômicos*, v. 28, n. 1, p. 33–75, 1998.

HOLSTI, K. J. *The State, War, and the State of War*. Cambridge: Cambridge University Press, 1996.

INDEPENDENT INTERNATIONAL COMMISSION ON KOSSOVO. *The Kosovo Report: Conflict, International Response, Lessons Learned.* Oxford, England: Oxford University Press, 2000.

IRWIN, D. A. The Truth About Trade: What Critics Get Wrong About the Global Economy. *Foreign Affairs*, v. 95, n. 4, p. 84–95, 2016.

KENNEDY, D. The Mystery of Global Governance. In: DUNOFF, J. L.; TRACHTMAN, J. P. (Eds.). *Ruling the world? Constitutionalism, International Law and Global Governance*. Cambridge: Cambridge University Press, 2009. p. 37–68.

KRISTOF, N. D. War in the Gulf: China; Beijing Backs Away from Full Support of the War. *The New York Times*, 1991.

NASSER, S. H. *Fontes e normas de direito internacional: um estudo sobre a Soft Law*. São Paulo: Atlas, 2005.

ROSENAU, J. N. Governance, Order and Change in World Politics. In: ROSENAU, J. N.; CZEMPIEL, E.-O. (Eds.). *Governance Without Government: Order and Change in World Politics*. Cambridge: Cambridge University Press, 1992. p. 1–29.

ROSENAU, J. N. Governance in the Twenty-first Century. *Global Governance*, v. 1, n. 1, p. 13–43, 1995.

ROSENAU, J. N. *Along the Domestic-Foreign Frontier: Exploring Governance in a Turbulent World*. Cambridge: Cambridge University Press, 1997.

SHAW, M. N. *International Law*. 5. ed. Cambridge: Cambridge University Press, 2003.

STOCK, J. T. Are humans still evolving? *European Molecular Biology Organization Reports*, v. 9, n. Special Issue, p. 51–54, 2008.

THORSTENSEN, V.; FERRAZ, L. O isolamento do brasil em relação aos acordos e mega-acordos comerciais. *Boletim de Economia e Política Internacional*, n. 16, p. 5–17, 2014.

TORELLY, M. Do Direito Internacional À Governança Global: Mudanças Estruturais Do Espaço Transnacional. *Revista de Direito Brasileira*, v. 15, n. 6, p. 20–46, 2016.

UNITED STATES OF AMERICA. DEPARTMENT OF STATE. BUREAU OF INTERNATIONAL ORGANIZATION AFFAIRS. *Report to Congress on Voting Practices in the United Nations, Submitted Pursuant to Public Law 98-151 and Public Law 98-164*. Washington, DC: Division of Publications, Office of Public Affairs, 1984. Disponível em: <https://archive.org/download/votingpracticesi1983unit/votingpracticesi1983unit.pdf>.

UNITED STATES OF AMERICA. DEPARTMENT OF STATE. BUREAU OF INTERNATIONAL ORGANIZATION AFFAIRS. *Annual Report to Congress on Voting Practices in the United Nations General Assembly (UNGA) and the Security Council.* Washington, DC: Division of Publications, Office of Public Affairs, 2000.

UNITED STATES OF AMERICA. DEPARTMENT OF STATE. BUREAU OF INTERNATIONAL ORGANIZATION AFFAIRS. Voting Practices in the United Nations 2015 – *Report to Congress Submitted Pursuant to Public Laws 101-246 and 108-447*. Washington, DC: Division of Publications, Office of Public Affairs, 2016.

Democracia e direito internacional: o alcance atual da cidadania na integração europeia e sul-americana

Marcela Benhossi
Daniel Campos de Carvalho

Introdução

Entre inúmeras características passíveis de destaque, pode-se afirmar que o termo democracia é um poderoso artifício retórico. Os múltiplos significados da noção permitem sua instrumentalização discursiva graças à carga positiva normalmente atribuída ao conceito. Tanto é assim que a semântica aberta da democracia lhe confere uma plasticidade de uso que não raramente presta testemunho do cinismo de parte dos agentes públicos.

Desta forma, o pressuposto de qualquer reflexão envolvendo o conceito de democracia é que a noção apresenta alta carga valorativa e retórica, o que também permite vislumbrar o seu potencial de intervenção e transformação da realidade. Tal afirmação pode ser comprovada pelo progressivo espraiamento de práticas democráticas (e seus efeitos) para searas e instâncias decisórias historicamente distantes do tema – como a gestão de organizações privadas e até os processos de tomada de decisão em instituições de ensino. Como não poderia deixar de ser, a disseminação dos imperativos da legitimidade democrática atinge com vigor as Relações Internacionais, uma vez que há um crescente câmbio relacionado ao reconhecimento da relevância da democracia para além do plano nacional.

Assim sendo, o objetivo deste texto é explorar um desdobramento específico do fortalecimento dos primados democráticos nas práticas e na retórica da governança internacional contemporânea, por meio da análise de certas repercussões fáticas que serão explicitadas abaixo. Vale apontar que o pano de fundo da discussão das próximas páginas é o recente adensamento de uma influência transversal de preceitos democráticos na tutela de bens jurídicos e na repercussão jurisprudencial atreladas ao fenômeno jurídico internacional (Fox; Roth, 2001). Entretanto, por conta das restrições inerentes a um texto de poucas páginas como o presente capítulo, seria certamente imprecisa e pretensiosa qualquer tentativa de sistematização rigorosa e ampla da interação entre direito e democracia nas Relações Internacionais[1] – daí a opção por um recorte determinado.

Ainda assim é possível engendrar uma breve enumeração não exaustiva e sem pretensões analíticas de alguns dos modos pelos quais o *topoi* democracia é apropriado pelo direito internacional contemporâneo. Vale pontar que engendraremos aqui uma panorâmica abordagem de perspectiva meramente dogmática, desconsiderando o importantíssimo enfoque zetético da relação entre direito internacional e democracia, expresso por exemplo no tema da legitimidade das normas (Franck, 1988; Franck, 1990; Clarck 2005; Carvalho; Jubilut, 2015) e das cortes (Bogdandy; Venzke, 2012; Bogdandy, 2013) internacionais.[2] Cabe, nos

1 Para os efeitos deste texto, assume-se o postulado de que a legitimidade do Direito Internacional está progressivamente atrelada ao protagonismo da questão democrática no plano internacional – ecoando a reflexão habermasiana de que a única forma de submissão ao poder admitida na contemporaneidade é a via democrática. Não problematizaremos tal questão, mas é inegável que a complexidade das interação entre legitimidade, direito e democracia no plano internacional permite outros arranjos. Neste sentido, ver Kumm (2004) e Moreira (2012).

2 "Instead the issue is how in the face of international community which "appropriates" and defines common material and spiritual assets and in the face of interna-

passos de Petersen (2008), levantar sumariamente algumas repercussões no direito internacional positivado, uma vez que é possível notar "*the infiltration of concerns for democratic legitimacy into virtually every aspect of international legal discourse*" (Fox; Roth, 2001, p.331).

Assim, um dos caminhos naturais seria, por exemplo, examinar de que forma os órgãos jurisdicionais de solução de controvérsias no plano internacional fazem remissão à noção de democracia nos seus julgados. Tal viés é especialmente interessante no tocante aos tribunais penais internacionais (Mayerfeld, 2004) e às cortes regionais de proteção dos direitos humanos, como a europeia (Pildes, 2016). Trata-se de um campo de pesquisa rico e subaproveitado, sobretudo considerando que qualquer análise que deite atenção às instâncias aplicadoras do direito internacional face à questão democrática tem por desafio: i) a dinâmica peculiar da atividade jurisprudencial internacional, ii) a complexidade política da sociedade internacional contemporânea e iii) a pluralidade de princípios, institutos e concepções passíveis de utilização no embate argumentativo para a limitação do alcance da própria atuação judicante, como por exemplo, as ideias de "domínio reservado do Estado" ou de "margem de apreciação".

Um segundo recorte de análise possível de ser feito aborda as formas pelas quais os preceitos democráticos interagem com o clássico tema dos sujeitos de direito internacional. Desconsiderando os sujeitos anômalos de direito internacional – as forças beligerantes, os movimentos insurgentes, a Santa Sé e a Ordem da Cruz de Malta –, o rol usual de detentores da personalidade jurídica internacional é composto por Estados, organizações internacionais e indivíduos (Dinh; Daillier; Pellet, 2003, p.413). Ainda que não seja novo o impacto sobre os entes esta-

---

tional governance increasingly appropriates administrative functions of the state, can establish mechanisms which, in the vocabulary of normative political theory, would legitimate such government. If an answer is not found to this, the huge gains attained in the systemic evolution of law making and law enforcement may be normatively and even politically nullified." (Weiler, 2004, p. 561).

tais do entrecruzamento entre direito internacional e democracia (como ilustrado pelo clássico tema do reconhecimento de governo), trata-se de uma relação em constante renovação (vide o surgimento da tese de que também o reconhecimento de Estado estaria condicionado ao respeito aos ditames democráticos[3]). Em contínuo desenvolvimento e com aspirações de consolidação, encontra-se também a ideia de um direito humano à governança democrática (Franck, 1992), concebido de uma perspectiva para além do Estado.

Apesar da importância dos temas envolvendo os Estados e os indivíduos, este trabalho focará na intersecção entre direito e democracia atinente a um sujeito de direito internacional específico: as organizações internacionais.[4] Contudo, será proposto um caso de estudo delimitado, passando ao largo de diversos temas relevantes nesta seara. Não serão abordadas, por exemplo, as questões atinentes à existência de cláusulas democráticas em organizações internacionais, as ações diretas das instituições na promoção da democracia em determinados contextos ou mesmo a exigência do prestígio à democracia na realidade política do postulador do ingresso em determinada organização (casos da Organização dos Estados Americanos e da União Europeia, por exemplo). Por seu turno, este texto empreenderá uma análise das iniciativas citadinas de certas organizações internacionais – já que as ações conexas a tais propostas têm vocação para a verificação fática da eventual aproximação material entre direito internacional e democracia.

Para tanto, será engendrada a apresentação de dois modelos de experiências regionais de promoção da cidadania para além do Estado: a cidadania no processo de integração da Europa e nas experiências sul-americanas. Preliminarmente, há de se apontar que a noção de cidada-

---

3 Para uma clareza de tal proposta e do conjunto de críticas passíveis, vide Vidmar (2013).

4 O termo organização internacional é utilizado neste texto como sinônimo de organização intergovernamental ou de organização governamental internacional, afastando-se da ideia de organização não-governamental.

nia cumpre, na União Europeia, no Mercado Comum do Sul (Mercosul) e na União das Nações Sul-americanas (Unasul), o mesmo papel: consubstanciar uma ferramenta institucional de adensamento das respectivas legitimidades. Para aclarar esta relação, usaremos como esteio teórico parte do repertório conceitual desenvolvido ao redor do problema do déficit democrático (Carvalho, 2012). A partir da apresentação de tais linhas-mestras, será fomentada a análise de alguns traços emblemáticos da cidadania nos referidos blocos regionais – com a única pretensão de explorar suas vicissitudes e clarificar se há correspondência entre a participação cidadã fabulada e a realidade. Tal discussão tem papel fundamental na contemporaneidade, uma vez que permite analisar a pertinência, a viabilidade. o sentido e do alcance de um "direito internacional democrático" (Besson, 2010, p.177).

Déficit Democrático nas Organizações Internacionais regionais e a abertura para a ação cidadã

As organizações internacionais correspondem a um aríete central das transformações do direito internacional público ao longo do século XX (Paulus, 2009, p.76). Ainda que seu advento possa ser localizado historicamente por volta de 1850, o primeiro grande experimento desta então novel forma de institucionalidade encontra-se previsto apenas no texto do Tratado de Versalhes em 1919 (Kennedy, 1987, p.841-42). Assim, a Liga das Nações ou Sociedade das Nações demarca não apenas a tentativa inaugural de construção de um amplo foro de concertação internacional com vistas à estabilização do sistema de Estados, mas também ilustra a pretensão de promover, visibilizar e normatizar outras dimensões da então nascente sociedade internacional.

Mesmo que a maior parte da historiografia considere a Liga das Nações como uma iniciativa frágil e ineficaz (Hobsbawm, 1995, p.44-45), o afastamento temporal torna nítido o quanto seu curto período de atividades foi fundamental na alteração da estrutura e da função do direito internacional contemporâneo – algo promovido pela instituição que a sucedeu: a Organização das Nações Unidas (ONU). O próprio texto fundante da Liga das Nações já demarcaria esta nova forma de articulação entre os agentes da comunidade internacional por meio do Direito:

> Art. 20. Os membros da Sociedade reconhecem, cada um no que o concerne, que o presente Pacto ab-roga as obrigações ou acordos inter se incompatíveis com seus termos e comprometem-se solenemente a não contrair semelhantes acordos ou obrigações para o futuro.
>
> Se antes de sua entrada na Sociedade, um membro assumiu obrigações incompatíveis com os termos do Pacto, deverá tomar medidas imediatas para delas se libertar.

Reforça a identificação da Liga das Nações com a pretensão de sedimentação de um *rule of law* na sociedade internacional, os avanços nos regramentos normativos e institucionais atinentes a inúmeros temas como "direitos especiais das minorias", proteção de refugiados, padrões trabalhistas e comércio de narcóticos. Ademais, sob os auspícios da organização, estruturou-se a Corte Permanente de Justiça Internacional – uma revolucionária conquista que alteraria profundamente o alcance do Direito para além das jurisdições estatais, desembocando na atual Corte Internacional de Justiça.

No pós-1945, os traços da ordem jurídica internacional do Entreguerras foram aprofundados com vigor, como demonstra emblematicamente o sistema de segurança coletiva erguido sob a tutela da ONU. A regulamentação expressa do uso da força foi (e é) o principal elemento de uma arquitetura internacional que reputa caráter decisivo ao fenômeno jurídico. O papel protagonista do Direito como vetor organizador da sociedade internacional auxilia na compreensão da explosiva proliferação das organizações internacionais após 1945 – e no consequente advento de novos polos de produção normativa e de destinatários de tais normas. Além do constante surgimento de novas instituições e de normas jurídicas, a proliferação de mecanismos de solução de controvérsias atrelados às organizações e o aumento do respectivo *enforcement* caracterizam este cenário, contribuindo para o adensamento de juridicidade do plano internacional e promovendo a passagem de um direito internacional de mera convivência, para um fenômeno jurídico internacional caracterizado pela cooperação (Amaral Júnior, 2012).

Ainda que seus efeitos sejam entendidos por autores de inclinação realista como retóricos e inócuos, a consolidação de uma ordem internacional que conceda papel destacado às organizações internacionais acarreta um inegável realinhamento dos comportamentos dos agentes e um reposicionamento do *locus* do poder internacional. Assim, tais instituições passam a ter um caráter central na condução dos destinos da sociedade global, influenciando decisivamente a realidade contemporânea. Deste modo, não há de se estranhar que o surgimento dos clamores por democratização dos centros deliberativos das organizações internacionais torne-se uma demanda de grande repercussão na atualidade – sobretudo pelo fato de que a única forma de sujeição ao poder amplamente aceita no nosso tempo é via uso público da razão, como prega o adágio habermasiano.

No âmbito das organizações internacionais, a demanda por democratização das instâncias decisórias pode apresentar diversas formas e roupagens, algo fruto da pluralidade de instituições, das peculiaridades de cada organograma e, claro, da mencionada diversidade conceitual acerca da democracia. Assim, exemplos de uma primeira leva deste tipo de pleitos podem ser reconhecidos nos movimentos em prol do aumento da acessibilidade de Estados Nacionais aos órgãos centrais das organizações internacionais – algo já presente na Liga das Nações, mas notadamente evidente a partir da crítica às limitações de participação em tais instâncias de Estados em desenvolvimento (uma constante da segunda metade do século XX).

Outra forma de promoção da democratização das organizações internacionais seria por meio da defesa de desenhos institucionais que permitissem o controle recíproco do exercício do poder pelos seus próprios órgãos, prestigiando o secular princípio do *checks and balances.* Também é possível compreender que a democratização das organizações internacionais exigiria o respeito aos direitos humanos e ao princípio da publicidade dos atos oficiais. Todavia, a forma mais tradicional de reconhecimento das limitações democráticas de uma organização internacional é por meio da falta de participação cidadã e/ou descolamento entre as pretensões da base social respectiva e a condução institucional. O próprio conceito de "déficit democrático", atualmente utilizado de forma indistinta para designar qualquer uma das vertentes vistas neste parágrafo[5], surgiu na década de 1970 para expressar o afastamento existente entre os nacionais dos Estados-membros e projeto europeu de integração.

De todo modo,

> Is global governance – the structure of international institutions – democratically legitimate, or does it suffer from a 'democratic deficit'? This is emerging as one of the central questions – perhaps the central question – in contemporary world politics (Moravcsik, 2004, p.336).

Ainda que seja possível operá-lo de diversos recortes, apenas lidaremos neste texto com o último aspecto do déficit democrático nas organizações internacionais, apresentado três casos contemporâneos de aplicação da noção: União Europeia, UNASUL e MERCOSUL. Mesmo que casos envolvendo o sistema ONU consubstanciem pautas interessantes de estudo do tema (Bummel, 2011, p. 104-105), a maior aderência da ideia de cidadania às realidades regionais nos impele a esse caminho.

O ponto de partida de qualquer análise que lide com a noção de cidadania é reconhecer que o conceito apresenta uma variada semântica teórica (Turner, 1993, p. 11) e histórica (Carvalho, 2008, p. 220). Metodologicamente, contudo, cumpre aclarar que neste trabalho será

5 Para uma sistematização mais acurada da diversidade semântica atrelada à ideia de déficit democrático no tocante às organizações internacionais, ver Carvalho (2012).

considerado como cidadania aquilo que os próprios projetos de integração identificam com o conceito – ainda que esta opção possa ser questionada por inúmeras perspectivas, ela serve ao interesse fulcral deste texto. Assim, a operacionalização da noção torna possível utilizá-la como instrumento de legitimação dos projetos de integração (tocando no tema do déficit democráticos das organizações internacionais), mesmo que o materialmente as iniciativas regionais tenham traços acentuadamente diferentes. Seja como for, fato é que a ideia de cidadania, "*an emotional glue between polity and citizen*" (Pomoell, 2000, p.94), consubstancia uma via reconhecida pelos condutores dos blocos regionais como fundamental para vencer os rechaços e críticas decorrentes das limitações de legitimidade dos processos de integração,

Experiências de promoção da cidadania na integração europeia

A concepção de uma cidadania comum passou a aparecer nos debates promovidos pelas instituições supranacionais apenas nos anos 1970 e 1980. A integração política não previa, até então, a existência de direitos específicos ligados à condição de cidadão europeu. A despeito desses esforços iniciais, foi só em 1990, durante a Conferência Intergovernamental sobre a União Política, realizada previamente à adoção do Tratado de Maastricht, que uma proposta formal acerca do caminho a ser traçado para a construção de uma cidadania europeia foi apresentada. O governo espanhol, responsável pela iniciativa, expressou a necessidade do estabelecimento de um tratamento diferenciado aos nacionais europeus quando no território de outro Estado-membro. Surgiam, assim, as bases para a construção jurídica da cidadania na integração (Chalmers, Davies, Monti, 2014).

Prevista no artigo 20 do Tratado sobre o Funcionamento da União Europeia (TFUE), a cidadania da União está intrinsecamente ligada à cidadania nacional: só é cidadão da União Europeia (UE) aquele que gozar de cidadania em um dos Estados-membros. Os direitos garantidos aos cidadãos da União, previstos nos artigos 21-4 do TFUE, são: I) o direito de circular e permanecer livremente no território dos Estados-membros; II) o direito de participar da vida política na UE, por meio da votação nas eleições para o Parlamento Europeu (PE), da participação nas eleições municipais nos Estados de residência e da Iniciativa de Cidadania Europeia (ICE); III) o direito de dirigir petições ao PE e de recorrer ao Provedor de Justiça Europeu ou a qualquer instituição ou órgão consultivo da UE com suas queixas; e IV) o direito de proteção por parte das autoridades diplomáticas e consulares de qualquer Estado-membro.

Com o propósito de compreender a manifestação da cidadania na integração, serão analisadas três de suas dimensões. Em um primeiro momento, será foco de estudo o direito de petição ao PE e o uso que tem sido feito desse mecanismo desde a sua implementação. Em seguida, explorar-se-á o papel que a ICE exerce na construção de políticas públicas da UE e o seu significado no projeto de inclusão do cidadão no processo legislativo. Por fim, a proposição de que a garantia de direitos sociais estaria atrelada à cidadania da União e serviria ao fortalecimento da legitimidade do bloco será pensada através da jurisprudência do Tribunal de Justiça da União Europeia (TJUE).

O direito de petição ao Parlamento Europeu

Ao longo de sua história, o PE sofreu significativas alterações no tocante às suas atribuições, tendo como objetivo conferir maior legitimidade ao desenho institucional da integração. De maneira geral, seus poderes foram alargados em duas áreas que são, tradicionalmente, fontes de autoridade em assembleias eleitas em democracias modernas: o controle do executivo e a criação legislativa (Hix; Noury; Roland, 2007, p. 13). Nos anos 1990, com a adoção do Tratado de Maastricht, o Parlamento vivenciou uma das mais relevantes mudanças em seu escopo com a adoção do processo de co-decisão, através do qual nenhuma legislação poderia ser aprovada sem o aval de ambos o Parlamento e a Comissão (Hix; Høyland, 2013, p. 172). Foi em meio a esse contexto, de atribuição de maior protagonismo ao PE com o propósito de tornar mais democrática a seara supranacional, que surgiu o direito de petição do Parlamento como um direito oriundo da cidadania da União.

O artigo 227 do TFUE estabelece que qualquer cidadão da União tem o direito de apresentar, a título individual ou em associação com outros cidadãos ou pessoas, petições ao Parlamento sobre qualquer questão que se integre nos domínios de atividade da União. O intuito é proporcionar um canal de fácil acesso para que os cidadãos da União e todos os residentes na UE possam direcionar suas aspirações e suas queixas às instituições da integração. A recepção, a apreciação e o seguimento de tais petições são de incumbência da Comissão de Petições, órgão parlamentar subsidiário do Parlamento (Marzocchi, 2017).

As repostas providas pela Comissão de Petições variam de acordo com as particularidades de cada caso, mas, de modo geral, compreendem desde o contato com autoridades competentes para a resolução de casos concretos que envolvam instituições dos Estados-membros até a moção de um processo no TJUE. Em se tratando de temáticas mencionadas em repetidas petições, o Parlamento e a Comissão podem optar por agir através de iniciativas políticas abrangentes (Marzocchi, 2017). É nesse sentido que a Comissão de Petições tem procedido, nos últimos anos, em relação aos temas de maior incidência, entre eles meio ambiente, justiça, direitos fundamentais e mercado interno (Vallina, 2016, p. 21).

Em relatório sobre as atividades da Comissão de Petições em 2015, de autoria de Ángela Vallina, é salientada a importância das petições no que tange à avaliação do impacto da legislação comunitária na vida quotidiana dos cidadãos. Ainda segundo o relatório, o processo funciona como um verdadeiro barômetro no controle da aplicação do direito da União ao facilitar a detecção de falhas e lacunas existentes na transposição dessa legislação, proporcionando a outras comissões informações valiosas para a elaboração de soluções no seu domínio de competência (Vallina, 2016, p. 9-12).

A própria Comissão de Petições, todavia, reconhece a existência de obstáculos que impedem a utilização plena do mecanismo por parte dos cidadãos da União. Sob uma primeira perspectiva, a sua utilização parece ser ainda limitada. O número de petições apresentadas por ano, que observou um crescimento significativo até o ano de 2013, quando atingiu-se o ponto máximo de 2891 petições, sofreu diminuições no último biênio analisado, chegando à cifra de 1431 petições em 2015 (Marzocchi, 2017). Por sua vez, o expressivo percentual de petições declaradas não admissíveis, tendência nos anos analisados pela Comissão, sugere certa confusão por parte dos peticionários no que diz respeito às competências europeias, que reiteradamente são misturadas com as competências nacionais e até mesmo com as atribuições do Conselho da Europa (Vallina, 2016, p. 31).

A Iniciativa de Cidadania Europeia

Prevista inicialmente no Tratado Constitucional, cujo processo de ratificação fracassou, a ICE entrou em vigor em 2012, um ano após a adoção do Regulamento (UE) n.º 211/2011, que regimentou a sua aplicação prática. Parte constituinte da cidadania da União, o direito à iniciativa está previsto nos artigos 11 do Tratado da União Europeia (TUE) e 24 do TFUE. A legislação possibilita que um milhão de cidadãos da UE, residentes em, pelo menos, um quarto dos Estados-Membros, convidem a Comissão a apresentar uma proposta de ato jurídico para efeitos de aplicação dos Tratados da UE. Não se trata, portanto, de uma proposta de lei direta: a Comissão mantém o monopólio da proposição legislativa na integração.

A Comissão tem como obrigações: i) o registro de iniciativas que atendam aos pré-requisitos do tratado; ii) o recebimento dos organizadores em audição pública para que expliquem detalhadamente as questões propostas; e iii) a apresentação, por meio de resposta formal, de suas conclusões jurídicas e políticas sobre a iniciativa em questão, das medidas que pretende tomar, se for o caso, e dos motivos que a levaram a tomar ou não essas medidas. Nesse sentido, a resposta dada pela Comissão aos organizadores da iniciativa não necessariamente envolve a formulação de um ato jurídico específico para a temática referida (Novak, 2017).

A ausência de um período longo de funcionamento do mecanismo impede qualquer análise mais precisa sobre o seu impacto em termos de mudanças efetivas. Contudo, algumas observações preliminares podem ser feitas a partir dos dados já existentes. Até o momento do presente estudo, 21 iniciativas haviam sido recusadas, 32 haviam sido arquivadas (muitas pela insuficiência de apoio), 7 estavam em andamento e apenas três podiam ser consideradas bem-sucedidas. Da análise das três iniciativas que foram apreciadas pela Comissão, podemos extrair duas conclusões. O tempo entre o registro da iniciativa e o envio da resposta formulada pela Comissão foi demasiadamente longo nos três casos, o que sugere uma falta de eficiência na fase de recolha. A própria Comissão dos Assuntos Constitucionais do PE, em relatório sobre a ICE publicado em 2015, reconheceu a dificuldade enfrentada por organizadores para angariar apoio em diferentes Estados-membros (Schöpflin, 2015, p. 5). Ademais, das três iniciativas, apenas uma resultou em produção normativa: o caso "*Right2Water*" e as decorrentes alterações na Diretiva Água Potável (EUROPEAN COMISSION, 2015).

Nessa perspectiva, a ICE aparenta ser um instrumento mais retórico e ideológico do que fático. Pensada como um "instrumento de uma democracia participativa transnacional, que permite aos cidadãos dialogar diretamente com as instituições da UE e participar ativamente na elaboração de políticas e de legislação europeias" (Schöpflin, 2015, p. 4), a iniciativa ainda não contribui de maneira significativa para a participação diária na política da integração (GIDDENS, 2014, p. 47).

Os direitos sociais como parte integrante da cidadania europeia

A identificação da participação política como a expressão mais contundente da cidadania europeia, não obstante a sua centralidade no discurso e na realidade jurídica da integração, não é a única interpretação possível dentro do debate acerca das formas através das quais se manifesta, ou deve se manifestar, a cidadania da União. Anthony Giddens, ao analisar o processo de legitimação da integração em meio à crise de confiança que acompanha a incerteza nos planos político e econômico, aposta na estreita relação entre cidadania e garantia de direitos sociais como forma de revitalização do projeto europeu (Giddens, 2007, p. 169).

A concepção da garantia de direitos sociais como parte integrante da cidadania está fortemente atrelada ao conceito de cidadania nos Estados modernos. Segundo Seyla Benhabib, são três os componentes que caracterizam essa cidadania: I) a identidade coletiva dos cidadãos, ancorada na língua, na religião, na etnicidade, na história comum e na memória; II) os direitos associados à participação política; e III) a garantia de direitos sociais. Esses aspectos, argumenta a autora, devem ser encarados, no contexto atual de instituições cosmopolitas, como realidades desagregadas umas das outras. A participação política na UE, por exemplo, não pressupõe uma identidade coletiva como tradicionalmente pensada (Benhabib, 2005, p. 675).

O terceiro elemento apresentado por Benhabib tem aporte importante na obra do historiador T. H. Marshall, que, ao estudar a evolução do conceito de cidadania, tendo por base o exemplo da Inglaterra, firmou a tese de que é somente através da suplementação dos direitos civis e políticos com direitos sociais que grandes parcelas da sociedade adquirem cidadania plena. Para o autor, as disparidades de classe, geradas pela distribuição desigual da riqueza, não poderiam ser equalizadas apenas pela igualdade perante a lei e pelo direito à participação política. Direitos sociais, como o direito à educação, seriam, desse modo, essenciais para a inclusão do indivíduo na comunidade política (Marshall, 1950).

Pensando os direitos sociais no plano da integração, Giddens rejeita a interpretação minimalista sobre a política social, segundo a qual os Estados-membros retém controle quase completo sobre os sistemas de bem-estar nacionais. Para o autor, existem variadas formas por meio das quais decisões tomadas pelas instituições europeias podem influenciar esses sistemas. De fato, a UE tem legislado em matérias importantes, como direitos laboral, medidas anti-discriminação e seguridade social. A agenda proposta pelo Tratado de Lisboa, por sua vez, demonstra uma preocupação crescente com as disparidades sociais e econômicas entre Estados-membros e entre regiões (Giddens, 2007, p. 164-171).

A realidade da integração nos últimos anos, entretanto, tem colocado em xeque essa perspectiva de que a União pode e tem por objetivo exercer o papel de provedora de direitos sociais. No âmbito do TJUE, dois casos emblemáticos parecem sugerir que uma agenda social, cujo cerne seja a proteção do cidadão da União em casos de violação de seus direitos sociais, não serve mais de norte para a atuação das instituições da UE.

O primeiro caso, julgado pela corte em 2014, gerou grande repercussão na mídia, em grande parte por conta da campanha do então primeiro-ministro britânico David Cameron contra migrantes chamados por ele de *benefit tourists*, ou "turistas sociais". Elizabeth Dano, cidadã romena de 25 anos de idade, e seu filho, Florin, residiam na Alemanha. Após terem pedido de assistência social negado pelo centro de trabalho local, buscaram o judiciário alemão para reclamar seus direitos. Apresentado diante do TJUE, o caso teve o seguinte desfecho: a corte entendeu que o Estado alemão somente estaria obrigado, nos termos da Diretiva 2004/38/CE da UE, a prover assistência financeira a residentes não nacionais que estivessem no país a mais de três meses e que estivessem empregados. Elizabeth Dano, por não ter um emprego, não tinha direito à assistência que havia pleiteado (COURT OF JUSTICE OF THE EUROPEAN UNION, 2014). Assim, ficou claro a partir do "caso Dano" que um Estado-membro pode rejeitar pedidos de assistência social feitos por cidadãos europeus que não tem intenção de trabalhar ou que não possuem condições de se sustentarem.

No ano seguinte, chegou ao tribunal o "caso Alimonovic". Quatro membros de uma mesma família, todos detentores de nacionalidade sueca e residentes na Alemanha, também buscaram o judiciário alemão, mas dessa vez por terem a assistência social não renovada por uma autoridade local. Diferentemente do "caso Dano", duas mulheres da família Alimonovic haviam trabalhado temporariamente e, portanto, haviam sido qualificadas para o recebimento de assistência no passado. A corte europeia mais uma vez julgou no sentido de eximir o Estado da obrigação de garantir direitos sociais. Aqui, a argumentação partiu do princípio de que, após seis meses desempregadas, mãe e filha já não teriam mais direito de tratamento igual no tocante à assistência social (COURT OF JUSTICE OF THE EUROPEAN UNION, 2015).

As repercussões da cidadania no processo de integração sul-americano

Como visto, os desdobramentos fáticos dão a medida do grau de dificuldade de verificação real das promessas da noção de cidadania na União Europeia. Cabe apontar, contudo, que o rosário de limitações da prática cidadã no bloco europeu apresenta uma nítida diferença de tom e de alcance se comparado às vicissitudes da integração sul-americana. Levando-se em conta a por ora insipiência das experiências citadinas do Mercosul e da Unasul, o projeto europeu de integração ganha alento, como veremos na sequência.

Sem sombra de dúvidas, o caso do Mercosul corresponde a um emblemático exemplo das dificuldades da participação da sociedade civil nos arranjos regionais contemporâneos. Desde seus movimentos instituintes, a integração mercosulina não foi caracterizada por uma franca abertura à participação dos atores sociais – opção que pode ser entendida como uma tentativa dos governos nacionais de manter o monopólio decisório na condução dos destinos do bloco.

Ainda que progressivamente seja possível reconhecer o advento de canais de diálogo entre a burocracia do bloco e a sociedade civil (Martins, Silva, 2011), fato é que há um descolamento histórico entre as instâncias tomadoras de decisão e a base social do projeto de integração (com a exceção pouco vigorosa dos temas envolvendo mão-de-obra e condições trabalhistas). Assim, é possível notar que iniciativas atreladas às diretrizes de um "Mercosul Social" ou de um "Mercosul Participativo" apenas podem ser identificadas a partir da segunda metade da década passada.[6]

Neste contexto, não é de se estranhar as dificuldades e a crise vocacional pela qual passa o Parlamento do Mercosul, ainda sem conseguir ter generalizado a eleição direta dos parlamentares como via de acesso para os representantes oriundos de todos os Estados do bloco (algo ilustrado pelo caso brasileiro). Mesmo que em algum momento próximo haja a exclusividade do voto direto como critério único para a composição da casa parlamentar, não são animadoras as perspectivas do Parlamento do Mercosul conseguir angariar um papel central na produção normativa, na formulação das políticas e, de forma mais ampla, na condução dos destinos do bloco.

Cabe destacar o conjunto de iniciativas que de alguma forma são reconhecidas como tendo pontos de contato com a noção de uma cidadania do Mercosul. Neste rol, é possível mencionar a criação do Acordo sobre Residência para Nacionais dos Estados Partes do Mercado Comum do Sul, a implementação do Acordo Multilateral de Seguridade Social (em 2005) e as facilidades no fluxo fronteiriço de nacionais do bloco. Também há de se considerar o Plano de Ação para efetivação da cidadania mercosulina (Estatuto da Cidadania) por ocasião da terceira década do Tratado de Assunção, nos moldes apresentados pela Declaração Sócio-laboral do Mercosul. Derradeiramente, cabe listar os parcos espaços de participação cidadã no bloco: a) as Cúpulas Sociais do Mercosul (caixa de ressonância da sociedade civil mercosulina, que se reúne semestralmente desde 2006); b) a Unidade de Apoio à participação social (em funcionamento desde 2013) e c) os foros participativos, como o Foro consultivo Econômico-Social e os outros foros temáticos específicos (como, por exemplo, o relacionado às questões de agricultura familiar).

---

6 Como demonstram, por exemplo, o advento do Instituto Social do Mercosul e a Declaração de Princípios do Mercosul Social, ambos de 2007,

Ainda que várias das ações listadas acima (como a criação das cúpulas sociais do bloco e a prolação do Estatuto da Cidadania) expressem uma tentativa de fortalecer um viés integrativo que não esteja marcado pela exclusividade da dimensão econômica (Martins, 2014, p.143), fato é que a apropriação política do bloco pela sua base social não parece plausível em um futuro próximo. Certamente não serão poucos os esforços necessários para retirar a cidadania mercosulina da esfera do possível, outorgando-lhe algum nível de correspondência fática.

Da dupla de exemplos tratada neste item, o caso relativo à Unasul consubstancia a tentativa mais recente de estruturar uma cidadania regional no continente. Reconhecida como a grande iniciativa do regionalismo pós-liberal sul-americano (Riggirozzi, 2010), a organização pretende adensar os laços continentais por uma via que não tome a dimensão econômica como motor e principal veio. Tal constatação pode ser comprovada na diversidade de canais institucionais existentes na Unasul, contemplando desde energia e defesa até cultura e saúde.[7]

Como não poderia deixar de ser, o tema da democracia tem um papel central na formatação, no funcionamento e nos propósitos da instituição. Isto pode ser comprovado com a incorporação de uma cláusula democrática no marco jurídico da organização (efetivada por meio do Protocolo Adicional ao Tratado Constitutivo, assinado em Georgetown em 2010) e na ação da Unasul em diversas situações, desde o acompanhamento de processos eleitorais nacionais até ações conciliatórias em contextos de ruptura institucional de Estados-membros (como o Paraguai, 2012).

No tocante à questão da cidadania, ainda que haja previsão normativa da participação cidadã no tratado constitutivo do bloco (vide os artigos 2º, 3º e 18), não houve grande repercussão concreta desde então – salvo o clamor pela consolidação da cidadania sul-americana presente na Reunião Ordinária de Chefes de Estado e de Governo da UNASUL de

7 Mesmo que a chamada "burocratização" da organização seja criticada e errática, ela demonstra a diversidade de propósitos da Unasul e serve de base estrutural para o aprofundamento e autonomização do processo de integração.

2012, a existência de algumas comissões temáticas afeitas a temas pertinentes e o advento do Foro de participação cidadã da Unasul (com primeira edição realizada em Cochabamba, no ano de 2014). Esta escassez de iniciativas mais vigorosas documenta as dificuldades para o estabelecimento da cidadania unasulina (Cunha, 2015) e demonstra inclusive a falta de uma clareza de abordagem do bloco sobre o tema, especialmente no tocante à abrangência e à repercussão institucional.

Conclusão

As vicissitudes na afirmação da cidadania para além do Estado Nacional são das mais diversas. Uma comparação meramente horizontal envolvendo as iniciativas citadinas da União Europeia, do Mercosul e da Unasul já deixa tal afirmação patente, como demonstrado por este trabalho. Mais que isso, nos três casos listados é possível notar que a promessa de construção de um liame de legitimidade entre o processo de integração e a respectiva base social apenas tem caráter discursivo e formal – estando longe de cumprir o seu potencial democrático.

Extrapolando tal constatação, se as noções de cidadania analisadas carecem de alcance material e podem ser compreendidas como exclusivas peças discursivas, abre-se a perspectiva de se considerar a interação entre direito internacional e democracia também como apenas artifício retórico. Mais do que evidenciar as dificuldades de legitimidade dos processos de integração, a cidadania dos blocos regionais seria capaz de sumarizar os limites do direito internacional enquanto ferramenta da governança global democrática. Note que a anomia da ação cidadã nos casos estudados implica a impossibilidade de participação efetiva dos cidadãos na produção normativa das instituições regionais, inabilitando a verificação por ora de um verdadeiro direito democrático. Contudo, há de se reconhecer que a democracia tende a cada vez mais ser considerada um princípio de direito internacional, o que eventualmente pode tanto auxiliar na promoção de uma ordem global mais justa, quanto servir de amparo para ações controversas – alicerçadas em um pretenso "direito de intervenção pró-democrática" ou em uma fictícia "responsabilidade de democratizar".

Referências

AMARAL JÚNIOR, Alberto do. *Curso de Direito Internacional.* São Paulo: Atlas, 2012.

BENHABIB, Seyla. Borders. Boundaries, and Citizenship. *Political Science and Politics*, v. 38, n. 4, p. 673-677, out. 2005.

BESSON, Samantha. Theorizing the sources of International Law. In: BESSON, Samantha; TASIOLAS, John (org). *The Philosophy of International Law.* Oxford: Oxford University, 2010.

BOGDANDY, Armin von; VENZKE, Ingo. In Whose Name? An Investigation of International Courts' Public Authority and Its Democratic Justification. *The European Journal of International Law*, v. 23 n. 1, p. 7-41, 2012.

BOGDANDY, Armin von. The Democratic Legitimacy of International Courts: A Conceptual Framework. *Theoretical Inquiries in Law*, v.14, n.36, pp. 361-379, 2013.

BUMMEL, Andreas. Towards a Global Democratic Revolution A Global Parliament and the Transformation of the World Order. *Cadmus*, v. 1 n.2, p.103-109, 2011.

CARVALHO, D. *Déficit Democrático na União Europeia.* Tese de doutorado apresentado ao Departamento de Direito Internacional da Faculdade de Direito do Largo de São Francisco da Universidade de São Paulo, 2012.

CARVALHO, Daniel Campos de; JUBILUT, Liliana Lyra. Nova fronteira de legitimidade? A arquitetura jurídico-política da Unasul e os pilares do novo regionalismo. In: MAZZUOLI, Valerio de Oliveira; GOMES, Eduardo Biacchi (orgs.). *Direito da Integração Regional.* São Paulo: Saraiva, 2015.

CARVALHO, José Murilo de. *Cidadania no Brasil: O Longo Caminho*. Rio de Janeiro: Civilização Brasileira, 2008.

CHALMERS, Damien; DAVIES, Gareth; MONTI, Giorgio. *European Union Law:* Texts and Materials. 3. ed. Cambridge: Cambridge University Press, 2014.

CLARK, I. *Legitimacy in International Society*. Oxford: Oxford University Press, 2005.

______. *International Legitimacy and World Society.* Oxford: Oxford University Press, 2007.

COURT OF JUSTICE OF THE EUROPEAN UNION. *PRESS RELEASE No 146/14*. Luxembourg, 11 nov. 2014. Disponível em: < http://curia.europa.eu/jcms/upload/docs/application/pdf/2014-11/cp140146en.pdf >. Acesso em: 30 mar. 2014.

______. *PRESS RELEADE No 101/15*. Luxembourg, 15 set. 2015. Disponível em: < http://curia.europa.eu/jcms/upload/docs/application/pdf/2015-09/cp150101en.pdf >. Acesso em: 30 mar. 2017.

CUNHA, J. S. Fagundes. Unasul e a cidadania cosmopolita. In: MAZZUOLI, Valerio de O.; GOMES, Eduardo B.. (Org.). *Direito da Integração Regional*. São Paulo: Saraiva, 2015, p. 579-589.

DINH, Nguyen *Quoc;* DAILLIER, Patrick; PELLET. Alain. *Direito internacional público*. Lisboa: Fundação Calouste Gulbenkian, 2003.

DOBSON, L. (2006), *Supranational Citizenship,* Manchester: Manchester University Press.

EUROPEAN COMISSION. *EU introduces more efficient monitoring of drinking water for better protection of public health.* Brussels, 28 out. 2015. Disponível em: < http://europa.eu/rapid/press-release_IP-15-5940_en.htm>. Acesso em: 30 mar. 2017.

FRANCK, T. Legitimacy in the international system. *American Journal of International Law*, v. 82, 1988.

______. *The Power of Legitimacy among Nations*. Oxford: Oxford University Press, 1990.

______. The Emerging Right to Democratic Governance. *The American Journal of International Law*, v. 86, n. 1, pp. 46-91, jan., 1992.

FOX, Gregory H.; ROTH, Brad R. Democracy and international law. *Review of International Studies*, v. 27, p. 327–352, 2001.

GIDDENS, Anthony. *Europe in the Global Age*. Cambridge: Polity Press, 2007.

______. *Turbulent and Mighty Continent*: What Future for Europe? Cambridge: Polity Press, 2014.

HABERMAS, Jurgen. Mudança estrutural da esfera pública, Rio de Janeiro: Tempo Brasileiro, 2003.

______. A Constelação Pós-Nacional, São Paulo: Littera Mundi, 2001.

HIX, Simon; HØYLAND, Bjørn. Empowerment of the European Parliament. *Annual Review of Political Science*, Londres, v. 16, p. 171-189, mai. 2013. Disponível em: < http://personal.lse.ac.uk/hix/Working_Papers/Hix-Hoyland-annurev-polisci-2013.pdf> Acesso em: 30 mar. 2017.

HIX, Simon; NOURY, Abdul G.; ROLAND, Gérard. *Democratic Politics in the European Parliament*. Nova York: Cambridge University Press, 2007.

HOBSBAWM, Eric J. *A era dos extremos*: o breve século XX: 1914-1991. Tradução: Marcos Santarrita. São Paulo: Companhia das Letras, 1995.

KENNEDY, David. The move to Institutions. *Cardozo Law Review*, v.8, n.5, abr.1987, p.841 -988.

KUMM, M. The legitimacy of international law: a constitutionalist framework of analysis. *European Journal of International Law*, v. 15, n. 5, Nov. 2004, pp. 907-931.

MARSHALL, T. H. *Citizenship and Social Class*. Cambridge: Cambridge University Press, 1950.

MARTINS, J. R. V. MERCOSUL: a dimensão social e participativa da integração regional In W. A. DESIDERÁ NETO (ed.), *O Brasil e Novas Dimensões do Regionalismo*, Rio de Janeiro: IPEA, pp. 101-144, 2014.

MAYERFELD, Jamie. The Democratic Legacy of the International Criminal Court. *The Fletcher Forum of Worl Affairs*, v.28, n.2, p.147-156, summer 2004.

MARZOCCHI, Ottavio. *O direito de petição*. Disponível em: < http://www.europarl.europa.eu/atyourservice/pt/displayFtu.html?ftuId=FTU_2.1.4.html>. Acesso em: 30 mar. 2017.

MORAVCSIK, Andrew. Is there a "democratic déficit in world politics? *Government and Opposition* , v.39 , n.2, p. 336-393, 2004.

MOREIRA, Felipe K. *Direito e Legitimidade na Sociedade Internacional.* Boa Vista: Editora da Universidade Federal de Roraima, 2012.

NOVAK, Petr. *Iniciativa de Cidadania Europeia*. Disponível em: < http://www.europarl.europa.eu/atyourservice/pt/displayFtu.html?ftuId=FTU_2.1.5.html >. Acesso em: 30 mar. 2017.

PAULUS, Andreas L.. The International Legal System as a Constitution. In DUNOFF, Jeffrey; TRACHTMAN, Joel P.. *Ruling the World? Constitutionalism, International Law and Global Governance.* Cambridge: Cambridge Press, 2009 , pp. 69-112.

PETERSEN, Niels. *The Principle of Democratic Teleology in International Law*. Bonn: Preprints of the Max Planck Institute for Research on Collective Goods: 2008.

PILDES, Richard H. Supranational Courts and the Law of Democracy: The European Court Of Human Rights. *Public Law & Legal Theory Research Paper Series*, Working Paper n. 16-43, 2016.

POMOELL, Jutta. *European Union Citizenship in Focus*. Helsinki: Forum Juris, 2000.

RIGGIROZZI, Pia. Region, Regioness and Regionalism in Latin America. Towards a new Synthesis. *LATN Working Paper*, n° 130, abril/2010.

SCHÖPFLIN, György. *RELATÓRIO sobre a Iniciativa de Cidadania Europeia*. Estrasburgo: Comissão dos Assuntos Constitucionais, 2015. Disponível em: < http://www.europarl.europa.eu/sides/

getDoc.do?pubRef=-//EP//NONSGML+REPORT+A8-2015-0284+0+DOC+PDF+V0//PT>. Acesso em: 30 mar. 2017.

TURNER, B. S. *Citizenship and social theory*. London: Sage, 1993.

UNASUL. *Tratado Constitutivo da UNASUL*. 2008. Disponível em: <http://docs.unasursg.org/alfresco/d/d/workspace/SpacesStore/c45e27d4-44c2-49fe-9027-d98b3a1d7979/UNASUR-CO-JEG-TRA-08-0001.pdf>.

______. *Protocolo Adicional ao Tratado Constitutivo da UNASUL sobre Compromisso com a Democracia*. 2010. Disponível em:

<www.itamaraty.gov.br/temas/america-do-sul-e-integracao-regional/unasul/protocolo-adicional-ao-tratado-constitutivo-da-unasul-sobre-compromisso-com-a-democracia Protocolo Adicional ao Tratado Constitutivo da UNASUL sobre Compromisso com a Democracia>.

VALENZUELA, O. I. S. "Hacia la construcción de un concepto de ciudadania en UNASUR". In P. L. A. MUTIZ, *Derecho de la Integración – Unión de Naciones Suramericas*. Bogotá: U. los Libertadores, 2011, p.271-306.

VALLINA, Ángela. *Relatório sobre as atividades da Comissão de Petições em 2015*. Estrasburgo: Comissão de Petições, 2016. Disponível em: < http://www.europarl.europa.eu/sides/getDoc.do?pubRef=-//EP//NONSGML+REPORT+A8-2016-0366+0+DOC+PDF+V0//PT >. Acesso em: 30 mar. 2017.

VIDMAR, Jure. *Democratic Statehood in International Law: The Emergence of New States in Post-Cold War Practice*. Oxford – Portland: Bloomsbury Publishing, 2013.

WEILER, J. H. H. The Geology of International Law – Governance, Democracy and Legitimacy. *ZaöRV*, n. 64, 2004.

WOUTERS, Jan; MEESTER, Bart De; RYNGAERT Cedric. Democracy and International Law. *Leuven Interdisciplinary Research Group on International Agreements and Development*, Working Paper n.5, 2004.

A hibridização das Forças Armadas no Brasil: as missões policializadas e as debilidades democráticas e estratégicas

David Succi Júnior
Samuel Alves Soares

Introdução

O presente texto tem como objeto o controle democrático do uso da violência, a ser debatido a partir da análise do uso do instrumento militar brasileiro no âmbito doméstico. O emprego da força pelos Estados, quer no âmbito doméstico ou na esfera externa, é questão clássica de análise e da ação no campo da política, fundamentalmente porque este uso, de um ponto de vista normativo-democrático, precisa ser regulamentado e mesmo limitado.

O tema transpassa séculos e encontra guarida nas definições políticas da antiga Roma, ao estabelecer o limite do Rubicão para a desmobilização das Legiões, uma forma de proteção quanto ao uso destas forças militares como uma ameaça interna. A questão permanece candente, e em países com fundamentos democráticos frágeis, é como se as forças militares tivessem sido criadas exatamente para atravessarem o Rubicão (Meynaud, 1961). Este quadro é peculiar a países latino-americanos em distintos momentos históricos, quer porque tais forças se apresentavam como modernizadoras em situações consideradas impeditivas do progresso, quer no auge da Guerra Fria, com a internalização do inimigo.

A análise é orientada por três níveis. No nível internacional-hemisférico – aqui considerados os países da América do Norte, Central e do Sul - residem as postulações dos Estados Unidos para uma definição do papel das forças armadas na América Latina e os impulsos derivados do sistema internacional. Em outro nível, regional sul-americano, as formulações para o uso da força militar advindas da criação da União das Nações Sul-Americanas e do Conselho de Defesa Sul-Americano e, por fim, no âmbito doméstico, de modo a indicar como foram estabelecidos os critérios formais e efetivos do emprego das forças armadas no âmbito interno.

O termo missão militar, segundo Aguilera (2010), pode ser entendido de duas formas. Do ponto de vista tático, representa uma manobra operacional, desenvolvida geralmente em situação de combate, com o a finalidade de alcançar um objetivo militar. Conceitualmente, refere-se às funções atribuídas ao instrumento militar em um marco histórico e social específico. O presente trabalho tem como foco as missões militares nos termos da segunda definição apresentada, mais especificamente a designação do instrumento castrense para tarefas de segurança pública.

O espaço de atuação das Forças Armadas é tradicionalmente balizado pelas figuras dos estados polêmico e agonístico (Freund, 1995). Estes são diferenciados com base na forma de resolução de conflitos. No primeiro caso, as partes não se encontram sob um mesmo ordenamento jurídico, considerando-se mutuamente como inimigos. Neste espaço, o uso da força visando a letalidade é considerado legítimo, uma vez que a incerteza e o risco à existência constituem uma constante nas relações entre os atores. Para Bobbio (2003), a construção do Estado moderno representa a passagem do estado polêmico para o agonístico. Neste segundo âmbito, busca-se eliminar o emprego da violência como instrumento de resolução de conflitos. As partes reconhecem-se como adversários, como iguais que se submetem às mesmas regras, e não mais inimigos, cuja eliminação é objetivada. Com base nesta diferenciação, são criados e mantidos instrumentos de força com finalidades diversas: Forças Armadas para o emprego da violência letal no âmbito externo, com o escopo de garantir a sobrevivência da unidade política; e forças policiais, cuja atuação restringe-se às fronteiras nacionais, com a finalidade de garantir a integridade física e moral dos cidadãos, sob um arcabouço legal específico.

Nas perspectivas convencionais das Relações Internacionais, é justamente a construção do espaço agonístico, em oposição a um espaço polêmico, que caracteriza o funcionamento da política internacional. Tem-se, portanto, o Estado, caracterizado pelo monopólio legítimo da violência, sob o qual assenta-se certa univocidade jurídica, em contraposição ao sistema internacional anárquico, no qual a guerra é iminente (Waltz, 2002). Neste quadro, como definido por Raymond Aron (2002), o militar e o diplomata consistem nos atores centrais responsáveis pelas gramáticas através das quais o Estado movimenta-se no ambiente externo, a estratégia e a diplomacia.

Apesar de a construção do instrumento militar estar tradicionalmente vinculada à ideia de interno e externo, as Forças Armadas na América Latina assumiram historicamente as mais diversas atribuições, desde o desenvolvimento nacional até a manutenção da ordem institucional e social, sendo a onda de ditaduras que se propagou nesta região entre as décadas de 1960 e 1980, o momento de maior penetração dos meios castrenses nas instâncias estatais (Rouquié, 1982).

Desde os processos de transição dos regimes de exceção para a democracia, a atuação dos militares em atividades internas – que não se limitam à segurança pública – constitui uma preocupação recorrente na literatura especializada. Há, naquele momento, a necessidade de inserir e institucionalizar as atividades militares em um regime democrático (D'Araujo, 2000). O debate neste contexto, e que ainda predomina no campo de estudo das relações civis-militares, refere-se ao controle das Forças Armadas pelos civis em termos institucionais. O principal conceito utilizado nas análises é o de controle objetivo, cunhado por Samuel Huntington (1996), o qual consiste em garantir a maximização do poder civil em relação ao dos militares. De acordo com o autor, o controle objetivo é construído através da profissionalização das forças militares, propiciando uma condição na qual os mesmos respondem instrumentalmente às diretrizes políticas do governo civil, ficando clara a delimitação entre a esfera de atuação do líder político civil e do chefe militar profissional.

As especificidades históricas da América do Sul são base para as primeiras críticas a esta concepção. Como apontam Lopez (2001) e Sain (1999), por ser produzido com base no caso estadunidense, a subordinação dos militares ao poder político no modelo huntingtoniano constitui um dado. A possibilidade de insubordinação está descartada. Por outro lado, Sain argumenta que Huntington tem como foco central os militares, deixando de lado o papel do governante civil. Defende que para analisar a realidade sul-americana faz-se necessário questionar não apenas a vontade de subordinação dos militares, mas também a vontade civil de controle ou direção política.

Nesta literatura, portanto, a eliminação do uso da força militar no interior do Estado, e o rechaço à ideia de inimigo interno, pelas quais passava a busca pela consolidação dos regimes democráticos da região, eram associadas diretamente ao controle político das instituições castrenses. Havia uma relação pressuposta entre o controle civil sobre os militares e a contenção do uso da força letal do Estado contra seus próprios cidadãos. Zaverucha (2005) considera a recorrente atuação das Forças Armadas em missões relativas à ordem e à segurança interna no Brasil como resultado de um processo de transição para a democracia imperfeito, cuja incompletude refere-se a uma falha no controle político das Forças Armadas, uma vez que, o fim do regime autoritário no país foi intensamente controlado pelos próprios militares.

Ainda que não se deva desconsiderar os espaços de autonomia resguardados pelos militares após o fim dos regimes autoritários na região, assim como sua incompatibilidade com as instituições democráticas (Mathias; Guzzi 2010), ao longo das últimas décadas, as instituições relativas ao controle civil sobre as forças militares, como o Ministério da Defesa e a atribuição da autoridade suprema sobre as Forças Armadas ao chefe do poder Executivo, difundiram-se pelos países da região. Estas, porém, não foram necessariamente acompanhadas pela redução do emprego do instrumento de letalidade do Estado (Pion-Berlin, 2005).

Os países da América Latina possuem uma longa tradição pretoriana que aponta como inimigos do Estado aqueles entes reconhecidos nas fronteiras internas – *os inimigos da ordem* – aos quais volta-se a atuação do poder armado, como sucedeu durante a Guerra Fria (Oliveira, Soares, 2000). No caso brasileiro, a definição constitucional de garantia da Lei e da Ordem quer significar, antes de mais nada, a manutenção de determinada ordem em um sistema político elitista e autoritário. O foco estabelecido na Carta de 1988 não visava, em seu artigo 142, a segurança pública ou o papel de guardas de fronteira, e sim a última reserva que o sistema poderia contar para evitar mudanças significativas. Um deslizamento jurídico ocorre para o artigo 144, este sim voltado para a esfera da segurança pública.

Alguns autores defendem que, mesmo não constituindo um fenômeno novo, verifica-se nos últimos anos um processo de expansão das missões militares (Battaglino, 2015). Observa-se uma intensa utilização dos meios castrenses em tarefas de segurança pública na região. Entre 2012 e 2013, na América Latina e Caribe, foram realizadas, por militares, 488 mil operações de segurança interna. Em 2014, 94% das Forças Armadas da região realizaram de forma regular algum tipo que atividade vinculada à segurança pública. Entre as ações desempenhadas pelas Forças Armadas estão: repressão e prevenção de atividades criminosas; patrulhamento; contenção de revoltas e manifestações populares; proteção das fronteiras contra delitos transnacionais, em especial o narcotráfico; e em alguns casos o controle de áreas penitenciárias (Donadio, 2014; 2016). A naturalização de práticas, treinamentos e armamentos militares para lidar com temáticas de segurança interna é considerado um processo de militarização da mesma.

O Brasil é, nesta esfera, um caso emblemático. Segundo o periódico Estado de S. Paulo (2017), nos últimos dez anos foram realizadas

67 operações de Garantia da Lei e da Ordem (GLO) em 17 estados do país. As atividades desempenhadas foram: auxílio ao desenvolvimento de eleições; segurança de reuniões de autoridades de Estado; segurança de eventos esportivos; e segurança pública. Entre 2005 e 2015, dos informes do Observatório Sul-Americano de Defesa e Forças Armadas referentes a missões militares, 46% estavam relacionados a atividades de segurança interna (Succi Junior, 2016). Neste âmbito, uma característica singular do Brasil em relação aos outros países da América do Sul, foi a criação, em 2005, do Centro de Instrução de Operações de Garantia da Lei e da Ordem, subordinado à 11° Brigada de Infantaria Leve – Garantia da Lei e da Ordem, com o objetivo de desenvolver doutrina e adestrar militares para o cumprimento de missões GLO, além de cooperar com os estabelecimentos de ensino das Forças Terrestres e das demais Forças Singulares e Auxiliares, entre as quais está a Polícia Militar.

Nos últimos anos, analistas passaram a questionar a relação direta estabelecida pela bibliografia especializada entre o controle institucional das Forças Armadas e a limitação do uso da força. Neste sentido, Levy (2016) defende a diferenciação entre controle dos militares e controle da militarização[1]. Ainda que os conceitos não estejam direcionados à região sul-americana, seu modelo analítico pode ser adequadamente utilizado para pensar o caso em questão. O autor afirma que controle dos militares refere-se à capacidade das instituições civis de determinar os limites da atuação militar em questões que tenham resultado político, como produção de doutrina, recursos e mobilização. O segundo diz respeito aos

1 Levy (2016) define militarização como o processo através do qual há um incremento do militarismo, o qual é, por sua vez, definido como uma perspectiva na qual a guerra e a preparação para a guerra são vistas como normal ou desejável nas atividades sociais. Para fins do presente trabalho, como indicado anteriormente, militarização será compreendida como a naturalização do emprego de práticas, treinamento e armamento militar para lidar com conflitos de determinada natureza.

mecanismos de legitimação do uso da força, o que envolve o discurso político e a aceitação pública.

Considera-se então, que a redução da utilização dos instrumentos de violência estatal não se encontra apenas na institucionalização de mecanismos de controle dos militares, mas em grande medida no processo político de legitimação de seu emprego. Nesta perspectiva, portanto, a problemática da inserção das instituições castrenses no espaço democrático desloca-se do debate procedimental, característico da concepção liberal de Schumpeter (1952), para uma lógica da democracia enquanto participação e debate público. Não se parte, porém, da premissa, característica das teorias liberais das Relações Internacionais, de que a democracia representativa e o debate público corroboram necessária e automaticamente na restrição ou negação do uso da força como forma resolução de conflito. Defende-se que a mobilização de forças militares para lidar com determinado conflito – no caso específico do presente trabalho, o emprego das Forças Armadas para atividades de segurança pública – deve ser visto como uma decisão política, ou seja, como uma escolha possível entre um amplo espectro de concepções concorrentes. Escolha esta, que se fundamenta em uma compreensão específica do papel da violência letal, das características que se atribui ao alvo da mesma e da natureza da ameaça que este representa.

Partindo da perspectiva de Robert Cox (1986), para o qual toda teoria é produzida por alguém com algum propósito, e da premissa de que a ação está pautada pelo modo em que se compreende a realidade, busca-se no presente trabalho, desenvolver uma análise crítica do modo em que se teoriza – e consequentemente legitima-se – a atuação militar em segurança pública no Brasil.

Na bibliografia analisada, foram identificadas duas grandes lógicas explicativas, ainda que os autores não se identifiquem explicitamente com as mesmas: o racionalismo e o construtivismo crítico. Estas são aplicadas aos três níveis de análise anteriormente indicados: internacional-hemisférico, regional sul-americano e doméstico. Defende-se que a perspectiva racionalista, por um lado, transforma o processo decisório em uma questão técnica. Por outro, estabelece um regime de inevitabilidade, no qual não há a possibilidade de uma ação alternativa. Elimina-se assim a possibilidade do debate público. O construtivismo crítico, por sua vez, amplia o espectro de escolhas possíveis. Uma vez que a realidade, nesta abordagem, não constitui um aspecto externo ao indivíduo, evidenciam-se as possibilidades de mudança a partir da agência. Assim, a legitimidade decisória encontra-se na esfera do político, e não do técnico, tornando-se passível de questionamento.

Lógicas Explicativas

Tanto a abordagem teórica racionalista, quanto a construtivista, não constituem perspectivas monolíticas, são heterogêneas (Fearon, Wendt,1991). O racionalismo será tratado nos termos em que se estabelece nas vertentes neorrealistas das Relações Internacionais (Waltz,2002; Merasheimer, 2001), enquanto o construtivismo é entendido nos termos postos por Guzzini (2013). Para os fins do presente trabalho, as perspectivas serão diferenciadas em três dimensões: ontologia; epistemologia; e teoria da ação.

Ontologicamente, o racionalismo, partindo de bases positivistas, considera a realidade como um dado externo ao indivíduo, cuja existência independe da consciência. Do ponto de vista epistemológico, defende a clara separação entre o objeto e o observador. Neste sentido, considera possível uma observação objetiva e neutra da realidade. Diante deste quadro, imputa aos atores a lógica do *homo economicus*, na qual estes, sob sólidas bases racionais, são capazes de observar a realidade objetivamente, e calcular a ação necessária para maximizar seus interesses. A ação racional corresponde, portanto, à adaptação a uma realidade autoevidente a fim de alcançar objetivos previamente estabelecidos. Deste modo, há apenas uma linha de ação válida e possível, diante da lógica das coisas, sendo qualquer desvio uma falha perante a realidade (Habermas, 2011). A ação adquire contornos de inevitabilidade.

A perspectiva construtivista, por sua vez, em sua vertente crítica, rompe com os pressupostos ontológicos e epistemológicos positivistas. Nega a existência de uma realidade externa aos indivíduos, por considerar que as normas de funcionamento societal são constituídas a partir da interação entre os indivíduos. O mundo social, portanto, não constitui uma realidade autoevidente, mas uma construção social, percebida pelos atores como objetiva (Berger, Luckmann, 2009). Por outro lado, rejeitam o pressuposto de que há uma clara separação entre aquele que observa e aquilo que é observado, negando a pretensão de neutralidade. A construção do conhecimento acerca do que se observa é interpretativa, e está pautada pela realidade social na qual se encontra o observador (Guzzini, 2013). Deste modo, a ação é explicada a partir da lógica do *homo sociologicus*, ou seja, age-se na realidade com base no modo em que se compreende a mesma. Uma vez que tanto a realidade quanto o conhecimento acerca da mesma não são estáticos, há possibilidades de de mudança. Uma linha de ação representa apenas uma escolha específica, ou a adequação a um conjunto de certas ideias compartilhadas, uma possibilidade entre tantas outras. Há assim, uma constituição mútua entre agente e estrutura, sendo a dimensão ideacional fundamental para a constituição do real. Deve-se evidenciar o aspecto crítico, que estabelece uma relação íntima entre a produção do conhecimento e as relações de poder.

Busca-se, na próxima seção, indicar as principais variáveis explicativas indicadas pela literatura para a compreensão do emprego das Forças Armadas sul-americanas em missões policiais, analisando-as com base nas duas perspectivas teóricas aqui apresentadas.

A dimensão internacional-hemisférica

Esta dimensão explicativa está vinculada às mudanças na dinâmica de funcionamento do sistema internacional decorrentes do fim da Guerra Fria. Com o fim das tensões Leste-Oeste, observa-se a intensificação dos processos de globalização, em especial da economia, o que estabeleceu uma maior porosidade das fronteiras nacionais e o aumento das atividades transnacionais. Nye (2009) defende que houve uma complexificação em relação às perspectivas convencionais dos três elementos centrais para qualquer teorização sobre a política internacional – os atores; os meios; e os fins.

Do ponto de vista da agenda de segurança internacional, há, por um lado, a dissolução do inimigo soviético, no qual se pautavam todas as hipóteses de conflito, e, por outro o surgimento da ideia de novas ameaças. Ainda antes do término da Guerra Fria, a Comissão Palme, vinculada à Organização das Nações Unidas (ONU), e presidida por Olof Palme, foi criada com a incumbência de identificar as ameaças que poderiam surgir a partir da mudança que estavam em processo. O informe, resultante dos trabalhos da Comissão, indicava que às ameaças convencionais, caracterizadas pelos conflitos interestatais, em que Forças Armadas nacionais enfrentam-se, somam-se "novas ameaças", de caráter multidimensional e não-estatal. O espectro das problemáticas indicadas é amplo, passando de questões que envolvem o uso da força como terrorismo, tráfico de drogas e armas, até problemáticas sociais e econômicas, como intensificação do fluxos migratórios e de refugiados, miséria e danos ambientais.

Com base nestas perspectivas, pode-se indicar duas consequências. A primeira é a intensificação das ações constabulares, ou seja, das atividades que, quando exigem o uso da força, encontram-se entre as esferas de ação policial (interna) e militar (externa) (Medeiros, 2010). A segunda consiste na securitização e militarização de questões sociais, econômicas e ambientais. Securitizar consiste no processo através do qual o caráter de segurança é atribuído a determinada temática (Buzan; Wæver; De Wilde, 1998). De acordo com Tickner (2016), os meios militares não consistem em uma estratégia automática diante da securitização, porém esta, em geral, favorece o uso das forças armadas para lidar com ameaças definidas como existenciais.

As interpretações para este quadro podem ser divididas em dois grandes grupos, com base nas lógicas explicativas anteriormente apresentadas. Do ponto de vista racionalista, pode-se indicar Mikkel Vedby

Rasmussen (2006), segundo o qual o panorama estratégico do século XXI não corresponde a uma construção social específica, mas a uma resposta racional às mudanças ocorridas na segurança internacional, o que promoveu uma reconsideração das funções das forças armadas. Sob esta lógica, a confusão entre as missões policiais e militares são reflexo de mudanças objetivas da realidade internacional diante da globalização. Como indica Derghougassian (2008), esta perspectiva pressupõe uma universalidade da transformação da agenda de segurança. Tal universalidade somente pode ser sustentada a partir de bases ontológicas positivistas, ou seja, considerando que há uma lógica de coisas do funcionamento social que independem dos atores, aos quais cabe compreender a realidade objetivamente, e se adaptar à mesma.

Do ponto de vista da literatura que enquadramos na lógica explicativa construtivista, a novidade consiste no modo em que antigas problemáticas passam, no contexto da reestruturação sistêmica do âmbito internacional, a ser compreendidas como ameaças aos Estados (Mathias; Soares, 2003). Neste sentido, deve-se observar o modo em que o fator ideacional tem repercussão na ação social. Sob uma ótica crítica, Derghogassian (2008) defende que a nova racionalização do panorama estratégico do século XXI serve para justificar e legitimar uma política estadunidense de expansão global de poder, em um contexto no qual o inimigo soviético não se faz mais presente, através da securitização perpétua.

No eixo hemisférico deve ser acrescentado um fator que incita o emprego regular das forças armadas no âmbito interno e que está presente, por exemplo, no auge da Guerra Fria e inserida na denominada Doutrina McNamara (Dockhorn, 2002), que postulava por um binômio inseparável: Segurança e Desenvolvimento. Esta perspectiva forneceu subsídios para o aprofundamento da Doutrina de Segurança Nacional, que, entre seus corolários, indicava a necessidade de freamento da atuação dos inimigos internos, já que os comunistas subvertiam a ordem, o que colocava em risco o desenvolvimento. Os Estados Unidos da América, por sua condição privilegiada, forneceriam as condições de segurança para os países periféricos. O resultado concreto foi a ampliação do emprego das Forças Armadas no combate ao inimigo interno.

Na década de 1990, agora ao fim da Guerra Fria, há um reposicionamento estadunidense. A busca por uma clara militarização da guerra ao narcotráfico proposta no governo de George Bush, para uma perspectiva mais abrangente e com responsabilidades compartilhadas no governo Clinton (Rodrigues, 2002). Embora certa reação de militares a este tipo de emprego, houve a ampliação do combate ao narcotráfico por parte das Forças Armadas, em particular na Amazônia, inclusive com a transferência de unidades militares para a região, ainda que não com este exclusivo fim.

A dimensão regional sul-americana

Nas análises feitas a partir do nível regional pode-se identificar dois elementos que se fazem presentes na quase totalidade dos trabalhos acerca das missões militares: a busca por descrever, por um lado, o alto índice de violência interna, e por outro, as especificidades nacionais para lidar com o mesmo; e o destaque à existência de arranjos regionais que tratam tal temática.

No primeiro caso, defende-se a existência de uma situação considerada paradoxal na América do Sul, que consiste na ausência de guerras interestatais – estabilidade externa – ao mesmo tempo em que se apresenta uma situação de instabilidade interna, marcada por altas taxas de violência (Medeiros, 2010b). No que se refere às diferentes respostas nacionais a este quadro, são apresentados os documentos normativos acerca das funções militares e as diferentes concepções acerca dos conceitos de defesa e segurança. Há uma preocupação em indicar os Estados em que a divisão entre as duas esferas se dá de modo enfático, tendo a Argentina como o principal exemplo, aqueles cujo entrelaçamento das mesmas se dá de modo explícito, tendo a Venezuela como ilustração, e os casos em que a distinção entre defesa e segurança se faz tênue, sendo ilustrativa a experiência brasileira (Bartolomé; 2009; Calderón Grosso, 2012; Soares, Soprano, 2014).

No que se refere aos organismos regionais, os estudos destacam dois: Organização dos Estados Americanos (OEA); e a União das Nações Sul-Americanas (Unasul). No que concerne à separação entre as esferas policial e militar, as duas organizações caminham em direções opostas. No âmbito da OEA, destacam-se as Conferências de Ministros de Defesa das Américas (CMDA). Desde de a conferência de Williamsburg, primeira CMDA, ocorrida em 1995, temáticas como crime organizado e terrorismo foram inscritos na esfera da defesa (Donadelli, 2016). Nota-se nos documentos resultantes das reuniões, uma linha argumentativa constante, cujos elementos principais são: ameaças unívocas aos países do hemisfério; possibilidade remota de guerra entre Estados da região, eliminando assim ameaças tradicionais; estabilidade jurídica das fronteiras territoriais; ameaças não-estatais e transnacionais, caracterizadas pela indiferença entre interno e externo; multidimensionalidade das ameaças; proposta de utilização das Forças Armadas nacionais, não mais necessárias para a defesa da soberania, para lidar com ameaças não-estatais; defesa convencional do continente sob tutela estadunidense (Saint-Pierre, 2012).

Em contrapartida, em 2008, sob a égide da Unasul, foi aprovada a criação do Conselho de Defesa Sul-Americano (CDS), como uma instância de consulta, cooperação e coordenação em matéria de defesa na região. Como indica Medeiros (2010a, p. 32, grifo do autor), "a proposta de um arranjo propriamente sul-americano, rompendo com essa longa tradição panamericana, por si só já confere ao CDS um interessante ineditismo geopolítico na América do Sul". Para o autor, uma das demandas que poderiam influenciar os rumos tomados pelo Conselho é a do combate ao crime organizado transnacional, o que corroboraria com o posicionamento cristalizado na OEA. No entanto, em 10 de agosto de 2009, foi criado, também no âmbito da Unasul, o Conselho sobre o Problema Mundial das Drogas (CSPMD), com o objetivo de desenvolver estratégias e mecanismos de coordenação e cooperação para lidar com a questão do narcotráfico (UNIÃO DE NAÇÕES SUL-AMERICANAS, 2008). No mesmo sentido, em 30 de novembro de 2012, estabeleceu-se o Conselho Sul-Americano em Matéria de Segurança Cidadã, Justiça e Coordenação de Ações contra a Delinquência Organizada Transnacional (DOT), tendo como objetivos fortalecer a segurança cidadã, a justiça e a coordenação de ações para enfrentar o crime organizado transnacional e propor estratégias, planos de ação e mecanismos de coordenação (UNIÃO DE NAÇÕES SUL-AMERICANAS, 2012). Deste modo, há indicativos de institucionalização da separação entre as questões de defesa e de segurança pública.

Diante deste quadro, pode-se dividir a bibliografia especializada em dois grupos, com base nas lógicas explicativas. Nas explicações racionalistas para o emprego do instrumento militar em atividades de segurança pública, há uma condição objetiva, uma lógica de coisas, diante da qual a mobilização dos meios castrenses torna-se necessária. Neste sentido, a capacidade bélica dos grupos criminosos, que, nesta visão, ultrapassaria as competências policiais, e o caráter transnacional dos mesmos, ou seja, sua intensa atuação nas áreas de fronteira, determinariam a escolha dos meios da força estatal a serem empregados. Neste sentido, para Norden (2015), manter uma distinção rígida entre defesa e segurança pública na região torna-se cada vez menos plausível. Nesta perspectiva, portanto, a utilização das Forças Armadas não é questionada como uma escolha política específica. A alocação do instrumento do Estado responsável pela letalidade aparece como uma mera resposta técnica em relação a uma realidade regional autoevidente. Despolitiza-se o processo de escolha. Por fim, evidencia-se a pretensão de neutralidade desta vertente, quando Bartolomé (2009) afirma que, caracterizações, por parte das abordagens críticas à ampliação das missões militares, como "militarização" da segurança pública ou "policialização" das Forças Armadas, constituem generalidades que atribuem carga valorativa à análise, não auxiliando na compreensão do estado de coisas vigente.

A perspectiva construtivista crítica, por outro lado, evidencia a possibilidade, em detrimento da inevitabilidade. O emprego interno de meios militares é considerado uma escolha específica, resultante da construção, intencional ou não, de um concepção específica acerca das Forças Armadas e do panorama da segurança internacional. Os trabalhos evidenciam a construção, através do discurso, de um conjunto de ideias, que levam a esta ação específica. O papel estadunidense na militarização do combate ao narcotráfico e na defesa do emprego dos militares latino-americanos em problemáticas internas é um elemento constante (Saint-Pierre, 2011; Villa, 2014; Rodrigues, 2012 ; Herz, 2000). Para Saint-Pierre (2011, p. 410),

> a versão onusiana da "multidimensionalidade" reaparece no continente americano como parte do pacote apresentado pela confluência de, por um lado, o Consenso de Washington com sua preocupação por diminuir o tamanho do Estado e, por outro, o intento norte-americano de recompor doutrinariamente o continente americano como sua área de segurança nacional. Com esse objetivo, é formulada a convocação das Conferências de Ministros de Defesa das Américas (CMDAs), como foro para discutir as questões da área e, especialmente, tratar de aprovar uma agenda hemisférica de segurança na qual era proposta uma lista comum de ameaças para todo o continente. A lista de ameaças propostas respeitava mais ou menos aquelas levantadas pela Comissão Palme, todavia, a ordem de prioridade ou de "periculosidade" respondia basicamente às necessidades norte-americanas.

Para Sanahuja e Verdes-Montenegro (2014), a dissolução do inimigo soviético exigiu uma nova hipótese de conflito que garantisse, como o primeiro havia feito, a manutenção da homogeneidade estratégica dos países da região. Esta foi encontrada no combate ao narcotráfico. É importante indicar que, o tráfico de drogas ilícitas é caracterizado como ameaça aos Estados Unidos ainda durante o período da Guerra Fria, quando Richard Nixon (1969-1974), caracterizou a atividade como ameaça à sociedade estadunidense, e declarou "guerra às drogas". Ronald Reagan (1981-1989) e George H. W. Bush (1989-1993), reafirmaram e ampliaram a classificação feita por Nixon, indicando o tráfico de drogas como ameaça não apenas à segurança nacional dos Estados Unidos, mas também a todos os países do hemisfério nos quais tal atividade estivesse presente. Segundo Herz (2000), o combate ao comércio de drogas ilícitas foi o carro-chefe da relação dos governos de Bush e Bill Clinton (1993-2001) com a região.

Villa (2014), por sua vez, defende que os atentados ocorridos no dia 11 de setembro de 2001, e a posterior "guerra ao terror", ofereceram aos Estados Unidos a possibilidade de passar da securitização do tráfico de drogas e do crime organizado transnacional, para um processo de macrossecuritização. Mudanças normativo-legais possibilitaram uma sobreposição entre os fenômenos do narcotráfico e do terrorismo, nos países andinos, deste modo, a ameaça passa a ser o narcoterrorismo. Tal alteração possibilitou o uso dos fundos destinados ao combate ao terror, e uma maior presença estadunidense na região. No Cone Sul, por outro lado, a macrossecuritização, pautada pelo narcotráfico e pela guerra ao terror, deu-se, segundo o autor, no âmbito da Tríplice Fronteira, entre Argentina, Brasil e Paraguai, região caracterizada pela concentração de organizações criminosas transnacionais. Para Villa, o máximo resultado que pode advir da securitização do tráfico de drogas ou da guerrilha é a possibilidade de emprego de forças tradicionais no combate aos mesmos. "A grande vantagem disso [militarização] consiste exatamente em manter a América do Sul no quadro menos centrado em preocupações estratégicas ou de ordem geopolítica" (Villa, 2014, p. 375), ou seja, garante a homogeneização estratégica do continente pautada pela agenda de segurança estadunidense.

Nesta perspectiva, os conselhos da Unasul – CDS, CSPMD e DOT – representam não apenas um modo diverso de lidar com um problema objetivo, mas uma resistência política significativa em relação os Estados Unidos, uma vez que, em um âmbito no qual o mesmo não está presente, nega-se a sobreposição entre defesa e segurança, cara às resoluções da OEA. Ainda que não tenham havido modificações substâncias no padrão de emprego das Forças Armadas dos países da região, em decorrência dos acordos firmados em nível sub-regional, autores como Martinez e Lyra (2015) defendem que a Unasul representa um processo de dessecuritização do narcotráfico.

Âmbito doméstico

Os argumentos apresentados no nível nacional, serão, assim como nas outras dimensões, agrupados em dois conjuntos. No primeiro, enfatizam-se aspectos estruturais. Considera-se que o emprego internos dos militares responde a um quadro de fatores constituído pela soma entre debilidade e ineficiência dos instrumentos policiais, aumento da violência e da sensação de insegurança, vinculadas a atividades criminosas. Para Pion-Berlin e Trinkunas (2005), os militares e os governantes civis não são guiados por grandes lógicas ideológicas, assim, a variação no escopo de atuação dos meios castrenses observada na região é explicada em função do grau de crise institucional e do controle civil. Neste sentido, Norden (2015) afirma que há uma maior probabilidade de designação de missões internas aos militares, nas ocasiões em que a capacidade de governar determinado espaço é posta em risco.

Por outro lado, há um debate particularmente relevante para os países da região: a intervenção das instituições castrenses na política. São inúmeros os exemplos de golpes de Estado perpetrados por militares na região. Destaca-se a onda de regimes autoritários que se estabeleceu na América do Sul entre as décadas de 1960 e 1980, sob as bases da Doutrina de Segurança Nacional, em concordância com o estado de coisas da Guerra Fria. O fim das ditaduras, como indicado anteriormente, colocou a necessidade de inserir as Forças Armadas em um ordenamento político democrático, neste sentido, enfatizam-se as especificidades das transições para a democracia, e os diversos padrões de relação civil-militar – maior ou menor autonomia militar – que se estabeleceram em decorrência destas (Linz,

Stepan, 1999; Saint-Pierre, Winand, 2007). A atuação das Forças Armadas em tarefas de segurança pública é então compreendida como uma falha na consolidação da democracia, por dois motivos: a) continuidade de um inimigo interno, ou seja, um grupo de cidadãos considerados uma ameaça à existência do Estado, e que, portanto, podem ser eliminados; b) não eliminação da presença militar em atividades internas estaria vinculado a um ímpeto castrense por manter sua autonomia e seu espaço na esfera de decisão política (Zaveruzha, 2005). Além dos objetivos de poder político, a necessidade de justificar o próprio orçamento na ausência de ameaças convencionais, é indicada como explicação para a aceitação, ou fomento, por parte dos militar de atividades características da segurança pública (Pion-Berlin, Trinkunas, 2005).

Ademais, a utilização interna dos meios castrenses torna-se útil politicamente, sendo ilustrativa a recente decisão do presidente brasileiro, Michel Temer, de, diante da crise prisional vivida pelo país, empregar soldados do Exército para realizar inspeções em presídios. O argumento utilizado por Temer baseia-se na credibilidade das Forças Armadas (Deutsche Welle Brasil, 18 jan 17). Como indicado por Dammert e Bailey (2005), o aumento da sensação de insegurança – que não se vincula diretamente a uma realidade objetiva – por parte da população civil, corrobora no clamor pela intensificação de medidas punitivas e de controle, entre as quais o emprego do aparato militar.

Tais perspectivas são aqui consideradas por uma perspectiva construtivista, na medida em que estes autores não apresentam o mundo fenomênico – material, objetivo e externo às relações sociais – como fonte da ação, no caso em questão, da escolha do instrumento militar para lidar com questões internas. O que está em jogo é o modo pelo qual o mundo social é compreendido e, em uma visão crítica, como ideias e discursos sobre este mundo social são construídos e propagados com o fim de gerar uma ação específica – promover a utilização interna das Forças Armadas com o objetivo de garantir autonomia, poder político ou justificativa orçamentária.

Implicações para a democracia

Alguns autores buscam compreender a relação entre as duas perspectivas não mais na forma de um debate entre visões irreconciliáveis, mas como abordagens complementares. Fearon e Wendt (1991) defendem uma visão pragmática da discussão acerca do racionalismo e do construtivismo, no sentido que estas devem ser vistas como instrumentos analíticos para a compreensão da realidade, não estabelecendo, assim, considerações metodológicas *a priori*. Os autores afirmam que a relação entre as perspectivas deve ser entendida como uma conversa e não um debate. Na mesma linha, Zurn e Checkel (2005) afirmam que as análises de casos estão sempre abertas a interpretações tanto racionalistas quanto construtivistas, de forma que a análise empírica não seria capaz de indicar um suposto vencedor em um pretenso debate.

Por outro lado, retomando a tese de Robert Cox, anteriormente apresentada, que nega a possibilidade de uma teoria dessinteressada, sendo não apenas uma ferramenta analítica, mas também um instrumento de poder, pode-se afirmar que os autores negligenciam uma questão central: as implicações políticas do modo em que se explica um fenômeno, o vínculo entre a produção do conhecimento e a ação política – uma vez que a percepção da realidade produz mobilização social, a ação está pautada pelo processo de cognição (Beck, 2008). Interessa-nos aqui as externalidades das lógicas explicativas apresentadas para o debate democrático acerca do emprego da força. Busca-se observar duas dimensões: a) quem possui legitimidade decisória? b) como a decisão é avaliada e legitimada?

Na primeira questão trata-se de compreender a relação entre o saber especializado e a política. Para tanto, Habermas (2011) apresenta três modelos: tecnocrático; decisionista; e o pragmático. Defende-se que a abordagem racionalista corrobora o primeiro, enquanto o construtivismo pode ser associado ao terceiro. O modelo tecnocrático fundamenta-se na cientificização da política. Há, neste caso, a redução da dominação política sobre a burocracia administrativa, considerada racional. Os políticos submetem-se a um "lógica das coisas", resultando em um estado no qual a "esfera pública política poderia, quando muito, legitimar o pessoal administrativo e dispor sobre a qualificação dos funcionários nomeados" (Habermas, 2011, p.160). A iniciativa política "permanece fadada a uma decibilidade fictícia (...) onde a iniciativa se converte em análise científica e planejamento técnico" (*Idem*, p. 154). De modo diametralmente oposto, apresenta-se o modelo decisionista. Neste caso, a escolha daquele que deve decidir refere-se apenas ao preenchimento de um cargo de autoridade, e não ao debate acerca das diretrizes com base nas quais as decisões futuras devem ser estabelecidas. "Segundo a concepção decisionista, pois, as decisões em si mesmas devem permanecer alheias à discussão pública" (*Idem*, p.159), cabendo exclusivamente àquele que ocupa o cargo de poder. Por fim, o autor afirma que o modelo pragmático consiste em uma inter-relação crítica entre o decisionismo e o tecnocratismo. Neste caso, cabe à esfera política a tarefa de traduzir as recomendações técnicas para a práxis. A instância político-decisória tem dois papeis: a) determinar a direção do progresso técnico-científico com base em necessidades práticas, que por sua vez estão vinculadas aos interesses sociais e orientações de valor de um mundo social específico; b) examinar e criticar as condições para alcançar a necessidade prática pela técnica adotada. Para o autor, o modelo pragmático é o único, entre os três apresentados, que se adéqua à lógica democrática.

A segunda dimensão refere-se ao significado atribuído a determinada ação e suas consequências. Ulrich Beck (2008), apresenta duas lógicas do risco global: da causalidade e da intencionalidade. A primeira é aqui considerada como lógica da inevitabilidade. Nesta, associada pelo autor a problemáticas como catástrofes ambientais ou financeiras, calculam-se os riscos com base na dialética entre custos e benefícios, sendo as consequências negativas, oriundas do processo de globalização, compreendidas como danos colaterais inevitáveis de um processo de tomadas de decisão em direção à modernização – objetivo maior. Assim, não se questiona a decisão tomada. A ideia de inevitabilidade permite a legitimação e redução dos custos políticos ao se adotar medidas impopulares ou que violam a normalidade institucional democrática. A posterior responsabilização do decisor devido a externalidades negativas é atenuada. Na lógica da intencionalidade, como defendido pelo autor, a boa vontade, associada à busca pela modernização, e a inevitabilidade, são substituídas pela má fé e pela intenção. É desta forma que são compreendidos os riscos vinculados ao terrorismo. Neste caso, a decisão de empregar a tática terrorista é condenada, na mesma medida em que a responsabilização, e o consequente clamor por punição, apresenta-se em grau elevado. Tais práticas são vistas como uma escolha entre tantas, e não como uma ação inevitável.

A abordagem racionalista, ao partir de bases ontológicas e epistemológicas positivistas, pressupõe que a função do decisor consiste em avaliar uma realidade dada, no caso, calcular objetivamente as ameaças ao Estado, e com base nesta análise supostamente neutra e descritiva, decidir os planos de ação de modo racional. A racionalidade, nesta perspectiva, restringe as possibilidades de ação. Há, nesse caso, apenas uma linha de ação política correta e racional, sendo qualquer desvio considerado irracional e, consequentemente, falho. Deste modo, o racionalismo vincula-se ao modelo tecnocrático. Pode-se depreender duas implicações política correspondentes às questões apresentadas.

Por um lado, o racionalismo pressupõem que, o modo mais adequado de compreender o mundo real, eliminando as distorções da subjetividade, consiste na utilização de métodos descritivos e empíricos, associados à ideia positivista de ciência. Estabelece-se assim uma separação entre especialistas e leigos. De modo que, "queda claro de qué lado se suponen los prejuicios y los errores (del de los legos) y qué lado esta exento de ellos (el de los expertos). La 'subjetividad del riesgo' se desahoga con los legos, que pasan por estar 'mal informados' en comparacion con los métodos de observacion 'precisos' y 'cientifico' de los expertos (Beck, 2008, p.30). A consequência lógica é a de que o técnico, detentor do saber especializado, possuem melhor condição, e portanto, maior legitimidade, do que o governante – cujo poder decisório baseia-se na eleição democrática – para determinar a alocação de um instrumento do Estado a uma função específica.

Tendo em mente a problemática aqui analisada, resulta que, do ponto de vista de uma análise racionalista, os atores mais aptos a decidir quais missões cabem às Forças Armadas seriam os próprios militares. Neste sentido, Paul Shemella (2006), ao tratar do espectro de funções militares, divide as mesmas em dois grupos: macro e micro. O primeiro refere-se à definição política do papel das Forças Armadas, enquanto a segunda está vinculada às definições operacionais. Shemella considera que a decisão acerca de qual tipo de força é adequado a cada situação inscreve-se no grupo das questões operacionais. Assim, a escolha de se empregar as Forças Armadas em segurança pública consistiria em uma questão meramente operacional, cuja consequência – ainda que o autor não a defenda – seria atribuir aos líderes militares a responsabilidade de deliberação. Amplia-se assim, o poder decisório das burocracias estatais em relação aos governantes eleitos, da mesma forma em que se exclui a opinião pública do processo de controle do uso da força.

Por outro lado, as críticas a este tipo de missão, vinculadas a inúmeras problemáticas como o uso desmedido da força e violação de direitos humanos, a construção de um inimigo interno, a (re)aproximação dos militares da esfera decisória do Estado, a "policialização" das Forças Armadas, entre outras, passam a ser compreendidas como consequências causais de uma ação inevitável. Para Habermas (2011, p. 156, grifo do autor), porém, "a autocompreensão tecnocrática dos novos *experts* (...) apenas escamotearia com uma roupagem de 'lógica das coisas' aquilo que é e sempre foi política".

A abordagem construtivista, por sua vez, ao romper com os preceitos ontológicos positivistas que, como indicado, restringem o espectro de escolhas políticas, amplia as possibilidades de decisão e ação. Uma vez que a realidade não se apresenta como um dado independente das interações sociais, a função da decisão política deixa de ser uma mera adequação técnica a um mundo autoevidente. Evidencia-se assim, que a escolha de mobilizar instrumentos militares para lidar com as problemáticas de segurança interna, representa apenas uma entre inúmeras possibilidades de alocação dos recursos do Estado. Explicita-se o caráter político das decisões públicas. Em detrimento de uma mera administração técnico-burocrática pretendida pela perspectiva da escolha racional, o processo decisório consiste na mediação entre valores e crenças concorrentes. Como apontado por Guzzini, o construtivismo não ignora o mundo fenomênico, de modo que não se reduz ao modelo decisionista. Vincula-se tal perspectiva ao modelo pragmático. A mediação feita pelo governante político depende do conjunto de normas, ideias, crenças e valores compartilhados intersubjetivamente. Portanto, as consequências para as dimensões políticas às quais aqui nos referimos, são: explicitar que a alocação dos instrumentos de força do Estado consiste em uma escolha eminentemente política – o que não lhe confere valoração negativa –, de modo que a outorga de prerrogativas decisórias a uma burocracia estatal significa um rompimento com a democracia representativa. Assim, cabe ao governante eleito a definição das missões militares, ou seja, a escolha de uma possibilidade entre tantas outras. Por outro lado, o político torna-se passível de responsabilização pelas possíveis externalidades negativas decorrentes de sua escolha. O debate público volta a integrar o processo de legitimação do uso da força.

Assim, ultrapassada a fase de regimes autoritários e indefinidas as ameaças ao Estado, novamente corre-se o risco de transformação das forças armadas em forças policiais, relação simbiótica inadequada para a consolidação democrática, ao fundar uma oposição entre Estado e parcelas da sociedade. Transformação esta que deve ser compreendida como uma escolha política específica, ainda que tenha sido fomentada por governos de direcionamentos contrastantes. Por outro lado, a inclusão das Forças Armadas em missões de natureza policial, dada a tradição republicana brasileira de ingerência militar na política, é uma dificuldade adicional para a efetivação do controle civil dos militares. Quando a ênfase do emprego da força militar recai sobre a dimensão externa, aquele controle é facilitado, ocorrendo o contrário quando o emprego militar é orientado para a arena interna (Desh; Goodman, 1996).

Considerações finais

O mote central da temática do uso da força refere-se aos direitos humanos. Os pontos de esgarçamento entre a busca da segurança e as imposições do uso da força, mais ainda quando é potencialmente letal, reservam um lugar essencial para a análise da temática. Forças preparadas doutrinariamente e com meios para aniquilar inimigos constituem uma reserva de poder dos Estados para um emprego finalístico em situações de conflitos bélicos contra o estrangeiro, o estranho.

Um processo de *hibridização* está em curso, ou já concluído, em países da América do Sul. Refere-se a um formato institucional em que as forças armadas já não podem mais ser caracterizadas como organizadas para emprego contra ameaças externas, ao tempo em que este papel que seria originário mescla-se ao seu uso como forças policiais na esfera da segurança pública ou como polícias de fronteira.

A *hibridização* ou, no limite, mesmo a inversão desta delicada equação, constitui-se na afronta a duas ordens de questões. De um lado é fragilizado ou ferido de morte o estatuto democrático, na medida em que o uso da força estatal em seu grau mais elevado arremete-se aos cidadãos, forma virulenta de tratar manifestações contrárias à ordem estabelecida como uma ameaça existencial, ou quando as infrações da lei se inserem no campo das batalhas, nas quais os objetivos são militarizados, isto é, no âmbito interno é que como se fosse mantida uma relação entre mandatários e cidadãos orientada por uma gramática aderente a um estado polêmico, sem que se transfigure em um estado agonístico. Em termos schmittianos, cidadãos, ainda que *hors la loi*, são tratados como inimigos que hostilizam a ordem, ou, mais precisamente, nos termos propostos por Habermas ao apresentar o Conceito de Político (Schmitt, 2008), há uma demarcação da identidade dos que se consideram inseridos na ordem, em *combate* contra a diversidade de um inimigo que ameaça sua existência. Os detentores da ordem vislumbram um estado de coisas em que há real "possibilidade de morte física", o que, nestes termos, impõe o uso da força máxima disponível.

O segundo afrontamento refere-se à dimensão estratégica. Ausente um movimento de externalização do conflito, debilita-se a condição estratégica dos Estados, incapazes de organizarem-se efetivamente em força contra inimigos externos. A hibridização das forças armadas transforma-as em entidades sem demarcações bem definidas. Organizadas com meios e doutrinas para o aniquilamento de inimigos equivalentes, passam a consistir em um limbo no qual não se afirmam enquanto forças estratégicas e se desprofissionalizam enquanto forças policiais.

A hibridização das forças armadas pode ser entendida complementarmente como um resultado estrutural de um processo colonialista vigente ao Sul, em que o estatuto democrático e estratégico é subtraído dos países, guindando suas forças armadas a um papel indistinto. Adicione-se, contudo, que se trata de uma posição de engajamento da força letal no âmbito interno, uma mazela condicionada por uma visão autoritária de elites locais. A busca por segurança gera ainda mais insegurança e os Estados nada mais são do que Leviatãs fragilizados, o que seria o caso brasileiro, duplamente afetado pelo emprego crescente de suas Forças Armadas no âmbito interno.

Referências

BARTOLOMÉ, Mariano César. Las Fuerzas Armadas suramericanas y las perspectivas de cooperación en la lucha contra el terrorismo y el crimen organizado. *Estudios Internacionalies*, 164, 2009.

BATTAGLINO, J. Políticos y militares en los gobiernos de la nueva izquierda sudamericana. *Política y gobierno*, v. 22, n. 1, p. 3-43, 2015.

BERGER, Peter L.; LUCKMANN, Thomas. *A Construção Social da Realidade*. 30 ed. Petrópolis: Editora Vozes, 2009.

BOBBIO, Norberto. Relações Internacionais. In: *O filósofo e a política: antologia*. Contraponto, Rio de Janeiro. 2003, pp. 317-382.

BUZAN, Barry; WÆVER, Ole; DE WILDE, Jaap. *Security: a new framework for analysis*. Lynne Rienner Publishers, 1998.

CALDERÓN GROSSO, Emilse. La impronta legal de la participación de las Fuerzas Armadas em la seguridad pública: luch contra el narcotráfico em América del Sur. URVIO, Revista Latinoamericana de Seguridad Ciudadana, n. 12, Quito, diciembre 2012. pp. 97-109.

COX, Robert W.. Social forces, States and World Orders: beyond international relations theory. In: KEOHANE, Robert O. (editor). *Neorealism and its critics*. Columbia University Press, New York, 1986.

DAMMERT, Lucía; BAILEY, John. La reforma policial y participación militar en el combate a la delincuencia: Análisis y desafíos para América Latina. *Revista Fuerzas Armadas y Sociedad*, Año 19, n. 01, 2005, p. 133-152.

DERGHOUGASSIAN, Khatchik. Las "nuevas amenazas" em la perspectiva estratégica del riesgo: una visión crítica. In: CENTRO DE ESTUDIOS LEGALES Y SOCIALES. *Construyendo Roles: Democracia y Fuerzas Armadas*. Buenos Aires: Cels, 2008.

Desch, Michael; Goodman, Louis. Threat Enviroments and military Missions and Miltary Roles Past and Present. In: DIAMOND, Larry, PLATTNER, Marc. *Civil-Relations and Democracy*. Baltimore, Maryland: John Hopkins, 1996.

D'ARAUJO, Maria Celina (Org.) . *Democracia e Forças Armadas no Cone Sul*. Rio de Janeiro: Editora FGV, 2000.

DIAMINT, Rut. A new Militarism in Latin America. *Journal of Democracy*, V. 26, n. 04, October 2015, pp.155-168.

DONADELLI, Laura M. *Segurança na América do Sul: uma abordagem histórico-conceitual*. Disseração (Mestrado em Relações Internacionais) – Programa de Pós-Graduação em Relações Internacionais (UNESP-UNICAMP-PUC-SP), 2016.

DOCKHORN, Gilvan Veiga. *Quando a Ordem é Segurança e o Progresso é Desenvolvimento 1964 - 1974*. Porto Alegre: Editora da PUCRS, 2002.

DONADIO, Marcela. (Org.). *Atlas Comparativo de la Defensa en América Latina y Caribe: Edición 2014*. Ciudad Autónoma de Buenos Aires: RESDAL, 2014.

DONADIO, Marcela. (Org.). *Atlas Comparativo de la Defensa en América Latina y Caribe*: Edición 2016. Ciudad Autónoma de Buenos Aires: RESDAL, 2016.

EXÉRCITO inicia ação no Rio; em 10 anos, tropa teve de ir às ruas em 1/3 dos dias. *Estado de S. Paulo*, 15 fev. 2017.

FREUND, Julien. *Sociología del conflicto*. Ministerio de Defensa de España, Secretaría General Técnica, 1995. 310p.

FEARON, J.; WENDT, A. Rationalism v. Constructivism: a skeptical view. In: CARLSNAES, W.; RISSE, T.; SIMMONS, B. (orgs.) *Handbook of international relations*. London: Sage, 1991. p. 52-72.

GUZZINI, S. Uma reconstrução do construtivismo nas Relações Internacionais. *Monções: Revista de Relações Internacionais da UFGD*, Dourados, v.2. n.3, jul. /dez., 2013.

HUNTINGTON, Samuel P. *O soldado e o Estado: teoria e política das relações entre civis e militares*. Rio de Janeiro: Biblioteca do Exército, 1996.

LEVY, Yagil. What is controlled by civilian control of the military? Control of the military vs. control of militarization. *Armed forces & society*, vol. 42, 2016. p.75-98.

LINZ, Juan; STEPAN, Alfred. *Transição e consolidação da democracia: a experiência do sul da Europa e da América do Sul*. São Paulo: Editora Paz e Terra, 1999.

LOPEZ, Ernesto. *Latin America: Objective and Subjective Control Revisited*. In PION-BERLIN (ed) Civil-Military Relations in Latin America: New Analytical Perspectives. The University of North Carolina Press, 2001.

MARTINEZ, Elias David Morales; LYRA, Mariana P. O. de. O Processo de dessecuritização do narcotráfico na Unasul. *Contexto Internacional*, v. 37, p.661-691, 2015.

MATHIAS, S. K. ; GUZZI, André C . Autonomia na Lei: as Forças Armadas nas Constituições Nacionais. *Revista Brasileira de Ciências Sociais* (Impresso), v. 25, p. 41-57, 2010.

MATHIAS, S. K. (Org.); SOARES, Samuel Alves (Org.). *Novas ameaças*: dimensões e perspectivas. São Paulo: Sicureza, 2003.

MEARSHEIMER, J. J. *The tragedy of great power politics*. New York: W. W. Norton & company, 2001.

MEDEIROS FILHO, OSCAR . *Conselho de defesa sul-americano: origens, demandas e propósitos*. In: Eduardo Munhoz Svartman; José Miguel Arias Neto; Tania Regina Pires de Godoy; Vágner Camilo Alves. (Org.). Defesa, Segurança Internacional e Forças Armadas III Encontro da ABED. Campinas: Mercado das Letras, 2010a.

MEDEIROS FILHO, O. *Entre a cooperação e a dissuasão: políticas de defesa e as percepções militares na América do Sul*. Tese (Doutorado em Ciência Política) – Faculdade de Filosofia, Letras e Ciências Humanas, Universidade de São Paulo, 2010b.

MEYNAUD, Jean. Les militaires et le pouvoir, *Revue française de sociologie*, Vol. 2, No. 2, Guerre, Armée, Société (Apr. - Jun., 1961), p. 75-87.

NORDEN, Deborah. Latin American Militaries in the 21st Century: civili-military relations in the era of disappering bounderies. In: MARES, David R.; KACOWICZ, Arie M. (Ed.). *Routledge Handbook of Latin American Security*. Routledge, 2015.

NYE, Joseph S. *Understanding international conflicts: an introduction to theory and history*. 7th ed. New York: Longman, 2009. (Longman classics in political science).

OLIVEIRA, Eliézer Rizzo de; SOARES, Samuel Alves. Forças Armadas, direção política e formato institucional. In: CASTRO, Celso;

D'ARAÚJO, Maria Celina. *Democracia e Forças. Armadas no Cone Sul*. Rio de Janeiro: FGV, 2000.

PION-BERLIN, David; TRINKUNAS, Harold. Democratization, social crisis and the impact of military domestic roles in Latin America. *Journal of Political and Military Sociology*, v. 33, p. 05-26, 2005.

RASMUNSSEN, Mikkel Vedby. *The risck society at war: terror, technology and strategy in the twenty-first century*. Cambridge: Cambridge University Press, 2006.

RAYMOND, Aron. *Paz e Guerra entre as Nações*. São Paulo: Editora Universidade de Brasília, Coleção Clássicos do IPRI, 2002.

RODRIGUES, Thiago. A infindável guerra americana: Brasil, EUA e o narcotráfico no continente, *São Paulo em Perspectiva*, vol.16, no.2, São Paulo, April/June 2002.

_____ Narcotráfico e militarização nas Américas: vício de guerra. *Contexto Internacional*, v. 34, p. 09-41, 2012.

ROUQUIÉ, Alain . *O Estado militar na América Latina*. São Paulo: Alfa-Ômega, 1982.

SAIN, Marcelo Fabián. *Alfonsin, Menem e as relações cívico-militare. A construção do controle sobre as Forças Armadas na Argentina democrática (1983-1995)*. Universidade de Campinas (Tese Doutorado), 1999.

SAINT-PIERRE, Héctor. 'Defesa'ou 'Segurança'? Reflexões em torno de Conceitos e Ideologias. *Contexto Internacional*, v.33, p. 407-433, 2011.

SAINT-PIERRE, Héctor. El concepto de la seguridad multidemensional: una aproximación crítica. In: MEJÍAS,Sonia A; RICAURTE, Verónica G. (Org.). *El concepto y las relaciones multilaterales de seguridad y defensa en el contexto de la UNASUR*. 01 ed. Madrid: Instituto Universitario General Gutiérrez Mellado - Ministéiro de Defensa Nacional del Ecuador, 2012.

SAINT-PIERRE ; WINAND, Érica C. . O legado da transcição na agenda democrática para a defesa: os casos brasileiro e argentino. In:

Héctor Luis saint-Pierre. (Org.). *Controle civil sobre os militares e política de defesa na Argentina, no Brasil, no chile e no Uruguai*. São Paulo: Editora Unesp - Programa de Pós-Graduação em Relações Internacionais UNESP - UNICAMP - PUC/SP, 2007.

SANAHUJA, José Antonio; VERDES-MONTENEGRO, F. J. Seguridad y defensa en Suramérica: regionalismo, cooperación y autonomía en el marco de UNASUR. In: Serbin A., Martínez L. y H. Ramanzini (Org.). *Anuario de la Integración de América Latina y el Gran Caribe*, 2014, v. 10: 2013-2014.

SCHMITT, Carl. *O conceito de político/Teoria do Partisan*. Belo Horizonte: Del Rey, 2008.

SCHUMPETER, Joseph A. *Capitalismo, Socialismo y Democracia*. Madrid: Aguilar S.A. de Ediciones, 1952.

SOARES, Samuel Alves; SOPRANO, Germán. Políticas de defesa de Argentina e Brasil no começo do século XXI: entre a confiança mútua e as culturas estratégicas em dissonância. In: PASSOS, Rodrigo Duarte Fernandes dos, VIEIRA, Noemi Ramos, y SIMONETTI, Miriam Cláudia Lourenção. (Orgs.). *Relações Internacionais Contemporâneas: novos protagonistas e novas conjunturas*, 1ed. Marília: Cultura Acadêmica Editora, 2014.

SUCCI JUNIOR, D. P.. A agenda de segurança estadunidense no pós--Guerra Fria e o emprego das Forças Armadas na Argentina e no Brasil. *Conjuntura Global*, v. 5, p. 566-585, 2016.

TEMER diz que militares não resolverão crise nos presídios. *Deutsche Welle Brasil*, 18 jan. 2017. Disponível em: http://www.dw.com/pt-br/temer-diz-que-militares-n%C3%A3o-resolver%C3%A3o-crise-nos--pres%C3%ADdios/a-37184337. Acesso em: 18 jan. 2017.

TICKNER, Arlene B. Securitization and the limits of democratic security. In: MARES, David R.; KACOWICZ, Arie M. (Ed.). *Routledge Handbook of Latin American Security*. Routledge, 2016.

UNIÃO DE NAÇÕES SUL-AMERICANAS. *Decisión para el Establecimiento del Consejo de Defensa Suramericano de la UNASUR*. Brasil, 2008. Disponível em: http://www.ceedcds.org.ar/Espanol/09-Downloads/ESTATUTO_CDS.pdf Acesso em: 17 jan 2017.

UNIÃO DE NAÇÕES SUL-AMERICANAS. *Declaración: VI Reunión Ordinaria del Consejo de Jefas y Jefes de Estado y de Gobierno de la Unión de las Naciones Suramericanas – Unasur*. Perú, 2012.

VILLA, Rafael Duarte. O paradoxo da macrossecuritização: quando a guerra ao terror não securitiza outras "guerras" na América do Sul. *Contexto Internacional*, v. 36, p. 349-383, 2014.

ZAVERUCHA, Jorge. *FHC, forças armadas e polícia: entre o autoritarismo e a democracia (1999-2002)*. Rio de Janeiro: Editora Redord, 2005.

WALTZ, Kenneth. *Teoria das Relações Internacionais*. Lisboa: Gradiva, 2002.

Os impasses da governança ambiental global: as políticas hídrica e energética

Fernanda Mello Sant'Anna
Júlia Abdalla Lunardi

Introdução

A preocupação com as questões ambientais nas últimas décadas evidenciou a dimensão da escala planetária em que vivemos. Se todos habitamos este mesmo planeta Terra, em que os ecossistemas e recursos são interdependentes, é importante que asseguremos sua capacidade de suporte da vida, para as atuais e futuras gerações. Essa nova solidariedade com as gerações futuras está presente no controverso e largamente debatido conceito de desenvolvimento sustentável. Além do que, assegurar as condições de vida para as atuais e futuras gerações é parte fundamental da cidadania hoje.

Todos temos direito à qualidade de vida, que só ocorre vivendo em um ambiente saudável. A negação do acesso aos recursos naturais, bem como a distribuição desigual dos resíduos e poluição é uma ameaça a este direito e tem gerado movimentos sociais por justiça ambiental. Devido à escala planetária que nos une independente das fronteiras políticas, a cooperação internacional parece fundamental para que os países possam coordenar suas ações para a sustentabilidade socioambiental. No entanto, a cooperação internacional não é tão simples e envolve vários elementos desde a estrutura do sistema internacional, como as especificidades dos problemas ambientais enfrentados. Desta forma, a governança ambiental global enfrenta diversos desafios para se concretizar e, principalmente, garantir as condições e qualidade de vida para as futuras gerações.

Entre as questões ambientais que afligem todo grupo humano estão dois recursos fundamentais e estratégicos nos tempos atuais que são a água e a energia, fundamentais para toda sociedade e para a qualidade de vida. Este capítulo discutirá a governança ambiental global na questão do acesso e uso dos recursos naturais, bem como os conflitos sociais envolvidos e o papel do Estado, e apresentará o caso do nexo entre água e energia e suas implicações para os países e a sociedade em geral.

Governança ambiental global: as instituições multilaterais e a justiça ambiental

Quando falamos em recursos naturais, a questão do acesso e uso pela sociedade está posta. A transformação da matéria em recurso já implica a sua utilidade para a sociedade. No entanto, vivemos em uma sociedade desigual que, de acordo com Martinez-Alier (2007), tem gerado conflitos ecológicos distributivos. Estes conflitos e os movimentos de resistência derivados da desigualdade na distribuição dos recursos e serviços ambientais, e também dos efeitos da poluição e degradação ambiental, quando relacionados a fatores como desigualdade econômica e social e discriminação racial ou de gênero, foram chamados de movimentos por justiça ambiental. Trata-se de um movimento preocupado com a sobrevivência humana em primeiro lugar, e que percebeu que determinados grupos sociais são mais afetadas negativamente pela desigual distribuição ecológica. Estes grupos são identificados, principalmente, por classe (desigualdade socioeconômica e de poder político), raça, etnia, e gênero.

Estes conflitos ecológicos distributivos tomam diversas formas e discursos, podendo ser locais e até globais. Alguns são marcados por um discurso claramente ambiental, e outros utilizam diferentes discursos.

Atualmente, observa-se que as ligações entre os conflitos locais e o movimento ambientalista global estão cada vez mais fortes. Muitas vezes os movimentos locais reforçam as redes globais e incorporam a linguagem e a força do ambientalismo global às suas lutas locais (Martinez-Alier, 2007).

Para Harvey (1999), o movimento por justiça ambiental está ancorado em uma retórica moral, na visibilidade dos meios de comunicação de massa, e na política simbólica. Entretanto, o movimento teria a potencialidade de superar esta fase e partir para uma ação revolucionária mundial. Este movimento de resistências, assim como outros movimentos ambientalistas fazem parte da chamada governança ambiental global, que é caracterizada por uma multiplicidade de atores, com diferentes objetivos, princípios e estratégias. Também participam desta governança os Estados e as instituições multilaterais internacionais.

A preocupação com a democratização e a participação social, em especial para a justiça ambiental, nos leva a questionar as instituições internacionais multilaterais. Diversas convenções e instituições foram criadas para tratar da temática ambiental desde 1970, embora já existissem algumas antes disso, levando a consolidação da temática ambiental na agenda internacional. Um exemplo disso, são as conferências das partes da Convenção sobre mudanças climáticas que têm ocupado os jornais e mídias em todo o mundo, divulgando as dificuldades dos países em acordar metas e compromissos para a redução dos impactos das mudanças climáticas. Essas reuniões se caracterizam pela participação dos representantes dos Estados, e a sociedade civil em geral se organiza em eventos paralelos, muitas vezes criticando a posição dos governos.

Hale, Held e Young (2013) acreditam que existe uma distância entre a nossa necessidade de soluções globais para os problemas globais como os ambientais e a habilidade das instituições multilaterais de encontrar essas soluções. Os autores sustentam que existe uma falência da cooperação global que eles chamam de "gridlock" ("impasse"). Eles argumentam que existem três características que definem esta situação. Em primeiro lugar há uma falta de governança; em segundo, este impasse ocorre em quase todas as áreas da governança global, portanto, o "impasse" é uma condição geral do sistema multilateral.

Esta falta de governança é um produto dos esforços de cooperação, por isso, historicamente contingente. Há um ciclo de interdependência autossustentada, em que as instituições multilaterais ajudaram a criar as condições que agora impedem a eficácia da cooperação global. A interdependência foi institucionalizada na cooperação internacional e criou as condições para que a globalização possa se aprofundar e acelerar, aumentando a interdependência.

A emergência de problemas globais mais difíceis que refletem o grau profundo de interdependência são: a economia global, a sustentabilidade do planeta, e a qualidade de vida. Não são problemas que afetam apenas aos diplomatas, são dilemas básicos de todas as pessoas em seu cotidiano. Com o aumento destes novos problemas, ocorre a criação de mais instituições globais e sua fragmentação. A proliferação destas instituições foi acompanhada pela redução da capacidade coletiva de resolver esses problemas.

A governança ambiental global encontra-se, portanto, em um impasse. Os problemas ambientais que enfrentamos hoje fazem parte do que os ecologistas chamam de Antropoceno: estamos vivendo um período no planeta Terra em que seus ecossistemas estão sendo profundamente afetados pelas ações do ser humano. Esta é uma forma totalmente nova de interdependência, a expansão da "comunidade que compartilha o mesmo destino", que deixou de ser a pequena vila para incluir todo o globo. Chegamos a uma situação em que a inabilidade de gerir os recursos do planeta de forma coletiva, nos levou a uma "tragédia dos comuns" (Hale, Held e Young, 2013).

A partir dos anos 1970 temos uma nova fase da governança ambiental global em termos de cooperação internacional e envolvimento dos Estados, destacando também a importante participação dos cientistas e comunidades epistêmicas e também da sociedade civil organizada. No entanto, na conferência de Estocolmo em 1972, a Conferência das

Nações Unidas sobre o Meio Ambiente Humano já apresentava elementos que levaram ao posterior impasse, como a divisão Norte-Sul. Os autores apontam as três características que criam obstáculos à governança ambiental, que seriam: o poder, isto é, a multipolaridade que gerou a divisão Norte-Sul e uma oposição entre os países ricos do Norte e os países pobres do Sul, ricos em recursos naturais e biodiversidade; o fato das questões ambientais serem mais difíceis, pois implicam perda de soberania nos territórios, se a máxima "pensar global e agir local" é seguida; e a fragmentação da temática na política internacional, em especial na ONU, já que o Programa das Nações Unidas para o Meio Ambiente (PNUMA) apresenta sérias fragilidades e está longe de representar uma organização internacional do meio ambiente. A fragmentação teria criado barreiras que impedem uma coerência nas ações para a sustentabilidade ambiental. Além disso, o sucesso de um regime inicial, que foi o da camada de ozônio, fez com que sua estrutura fosse copiada em outros temas, que não tinham as mesmas características, gerando uma inadequação, como no caso das florestas e das mudanças climáticas.

Apesar dos problemas ambientais serem cada vez mais sistêmicos e globais, e portanto, mais perigosos, a governança ambiental é bastante fragmentada. Mesmo no âmbito doméstico é muito difícil que o meio ambiente seja tratado como um tema transversal. Pelo contrário, as políticas dos Estados continuam setoriais, embora os temas estejam inter-relacionados, não existe uma coordenação conjunta destas políticas. Este é o caso que será tratado neste trabalho, entre os setores de recursos hídricos e energia. Por mais que os Estados tenham políticas separadas é inegável como cada setor afeta o outro gerando conflitos e até mesmo agravando problemas nos dois setores.

Se os problemas são cada vez mais globais e sistêmicos como o Estado poderia englobar de maneira eficaz a governança ambiental?

O papel do Estado na governança ambiental

Em meio ao crescente espaço de risco ambiental e das injustiças ambientais, faz-se necessário pensar e agir sobre uma configuração política que seja capaz de abarcar uma multiplicidade de discursos e "bolsões de realidade" e, ao mesmo tempo, orientá-los a um objetivo comum.

Robyn Eckersley, em *The green state: rethinking democracy and sovereignty*, explora em detalhes como se daria a organização política, econômica, social e ambiental sob esse novo prisma.

Segundo a autora, o Estado democrático haverá de passar por várias transformações, na direção da progressão democrática, a fim de que a justiça ambiental e toda a racionalidade contemporânea seja incrementalmente desenvolvida. Eckersley ecoa a ideia de racionalidade ambiental de Enrique Leff (2006), que, sucintamente, sugere uma alteração moral e de significados a partir dos quais baseamos todo o funcionamento da sociedade. Assim, o processo em direção a um Estado ecológico não estaria restrito às mudanças em instituições, mas também operante em relação a toda a atribuição de valores da sociedade contemporânea.

Eckersley argumenta que este novo Estado democrático, o qual chama de democracia ecológica, terá de rever toda sua postura representativa e comunicativa, pois terá de dar conta de *todos* os seres envolvidos nas comunidades representadas, humanos e não-humanos, presentes e futuros. Nesse sentido, a própria organização sociopolítica que observamos atualmente seria reestruturada, uma vez que limites territoriais não são representações adequadas desses "bolsões de realidade", e, portanto, não contêm populações e outros seres baseados em critérios como risco e situação ambiental.

O Estado democrático ecológico segundo Eckersley, não seria um substituto do Estado democrático liberal, mas uma expansão do mesmo. O grande princípio desse Estado é a representatividade global, principalmente de segmentos marginalizados da sociedade, como aqueles sob risco ambiental ou que vivem em péssimas condições ambientais, geralmente não contemplados pelo Estado. Ademais, o Estado verde necessitaria de instituições e mecanismos sólidos para fiscalizar, implementar e inserir de forma concreta os problemas ambientais na pauta política, tornando-os tão presentes e validados como, por exemplo, a própria economia.

Matthew Paterson, em *The 'normal and mundane practices of modernity': Global power structures and the environment* também discorre acerca da relação entre instituições e meio ambiente no panorama global. Segundo o autor, a configuração das instituições internacionais, junto do conceito de desenvolvimento sustentável, são incompatíveis com o bem-estar ambiental, ou mesmo com a intenção de frear a degradação ambiental. Explorando os quatro pilares que identifica como alicerces do poder político mundial — a saber, sistema de estados, capitalismo, conhecimento e patriarcado —, Paterson conclui que as formas de poder dominantes são antiecológicas, e devem ser repensadas. O autor sugere que a descentralização conectada do poder, na qual a organização política se assemelha a uma rede de pequenas comunidades, seria uma possível resposta institucional ao problema ambiental. Isto não significaria o desaparecimento do Estado, mas uma reconfiguração do mesmo a fim de que as estruturas antiecológicas observáveis atualmente não tenham margem para nascer e se desenvolver.

Assim, como é de conhecimento geral, a conexão entre política ambiental e Estado é, atualmente, muito aquém do necessário para assegurar bem-estar a todos os seres envolvidos na biosfera, presentes e futuros. A resposta para que essa conexão seja concretizada, estabilizada, e expandida em termos de materializações na realidade política — adequadamente, também, fiscalizadas e mantidas —, é a progressiva reconfiguração do Estado em direção ao Estado verde proposto por Eckersley. Esse Estado seria tanto verde quanto mais democrático que o observado atualmente, e garantiria que a política ambiental ocupasse uma posição de reconhecimento e respaldo concreto, presente e fixo nos âmbitos social, político e econômico.

Esse tipo de transformação é realizado vagarosamente, passo a passo. Por isso, *começar* é imprescindível e inadiável: essa reconfiguração e as consequentes mudanças são um objetivo a longo prazo. Embora seja costumeiro dizer que as mudanças estruturais e da própria racionalidade da sociedade contemporânea sejam *para ontem*, é necessário pensar também nos objetivos a longo prazo e dar os primeiros passos em direção a essa nova configuração sociopolítica, *in tandem* com as ações políticas ambientais imediatas segundo a capacidade atual do Estado em realizá-las e dos mecanismos atuais — políticos ou sociais — em fiscalizá-las.

Ainda que os Estados tenham incorporado as políticas ambientais, criado ministérios do meio ambiente e várias outras instituições para lidar com problemas ambientais, em geral essas instituições apresentam grande fragilidade institucional e estão abaixo hierarquicamente das instituições econômicas, por exemplo. Em alguns casos persiste o discurso de que o meio ambiente é um tema transversal e deve estar presente em todos os setores, no entanto, a prática é outra. O nexo entre água e energia se propõe a demonstrar a inadequação do tratamento de políticas setoriais para tratar das questões ambientais, bem como as consequências para a justiça ambiental.

O nexo água-energia e a justiça ambiental

Desde o início do novo milênio, o nexo água-energia tem conquistado espaço no meio científico e em organizações internacionais — ONU, por exemplo —, se tornando, também, um importante problema na política hídrica e energética. Já existem vários casos em que os dois "setores" parecem entrar em conflito entre si e com outros conflitos sócio-ambientais relacionados a esse nexo. De diferentes formas, água e energia são interdependentes: ambos são recursos naturais estratégicos que são essenciais e importantes para produção e crescimento econômico e para a qualidade de vida, sendo utilizados em atividades humanas básicas como consumo de água para seres humanos e animais e nutrição.

Embora sejam tratados em setores separados e diferentes, com políticas independentes, água e energia se interpelam de várias maneiras. Tipos diferentes de fontes energéticas e de produção energética utilizam água de alguma forma. A mais evidente destas é a hidreletricidade, que usa a força da água para gerar eletricidade. Outras formas de produção energética também necessitam de água para sistemas de aquecimento e vaporização, e a energia nuclear utiliza água para resfriar o sistema. A extração e produção de combustíveis fósseis requer água no processo. Biocombustíveis, como o etanol, utilizam água para irrigação. É importante notar que alguns desses processos produzem grande quantidade de poluição e contaminação hídrica, como despejos que degradam a qualidade da água, comprometendo outros usos desse recurso, como é o caso da exploração do petróleo.

Um grande problema relativo a essa situação é que, embora água e energia sejam interdependentes, os dois setores carecem de coordenação, comunicação e intercâmbio de informações. De acordo com a Agência Internacional de Energia, em 2012 "globalmente, aproximadamente 15% das retiradas de água foram para produção energética, e é previsto que esta porcentagem suba para 20% até 2035" (Schuster-Wallace *et al.* 2015: 1).

É importante mencionar que a água é um recurso natural essencial à vida humana e toda a vida no planeta. É um recurso sem o qual não podemos viver e ao qual não há substituto. A água é utilizada para uma miríade de propósitos e atividades e é primordial para todas as funções e sustentabilidade dos ecossistemas. Os múltiplos usos da água incluem o abastecimento doméstico, industrial, para agricultura, turismo e lazer, hidroeletricidade, navegação, etc. Os recursos hídricos têm sido apontados como um dos recursos naturais com maior potencial para causar conflitos, doméstico e internacional, no futuro, já que sua quantidade no planeta é fixa e a demanda é crescente.

Todas as formas em que a energia depende da água demonstra que ela é vulnerável as variações naturais e outros constrangimentos como a disponibilidade e regulações. Outra variável que pode interferir na disponibilidade de água é as mudanças climáticas e o crescimento econômico e da população que podem aumentar a demanda tanto por água quanto por energia. As mudanças climáticas irão alterar o padrão de chuvas em várias partes do mundo, que combinado com as demandas crescentes por biocombustíveis e outros cultivos que dependem das chuvas e da irrigação, terá consequências para a produção de alimentos e expansão dos biocombustíveis. A hidroeletricidade também será impactada pela variabilidade das chuvas causadas pelas mudanças climáticas, no Brasil, uma grande seca no ano de 2014, na região sudeste do país, teve um impacto negativo sobre as usinas hidrelétricas e para o abastecimento doméstico e industrial, afetando não apenas o setor energético, como também todas as atividades que dependem da água. O mesmo tem sido observado em outras partes do mundo, pois várias usinas de energia foram forçadas a encerrar suas atividades nos Estados Unidos, Índia, França e outros países, devido à falta de água e altas temperaturas comprometendo os processos de resfriamento. Projetos de termoelétricas têm sido reavaliados devido ao seu impacto para os recursos hídricos regionais e a vulnerabilidade às mudanças climáticas. Secas mais longas e recorrentes têm ameaçado a capacidade hidroelétrica de muitos países como o Sri Lanka, China e Brasil (Rodrigues *et al.*, 2013, V-VI).

Este cenário demonstra a vulnerabilidade mútua entre os projetos energéticos e hídricos, pois a água também depende da energia de diversas formas como para transporte, extração, etc. Estas vulnerabilidades têm gerado custos adicionais em relação às medidas de adaptação para cenários futuros, incluindo as consequências das mudanças climáticas, como inundações e secas, que podem afetar o desenvolvimento (IEA, 2012). Além disso, "as mudanças climáticas aumentarão a vulnerabilidade dos países já que o aumento da temperatura acelera a evaporação e a precipitação. [...] o padrão de chuvas mudará e se intensificará, aumentando a incerteza no desenvolvimento energético". Outras fontes de energia renovável como a solar e eólica, combinadas com a eficiência energética pode contribuir para gerar energia com menos demanda de água. Neste contexto de aumento da restrição dos usos da água, que os recursos hídricos se tornaram um critério importante para determinar a viabilidade de novos e atuais projetos energéticos.

A geração de energia hidrelétrica é a forma renovável de energia mais comum no mundo e consiste numa parte importante da geração global de energia. A hidroeletricidade representava em 2008 cerca de 16% da produção total de energia no globo, produzindo 3.288 TWh. Embora a Agência Internacional de Energia (AIE) estima que, o potencial técnico da hidroeletricidade é mais de 16.400 TWh por ano. A produção global total de energia hidrelétrica merece uma atenção especial já que dois terços dela provêm de apenas 10 países (China, Canadá, Brasil, Estados Unidos, Rússia, Noruega, Índia, Venezuela, Japão e Suécia). Os cinco primeiros, que incluem os cinco primeiros citados acima, produziram em 2008, 8360 TWh por ano, e o Brasil sozinho produziu 11% da hidroeletricidade total neste ano, mas é importante apontar que desde então o Brasil construiu três grandes hidrelétricas na Bacia Amazônica (as usinas de Santo Antônio, Jirau e Belo Monte). Duas delas já estão em funcionamento, e fazem parte da Iniciativa para a Integração da Infraestrutura Regional na América do Sul (IIRSA), e Belo Monte está quase completa. A construção destas usinas gerou sérios conflitos socioambientais e tensões entre a Bolívia e o Brasil em relação à bacia do rio Madeira na Amazônia. Ainda que a AIE tenha apontado as variações hídricas previstas para ocorrerem devido às mudanças climáticas, estas não terão um impacto uniforme em todo o globo e algumas partes serão mais afetadas que outras.

Apesar da evidência crescente sobre o nexo entre água e energia, estes recursos têm sido tratados como dois setores separados com pouca integração entre eles. Em alguns países da América do Sul pode ser observado a priorização de um dos setores, geralmente o energético em detrimento do hídrico. O primeiro Código de Águas brasileiro, de 1934, por exemplo, apresentava a sua maior parte dedicada a geração de eletricidade. Desde então, a política de recursos hídricos foi subjugada pelo setor energético, ainda que os múltiplos usos da água já gerassem conflitos. Os setores de água e energia embora sejam interdependentes sofrem com a falta de coordenação política e integração, pois são tratados como setores independentes, e apenas um esforço limitado se dedica a tratar das relações entre eles (Hussey e Pittock, 2012).

Entre os recursos naturais que tem causado mais conflitos e representa sérias ameaças para a segurança, a água tem sido apontada como a número um entre os recursos renováveis (Gleick, 1993; Homer-Dixon, 1994, Gleditsch *et al.* 2006; Yoffe *et al.* 2004). Os recursos hídricos estão sofrendo um processo de securitização em muitas partes do mundo, consolidando o conceito de segurança hídrica que está presente em diversos documentos governamentais e de organizações internacionais. Deste modo, a segurança hídrica internacional é um termo complexo que envolve múltiplas metas tais como assegurar a paz, a segurança humana e a proteção ambiental no processo de planejamento e implementação da gestão dos recursos hídricos em bacias compartilhadas por dois ou mais países (Pachova e Jansky, 2008, p. 61).

Várias instituições têm usado o conceito de segurança hídrica, o que tem levou a múltiplas definições do conceito, especialmente de organizações internacionais como o Global Water Partnership, o Fórum Econômico Mundial, o Instituto da UNESCO para Educação sobre Recursos Hídricos, o Conselho Mundial da Água, etc. No âmbito doméstico, a segurança hídrica tem se tornado uma questão importante para a gestão hídrica local e nacional (Jansky *et al.*, 2008; Mirumachi, 2008). Acadêmicos e a comunidade epistêmica também tem cada vez mais utilizado o conceito (Cook e Bakker 2012). Para o Relatório do Desenvolvimento Humano de 2006 (UNDP, 2006), a segurança hídrica almeja assegurar que cada pessoa tenha uma quantidade suficiente de água de qualidade por um preço acessível, contribuindo para uma vida saudável e produtiva, enquanto também mantém os ecossistemas ecológicos permitindo a continuidade do ciclo da água, necessário para a sobrevivência. É importante notar que a água também pode levar a competição e conflitos e, portanto, também está relacionada à paz, especialmente os recursos hídricos transfronteiriços, já que com o aumento do número de atores e interesses aumenta também as ameaças pois inclui as escalas nacionais e internacional. Assim, a habilidade política dos países que compartilham bacias hidrográficas tem um papel importante para a segurança hídrica (Mirumachi, 2008).

O mesmo processo de securitização da água pode ser visto no discurso sobre a energia. A segurança energética é geralmente entendida como a segurança do fornecimento de energia (Baumann, 2012). No entanto, é importante ressaltar que se trata de um conceito multidimensional, excedendo a noção polarizada de demanda-oferta que não permite uma compreensão mais ampla e inclusiva desta questão. Portanto, a segurança energética é uma questão complexa constituída pela segurança tradicional do fornecimento a preços acessíveis, juntamente com as circunstancias econômicas, geopolíticas, ambientais e internas que formam o status energético de um país ou região. Pode ser observado nos discursos de governos nacionais na América do Sul que o aumento da produção energética é visto como uma matéria de sobrevivência, especialmente sobrevivência econômica. Os países sul-americanos devem encontrar novas fontes de energia, devem construir mais usinas hidrelétricas, para alcançar a segurança energética. Estas metas também podem ser iniciativas regionais, como vem sendo desenvolvido na região nas últimas décadas com a integração energética.

Cabe ressaltar que a utilização dos recursos hídricos para geração de energia tem gerado conflitos e movimentos por justiça ambiental, como nos casos das barragens de usinas hidrelétricas, e também na contaminação da água na exploração do petróleo. No caso das barragens, sua construção sempre foi realizada com resistências, em especial, das pessoas afetadas pelas barragens, mas se tratava de uma oposição localizada. Esta oposição começou a se organizar de forma transnacional a partir dos protestos para uma reforma do Banco Mundial em suas ações de financiamento de projetos com grande impacto ambiental e humano, na segunda metade da década de 1980. Juntamente com a emergência de ONGs como a International Rivers Network (IRN) a transnacionalização do movimento anti-barragens foi se consolidando. Em 1996 o Banco Mundial publica a primeira fase da revisão de seu Departamento de Avaliação de Operações intitulado "World Bank's Experience with Large Dams: a preliminar review of impact", que recebe muitas críticas inclusive da IRN. No ano seguinte o Banco Mundial realiza em conjunto com a World Conservation Union (IUCN) e outros stakeholders relacionados às barragens para um workshop. Neste ano de 1997, foi realizada também a Primeira Reunião Internacional de Afetados por Barragens, onde se reuniram ativistas em Curitiba, Brasil. Esta reunião foi organizada pelo Movimento dos Atingidos por Barragens (MAB) brasileiro (Conca, 2006; Dubash *et al.*, 2001).

Embora a água seja um recurso natural essencial à vida e insubstituível o direito ao acesso à água potável e ao saneamento somente foi reconhecido pela Assembleia Geral da ONU em julho de 2010, por meio de sua Resolução 64/292, como um direito humano. Milhões de pessoas em todo o mundo ainda sofrem com a falta de água potável e saneamento, resultando em enfermidades facilmente evitadas com um saneamento adequado. A falta de energia elétrica também acomete mais de um bilhão de pessoas em todo o mundo. Além do que, não basta ter energia, é preciso desenvolver as fontes renováveis e menos poluentes se quisermos garantir a sua sustentabilidade e a qualidade de vida (ONU, 2017).

Desta forma, a degradação e distribuição irregular de recursos hídricos, junto da tendência à apropriação e utilização dos mesmos em pólos com oportunidade econômica — ou concentrações populacionais — marginaliza setores que muitas vezes não têm condições de representação e/ou diálogo e, principalmente, que necessitam do recurso para sobrevivência física ou produção econômica. O nexo água-energia amplifica o conflito do econômico *versus* o humano ou ecológico, tornando necessário e urgente o desenvolvimento e presença da justiça ambiental nos âmbitos político, social e econômico, aliada a coordenações de políticas ecológicas que visem a preservação desses recursos frente à exploração econômica.

Considerações Finais

Este capítulo procurou expandir as questões de governança global e justiça ambiental, principalmente aplicadas aos recursos hídricos e energéticos. Como vimos, a governança global ambiental enfrenta o problema de ter uma área de atuação ampla inserida em uma repartição setorial internacional rígida e estabelecida, tornando sua presença transversal nesses setores uma tarefa árdua e ainda em progresso. Enquanto isso, a degradação ambiental perdura e evolui, causando mais e mais danos irreparáveis aos ecossistemas terrestres e a consequente criação de um ambiente instável e deteriorado para as gerações atuais e futuras. Ademais, a justiça ambiental esbarra em formações estruturais anti-ecológicas e anti-sociais em vários níveis: desde a racionalidade econômica até as instituições multilaterais globais e os próprios Estados atrofiados em termos de políticas ambientais e socio-ambientais. Nesse contexto, as políticas hídrica e energética, apesar de serem interligadas, encontram o ambiente institucional para que continuem a ser tratadas setorialmente, perpetuando a abertura para danos ambientais e para injustiças ambientais que assolam populações marginalizadas.

Referências bibliográficas

CONCA, Ken. *Governing water: contentious transnational politics and global institution building*. Massachusetts: MIT Press, 2006.

COOK, C. e BAKKER, K. *Water security: debating and emerging paradigm. Global Environmental Change*. V. 22, 2012, p. 94-102.

DUBASH, N. K.; DUPAR, M.; KOTHARI, S. e LISSU, T. *A Watershed in Global Governance? An Independent Assessment of the World Comission on Dams*. World Resources Institute, 2001.

ECKERSLEY, Robyn. Green Theory. In: DUNNE, T.; KURKI, M.; SMITH, S. *International Relations Theories: discipline and diversity.* Oxford: Oxford university Press, 2013, p. 266-286.

ECKERSLEY, R. *The Green State: rethinking democracy and sovereignty. Londres*: The MIT Press, 2004, 331 p.

GLEDITSCH, N. P. e BROCHMANN, M. *Shared river – a reconsideration. Political Geography.* V. 31, 2012, p. 519-527.

GLEICK, P. Water and conflict: freshwater resources and international security. *International Security.* MIT Press, v. 19, n. 1, 1993, pp. 79-112.

HARVEY, D. The environment of justice. In: FISCHER, F; HAJER, M. A. *Living with Nature: environmental politics as cultural discourse.* Oxford: Oxford University Press, 1999.

HOMER-DIXON, T. F. *Environmental scarcities and violent conflict: evidence from cases. International Security.* MIT Press, V. 19, n. 1, 1994, pp. 5-40.

Hussey, K. e Pittock, J. The Energy–Water Nexus: Managing the Links between Energy and Water for a Sustainable Future. *Ecology and Society.* V. 17, n. 1, 2012.

IEA. International Energy Agency. *Water for Energy. Is energy becoming a thirstier resource?* IEA: 2012.

JANSKY, L., NAKAYAMA, M., e PACHOVA, N. I. Introduction: from domestic to international water security. In: JANSKY, L., NAKAYAMA, M., e PACHOVA, N. I. (eds.). International water security: domestic threats and opportunities. New York: United Nations University Press, 2008, p. 1-5.

LEFF, H. *Racionalidade Ambiental: a reapropriação social da natureza.* Rio de Janeiro: Civilização Brasileira, 2006.

MARTINEZ-ALIER, Joan. *O ecologismo dos pobres: conflitos ambientais e linguagens de valoração.* São Paulo: Contexto, 2007.

MIRUMACHI, N. Domestic issues in developing international waters in Lesotho: ensuring water security amidst political instability. In: JANSKY, L., NAKAYAMA, M., e PACHOVA, N. I. (eds.). *International water security: domestic threats and opportunities*. New York: United Nations University Press, 2008, p. 35-60.

PACHOVA, N. I. e JANSKY, L. Domestic drivers of international water security on the Danube. In: JANSKY, L., NAKAYAMA, M., e PACHOVA, N. I. (eds.). International water security: domestic threats and opportunities. New York: United Nations University Press, 2008, p. 61-78.

PATERSON, Matthew. *Understanding Global Environmental Politics: domination, accumulation, resistance*. Londres/Nova Iorque: Palgrave Macmillan, 2000. Capítulo 3: The 'normal and mundane practices of modernity': Global power structures and the environment. P. 35-65.

ONU. *Banco Mundial: 1,2 bilhão de pessoas ainda vivem sem eletricidade e 663 milhões sem água potável*. Disponível em: <https://nacoesunidas.org/banco-mundial-12-bilhao-de-pessoas-ainda-vivem-sem-eletricidade-e-663-milhoes-sem-agua-potavel/>. Acesso em: 30 março 2017.

RODRIGUES, d. J.; DELGADO, Anna; DELAQUIL, P.; SOHNS, A. Thirsty energy. *Water Papers*. Water Partnership Program. Washington: World Bank, 2013.

Schuster-Wallace, C. J.; Qadir, M.; Adeel, Z.; Renaud, F.; e Dickin, S. K. *Putting water and energy at the heart of sustainable development*. Hamilton (CA): United Nations University, 2015

UNDP. *Human Development Report*. UNDP: 2006.

YOFFE, S.; FISKE, G.; GIORDANO, M.; GIORDANO, M.; KELLI, L.; STAHL, K. e WOLF, A. Geography of international water conflict and cooperation: data sets and application. *Water Resources Research*. V. 40, 2004.

Os desafios da construção de políticas de enfrentamento aos riscos de desastres: reflexões sobre a inclusão da participação efetiva dos afetados

Maria Galleno de Souza Oliveira
e José Carlos de Oliveira

Introdução

Na concepção normativa oficial, os desastres são resultados de eventos adversos, naturais ou provocados pelo homem sobre um cenário vulnerável, causando greve perturbação ao funcionamento de uma comunidade ou sociedade, envolvendo extensivas perdas e danos humanos, materiais, econômicos ou ambientais, que excedem sua capacidade de lidar com o problema usando meios próprios (BRASIL, 2012).

Sob o ponto de vista social, os desastres são eventos concentrados no tempo e no espaço, em que uma sociedade ou uma parte relativamente autossuficiente dessa sofre grave perigo e incorre em grandes perdas e danos, que afetam a estrutura social a tal ponto que a execução total ou parcial de serviços e funções essenciais para a sociedade é interrompida (Frizt, 1961), rompendo o cotidiano social. Ou seja, eles são o resultado da associação simultânea entre causas naturais imediatas somadas aos processos intrínsecos de causalidade sistémica ou estrutural, decorrentes do sistema social e das suas relações com o ambiente construído (Ribeiro, 1995).

Portanto, apesar da "aparência" de natural, mesmo no caso dos desastres provocados por fenômenos naturais, um desastre não é natural, pois para que ele ocorra, deve haver correlação entre os riscos naturais (como um terremoto, um furacão, um tsunami, etc.) e certas condições físicas socioeconômicas, culturais e vulneráveis (tais como uma precária situação econômica, más condições de habitação, tipo de solo instável, má localização da habitação, etc.), o que significa que há um alto risco de haver o desastre quando um ou mais perigos naturais ocorrem em situações vulneráveis.

A partir desta perspectiva, depreende-se que o desastre é tanto um produto como resultado de processos sociais, econômicos culturais e históricos, e territorialmente confinados e em forma. Uma consequência importante desta visão é que um desastre, além de ser considerado em si mesmo como um fenômeno "anormal", também deve ser visto como a consequência de uma organização social, política e cultural (Lavell, 1993).

A governança dos desastres socioambientais

O termo governança tem múltiplas dimensões com significados e visões diversificados, podendo ser empregado no setor público e no setor privado. Em termos gerais, o Banco Mundial (World Bank, 1992) conceitua governança como a maneira pela qual o poder é exercido na gestão, administração e utilização dos recursos do património económico e social visando ao desenvolvimento do país, e identifica quatro áreas de governança: gestão do setor público, prestação de contas, quadro jurídico para o desenvolvimento, a informação e a transparência.

O conceito de governança envolve três dimensões: autoridade, tomada de decisões e prestação de contas. Sob essas dimensões, a governança é a forma como o poder é exercido, quem tem o poder e toma as decisões e como os cidadãos se fazem ouvir e como as decisões são tomadas (INSTITUTE ON GOVERNANCE, 2015). Assim, a governança engloba a gestão administrativa do Estado e a capacidade de articular e mobilizar os atores estatais e sociais, visando ao melhor desempenho das políticas para resolver os problemas de ação coletiva (Lima; Abrucio & Silva, 2014). No âmbito da governança nos setores públicos, compete examinar o papel das instituições, dos cidadãos, da sociedade civil, das normas e dos processos que afetam o que é prioridade na sociedade e a prestação de serviços públicos.

A partir desses conceitos e das orientações do Marco de Sendai (2015), compreende-se que a governança nos desastres socioambientais envolve vários grupos e elementos em nível nacional, regional e global, com a participação dos setores públicos e privados, organizações da sociedade civil, comunidade acadêmica e instituições científicas e de pesquisa, trabalhando em conjunto para promover a colaboração e implementar os instrumentos relevantes para a redução do risco de desastres.

No âmbito brasileiro, a governança dos desastres socioambientais é compartilhada entre a União, os Estados, o Distrito Federal e os Municípios, com a participação da sociedade civil. O Sistema Nacional de Proteção e Defesa Civil é constituído por órgãos e entidades da administração pública federal, dos Estados, do Distrito Federal e dos Municípios, e pelas entidades públicas e privadas que atuem significativamente na área de proteção e defesa civil.

Não obstante o avanço na governança mundial para diminuir os efeitos dos desastres, adotado desde a Resolução Nº 42/169 que instituiu a década de 1990 como "Década Internacional para a Redução das Catástrofes Naturais", passando pelas I Conferência Mundial para Redução de Risco de Desastres – Conferência de Yokohama (1994) e da II Conferência Mundial para a Redução de Risco de Desastres – Conferência de Hyogo (2004) até chegar na III Conferência Mundial para a Redução de Risco de Desastres – Conferência de Sendai (2015), constata-se que eles continuam a atingir milhões de pessoas por todos os continentes da terra.

No mundo inteiro, no período que compreende entre 2005-2015, quando foi adotado o Marco de Hyogo, mais de 700.000 pessoas morreram, acima de 1.4 milhão de pessoas foram feridas, aproximadamente 23 milhões foram desalojadas e mais de 1.500 milhão de pessoas, de uma forma ou de outra, foram prejudicadas pelos mais diversos tipos de desastres. Além disso, as mulheres, crianças, pessoas com necessidades especiais e em situação de vulnerabilidade foram desproporcionalmente as mais afetadas. As perdas econômicas totais ultrapassaram a soma de 1.3 bilhão de dólares, sendo que entre 2008-2012, 144 milhões de pessoas sofreram deslocamentos forçados em consequência dos desastres.

Conforme o Relatório Anual de Catástrofes Naturais de 2016 da Munich Re (2016), após a adoção do Marco de Sendai (2015-2030), no ano de 2016, houve o decréscimo mundial de óbitos causados por desastres ambientais em relação ao ano de 2015, passando de 25.400 mortes para 8.700 em 2016. Por outro lado, sob o ponto de vista econômico, ocorreu o aumento de quase 70% de impactos financeiros causados por desastres, que atingiu o valor de aproximadamente 17,5 bilhões de euros em prejuízos econômicos. Interpretando o gráfico da Figura 1, observa-se que, em 2016, ocorreram 750 desastres naturais e tanto as perdas globais quanto as perdas com seguro foram superiores à média ajustada pela inflação nos últimos dez anos (US $ 154 bilhões e 45,1 bilhões, respectivamente), sendo que os países mais atingidos pelas perdas econômicas foram: Japão, China, Caribe, Estados Unidos da América e Europa.

Figura 1: Catástrofes Naturais em 2016

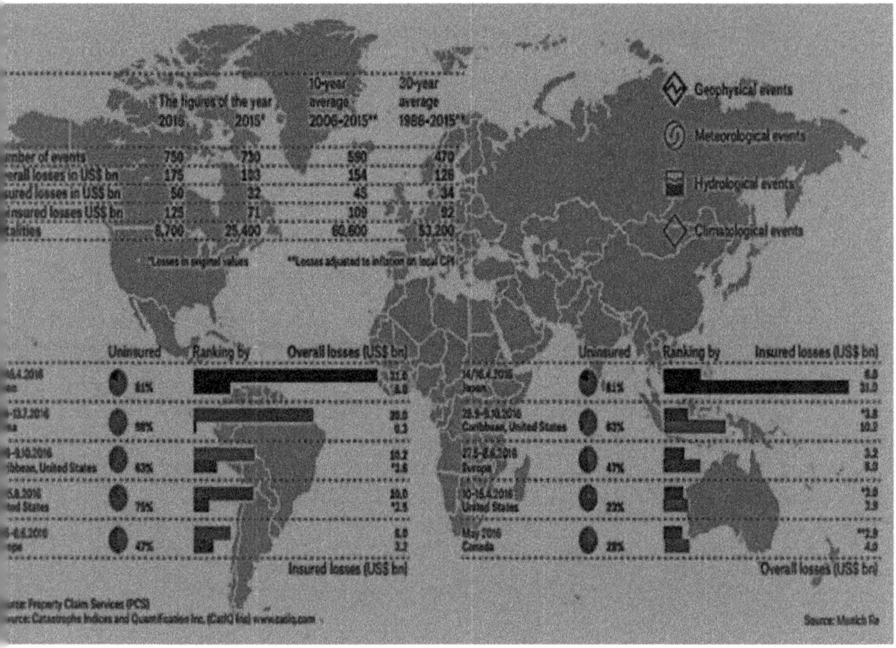

Fonte: Munich Re – Press Release.
Disponível em: https://www.munichre.com/site/corporate/get/params_E-192025720_Dattachment/1351568/20160103_RZ_Big-five-overview-en.pdf

O elevado número de inundações, incluindo inundações de rios e inundações repentinas, foi excepcional e representou 34% das perdas globais, em comparação com a média de 21% nos últimos dez anos (Munich RE, 2016). Os desastres denominados de "pequenas escalas" e de "evolução lenta" incidiram particularmente sobre as comunidades, as famílias, as pequenas e médias empresas, o que constituiu uma alta percentagem de perdas totais, expondo-os ainda mais aos riscos e vulnerabilidades.

Os desastres socioambientais e seus tipos

De modo geral, os desastres podem ser classificados em dois grupos de estrutura genérica (natural e tecnológico), que são subdivididos em subgrupos, considerados por tipos e subtipos.

Os desastres classificados como naturais (Quadro 1) são aqueles consequentes de eventos geológicos, hidrológicos, meteorológicos, climáticos e biológicos. Os desastres tecnológicos (Quadro 2) são provenientes de ações antrópicas e relacionados a substâncias radioativas, produtos perigosos, incêndios urbanos, obras civis, transportes de passageiros e cargas não perigosas.

Quadro 1: Classificação dos desastres naturais

Biológicos	Geofísicos	Hidrológicos	Meteorológicos
Epidemias - Doença infecciosa viral - Doença infecciosa bacteriana - Doença infecciosa parasitária - Doença infecciosa fúngica - Doença infecciosa de príon	**Sismos** **Vulcões** **Movimento de massa (seco)** - Queda de rocha - Desmoronamento - Avalanche - Sedimentação	**Chuvas** - Inundação - Cheias - Tempestade marítima/ inundação costeira	**Tempestades** - Ciclone tropical - Ciclone extratropical - Tempestade local
Infestação de Inseto		**Movimento de massa (úmido)** - Queda de rocha - Desmoronamento - Avalanche - Sedimentação **Hidro Meteorológico**	**Climatológicos**
Ataque de Animal			**Temperatura Extrema** - Onda de calor - Onda de frio - Condição extrema de inverno
			Seca
			Incêncio - Incêndio florestal - Incêndio terrestre
			Extraterrestre
			Impacto - Meteoro - Asteroide - Cometa - Clima espacial

Fonte: *Annual Disaster Statistical Annual*: The numbers and Trends. GUHA-SAPIR, Debarati *et al.*, 2015.

Quadro 2: Classificação dos desastres tecnológicos

<table>
<tr><th>Substâncias radioativas</th><th>Produtos perigosos</th><th>Incêndios urbanos</th><th>Obras civis</th></tr>
<tr><td>Siderais com riscos radioativos
- Queda de satélite</td><td rowspan="2">Desastres em plantas e distritos industriais, parques e armazenamentos com extravasamento de produtos perigosos
- Liberação de produtos químicos para a atmosfera causada por explosão ou incêndio</td><td rowspan="2">Incêndio em planta e distritos industriais, parques e depósitos</td><td rowspan="2">Colapso de edificações</td></tr>
<tr><td rowspan="2">Substâncias e equipamentos radioativos de uso em pesquisas, indústrias e usinas nucleares
- Fontes radioativas em processo de produção</td></tr>
<tr><td>Contaminação da água
- Liberação de produtos químicos nos sistemas de água potável
- Derramamento de produtos químicos em ambiente lacustre, fluvial, marinho e aquíferos</td><td rowspan="3">Incêndio em aglomerados residenciais</td><td>Rompimento/ colapso de barragens</td></tr>
<tr><td rowspan="2">Risco de intensa poluição ambiental provocada por resíduos radioativos</td><td>Conflitos bélicos
- Liberação de produtos químicos e contaminação como consequência de ações militares</td><td rowspan="2">Transporte de passageiros e cargas não perigosas
- Rodoviário
- Aéreo
- Ferroviário
- Marítimo
- Aquaviário</td></tr>
<tr><td>Transporte de produtos perigosos
- Rodoviário
- Aéreo
- Ferroviário
- Duto viário
- Marítimo
- Aquaviário</td></tr>
</table>

Fonte: Instrução Normativa nº2, de 20 de dezembro de 2016 – Anexo V – COBRADE. Ministério da Integração, 2016.

A Instrução Normativa nº 1, de 24 de agosto de 2012, classificava os desastres quanto à intensidade em dois níveis: nível I – desastres de média intensidade e nível II – desastres de grande intensidade (art. 3º). Entretanto, em 20 de dezembro de 2016, o Ministério da Integração publicou a Instrução Normativa nº2, que fez uma pequena alteração, classificando os desastres, quanto à intensidade, em três níveis: a) nível I – desastres de pequena intensidade, b) nível II – desastres de média intensidade e c) nível III – desastres de grande intensidade (art. 2º).

A IN nº 2, de 20 de dezembro de 2016, conceitua os desastres de pequena intensidade como sendo aqueles em que existem apenas danos humanos consideráveis, e a situação de normalidade pode ser reestabelecida pelo governo local ou complementado por recursos estaduais e federais, e será decretado estado de emergência.

Os desastres de média intensidade são aqueles em que os danos e prejuízos são suportáveis e superáveis pelo governo local, e o restabelecimento da situação de normalidade poderá ser com recursos locais, ou complementados com recursos estaduais e federais. São caracterizados pela ocorrência, de ao menos, dois danos, sendo obrigatório que um deles seja dano humano, que importem em prejuízo econômico público ou prejuízo econômico privado que afete a capacidade do poder público local em responder e gerenciar a crise instalada. Neste caso, será decretado estado de emergência.

Nos desastres de grande intensidade, os danos e prejuízos não são suportáveis e superáveis pelo governo local, necessitando, para o restabelecimento da situação de normalidade, da mobilização e ação coordenada das três esferas de atuação do Sistema Nacional de Proteção e Defesa Civil, e, em alguns casos, até de ajuda internacional, sendo decretado estado de calamidade pública.

Essas alterações não melhoraram o conceito de desastres, pelo contrário, tornou-os vagos e confusos, além de não seguir a orientação da EM-DATA e da UNISDR, que elaborou o conceito de desastres universal e que era adotado pela Instrução Normativa nº 1, de 24 de agosto de 2012. Ou seja, houve uma regressão quanto ao conceito e classificação oficial dos desastres no Brasil.

Quanto às mudanças climáticas, estas também são consideradas como um dos fatores que geram risco de desastres, interferindo no clima global e causando grandes secas (Etiópia e o Nordeste do Brasil) e invernos com temperaturas extremas (Estados Unidos, Europa), ondas de calor e fome (Etiópia), ciclones catastróficos (leste e sudeste da Ásia e dos

Estados Unidos) e graves inundações (Tailândia, Brasil, Índia, Estados Unidos, Inglaterra, Itália).

Outro tipo de desastre, que é classificado na categoria de tecnológico relacionado a obras civis, e que frequentemente atinge a sociedade, são aqueles causados por rompimento de barragens e diques, como exemplo cita-se o recentemente ocorrido na Barragem da Samarco, que arrasou vários distritos da região do Município de Mariana (MG) e destruiu grande parte do ecossistema da bacia do Rio Doce, além de causar a morte de 19 pessoas e grandes prejuízos econômicos e sociais.

Neste contexto de desastres antrópicos que afligem as populações e aumentam seus sofrimentos, inserem-se os conflitos armados de diferentes magnitudes, tais como a invasão do Afeganistão e do Iraque pelos Estados Unidos no início dos anos dois mil, a atual guerra civil na Síria e a crescente atividade terrorista do Estado islâmico. Em consequência desses conflitos, ocorre o deslocamento forçado de pessoas, levando-as a migrações em massa a outros países, principalmente os países europeus, o que coopera para aumentar a situação de vulnerabilidade desses grupos de pessoas.

O quadro brasileiro dos desastres socioambientais

No que se refere ao Brasil, ao longo dos anos, o País foi atingido por vários tipos de desastres, causados principalmente por vendavais (Taquarituba-SP), tornados (Santa Catarina), tremor de terra (Ceará), inundações (Porto Alegre, São Luiz do Paraitinga-SP), desmoronamentos (Rio de Janeiro), rompimento de barragem (Mariana-MG), maré vermelha (Bahia) e secas (Acre, Alagoas, Bahia, Ceará, Espírito Santo, Pernambuco, Mato Grosso, Maranhão, norte de Minas Gerais, Paraíba, Pernambuco, Piauí, Rio Grande do Norte, Sergipe, Tocantins, entre outros).

Somente no ano de 2016, 1.083 municípios brasileiros estiveram sob situação de emergência em todo o Brasil, conforme levantamento realizado pelo G1 (Quadro 3).

Quadro 3 – Estados Afetados pela Seca/2016 –
Parcela dos municípios em situação de emergência

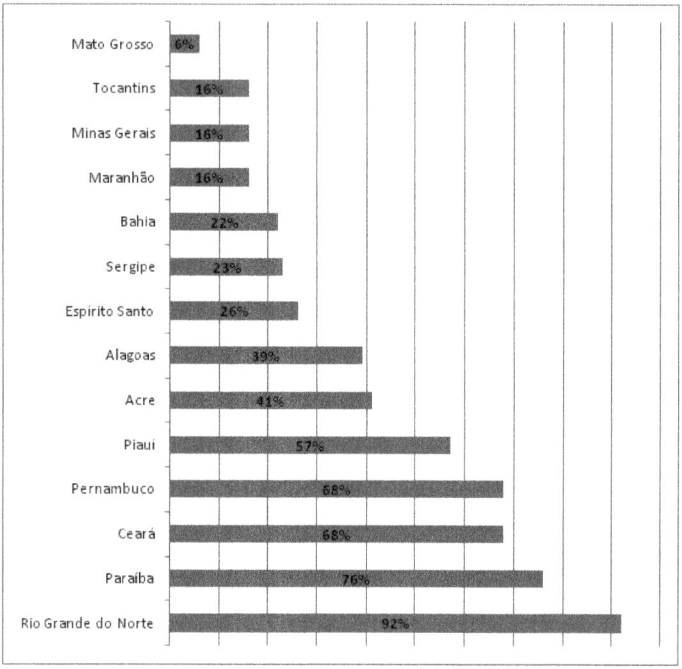

Fonte: Portal G1 – Disponível em: http://g1.globo.com/politica/noticia/2016/10/seca-coloca-quase-11-mil-cidades-em-situacao-de-emergencia-no-pais.html

O Nordeste (Figura 2) foi a região que teve o maior número de municípios afetados, todavia há registro de estiagem e seca nos Estados de Mato Grosso e Goiás (região Centro-Oeste), Acre, Amazonas e Roraima (região Norte), Espírito Santo (região Sudeste).

Figura 2: Monitor de Secas no Nordeste do Brasil – Dez.2016

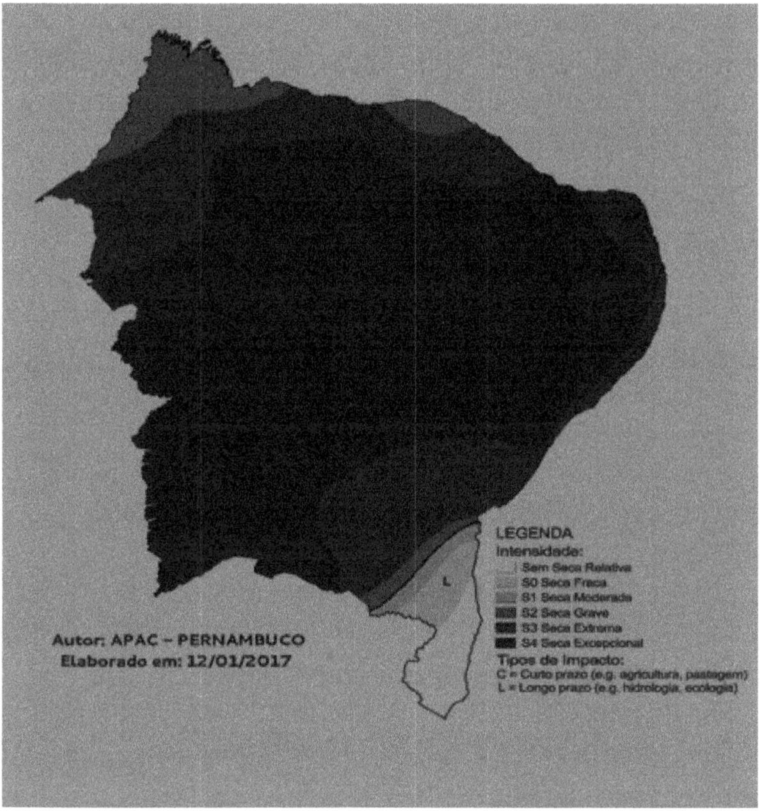

Fonte: Monitor de Secas do Nordeste do Brasil. ANA.
Disponível em: http://monitordesecas.ana.gov.br/

Apesar da frequente ocorrência destes tipos de desastres, ainda persiste a cultura de que não ocorre desastre no Brasil, pois eles são provocados pela "natureza" ou "vontade de Deus". Porém, nos últimos quinze anos, essa percepção aos poucos está sendo alterada, principalmente porque os poderes públicos são cada vez mais confrontados pelos órgãos internacionais especializados na redução de risco de desastres e pela própria sociedade local, que, ao exercer sua cidadania, exige respostas e soluções eficientes, eficazes e rápidas aos problemas acarretados pelos desastres. Por outro lado, a sociedade cidadã também não aceita a ideia de que não existem responsáveis pelos desastres e que os "custos" devem ser diluídos entre todos, e exige a identificação das causas e que seja responsabilizado quem os provocou.

Os meios de enfrentamento aos desastres: desafios e respostas

Em resposta a desafios significativos expostos pelos desastres socioambientais, a comunidade internacional busca meios para enfrentá-los e superá-los através de uma série de iniciativas globais, designadamente no âmbito da III Conferência de Sendai para a Redução do Risco de Desastres de 2015, os Objetivos de Desenvolvimento Sustentável da ONU de 2015, a Conferência sobre Mudança Climática da ONU de 2015, e a Cúpula Mundial da Ajuda Humanitária de 2016, visando a fortalecer a governança na área de gestão e redução do risco de desastres.

No caso do Brasil, há vários mecanismos jurídicos, políticas públicas e sociais voltados para prevenir, preparar, mitigar, responder e recuperar a sociedade e a população atingida pelos desastres, entre os quais se elenca a Política Nacional de Proteção e Defesa Civil – Lei nº 12.608/2012, a Política Nacional de Segurança de Barragens – Lei nº 12.334, de 20 de setembro de 2010, a Política Nacional de Mudanças Climáticas – Lei nº 12.187/2009, e a Constituição Federal do Brasil de 1988. E, mais recentemente, a Política Nacional de Combate à Desertificação e Mitigação dos Efeitos da Seca – Lei nº 13.153/2015.

Nos vários níveis da estrutura estatal brasileira (federal, estadual e municipal), foram criados órgãos de monitoramento e de implementação para desenvolver ações efetivas voltadas aos desastres. No meio científico, há vários centros de pesquisa com o objetivo de analisar as causas e as consequências dos desastres no Brasil.

De acordo com Margareta Wahlström (ex-Presidente da UNISDR), em discurso proferido durante a Terceira Conferência da ONU para Redução do Risco de Desastres (SENDAI, 2015):

> Apesar de muitos sucessos e a melhora do desempenho na gestão de desastres, é decepcionante notar que 700.000 pessoas morreram em eventos de desastres ao longo dos últimos dez anos. Um total de 1,7 mil milhões de pessoas tiveram suas vidas interrompidas de alguma forma. É de grande preocupação que as perdas económicas nos principais eventos de desastres relatados chegam a US $ 1,4 trilhão.

Isto é, mesmo com os avanços obtidos na gestão do risco de desastres, tanto no contexto global quanto no local, perdura a percepção de que a intensidade e frequência de desastres 'naturais' e 'antrópicos' se aceleraram e aumentaram nas últimas décadas.

No Brasil, conforme estudos técnicos realizados pela Confederação Nacional dos Municípios, os prejuízos econômicos causados por fenômenos naturais extremos (secas e chuvas), no período de 2005-2015, ultrapassaram o montante de R$ 173,5 bilhões (Tabela 1), sendo que a União, os Estados e Municípios não conseguiram suprir tais prejuízos econômicos, que acumularam o total de R$ 161,2 bilhões nos setores do agronegócio, pecuária, indústrias e comércio.

Tabela 1 – Prejuízos causados por desastres – Todas as regiões

Tabela 1 – PREJUÍZOS CAUSADOS POR DESASTRES - TODAS AS REGIÕES				
Ano	**2012**	**2013**	**2014**	**2015**
Centro-Oeste	8.127.500,00	570.833.745,98	1.039.380.416,41	44.998.455,05
Nordeste	513.708.761,74	40.781.016.477,29	50.230.962.590,61	14.170.903.448,01
Norte	1.900.798,00	1.556.720.728,08	1.259.320.106,04	1.936.473.050,96
Sudeste	106.620.554,65	27.033.235.938,00	24.590.914.187,56	3.444.241.590,33
Sul	78.184.800,00	1.635.856.053,92	3.454.989.793,75	1.069.955.948,02
Total	**708.542.414,39**	**71.577.662.943,27**	**80.575.567.094,37**	**20.666.572.492,37**

Fonte: Estudo Técnico: Prejuízos causados por desastres naturais – 2012-2015, CNM, 2016.

O estudo técnico da Confederação Nacional de Municípios (CNM), ao avaliar sobre os danos humanos, observa que o número de pessoas atingidas pelos desastres no Brasil ultrapassou *53,6 milhões* de afetados, com *864 vítimas fatais*, incluindo as 242 pessoas que morreram no incêndio ocorrido na *boate Kiss* (Santa Maria-RS) em 2012 (Tabela 2).

Tabela 2 – Danos Humanos (R$)

Tabela 2 – Danos Humanos (R$)				
ANO	**2012**	**2013**	**2014**	**2015**
Centro-Oeste	5.296	1.345.286	536.222	76.164
Nordeste	446.648	15.344.249	11.612.924	6.527.868
Norte	3.963	624.420	833.310	900.663
Sudeste	64.644	5.736.005	1.963.642	1.421.947
Sul	93.904	2.210.781	3.108.934	795.759
Total	**614.451**	**25.260.741**	**18.055.032**	**9.633.417**

Fonte: Estudo Técnico: Prejuízos causados por desastres naturais – 2012-2015, CNM, 2016.

Portanto, para continuar os progressos obtidos na redução do risco de desastres, tem de haver investimento custo-eficiente na prevenção. E, para isso ocorrer, é necessário o trabalho contínuo e conjunto entre governos, iniciativa privada, meio científico e a sociedade, em todos os níveis e graus, e também que se disponibilizem tecnologia, conhecimento e instrumentos normativos, a fim de embasar as políticas públicas, preparar, envolver e criar oportunidade a todos os afetados, principalmente aos mais vulneráveis, entre os quais se encontram as mulheres, os idosos, as crianças, os povos indígenas e quilombolas, os portadores de necessidade especial e os imigrantes.

Outros desafios e respostas – a vulnerabilidade e a perda do bem-estar em casos de desastres socioambientais

O relatório *Unbreakable: Bulding the Resilience of the Poor in the Face of Natural Disaster* (Hallegatte *et al.*, 2017), publicado pelo Banco Mundial, expôs que as perdas econômicas advindas por desastres naturais e antrópicos chegaram a 92 bilhões de dólares no ano de 2015. Todavia, esse tipo de avaliação tradicional, que mede a gravidade dos desastres e seus impactos socioeconômicos com base nos danos causados aos edifícios, produção agrícola, infraestrutura e equipamentos, não considera o quanto é suportável ao bem-estar das populações, tendo em vista que o grau maior ou menor da perda que será sentido depende de quem o experimente, pois um dólar perdido para um país (comunidade ou pessoa) rico não terá o mesmo impacto que causará a um país (comunidade ou pessoas) pobre.

Assim, além de avaliar as perdas em ativos e em produção, deve-se considerar a perda do bem-estar, tendo em vista que a pobreza aumenta desproporcionalmente o risco de desastres, pois as populações mais pobres são mais expostas às ameaças e têm maior vulnerabilidade, havendo menor capacidade e resiliência de enfrenta-los e recuperar-se.

Portanto, há necessidade de que existam políticas efetivas de redução da pobreza e que façam parte do conjunto de ferramentas das ações de redução do risco de desastres. O relatório do Banco Mundial observa que três indicadores devem ser considerados no desenvolvimento de políticas públicas voltadas à redução do risco de desastres:

1) complementariedade entre os esforços para a redução da pobreza e dos riscos de desastres – os países mais pobres (e as populações pobres) sofrem mais desproporcionalmente os efeitos negativos dos desastres, pois encontram-se mais expostos às ameaças e riscos, o que os tornam mais vulneráveis. Além disso, estão sujeitos a efeitos irreversíveis sobre a educação e a saúde, aumentando a transmissão intergeracional de pobreza e, com isso, tornando-os mais vulneráveis aos desastres, criando assim um ciclo que tende a aumentar e crescer. Portanto, para reduzir o risco de desastres, deve ocorrer concomitantemente com ações políticas para a redução da pobreza.

2) os desastres socioambientais afetam o bem-estar mais do que sugerem as estimativas tradicionais (baseadas em danos aos ativos e à produção) – estudos realizados pelo Banco Mundial em 117 países, com base em estimativas de resiliência socioeconômica (Mapa 1), incluindo na análise os elementos pobreza e falta de capacidade para lidar com os desastres, demonstraram que as perdas de bem-estar (Mapa 2) devido aos desastres naturais que atingem os países mais pobres ou em desenvolvimento, equivalem a 520 bilhões de dólares de queda no consumo

anual, o que corresponde a 60% a mais do que as perdas com ativos. Desse modo, o projeto da gestão de risco de desastres não deve depender apenas de perdas de ativos, mas também abranger as perdas com o bem-estar das populações.

Mapa 1: A resiliência socioeconômica mede a capacidade de uma população para perda de ativos - Resiliência socioeconômica (percentual) de 117 países

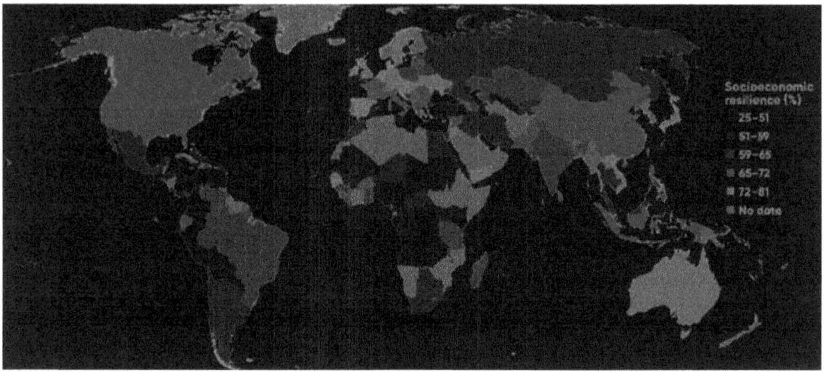

Fonte: Hallegatte *et al.*, 2016.

Mapa 2: O risco para o bem estar combina ameaça, exposição, vulnerabilidade dos ativos e resiliência socioeconômica – O risco para o bem estar como porcentagem do PIB anual de 117 países

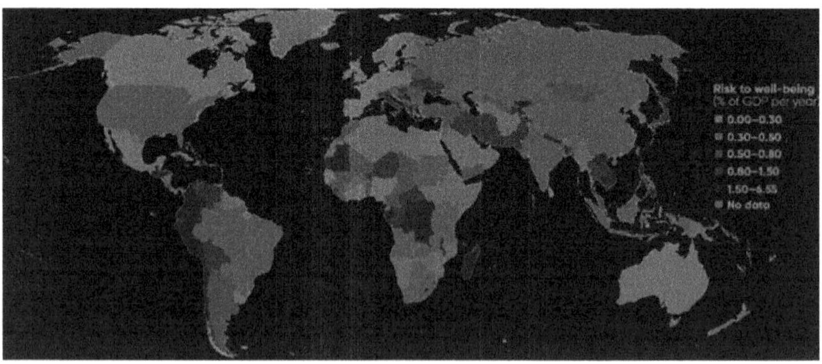

Fonte: Hallegatte *et al*, 2016.

3) políticas públicas voltadas para tornar os países e as pessoas mais resilientes – significa que a gestão dos riscos de desastres deve incluir um conjunto diversificado de ferramentas para diferentes tipos de desastres e de lugares. Portanto, as políticas de aumento da resiliência devem abranger inclusão financeira, acesso ao seguro de saúde e outros tipos de seguros, maior proteção social e redes de segurança adaptativas às situações de desastres para garantir o reestabelecimento dos afetados, e instrumentos financeiros que assegurem que os governos e as autoridades locais tenham recursos necessários e suficientes para atuar em situações de crise.

Considerações finais

Os desastres socioambientais atingem indistintamente os países e a sociedade civil mundial, porém, devido a maior exposição aos riscos, como consequência de maiores vulnerabilidades e menor resiliência, são as populações de países em desenvolvimento ou subdesenvolvidos que são as mais impactadas, criando assim um ciclo contínuo e gradual de aumento das vulnerabilidades e de pobreza.

O relatório *Unbreakable: Bulding the Resilience of the Poor in the Face of Natural Disaster* (Hallegatte *et al.*, 2017) alerta para o fato de que os desastres naturais afetam o bem-estar das pessoas, principalmente daquelas que se encontram em extrema pobreza. Com base em estimativas realizadas em 89 países, o relatório conclui, que se pudessem ser evitados todos os desastres no próximo ano, haveria uma diminuição em 26 milhões do número de pessoas que subsistem com menos de 1,90 dólar/dia. Pois o impacto sobre a pobreza é muito maior devido ao fato de que as pessoas pobres estão muito mais expostas aos riscos, perdem muito mais em relação à sua riqueza, quando são atingidas, e recebem menos apoio de seus familiares, amigos, sistemas financeiros e dos governos. Além disso, os desastres podem levar as pessoas à pobreza, por isso a avaliação das políticas públicas voltadas para a redução dos desastres deve combinar as perdas em ativo (que é a combinação de ameaça+exposição+v ulnerabilidade) e as perdas de bem-estar (que engloba ameaça+exposição+vulnerabilidade+resiliência socioeconômica), utilizando diferentes instrumentos de políticas para diferentes tipos de desastres e populações, aumentando a resiliência e a capacidade de resposta aos riscos de desastres, o que diminuirá a vulnerabilidade.

Os desastres socioambientais seguirão existindo, portanto é relevante investir e efetivar os quadros normativos, as políticas e as ações que abordam sobre a eficácia da gestão de riscos dos desastres; desenvolver os mecanismos utilizados para proteger e integrar as pessoas, as comunidades, os países, os meios de subsistência, a saúde, o patrimônio cultural, os ativos socioeconômicos, financeiros e o ecossistema; reforçar a resiliência e diminuir as vulnerabilidades; e incorporar, nesse processo, a experiência, o conhecimento tradicional, as habilidades e as capacidades das populações e povos locais.

De modo geral, o esforço da sociedade mundial diante do grande desafio para minimizar os riscos dos desastres, para melhorar o bem-estar social e diminuir a pobreza em consequência dos desastres, deverá superar as resistências estatais e as da sociedade civil, incrementar as ações para identificar e atribuir as responsabilidades múltiplas, dar condições para inserir e aumentar o protagonismo da população local na construção de políticas públicas sob o ponto de vista dos afetados, associadas às relações entre direito, marco regulatório, saberes tradicionais, vulnerabilidades e riscos.

Referências

BRASIL (2012). *Lei nº 12.608, de 10 de abril de 2012*. Disponível em: http://www.planalto.gov.br/ccivil_03/_Ato2011-2014/2012/Lei/L12608.htm. Acesso em: 30 ago.2016.

BRASIL (2010). *Lei nº 12.334, de 20 de setembro de 2010*. Disponível em: http://www.planalto.gov.br/ccivil_03/_Ato2007-2010/2010/Lei/L12334.htm. Acesso em: 10 set.2016.

BRASIL (2009). *Lei nº 12.187, de 29 de dezembro de 2009*. Disponível em: http://www.planalto.gov.br/ccivil_03/_ato2007-2010/2009/lei/l12187.htm. Acesso em: 30 ago.2016.

BRASIL. MINISTÉRIO DA INTEGRAÇÃO (2012). Instrução Normativa nº 1, de 24.08.2012 – Anexo I – COBRADE. Disponível em: http://mi.gov.br/documents/10157/3776390/Instru_Normativa_01.pdf/8634a6e3-78cc-422a-aa1d-7312ce7f1055. Acesso em: 10 set.2016.

BRASIL. MINISTÉRIO DA INTEGRAÇÃO (2016). Instrução Normativa nº 2, de 20 de dezembro de 2016 – Anexo V – COBRADE. Disponível em: http://mi.gov.br/documents/3958478/0/Anexo+V+-+Cobrade_com+simbologia.pdf/d7d8bb0b-07f3-4572-a6ca-738daa95feb0

CONSELHO NACIONAL DE MUNICÍPIOS – CNM (2015)). *Estudo Técnico*: Os prejuízos causados por desastres naturais – 2012 a 2015. Disponível em: http://www.cnm.org.br/portal/dmdocuments/Preju%C3%ADzos%20causados%20por%20desastres%20naturais%20-%202012%20a%202015%20(2016).pdf. Acesso em: 30.06.2016.

FREY, K (2000). Políticas públicas: um debate conceitual e reflexões referentes à prática da análise de políticas públicas no Brasil. *Planejamento e Políticas Públicas*, Brasília-DF, n. 21, p. 212-259, jun.

FRITZ, Charles E (1961). Disaster. In: *Contemporary Social Problems*: An introduction to the sociology of deviant behavior and social disorganization contributors. MERTON, R. K.; NISBET, R. A. (Orgs) New York: Haarcourt, Brace & World Publisher, p. 651-694.

GUHA-SAPIR, Debarati; HOYOIS, Philippe; BELOW, Regina (2015). *Annual Disaster Statistical Review 2015*: The numbers and trends. Bussels: CRED. Disponível em: http://cred.be/sites/default/files/ADSR_2015.pdf. Acesso em: 12 ago.2016.

HALLEGATE, Stephane; VOGT-SCHILB, Adrien; BANGALORE, Mook; ROZENBER, Julie (2017). Unbreakable: Building the Resilience of the Poor in the Face of Natural Disasters. Washington D.C: World

Bank. Disponível em: https://openknowledge.worldbank.org/handle/10986/25335. Acesso em: 20 ago.2016.

HAPER, Erica (2015). *International Law and Standards Applicable in Natural Disaster Situations*. Rome: International Development Law Organization, 2015.

INSTITUTE ON GOVERNANCE (2015). *Defining Governance*. Disponível em: http://iog.ca/defining-governance/ Acesso em: 02 ago.2015

LAVELL, Allan (1993). Ciencias Sociales y Desastres Naturales en América Latina: un encuentro inconcluso, p. 111-127. IN: MASKEY, Andrew (compilador). *Los Desastres non son naturales. LA RED* – Red de Estudios Sociales en Prevención de Desastres en América Latina. Disponível em: http://www.desenredando.org/public/libros/1993/ldnsn/LosDesastresNoSonNaturales-1.0.0.pdf. Acesso em: 12 ago.2016.

LIMA, Angelo José Rodrigues; ABRUCIO, Fernando Luiz; SILVA, Francisco Carlos Bezerra(2014). *Governança dos recursos hídricos*: proposta de indicador para acompanhar sua implementação.

Disponível em: http://d3nehc6yl9qzo4.cloudfront.net/downloads/wwf_fgv_governanca_dos_recursos_hidricos.pdf. Acesso em: 20 out.2016.

MASKEY, Andrew (1993). Vulnerabilidad y mitigación de desastres, p. 93-110. In.: MASKEY, Andrew (compilador). *Los Desastres non son naturales. LA RED* – Red de Estudios Sociales en Prevención de Desastres en América Latina. Disponível em: http://www.desenredando.org/public/libros/1993/ldnsn/LosDesastresNoSonNaturales-1.0.0.pdf. Acesso em: 12 ago.2016.

MONITOR DE SECAS DO NORDESTE DO BRASIL, ANA (2016). Disponível em: http://monitordesecas.ana.gov.br/. Acesso em: 30 dez.2016.

MUDANÇAS climáticas – *Sociedade de risco*, 2011, Ano 8. 68 ed. – 2011. Disponível em: http://www.ipea.gov.br/desafios/index.php?view= article&catid= 28%3 Areportagensmaterias&id=2600%3Amudancas-climaticas-sociedade-de-risco&tmpl =component&print=1&layout=default&page=&option=com_content&Itemid=23. Acesso em: 10 ago.2016.

MULUGETA, Genene; AYHONGE, Samuel; DABY, Deolall; DUBE, Opha P.; GUNDYANGA, Francis; LUCIO, Filipe; DURRHEIM, Ray (2007). *Natural and Human-induced Hazards and Disasters in sub--Saharan Africa*. Disponível em: http://www.icsu.org/africa/publications /ICSUROAScienceP lanonHazardsandDisasters.pdf. Acesso em: 20 set.2016.

MUNICH RE (2016). Press release: Natural catastrophe losses at their highest for four years, Germany. Disponível em: https://www.munichre.com/site/corporate/get/params_E-192025720_Dattachment/1351568/20160103_RZ_Big-five-overview-en.pdf. Acesso em: 06 jan.2017.

OPAS (1994). Hacia un mundo más seguro frente a los desastres naturales: la trayectoria de América Latina y el Caribe. Washington: OPAS. Disponível em: http://www.paho.org/disasters/index.php?option=com_content&view=article&id=668%3Aa-world-safe--from-natural-disasters&catid=895%3Abooks&Itemid=924&lang=es. Acesso em: 20 jul.2016.

PORTAL G1 (2016). *Seca coloca quase 1, 1 mil cidades em situação de emergência no país*. DISPONÍVEL EM: http://g1.globo.com/politica/noticia/2016/10/seca-coloca-quase-11-mil-cidades-em-situacao-de--emergencia-no-pais.html. Acesso em: 20 nov.2016.

RADIO ONU (2015). *Desastres naturais afetaram 100 milhões de pessoas no mundo em 2015*. Disponível em: http://www.unmultimedia.org/radio/portuguese/2016/02/desastres-naturais-afetaram-100-milhoes-de-pessoas-no-mundo-em-2015/#.V-pnzigrLIV. Acesso em: 20 jul.2016.

RENAUD, Fabrice G.; SUDMIER-RIEUX, Karen; ESTRELLA, Marisol. UNEP (2013). *The role of ecosystems in disaster risk reduction*. Tokyo:

United Nations University Press. Disponível em: https://collections.unu.edu/eserv/UNU:1995/text_808710_9789280812213.pdf. Acesso em: 20 ago.2016.

RIBEIRO, João Manuel (1995). Sociologia dos Desastres. *Sociologia – Problemas e Práticas*, n. 18, p.23-43.

UNEP (2015). *DISASTERS & CONFLICTS: Field and policy updates* – July/December. Disponível em: http://www.unep.org/disastersandconflicts/portals/155/dnc/docs/qpr/UNEP_Policy_Field_Updates_Dec_2015.pdf. Acesso em: 05 set.2016.

UNEP. *From conflict to peacebuilding* - The role of natural resources and the environment. Disponível em: http://postconflict.unep.ch/publications/pcdmb_policy_01.pdf. Acesso em: 19 jul.2016.

UNISDR (2015). *2015 Disasters in numbers*. Disponível em: http://www.unisdr.org/files/47804_2015disastertrendsinfographic.pdf. Acesso em: 20 jul.2016.

UNISDR 2015). *GAR2015 – Evaluación Global sobre Reducción del Riesgo de Desastres 2015*. Diponível em: http://www.preventionweb.net/english/hyogo/gar/2015/en/gar-pdf/GAR2015_SP.pdf. Acesso em: 30 ago.2016.

UNISDR. *GAR2015 – resumo*. Disponível em: http://www.preventionweb.net/english/hyogo/gar/2015/en/gar-pdf/GAR15_at_a_glance_ES.pdf. Acesso em: 1º set.2016.

VEJA ON LINE. *Especial on line – Desastres Naturais*. Disponível em: http://veja.abril.com.br/especiais_online/desastres_naturais/index.html. Acesso em: 1º set.2016.

WORLD BANK (1992). *Governance and Development*. Disponível em: http://documents.worldbank.org/curated/pt/604951468739447676/pdf/multi-page.pdf. Acesso em: 15 fev.2013.

As condições histórico-sociais de exercício da cidadania no Brasil: a cidadania bloqueada

Murilo Gaspardo e Liz Marina Tamião Santana

Introdução

O crescimento constante das abstenções e votos brancos e nulos nas últimas eleições, os diversos escândalos de corrupção, as crises fiscal e econômica, as deficiências na prestação dos serviços públicos e no funcionamento da Administração Pública, e a disfuncionalidade do "presidencialismo de coalizão", dentre outros problemas que marcam o sistema político brasileiro contemporâneo, suscitam debates nos meios acadêmico, jornalístico e político sobre a necessidade de reformas das instituições políticas, tanto no que se refere à representação partidária-eleitoral, como a um possível aperfeiçoamento e incremento dos institutos participativos, por exemplo: conselhos, conferências, audiências e consultas públicas; plebiscitos, referendos e iniciativa popular; orçamento participativo e Emendas às Leis Orgânicas do Programa de Metas.[1]

1 A Emenda à Lei Orgânica do *Programa de Metas* é uma inovação institucional aprovada de forma pioneira no Município de São Paulo no ano de 2008, por iniciativa do Movimento Nossa São Paulo (MNSP) – posteriormente denominado de Rede Nossa São Paulo (RNSP), que também realiza o monitoramento de sua aplicação. A norma instituiu a obrigatoriedade de Prefeitos apresentarem pro-

Questões semelhantes encontram-se na ordem do dia por todo o mundo, tanto naqueles Estados de regimes democráticos maduros, como nos que ainda há grandes fragilidades. Há uma dimensão global nas explicações para esse fenômeno relacionada com a globalização neoliberal, a desterritorialização da política e o policentrismo do poder. Por outro lado, há questões históricas, políticas, culturais e socioeconômica de ordem interna que necessariamente devem ser consideradas.

A Teoria do Estado analisa esse problema combinando as perspectivas nacional e global, jurídica e política. Isso porque, trata-se de uma disciplina cujo campo de investigações abrange as questões pertinentes à região limítrofe entre o direito e a política, especialmente da perspectiva da legitimidade, pode cumprir um papel científica e politicamente relevante neste contexto, por meio de um trabalho de engenharia institucional devidamente fundamentado em uma visão realista.

Nesse sentido, este artigo reflete sobre as condições histórico-sociais de exercício da cidadania no Brasil, sintetizadas pela ideia de cidadania bloqueada, que deve ser tomada como condicionante (não determinante) em quaisquer projetos de reforma institucional do sistema democrático. Termos clareza sobre o que explica a permanência de bloqueios à cidadania e sobre sua forma de atuação é indispensável tanto para explicações coerentes sobre os processos em curso, como para prescrições adequadas para enfrentar os problemas diagnosticados. Trata-se de considerarmos seriamente a realidade sem nos prostrarmos diante dela.

O conceito de cidadania, tal como o empregamos, é uma criação recente na sociedade ocidental moderna e compreende três dimensões, correspondentes aos direitos civis, políticos e sociais. Essas dimensões não necessariamente coexistem em um mesmo contexto político, mas

---

gramas de metas baseados nas propostas que defenderam durante as campanhas eleitorais, o que, associado a um conjunto de institutos complementares, tem como objetivos expressos: qualificar o debate eleitoral, contribuir com a prática do planejamento na Administração Pública e fortalecer o controle social das políticas públicas.

a inexistência ou as limitações de uma delas têm implicações sobre as demais. O cidadão completo é aquele que desfruta dessas três dimensões da cidadania, enquanto o incompleto possui apenas alguns destes direitos, e aquele que não possui nenhum deles pode ser considerado um não-cidadão. Os direitos civis são aqueles que garantem uma convivência civilizada entre as pessoas, dos quais depende a existência de uma sociedade civil: direito à vida, à liberdade, à propriedade (enquanto elemento e nos limites necessários para assegurar a dignidade humana) e à igualdade formal. Os direitos políticos, por sua vez, referem-se à participação do cidadão no governo da sociedade, de maneira que são eles que "conferem legitimidade à organização política da sociedade". Nem todos os habitantes de um Estado possuem direitos políticos pois, ao longo da história, frequentemente foram estabelecidas limitações, como de idade (ainda vigente) ou de renda. Os direitos políticos não se restringem ao voto, mas incluem, por exemplo, o direito à organização partidária, a ser votado para um cargo público e às manifestações públicas. Enfim, os direitos sociais "garantem a participação na riqueza coletiva" (Carvalho, 2001, p. 9 – 10), abrangendo o direito à educação, à saúde, ao trabalho e à previdência social, dentre outros.[2] O objetivo desses direitos é diminuir a desigualdade social e minimizar os efeitos do capitalismo moderno, garantindo a todos um bem-estar mínimo. Além disso, revelam-se condições imprescindíveis para a igualdade política real e para a efetividade dos próprios direitos civis.

---

2 T. H. Marshall, em "Cidadania, Classe Social e Status", é a principal referência quando falamos nas três dimensões de direitos de cidadania. Sua ideia original é que cada dimensão destes direitos está associada a uma instituição do Estado moderno. Assim, os direitos civis estariam ligados aos tribunais de justiça; os direitos políticos, ao parlamento e conselhos do governo local; e os direitos sociais, ao sistema educacional e demais serviços sociais. Segundo ele, a divisão das três dimensões só pode ser traçada a partir do momento em que surgem, no Estado, as divisões das instituições e funções deste; antes do século XII (que marca o nascimento dos tribunais de justiça especializados na Inglaterra), não se pode falar em três faces da cidadania, mas em apenas um direito.

A construção da cidadania é um processo histórico que varia em cada país. No Brasil, além de ter se iniciado no final do século XIX, portanto, de forma bem mais tardia do que as experiências inglesa e norte-americana (já bastante amadurecidas no século XVIII), a cronologia de afirmação dos direitos também é peculiar: enquanto nos países centrais ocorreu primeiramente o reconhecimento dos direitos civis, seguidos pelos políticos e muito posteriormente os sociais, por aqui, a afirmação jurídica da universalização dos direitos sociais ocorreu primeiro. E isso tem consequências para a forma como a cidadania é exercida nos dias atuais (Carvalho, 2001, pp. 11 – 12).

No desenvolvimento deste capítulo, consideraremos, inicialmente, os bloqueios históricos à cidadania vinculados à formação do Estado brasileiro, notadamente a escravidão e o patrimonialismo. Em seguida, trataremos da ideia de cidadania concedida (ou ausência de cidadania), alimentada pelas práticas do coronelismo, do clientelismo, da cultura do favor, que também bloqueiam o processo emancipatório. Em terceiro lugar, discorreremos sobre como a persistente desigualdade e a exclusão social restringem a cidadania não apenas na dimensão social, mas também na política. Enfim, destacaremos a relação entre o atual contexto de crise política e a demanda por uma nova institucionalidade democrática.

Escravidão, patrimonialismo e a formação do Estado brasileiro: bloqueios históricos à cidadania

O sistema escravista, que vigorou por cerca de três séculos no território brasileiro, marcou de forma profunda as relações sociais e tradição política do país, de maneira que suas consequências ainda se fazem presentes contemporaneamente.

A importação de escravos africanos e a escravização dos povos indígenas locais, base do sistema, foi favorecida pela produção de açúcar, tabaco e produtos afins em latifúndios monocultores, que exigiam muita mão-de-obra (Carvalho, 2001, pp. 18 – 19). Ao longo dos anos, a população escrava superou em quase o dobro o número de homens livres.

Legalmente, os escravos não eram pessoas, não possuíam direitos civis. Para todos os efeitos, eram equivalentes a animais – podiam ser comprados e vendidos, espancados, castigados; não eram iguais a seus senhores ou a quaisquer homens livres e, em alguns casos, sequer possuíam direito à vida, podendo os donos matá-los sem qualquer tipo de consequência (Carvalho, 2001, p. 21). Os donos de escravos os viam como humanos, mas não como iguais (Costa, 1999, pp. 347 – 355).

Com a escravatura, era virtualmente impossível que a população brasileira exercesse sua cidadania; não só pela maioria da população estar na situação de escravidão, mas também porque à população que era livre faltavam condições básicas para que seus direitos civis fossem exercidos. Dependia-se muito dos grandes proprietários para escapar dos abusos do governo e ter qualquer chance de viver com um mínimo de dignidade; os únicos que não dependiam dos grandes proprietários eram eles mesmos, ou os que aspiravam ser um e escapavam para o interior. Os senhores, por sua vez, também não poderiam ser considerados cidadãos: a cidadania pressupõe o reconhecimento da igualdade – como eles não se consideravam iguais aos demais homens e não se submetiam aos mesmos deveres, ocupavam uma posição de privilégio, acima ou fora da cidadania (Carvalho, 2001, p. 21). Esse fenômeno também tem uma dimensão ético-cultural: o convívio constante com a violência reservada aos escravos, além da ignorância e miséria inerentes à posição de escravidão, moldavam o caráter e a cultura dos senhores par ao não reconhecimento e o não exercício da cidadania (Silva, 1998, p. 28).

As relações de mando e dominação também se faziam presentes no meio familiar, regido pelo patriarcalismo. A cultura de negação da cidadania e personalismo vigentes na esfera privada manifesta-se no comportamento político por meio do patrimonialismo (Holanda, 2014, p. 175). E um Estado regido pelo personalismo e pelo patrimonialismo não combina com a cidadania.

Na explicação de Faoro (1979, p. 733),

> a comunidade política conduz, comanda, supervisiona os negócios, como negócios privados seus, na origem, como negócios públicos depois, em linhas que se demarcam gradualmente. O súdito, a sociedade, se compreendem no âmbito de um aparelhamento a explorar, a manipular, a tosquiar nos casos extremos. Dessa realidade se projeta, em florescimento natural, a forma de poder, institucionalizada num tipo de domínio: o patrimonialismo, cuja legitimidade assenta no tradicionalismo – assim é porque sempre foi.

A tendência dos governantes em tratar temas públicos como se fossem "seus", e não do povo, fazia com que este se retraísse dos negócios públicos. A participação não era estimulada e não havia direitos propriamente ditos, garantidos pelo Estado; bens e cargos públicos eram usados para benefício pessoal dos membros da classe governante (Faoro, 1979, p. 745).

A tentativa de estimular um ambiente político mais receptivo à ideia de participação política, incentivada pelo regente Diogo Feijó, não foi capaz de melhorar a situação neste aspecto; a ampliação da margem legal dos poderes locais, ao invés de proteger os mais necessitados, aumentou o grau de arbítrio com que os grandes proprietários de terras agiam (Caldeira, 1999, p. 35).

À ausência de direitos civis e políticos para a maioria da população colonial, somava-se a dificuldade do acesso à justiça. Mulheres e escravos estavam submissos à vontade de seus senhores; os homens livres não conseguiam justiça porque ela funcionava de forma arbitrária, dominada quase sempre pela vontade dos grandes proprietários e representantes da Coroa. Sendo a justiça uma maneira de garantir os direitos civis, estes já ficavam largamente prejudicados (Marshall, 1967, p. 67). Mesmo que o indivíduo conseguisse acesso à justiça, dificilmente ele teria o conhecimento necessário para defender seus direitos; a educação primária não era estimulada, nem pela administração colonial nem pelos grandes latifundiários (Carvalho, 2001, p. 22).

A independência do Brasil de Portugal ocorreu em um contexto em que não havia propriamente cidadãos. Remanesceram o patrimonialismo, o personalismo, a ausência de consciência política, a baixo integração social e a negação da cidadania nas relações sociais e na gestão da coisa pública (Carvalho, 2001, p. 23 – 25, Faoro, 1979, p. 736 – 737). Os direitos sociais, assim como na época colonial, ainda eram pouco discutidos: ações nos campos da saúde, da educação e da assistência não se davam a partir da dimensão do direito, mas sim da caridade e da filantropia (Carvalho, 2001, p. 24).

A escravidão foi mantida com a independência política e os senhores de escravos, não obstante as pressões da Inglaterra, conservaram seu poder e defendiam o sistema escravista com o argumento de sua necessidade para sustentar a economia brasileira (Costa, 1999, p. 359). A manutenção desse sistema, obviamente, impedia o avanço da cidadania. Os valores da escravidão continuavam a se infiltrar por todas as camadas sociais, a ponto de até mesmo os escravos libertos terem escravos. A tradição ibérica não favorecia a ideia de liberdade como direito inalienável do indivíduo, a hierarquia e o coletivo eram mais fortes do que a igualdade e a pessoa (Carvalho, 2001, p. 19 – 20, 28, 50 – 51).

A manutenção da escravidão também constituída um grande obstáculo para a afirmação da soberania estatal, pois esta tem como elemento constitutivo o monopólio dos poderes legislativo e coercitivo, o que esbarrava no exercício do arbítrio pelos grandes proprietários de terra sobre a população escrava (Silva, 1998, pp. 25 – 26). E tudo isso se passava permeado por um discurso liberal que acompanhava as tendências europeias, porém sem nenhum enraizamento nas relações sociais e políticas, esvaziado, pois, de toda substância (Caldeira, 1999, p. 37).

A Constituição brasileira de 1824 é outra prova da resistência das elites em construir um Estado de direito liberal e representativo. Além de ter sido outorgada pelo Imperador, o Poder Moderador e suas competências suplantava qualquer possibilidade de efetivo controle recíproco entre os Poderes, elemento essencial de um Estado liberal, tratava-se de verdadeira "constitucionalização do absolutismo". Além disso, o texto constitucional não correspondia à realidade social e a monarquia sustentava-se por meio de um pacto com os senhores de escravos, que continuaram a exercer seu poder privado sem subordinação à Constituição (Bonavides, Andrade, 2004, p. 15, 101).

É verdade, porém, que em termos formais, a nova ordem incorporou alguma expansão dos direitos políticos: estabeleceu que todos homens, maiores de 25 anos (*régime capacitaire*) e que ganhassem pelo menos 100 mil réis por ano (*régime censitaire*) teriam o direito e o dever de votar . Os analfabetos também tinham direito de voto. A primeira lei eleitoral do Império estabelecia eleições indiretas e dois tipos de participação política: os votantes, aqueles que cumpriam os requisitos legais, escolhiam os conselheiros de seu município e os eleitores. Os eleitores, por sua vez, eram aqueles que votavam de fato para cargos públicos em nível nacional (Love, 1970, p. 6, Carvalho, 2001, pp. 29 – 30). Apesar das restrições, tratava-se, pois, de uma legislação eleitoral muito avançada para a época.

Entretanto, não havia uma consciência de cidadania na época, o que, somado às condições socioeconômicas, constituiu terreno fértil para o desenvolvimento da prática da fraude eleitoral, esvaziando de substância a cidadania política formalmente reconhecida para os homens livres.

Diante das dificuldades para a conservação do poder por meio de instituições e práticas abertamente despóticas, logo os chefes políticos perceberam as vantagens de concorrerem às eleições facilmente fraudadas. Por meio de um cargo eletivo poderiam continuar a exercer seu poder de forma ilimitada, mas com a vantagem de um revestimento liberal que conferia ares de legitimidade a seu domínio (Caldeira, 1999, p. 35). Os que concorriam usavam de toda a sua influência para ganhar as eleições locais. Perdê-las significava perda de prestígio e controle de cargos importantes, como os de delegado de polícia, juiz municipal, coletor de impostos e postos na Guarda Nacional. Eles se valiam, portanto, de todo tipo de artifício para conseguir o que desejavam. Os votantes da época não possuíam, ainda, nenhuma noção sobre como fazer parte de uma sociedade política; seus votos eram atos de lealdade ou de obediência ao chefe político local. Conforme o votante ganhava consciência do valor de seu voto, passava a cobrar por ele. As eleições eram, desta forma, uma oportunidade de ganhar dinheiro, uma boa refeição, ou itens novos que eram necessários, ao invés de um ato cívico (Carvalho, 2001, p. 32 – 36, Leal, 2012, p. 25)(Carvalho, 2001, p. 35 – 36).

A norma eleitoral do Império permaneceu quase inalterada até 1881. O excesso de corrupção que existia no processo eleitoral não passava despercebido à Câmara dos Deputados e ao Senado Federal. A primeira grande mudança na lei eleitoral aconteceu em 1881, com a aprovação do que ficou conhecida como a Lei Saraiva – pois foi aprovada e patrocinada pelo governo de José Antônio Saraiva. A lei ampliava os requisitos para o voto, subindo o valor anual do salário para 200 mil réis, proibindo o voto dos analfabetos e tornando o voto facultativo; e estabelecia as eleições diretas (Carvalho, 2001, pp. 38 – 39; Love, 1970, p. 6). Foi uma lei conservadora aprovada em uma Câmara liberal, com poucas vozes se erguendo contra ela. Devido à proibição do voto dos analfabetos, 80% da população que podia votar anteriormente perdeu seus direitos políticos (Carvalho, 2001, p. 39).

Enquanto todas essas mudanças aconteciam no campo dos direitos políticos, a população negra sofria. Ainda que a elite governante do país não sentisse necessidade de estabelecer um sistema de segregação racial legal e aceitasse eventualmente um negro descendente da miscigenação entre escrava e senhor de terras (Costa, 1999, pp. 356 – 358), nada fez pela efetiva inclusão social do negro ex-escravo – na verdade, muitas dificuldades foram criadas.

Depois da libertação, muitos ex-escravos se viram forçados a voltar para suas fazendas, onde trabalhavam por um salário baixo, e seus descendentes continuaram a viver e trabalhar ali, com uma situação pouco diferente da de seus pais e avós (Carvalho, 2001, p. 52). Outros foram para as cidades, sem conseguirem emprego fixo, e sobrevivendo de forma precária – pois nenhum tipo de programa social foi estabelecido pelo governo para apoiar a massa de ex-cativos. Se os brancos pobres tinham dificuldade em terem reconhecidos seus direitos civis, para os negros as coisas eram ainda piores, pois grande parte dos brasileiros ainda tinha dificuldade em aceitar a libertação e dificultava o quanto podia a inserção do negro na vida social e política do país, bloqueando, pois, o exercício de sua cidadania.

Evidentemente, esse processo histórico deixou marcas na sociedade brasileira, remanescendo bloqueios ao exercício pleno da cidadania de negros e pobres em geral, os quais são facilmente perceptíveis nas relações sociais e políticas contemporâneas.

O reconhecimento de direitos civis, políticos e sociais não existia para a parcela negra da sociedade até muito recentemente (Souza, 2009, p. 371). Com o passar do tempo, houve avanços na garantia jurídica dos direitos civis, políticos e sociais fundados na noção de igualdade e foram abertas algumas portas para a inclusão social, inclusive em razão da luta de movimentos sociais. Porém, em termos substanciais, ainda não é possível afirmar que exista uma cidadania plena para os negros e os pobres.

O sistema patrimonialista instalado na gênese do Estado brasileiro, da mesma forma, ainda apresenta efeitos na política atual. Observa-se, por exemplo, a maneira como se constrói o *presidencialismo de coalizão*: não se trata de alianças políticas programáticas, mas de comunhão oportunista de interesses fundada no fisiologismo, no clientelismo, na distribuição de cargos públicos e cotas do orçamento do Estado – nem sempre a partir de critérios republicanos e, não raro, pelo recurso à corrupção.

Apesar disso, não podemos afirmar que o patrimonialismo tenha hoje o mesmo papel que tinha na segunda metade do século XX ou anteriormente. Nesse sentido, Jessé Souza (2009, p. 61 – 62, 70) apresenta a seguinte sugestão: a tese segundo a qual o personalismo e o patrimonialismo seriam características permanentes e imutáveis do brasileiro nada faz além de remover a culpa dos que de fato prejudicam a sociedade e jogá-la em um "ente" abstrato e incontrolável à população, desresponsabilizar a sociedade civil em relação a seus erros e demonizar o Estado (Souza, 2009, p. 70). O autor, assim, se recusa a crer no patrimonialismo como algo inerente à cultura política brasileira, afirmando a possibilidade de mudança e reafirmando que já houve mudança – não tendo o fenômeno a mesma influência de antes.

De fato, não podemos desresponsabilizar as escolhas presentes pela estrutura social desigual, injusta e de cidadania bloqueada, como se fossem resultantes de uma cultura forjada definitivamente no momento fundante do Estado brasileiro, em uma visão determinista da história. Entretanto, a escravidão e o patrimonialismo não podem ser desprezados enquanto elementos condicionantes do exercício da cidadania do Brasil. Superar a desigualdade e os bloqueios ao exercício da cidadania é um imperativo para os verdadeiramente democratas (não para os cínicos), mas até por isso, aqueles que se dedicam ao trabalho de engenharia institucional com tal propósito precisam considerar seriamente tais marcas deixadas pela história.

Coronelismo, clientelismo e autoritarismo: cidadania concedida ou ausência de cidadania?

A Primeira República (1889 – 1930) foi instalada por meio de um golpe militar que derrubou o Imperador e colocou Deodoro da Fonseca, marechal do Exército, no comando do Poder Executivo. Pretendia-se, em tese, imitar o modelo de federação existente nos Estados Unidos, a fim de descentralizar o poder para aproximar o governo da população e aprimorar a participação política. Contudo, os efeitos de tal descentralização restringiram-se às elites políticas, formando, eventualmente, poderosas oligarquias estaduais, que se apoiavam em partidos estaduais únicos (Carvalho, 2001, p. 41, Love, 1970, p. 7). Nasce, assim, um estilo de política que marcou as regiões interioranas do país por décadas – o coronelismo.

Resumidamente, o coronelismo era a prática política que aliava os chefes políticos locais com os governadores dos estados, e os governadores com o presidente da República (Carvalho, 2001, p. 41, Leal, 2012, p. 20, 49 – 50). O fenômeno relaciona-se com o clientelismo, que ocorre quando o indivíduo (cliente) fica dependente e submisso ao poder do coronel (patrão), independente de ter com ele qualquer relação familiar ou empregatícia. Longe de diminuírem as fraudes eleitorais com o endurecimento da legislação eleitoral em 1881 e 1891, elas aumentaram. Nenhum "coronel", como eram chamados os líderes locais, aceitava perder as eleições; e, igualando-se a seus antecessores coloniais, recorriam a qualquer meio para não fazê-lo. Da mesma forma que antes da proclamação da República, o coronelismo impedia o exercício adequado dos direitos políticos porque negava os direitos civis (Carvalho, 2001, p. 41 – 42. 56).

Dentro das terras que pertenciam ao coronel, era ele quem fazia a lei. O poder do Estado parava em sua cerca, como era antes com os grandes latifundiários. Os que trabalhavam para ele, antes de serem cidadãos brasileiros, eram seus mandados, que obedeciam a suas vontades – inclusive votando nele e em seus candidatos. Como consequência disso tudo, não só os direitos políticos dos cidadãos eram negados, mas também seus direitos civis: a liberdade de ir e vir, a liberdade de expressão, o direito de propriedade, o direito à dignidade e à honra – tudo ficava nas mãos do coronel, pois ele tinha o controle privado dos juízes, dos delegados e da justiça (Carvalho, 2001, p. 56 – 57; Leal, 2012, p. 25, 44). Os amigos do coronel possuíam sua proteção e eram virtualmente inatingíveis; seus inimigos eram perseguidos ou ficavam sujeitos à lei comum (Leal, 2012, p. 38 – 39). O direito, que deveria servir para a proteção das pessoas, tornava-se um instrumento particular do líder (Carvalho, 2001, p. 56 – 57). Assim, mesmo que os cidadãos tivessem direito ao voto, eles não conseguiriam exercê-lo adequadamente, por lhes faltarem as condições efetivas para tal.

Vê-se aqui que o coronelismo costura-se e funde-se com o patrimonialismo. Pode-se, inclusive, afirmar que o primeiro é filho do segundo: a cultura do poder privado sobrepondo-se ao poder público une-se ao poder político da grande propriedade, característica do Brasil colônia e do Brasil imperial, para formar o sistema coronelista. O coronel usava de seu poder para favorecer seus aliados e prejudicar os inimigos, ficando clara a relação com o patrimonialismo colonial, ainda que não seja idêntica devido à decadência do poder privado durante a Primeira República (Leal, 2012, p. 252) e ao fortalecimento do Estado e do poder público, fruto direto da segunda Constituição brasileira.

A primeira Constituição republicana, a de 1891, excluiu o critério de renda para a votação, mas manteve o limite de idade e de alfabetismo, já presentes na lei Saraiva de 1881. Em teoria, portanto, os direitos políticos foram expandidos; na prática, os cidadãos não tinham liberdade para votar em quem quisessem, justamente devido ao controle que o coronel exercia sobre a população rural (que era a maioria). Além disso, com frequência recorria-se a fraudes para a vitória nas eleições: via-se analfabetos votando, falecidos, cidadãos inexistentes ou não-cidadãos – aqueles que não possuíam direitos políticos (Love, 1970, p. 7 – 10, Leal, 2012, p. 254).

A partir de 1930, depois do golpe que levou Getúlio Vargas ao poder, apareceram pela primeira vez em legislação constitucional os direitos sociais, que diziam respeito principalmente ao trabalhador: direitos trabalhistas e previdenciários. Já os direitos políticos foram ora ampliados e ora reduzidos, ao longo de golpes de Estado e instabilidade política, até 1945, quando o último golpe derrubou Vargas e iniciou o primeiro período verdadeiramente democrático do país. Os direitos civis foram formalmente garantidos pelas três Constituições da era Vargas, mas não foram efetivados, pois as restrições permaneceram na prática e até mesmo o acesso à Justiça era cerceado à maioria da população, especialmente no período ditatorial (Carvalho, 2001, pp. 87 – 88).

A revolta paulista de 1932, com a demanda por uma reforma social e política, foi derrotada em batalha, mas não no campo político. Devido a ela, foram convocadas eleições para a Assembleia Constituinte e para Presidente da República, que aconteceram já regidas por nova legislação eleitoral. Tal legislação representou um incrível avanço para os direitos políticos, pois foram introduzidos o voto secreto, para reduzir as fraudes, e uma Justiça Eleitoral, que delegava a juízes a fiscalização do alistamento eleitoral, da votação, da apuração dos votos e do reconhecimento dos eleitos. Além disso, pela primeira vez, permitiu-se que as mulheres votassem (Carvalho, 2001, p. 101).

Apesar de todos os avanços nos direitos civis, políticos e sociais, e a maior participação da população na vida política do país, o golpe de Estado de 1937 aconteceu com pouca resistência popular. Durante a ditadura de Vargas, que vigorou entre 1937 e 1945, ele reforçou sua imagem histórica de "pai dos pobres", ampliando largamente os direitos sociais. Contudo, a introdução de tais direitos em um ambiente insalubre para o exercício de direitos civis e políticos torna sua natureza democrática questionável. Eles não foram, portanto, conquistas das lutas populares, mas um "presente" de um governo populista, paternalista e autoritário; ao invés de contribuírem para uma cidadania ativa, eles serviram para desenvolver uma população dócil e bestializada. Os direitos trabalhistas e previdenciários reconhecidos durante a era Vargas eram mais semelhantes a privilégios do que a direitos, pois beneficiavam um grupo específico de trabalhadores (os urbanos sindicalizados) e deixavam os demais desprotegidos, os quais, aliás, formavam a maioria da população trabalhadora da época (rurais, autônomos e domésticas) (Carvalho, 2001, p. 106 – 115).

O avanço dos direitos sociais à frente dos políticos, por mais que tenha sido positivo para parte da população, contribuiu com o desenvolvimento de uma cidadania passiva e para a continuidade da tradição de exercício dos direitos políticos como "moeda de troca" para o candidato, algo semelhante ao clientelismo que precedeu à ditadura varguista. A população votava em determinado político não por acreditar em suas convicções e em seu programa de governo, mas como agradecimento por ele ter implantado determinada política ou realizado algum favor (Carvalho, 2001, pp. 125 – 126).

O clientelismo e o coronelismo foram aspectos da história política do Brasil extensos e marcantes. A tendência do eleitor brasileiro em observar direitos sociais não como direitos, mas como benefícios concedidos por um indivíduo, persiste até hoje. Apesar de podermos observar que o pensamento começou a mudar nos últimos anos a partir de campanhas de conscientização civis e do esforço de movimentos sociais, por exemplo, o clientelismo ainda é bastante presente (Carvalho, 2001, p. 224), e condiciona o potencial emancipatório de inovações institucionais como conselhos de políticas públicas, orçamento participativo e a Emenda do *Programa de Metas,* os quais, em grande medida, dependem de uma sociedade civil autônoma e mobilizada para que seus objetivos sejam atingidos.

A Constituição posterior ao fim da era Vargas, a de 1946, deu continuidade às conquistas sociais do ex-presidente e garantiu direitos civis e políticos que antes foram cerceados em razão do regime ditatorial. Com ela, iniciou-se o período democrático mais longo da história do Brasil com exceção do atual. As eleições para Presidente, Deputados Federais, Senadores, Governadores, Deputados Estaduais, Prefeitos e Vereadores foram constantes e, no geral, ilibadas. Havia algumas restrições ao exercício da cidadania, como o controle do direito de greve e a proibição do Partido Comunista, mas ocorreu uma expansão significativa em relação à Constituição de 1934. O voto dos analfabetos ainda era proibido, mas para o restante da população, homens e mulheres maiores de 18 anos, era obrigatório e secreto, excetuando-se os soldados das forças armadas. Como consequência, a participação política aumentou gradativamente a partir de 1945, não só por meio do voto, mas também das organizações sindicais e dos partidos políticos (Carvalho, 2001, p. 127, 144 - 146, Love, 1970, p. 19).

O aumento da participação política tornou o processo eleitoral progressivamente mais limpo e transparente. Além do interesse da população em provocar uma maior fiscalização e cuidado por parte do poder público, a crescente urbanização modificava o eleitor médio. O cidadão urbano era menos propenso a ser aliciado e coagido a votar em um determinado candidato, como ocorria com seus semelhantes que viviam em área rural. Contudo, ele tendia a comprar a propaganda populista dos políticos, o que, virtualmente, culminava na mesma situação de manipulação política. Apesar disso, a democracia evoluiu e amadureceu durante este breve período democrático, com partidos políticos se consolidando e convicções políticas amadurecendo na população (Carvalho, 2001, p. 147-148).

Em um momento de aumento da participação política, o golpe militar de 1964 representou a reação das elites militares, políticas e econômicas aos "riscos" da democracia. A repressão aos direitos civis e políticos foi imediata, mantendo-se, entretanto, formalmente as eleições e o funcionamento do Congresso Nacional. Quanto aos direitos sociais, de forma semelhante ao que ocorreu durante a ditadura de Getúlio Vargas, foram ampliados (Carvalho, 2001, p. 157, 167).

A princípio, tal dado parece contraditório. Como pode um governo autoritário, que suprimiu violentamente os direitos civis e políticos de sua população, ter mantido as eleições e o Congresso Nacional? A resposta está no fato de que manter a aparência de um governo aberto e democrático era importante para os militares e para a parcela das elites civis que apoiou o golpe. Além disso, o Governo sabia que não seria fácil nem apropriado suprimir completamente os direitos políticos depois de uma mobilização tão grande da população como a que aconteceu entre 1945 e 1964.

A tática de suprimir os direitos civis e políticos enquanto se aumentava os direitos sociais foi a grande marca dos governos autoritários brasileiros do século XX. Durante a ditadura militar de 1964, contudo, a eficácia da tática foi menor do que a experiência de Getúlio Vargas, justamente pela prévia mobilização política já mencionada e pelo foco do governo militar em cooptar a população rural, que era menos numerosa e relevante do que o operariado urbano (Carvalho, 2001, pp. 190 – 191).

A decadência do regime militar e das restrições às liberdades civis e políticas criou a necessidade de substituir a Constituição do período por uma nova Carta, que refletisse uma nova era de proteção aos direitos dos cidadãos e a construção de uma tradição democrática estável para o país. Essa foi a missão atribuída à Assembleia Nacional Constituinte de

1987. A Constituição Federal de 1988, resultante desse processo, prescreveu garantias para os direitos civis, políticos, sociais e econômicos, promoveu a descentralização administrativa, estabeleceu as condições de funcionamento para a democracia representativa e abriu várias possibilidades para a participação popular.

Contudo, o esforço jurídico empenhado em garantir os direitos da população não foi o suficiente para compensar a tradição histórica do Brasil de bloqueio à cidadania. A tradição autoritária continua a condicionar as práticas políticas e a bloquear o pleno exercício da cidadania.

Por essas razões, como ressalta Bonavides (2009, p. 830, 835 – 836), "a democracia do sistema constitucional brasileiro se mostra, na essência, o reverso, em virtude da execução que lhe tem dado por obra do bloqueio representativo – quase total – que obscurece, usurpa e invalida o teor de democracia direta constante dos artigos 1º e 14 da Carta Magna de 1988". Não obstante os quase trinta anos de vigência da Constituição Federal de 1988, ainda "somos uma democracia bloqueada, uma democracia mutilada, uma democracia sem povo; o que, aliás, é singular contradição de forma e substância". Permanece, pois, o domínio da elite hegemônica.

E as restrições ao exercício da cidadania atingem até mesmo os mais elementares direitos civis. Observa-se, por exemplo, que os direitos civis dos moradores da periferia das cidades sempre foram desrespeitados. A rápida urbanização do país durante a ditadura militar foi marcada pela precarização das condições de moradia, trabalho e acesso a serviços básicos, como saneamento, energia elétrica, transporte e saúde. Depois da redemocratização e da Constituição de 1988, cresceu a pressão dos moradores das cidades sobre o Poder Público pela garantia de atendimento a demandas sociais, segurança pública, justiça e proteção aos direitos civis. Embora tenham ocorrido avanços, sobretudo na área social, a política de segurança ainda é marcada por práticas recorrentes de abusos policiais, em flagrante violação aos direitos civis, o que constitui um importante resquício do autoritarismo (Carvalho, 2001, p. 194).

O acesso à justiça pelos mais pobres e excluídos, não obstante os avanços institucionais ocorridos, como a criação das Defensorias Públicas e dos juizados especiais, ainda sofre restrições e é marcado pela desigualdade. Como pode um cidadão participar de forma plena de instâncias como conselhos e conferências de políticas públicas, ou das assembleias de orçamento participativo e audiências públicas do *Programa de Metas*, quando nem mesmo seus direitos civis são assegurados? Não se trata de um impedimento absoluto, mas é uma restrição que precisa ser considerada. A experiência dos sujeitos com as práticas autoritárias inibe o envolvimento com as questões públicas, o engajamento nos espaços políticos participativos.

Soma-se a tudo isso a persistente desigualdade e exclusão social que também restringem o exercício da cidadania, assunto que abordaremos na próxima seção.

Desigualdade, exclusão e as restrições à cidadania no Brasil

Durante a redemocratização, o Brasil encontrava-se mergulhado em uma crise econômica que já durava décadas e o abismo social produzido por esta crise e por outros fatores históricos aumentava a cada ano. A modernização nacional, promovida pelos governos que sucederam a ditadura, não impediu a persistência da desigualdade abissal existente na sociedade brasileira; pelo contrário, ela criou uma classe social que era "não só sem capital cultural nem econômico em qualquer medida significativa, mas desprovida, esse é o aspecto fundamental, das precondições sociais, morais e culturais que permitem essa apropriação" (Souza, 2009, p. 21). Essencialmente, é uma classe social abandonada política e socialmente, ignorada pelas camadas superiores, que tentam elaborar soluções paliativas ou parciais para o problema e jamais atacam ou resolvem de fato as situações que exigem atenção. A redução temporária das desigualdades, ocorrida principalmente a partir do Governo Lula, em razão da ampliação do emprego, da política de valorização real do salário-mínimo e de programas sociais como o "Bolsa Família" também não enfrentou as causas estruturais da desigualdade – prova disso é que diante de nova crise econômica e fiscal, especialmente a partir de 2014 e 2015, retrocessos sociais já são evidenciados.

A classe a que nos referimos aqui, e à qual Jessé de Souza se refere como "ralé", não está em sua posição social somente devido ao abandono político que sofre. A "fórmula do sucesso" meritocrático não envolve somente aspectos sociais ou educacionais; é uma tradição cultural, algo enraizado no indivíduo. São fatores que crianças de classe média e alta aprendem desde cedo com seus pais – capacidade de concentração, disciplina, pensamento prospectivo – e que as tornam, desde muito cedo, mais capazes de competir no mercado de trabalho do que suas semelhantes de classes baixas (Souza, 2009, p. 22 – 23). Pode-se dizer, a partir disto, que as diferenças sociais são reproduzidas ao longo das gerações; talvez a melhoria nos índices de educação e demais serviços públicos consiga fazer alguma diferença, mas ela não resolve o problema apresentado.

Essa camada de excluídos se reproduz continuamente, e reproduz, dessa forma, as mesmas desigualdades, geração após geração. Ainda que esforços estatais sejam feitos, eles não conseguem compensar a total e completa exclusão que centenas de milhares de membros da "ralé" sofrem a cada ano. O grau de crueldade de tal exclusão é aumentado quando se vê que não basta excluí-los; deve-se culpá-los pelo seu próprio destino, dizendo que, numa sociedade "meritocrática" como a nossa, a pobreza só é perpetuada pela falta de esforço ou de capacidade daquele que falha em ser bem-sucedido. Ignora-se o fato de que os privilégios são transmitidos por herança familiar ou de classe, sendo ele percebido como esforço individual e mérito (Souza, 2009, p. 42 – 44).

Não se pode entender, portanto, nossa situação de desigualdade social extrema como sendo apenas fruto de fatores históricos e abandono governamental dos mais pobres. Existem raízes muito mais profundas do problema, que são parte de fatores culturais despercebidos tanto por aqueles que deles se favorecem como por aqueles que por eles são prejudicados; há uma preferência em associar nossa desigualdade com um "mal de origem", ao mesmo tempo em que diz-se que ela diminuirá "naturalmente" através do progresso econômico (Souza, 2009, p. 59 – 60). Com isto, tanto o governo pode "lavar as mãos", afirmando que a elaboração de políticas públicas eficientes de distribuição de renda não resolverá o problema, como a sociedade pode "esquecer" de pensar em sua parcela de responsabilidade no problema. Tudo é, no fim, atribuído à política econômica do governo, e cria-se um hábito de pensar na resolução dos dilemas sociais e individuais somente por meio do sucesso ou fracasso do crescimento da economia nacional.

O fator de dominação social moderno é, justamente por passar a impressão de justiça e equidade, mais perigoso e mais amplo do que as dominações sociais que o precederam (Jessé de Souza refere-se a elas como "dominação de sangue"). Inevitavelmente, apesar de afetar muito mais as classes inferiores do que as superiores, ela também se espalha nestas últimas, sendo a sociedade como um todo prejudicada por tal "dominação impessoal e sem sujeito que envolve a todos" (Souza, 2009, p. 388 – 389). Apesar de os princípios da dignidade do trabalho e da liberdade individual terem sido os pilares construtores das sociedades ocidentais modernas, isto não significa que todas as pessoas tenham acesso real a eles; de fato, a maioria não tem, mas ainda os usam para justificar diferenças sociais entre indivíduos e classes (Souza, 2009, p. 396 – 397).

A dominação social moderna afeta também o exercício da cidadania. Os fatores que produzem um trabalhador produtivo, aqueles mesmos que são internalizados na criança privilegiada desde pequena – autocontrole, disciplina e noção de corresponsabilidade – são necessários para uma cidadania ativa, em que o cidadão percebe onde ele pode atuar e onde ele não pode (Souza, 2009, p. 400). Sem acesso efetivo a tais valores, não se pode afirmar que os membros da "ralé" possuam o mesmo poder político e a mesma noção de cidadania do que os membros das classes média e alta.

Tornam-se indiferentes as garantias de direitos civis e políticos se aqueles que as têm não sabem como nem porque eles deveriam usá-las. Políticas públicas pouco fazem para mudar este quadro, até mesmo porque elas dificilmente são pensadas a longo prazo (Souza, 2009, p. 401). Mesmo quando existem instrumentos teoricamente eficazes para estimular a emancipação política e a participação popular generalizada, eles deparam-se com bloqueios impostos pelo abismo social entre classes. Isso não significa que sejam intransponíveis, mas que devem ser seriamente considerados na análise e da edificação de instituições voltadas para o estímulo à cidadania participativa.

Considerações finais: democracia em crise e a demanda por uma nova institucionalidade

O recente período de recessão econômica e a crise política que o país enfrenta desde 2013 contribuíram para o surgimento de um semi-consenso entre os cidadãos de que as instituições governamentais como estão organizadas hoje não conseguem responder às suas necessidades e desejos. O Governo é encarado como parte do problema, e não da solução, e a participação política por meio dos instrumentos convencionais enfrenta "um grave problema de funcionalidade" (Subirats, 2015, p. 448).

O modo como o sistema político brasileiro foi construído exigiu a prática do "presidencialismo de coalizão": a necessidade de o Presidente, para alcançar uma governabilidade, ter uma esmagadora maioria suprapartidária no Congresso Nacional a qual, ao mesmo tempo em que lhe dá sustentação política, bloqueia qualquer projeto que possa implicar transformações sociais mais profundas (Nobre, 2013, p. 12). Essa maioria é formada por partidos que compuseram o "Centrão" na Assembleia Constituinte de 1987 e seus desdobramentos. Marcos Nobre denomina esse fenômeno de "pemedebismo". Apesar de ter sido bem tolerado pela população brasileira ao longo das últimas décadas, a impaciência e indignação do povo têm se mostrado devido às consequências de tal arranjo, principalmente "os custos crescentes da fragmentação partidária;

a desorganização administrativa gerada pela distribuição de cargos no governo; e a propensão à corrupção gerada pela distribuição desses cargos" (Avritzer, 2016, p. 11).

Por outro lado, e não obstante as restrições ao exercício da cidadania sobre as quais discorremos, e talvez até mesmo em razão delas, estamos diante do nascimento de um novo tipo de cidadão, um indivíduo bem informado pela ampla variedade de mídias disponíveis, que é ciente de seus direitos e anseia pelo seu exercício, e não se contenta com a delegação de poder. Este novo cidadão exige e precisa de um espaço mais amplo de participação política. Ele sente a necessidade de uma reforma política que "amplie o papel do engajamento da sociedade no sistema político como um todo" (Avritzer, 2016, p. 16). Para ele, o exercício de seus direitos políticos não se limita ao voto, mas precisa ir além: as ideias de política e democracia devem ser expandidas para além do círculo institucional, gerando um debate que envolva não somente o aspecto político da sociedade, mas também o cultural. As novas ferramentas de comunicação surgidas no fim do século XX e começo do século XXI fornecem a infraestrutura material para tanto – mas as condições políticas e institucionais ainda estão por ser construídas.

A internet tem sido o principal meio de mobilização política no Brasil nos últimos anos. Por meio dela, o debate político ocorre livremente e de forma não hierarquizada, horizontal, sem intermediários e com lideranças difusas (Castells, 2013, p. 15 – 16). Entretanto, é necessário ponderar que os meios de comunicação de massa, bem como uma elite de lideranças políticas e sociais que dispõe de recursos materiais para tanto, acabam por exercer um papel privilegiado na formação da opinião pública, mesmo nas redes sociais.

Registramos que essas novas formas de exercício da cidadania, de organização e de mobilizações sociais, influenciados pelas tecnologias da informação e da comunicação, não são exclusividades brasileiras – ao contrário, trata-se de um fenômeno que ocorre em diversas partes do mundo.

Castells (2013, p. 163 – 169) analisou diversas revoltas populares ocorridas ao redor do mundo nos últimos anos[3] e assinalou as seguintes características comuns: a) são conectados em rede de diversas maneiras, não somente "on-line", mas também "off-line"; b) acontecem num "espaço de autonomia", que é um híbrido entre espaço urbano e espaço cibernético; c) começam localmente, mas se comunicam com o mundo inteiro; d) iniciam-se espontaneamente, normalmente devido à indignação com o Governo; e) são virais, ou seja, espalham-se com facilidade e inspiram outros movimentos semelhantes em outros lugares; f) são movimentos sem liderança, devido à desconfiança em relação a chefes e instituições; g) são movimentos autorreflexivos, que se questionam constantemente sobre métodos e objetivos; h) no geral, não são violentos, normalmente agindo por meio da desobediência civil; i) são movimentos sem uma demanda específica, possuindo, em geral, demandas plurais e desordenadas; j) são movimentos voltados para a mudança de opinião pública ou de valores da sociedade, não se concentrando num partido específico; k) apesar de não se envolverem com nenhum partido, são políticos no sentido de que querem e discutem a democracia participativa.

Quase todas estas características, senão todas elas, estiveram presentes não só durante a Primavera Árabe, em 2011, como também nos protestos brasileiros de junho de 2013 (também conhecidas como "Jornadas de Junho") e de março de 2015, que foram organizadas pela Internet, o que por si só já prova sua importância como instrumento de mobilização.

As Jornadas de Junho, iniciadas como um protesto contra o aumento da passagem do ônibus municipal de São Paulo, atingiram proporções nunca antes vistas em mobilizações sociais brasileiras. Formadas por uma nova classe social[4], os protestos estavam ligados a um sentimen-

---

3 São elas: Primavera Árabe (Tunísia, Egito, entre outros países); os Indignados na Espanha; Occupy Wall Street, nos Estados Unidos; e o movimento islandês para a elaboração de uma nova Constituição.

4 André Singer faz uma análise das Jornadas de Junho e elabora a hipótese de que o "novo proletariado" era a parcela principal de participação no movimento. O

to de impotência e indignação perante a ausência de punição de casos grandes de corrupção política, além de uma crise econômica que afetava profundamente os presentes e que prejudicava o prospecto de vida pensado para a classe média. Dali, germinou uma crise de legitimidade pouco antes vista no país, à qual teve continuidade nas eleições de 2014, nos protestos de março de 2015 (Avritzer, 2016, p. 19) e que atravessam o ano de 2016.

Tais movimentos demonstram, por um lado, que a cidadania passiva, aquela que se resume ao voto e à aceitação dócil dos arbítrios de membros da classe política e do governo, enfraqueceu nos últimos anos. Por outro lado, grande parte da população brasileira continua excluída desses processos, notadamente os mais pobres, menos educados e moradores das periferias. De qualquer forma, a participação política não é mais restrita às elites políticas e econômicas, como foi durante grande período da história brasileira. Trata-se de um sinal de esperança, ou de uma oportunidade transformadora, que precisa ser reconhecida para o rompimento dos bloqueios ao exercício da cidadania. Para isso, todavia, é preciso que a demanda por uma nova institucionalidade democrática seja satisfatoriamente respondida. Caso contrário, não é desprezível o risco de ampliação dos bloqueios ao exercício da cidadania, com a entrega de cada vez maiores poderes decisórios a elites tecnocráticas, judiciárias e financeiras, ou mesmo a algum "salvador da pátria" - opção que a história já demonstrou ser desastrosa para a democracia e o Estado de Direito.

É neste contexto nacional e global que devemos procurar compreender melhor o sentido contemporâneo, os bloqueios ao exercício da cidadania, e as respostas políticas e alternativas jurídicas necessárias para superá-los.

---

novo proletariado é caracterizado como jovens com alto nível educacional, mas baixa remuneração (Singer, 2013, p. 31), o que pode ser um dos motivos para a indignação.

Referências

ANDRADE, Paes de, BONAVIDES, Paulo. *História Constitucional do Brasil*. Brasília: OAB Editora, 2004.

AVRITZER, Leonardo. *Impasses da democracia no Brasil*. Rio de Janeiro: Civilização Brasileira, 2016.

BONAVIDES, Paulo. A Democracia Participativa e os Bloqueios da Classe Dominante. In: BENEVIDES, Maria V. M., BERCOVICI, Gilberto e MELO, Claudineu (org.). *Direitos Humanos, democracia e República - Homenagem a Fábio Konder Comparato*. São Paulo: Quartier Latin, 2009, p. 825 – 840.

CALDEIRA, Jorge. *Diogo Antônio Feijó*. São Paulo: Editora 34, 1999.

CARVALHO, José Murilo de. *Cidadania no Brasil: o longo caminho*. Rio de Janeiro: Civilização Brasileira, 2001.

CASTELLS, Manuel. *Redes de indignação e esperança: movimentos sociais na era da internet*. Rio de Janeiro: Zahar, 2013.

COMPARATO, Fábio Konder. *A Escola de Governo: do berço à idade adulta*. In: Estudos Avançados. Universidade de São Paulo: Instituto de Estudos Avançados; vol. 30, n. 87. Maio/Agosto 2016.

COSTA, Emília Viotti da. *Da Monarquia à República*. 6ª ed.. São Paulo: UNESP, 1999.

FAORO, Raymundo. *Os Donos do Poder: formação do patronato político brasileiro*. 5ª ed. Porto Alegre: Editora Globo, 1979.

HOLANDA, Sérgio Buarque de. *Raízes do Brasil*. 27ª ed. São Paulo: Companhia das Letras, 2014.

LEAL, Victor Nunes. *Coronelismo, Enxada e Voto: o município e o regime representativo no Brasil*. 7ª ed.. São Paulo: Companhia das Letras, 2012.

LOVE, Joseph L. Political Participation in Brazil, 1881 – 1969, *Luso-Brazilian Review*, v. 7, n. 2, p. 3 – 24, 1970.

MARSHALL, T. H. *Cidadania, Classe Social e Status*. Rio de Janeiro: Zahar Editores, 1967.

NOBRE, Marcos. *Imobilismo em Movimento: da abertura democrática ao governo Dilma*. 1ª ed. São Paulo: Companhia das Letras, 2013.

SILVA, José Bonifácio de Andrada e. *Projetos para o Brasil*. Org. Miriam Dolhnikoff. São Paulo: Companhia das Letras, 1998.

SINGER, André. Brasil, Junho de 2013: Classes e Ideologias Cruzadas, *Novos Estudos CEBRAP*, v. 97, p. 23 – 40.

SORJ, Bernardo. On-line / off-line: la nueva onda de la sociedade civil y la transformación de la esfera pública. In: SORJ, Bernardo; FAUSTO, Sérgio. *Internet y movilizaciones sociales: transformaciones del espacio público y de la sociedad civil*. São Paulo: Plataforma Democrática, 2015. p. 35 – 60.

SOMMA, Nicolás; SORJ, Bernardo (org.); FAUSTO, Sergio (org.). Participación ciudadana y activismo digital em América Latina. In: SORJ, Bernardo; FAUSTO, Sérgio. *Internet y movilizaciones sociales: transformaciones del espacio público y de la sociedad civil*. São Paulo: Plataforma Democrática, 2015, p. 103 – 146.

SOUZA, Jessé. *Ralé brasileira: quem é e como vive*. Belo Horizonte: UFMG, 2009.

SUBIRATS, Joan. ¿Nueva política? Argumentos a favor y dudas razonables. *Informe España* 2015, v. 1, n. 22, p. 447 – 464.

Comissões Parlamentares de Inquérito no Senado Federal (Instrumentos de Cidadania): 52ª e 53ª Legislaturas (uma análise empírica)

José Duarte Neto e Guilherme Pinho Ribeiro

Introdução

É evidência, verdadeira obviedade, a permanente expansão da globalização enquanto fenômeno de interconexão dos vários níveis da vida cotidiana – econômico, político, social, ambiental e cultural – a diversos e longínquos lugares do mundo. Também é fato que o nexo econômico é aquele que confere orientação e aceleração às dimensões conectadas. Esta transposição tem produzido ganhadores e perdedores nos diversos Estados em que opera, um desenvolvimento assimétrico e um aprofundamento das desigualdades existentes nos Estados. A prosperidade é compartilhada de modo desigual.

O dilema deste mundo globalizado – requisito para o exercício pleno da cidadania no espaço local e mundial – encontra-se no desenvolvimento sustentável. Existem, contudo, diversos entraves e obstáculos a serem transpostos para o desenvolvimento adequado e simétrico e para o exercício pleno da cidadania (também em nível global). A corrupção é compreendida hoje como uma dessas maiores dificuldades. Consiste, por vezes, no principal fator de dilapidação do patrimônio público (republicano), de cometimento de crimes nas burocracias nacionais e internacionais e de ineficiência dos serviços e de políticas públicas de saúde, educação e meio-ambiente sustentável. Acaba sendo uma disfunção institucional. Disfunção que tem características de problemas sistêmicos, no qual convergem instituições estatais, instituições entre si e um espaço globalizado (Clammer, 2012, p 113).

A despeito, e anteriormente a vastidão do problema internacional, a corrupção é uma velha tradição em nosso sistema constitucional e, vez e outra, a causa subjacente de rupturas institucionais e instabilidades de ampla tipologia. À guisa de exemplo, a disfuncionalidade pode ser encontrada (direta ou indiretamente): a) nas denúncias que justificaram o suicídio de Vargas (1954); b) na construção de Brasília por Juscelino; c) no mote de campanha da eleição presidencial de Jânio Quadros; d) na ruptura do regime pela força em 1964; e) no impeachment de Fernando Collor de Mello; f) na compra de votos pela reeleição de Fernando Henrique Cardoso; g) na mercancia do apoio popular no episódio Mensalão; h) no objeto de investigação da operação Lava-Jato (*Operation Car Wash*).

A solução do problema não é de fácil diagnóstico e desenlace. Mas, certamente, começa em nível local. Mesmo que a globalização tenha fragilizado a soberania estatal, que tenha colocado em xeque a efetividade do exercício cidadão dentro do espaço democrático, é por essas cercanias que a solução mostra-se provável. A soberania do Estado ainda remanesce como trincheira factível para qualquer combate em âmbito global. O combate se principia *Urbi et Orbi*, se invocada uma expressão da língua mãe dos juristas.

Nesta perspectiva, o objeto deste é auditar um dos principais mecanismos de *accountabilitty* vertical (no controle das práticas sociais e estatais): a atribuição de fiscalização dos Parlamentos. É investigação que se faz no âmbito das Comissões Parlamentares de Inquéritos (órgão de expressão desta competência constitucional). O recorte também se dará no âmbito daquelas que foram criadas e instaladas nas 52ª e 53ª legislaturas no Senado Federal. Isso porque em levantamento feito nos arquivos das CPIs na Câmara dos Deputados e no Senado Federal apuraram-se em relação à sua conclusão, ou seja, ao término das CPIs com a apresentação de relatório, o seguinte quadro[1]:

Casa	Relação CPIs Concluídas/ Instaladas do período da CF 88-2002	Relação CPIs Concluídas/ Instaladas do Período de 2002-2010
Senado Federal	15/17 (88,23%)	4/14 (28,57%)
Câmara dos Deputados	35/39 (89,74%)	15/17 (88,23%)
Congresso Nacional	19/20 (95,00%)	8/10 (80,00%)

Este levantamento permitiu inferir que: a) da promulgação da CF/88 até o ano 2002, o número de CPIs concluídas no Senado Federal, na Câmara dos Deputados e no Congresso Nacional permaneceu proporcional (média de 90,99%); b) entretanto, a proporção de instalação de CPIs, nos últimos dez anos, foi menor no Senado Federal do que Câmara dos Deputados e no Congresso Nacional (CPMIs); c) nos últimos dez anos, proporcionalmente houve um decréscimo na conclusão de CPIs no Senado Federal quando comparado com a Câmara dos Deputados.

Daí, ser objetivo deste descobrir as razões empíricas e institucionais (e não sociológicas) do decréscimo na apresentação dos relatórios finais das CPIs constituídas no Senado Federal de 2003-2010. O texto se vergará sobre as atas das reuniões das Comissões Parlamentares de Inquérito que foram instaladas e sobre os motivos de sua instalação, desenvolvimento dos trabalhos e conclusão. Obtidos os dados, extraídos de suas atas de trabalho e do Diário Oficial, serão confrontados e esquematizados para descortinar as razões da conclusão de umas e do não resultado de outras. É o objeto do terceiro capítulo. Por óbvio que, antes deste enfrentamento, discorrer-se-á

1 CÂMARA DOS DEPUTADOS. *Resposta à solicitação nº 7261102899437*. Anexos das informações sobre as CPIs. Mensagem recebida por guilhermepinho1@yahoo.com.br em 6 mar. 2013.

sobre a arqueologia do instituto (capítulo 1) e sobre sua construção dogmática (capítulo 2). Aparato necessário para uma conclusão crítica aferida da observação dos dados levantados (capítulo 3).

É crítica que se faz na crença da possibilidade de se aprimorar um mecanismo de fiscalização e supressão de disfuncionalidade (corrupção) que se opõe a um exercício pleno da cidadania democrática.

A emergência histórica das Comissões Parlamentares de Inquérito

Aliada a suas funções precípuas, o Parlamento tem a tarefa de controlar o Governo (aqui compreendido como o Poder Executivo). A função fiscalizadora deita suas raízes na Idade Média e na eclosão do Poder Legislativo como órgão contraposto às funções do monarca. Esta função fiscalizadora se especializa internamente, destaca-se e ganha em funcionalidade com a emergência das Comissões Parlamentares de Inquérito. Órgãos, colegiados, criados no interior dos Parlamentos com a finalidade específica de investigar e esclarecer fatos, atribuir responsabilidades e exigir providências. Como o aparecimento dos Parlamentos se confunde com a história da ascensão do Estado de Direito, e das Comissões Parlamentares de Inquérito como instrumentos de sua concretização, não se dispensa uma revisitação de sua gênese e uma análise detida de seus poderes, instrumentos e dinâmica. A soberania do Parlamento na Inglaterra e a importância do Congresso americano enquanto contrapeso em um Sistema de Governo Presidencialista sugere o início do percurso.

A organização constitucional inglesa é o berço das Comissões Parlamentares de Inquérito. Em 1604 o Parlamento já ouvia testemunhas, consultava e confrontava documentos após a invalidação da eleição de Sir Francis Goodwin pelo rei James I (*Goodwin's Case*)(Dimock, 1929, p. 48). No final do século XVII uma comissão foi especialmente instituída para investigar, julgar e, ao final, condenar o comandante Lundy por ilícitos perpetrados na Guerra da Irlanda (Souza, 2006, p. 23). Foi tradição que se sedimentou de duas formas, ou pela eleição de um órgão com função investigatória própria (*Select committe*), ou, excepcionalmente, pela investigação empreendida pela totalidade dos parlamentares (*Committes of the whole House*). Seus poderes, entretanto, foram granjeados a partir da promulgação de uma lei em 1858 que impunha o dever da verdade às testemunhas convocadas e de outra em 1871 que lhes dava imunidade pelo testemunho prestado (Sproesser, 2008, pp 149-150). Suas principais funções cingiam-se a obter informações para embasar a atividade legislativa, fiscalização financeira (exercício orçamentário) e supervisão de repartições e servidores públicos (Costa Pereira, 1948, p 16).

Curiosamente, apesar do surgimento precoce, cairiam em desuso. Hodiernamente investigações e estudos temáticos são comumente executados por Comissões externas ao Parlamento (*Royal Comissions*) criadas pela Coroa a pedido do Gabinete. Gozam de grandes poderes investigadores, em algumas situações maiores do que a autoridade judicial e superiores, portanto, às antigas Comissões Parlamentares. Como estas, contudo, circunscrevem-se à matéria para a qual foram criadas. Recorrem-se com frequência à convocação de membros externos, não parlamentares, o que lhes confere tecnicidade e independência, mas, ao mesmo tempo, desvinculação do Parlamento. Sua grande independência, por outro lado, fazem-nas perpetuarem no tempo, o que se mostra impossível com uma Comissão Parlamentar de Inquérito que vige durante uma respectiva legislatura (Martinelli, 2003, p 104).

A herança do *Common Law* e a condição de ex-colônia inglesa possibilitaria que o instituto deitasse raízes e florescesse na República constitucional americana. Surgidas lá, foram aqui que conquistaram prestígio como mecanismo de fiscalização. Uma explicação aceitável são as peculiaridades do Sistema de Governo. No Parlamentarismo de Westminster uma maior colaboração e interdependência funcional de poderes, no Presidencialismo americano uma separação e maior independência funcional, o que possibilita o amadurecimento de um sistema de freios e contrapesos e de instrumentos de fiscalização de um poder por outro. As Comissões Parlamentares de Inquérito seriam uma delas.

Mesmo antes da independência, sabe-se de caso de testemunha que foi presa por se recusar a depor perante a Assembleia de Nova York em 1761. As Constituições dos Estados de Maryland e Massachussets previram a possibilidade de seus legislativos instaurarem órgãos de investigação. A Constituição federal de 1787 e a maioria das Constituições dos Estados Americanos não explicitaram em normas o instrumento. O que não impediu a sua larga expansão (Sampaio, 1988, p 1). Após a promulgação da Constituição, em 1792, fora instalada uma investigação para apurar a responsabilidade militar e civil do General St. Clair em guerra travada contra os índios. E, desde então, todo conflito armado justificou a instalação de uma delas. Exceção feita a Guerra hispano-americana, prevendo-se a enormidade da conflagração, a investigação foi instalada por iniciativa do Presidente Mckinley (Baracho, 2001, p 5).

A importância das Comissões Parlamentares de Inquérito enquanto instrumento de fiscalização do legislativo provêm, sobretudo, da gama de atribuições e poderes que enfeixam. As leis de 1857 e 1862 davam-lhes *power to send for person, papers and records,* assim como no direito inglês, e, tipificava como crime e cominava pena multa e prisão às testemunhas relutantes (penas aplicadas aos Tribunais). Modernamente seu estatuto jurídico está incorporado ao US CODE (Seções 192 a 194), estabelecendo os deveres de testemunhas convocadas e a possibilidade de requisição de documentos, as imunidades daqueles que são chamados a depor (garantia contra a autoincriminação), as penas e penalidades a serem aplicadas nas hipóteses de falsidade ou recusa imotivada em depor e procedimento a ser adotado quando diante da constatação de infrações, à guisa de exemplo, ciência ao órgão de acusação, *Prosecutor ou Attorney,* para que promova o devido processo legal para a imposição da sanção (Sproesser, 2008, p 156).

Não se desconhece que em algumas situações seu adequado emprego foi causa da garantia de Direitos. Logo após a Guerra Civil, em 1871, uma Comissão de Inquérito investigou as condições em que viviam os afrodescendentes americanos e os obstáculos à sua participação política nos Estados da Carolina do Norte e do Sul, Mississipi e Flórida. Seus trabalhos permitiram uma produção legislativa sobre normas eleitorais, de resguardo da cidadania negra e coibição de associações ilegais racistas (*Civil Rights Act of 1871*)(Sproesser, 2008, p 109).

Todavia, o prestígio, mesmo o excesso de independência, fê-las não raras vezes veículo do arbítrio e da opressão. Dois exemplos, ao menos, corroboram a afirmação. A instalação da Comissão de Atividades Antiamericanas na Câmara dos Deputados em 1938, sob a presidência de Martin Dies, que devassou a vida dos americanos e os submeteu à execração pública e a Subcomissão Permanente de Inquérito do Senado Federal, instalada em 1945 sob a presidência de Joseph McCarthy e que espreitou e perseguiu toda a *intelligentsia* norte-americana (Martinelli, 2003, p 113).

Daí a contraofensiva da Suprema Corte Americana para impor alguns limites a este importante mecanismo de apuração do ilícito. Em McGrain vs Daugherty (1927) decidiu-se que qualquer investigação empreendida pelo Congresso Americano ou por qualquer de suas casas deve ter um propósito genuinamente legislativo. Em *Quinn* vs *United States* e Sweezy vs *New Hampshire* se reafirmou o *Bill of Righs* em defesa da liberdade de cátedra e de manifestação política no interior do ambiente universitário (Martinelli, 2003, p 114). Travas jurídicas que não interferiram e não interferem na criação e exercício da função fiscalizadora pelo legislativo.

Atualmente encontram-se instaladas no Senado Americano três Comissões de Investigação (*Select Committe* ou *Special Comittees*). A *Select Commitee on Ethics* de caráter permanente e criada em 1977 tem por fim investigar irregularidades praticadas por membros do senado (senadores, funcionários e assessores). Existindo informações de irregularidades a comissão designa presidente e vice-presidente de uma preliminar *enquirity*[2] para apuração dos fatos e, encontradas evidências não só senadores, mas

2 UNITED STATES SENATE. *Select Committee on Ethics*. Disponível em: < http://www.ethics.senate.gov/public/>. Acesso em: 12 nov. 2014.

funcionários e assessores. Em verdade, a comissão de inquérito é um das ferramentas utilizadas em seu procedimento. Quando há denúncias de irregularidades praticadas dentro do Senado, esta comissão de ética designa presidente e vice-presidente para a condução de um *preliminar enquiry*, para se determinar se há ou não evidências suficientes para a abertura de uma *adjudicatory review* e que possibilitará recomendações ao plenário do Senado[3]. A *Special Committee on Aging*, inicialmente criada como temporária em 1961, tornou-se permanente a partir de 1977. Tem como objetivo o tratamento da questão social dos idosos, com a apuração e investigação de fraudes, desperdícios, cobertura securitária e abusos perpetrados[4]. Há, por fim, a *Select Committee on Intelligence* que foi criada para vigilância da conformidade constitucional dos serviços de inteligência e contrainteligência. Suas reuniões são secretas em virtude do acesso a documentos sigilosos de segurança governamental[5].

A Câmara dos Deputados conta com duas comissões. Uma permanente desde 1977 e com as mesmas atribuições da *Select Committee on Intelligence*[6] e a *Select Committee on Benghazi*, temporária, criada em 2012 para investigar o atentado terrorista contra a embaixada americana em Bengazhi na Líbia[7].

---

3 UNITED STATES SENATE. *Rules of Procedure: Select Committee on Ethics.* Disponível em: < http://www.ethics.senate.gov/public/index.cfm/files/serve?File_id=551b39fc-30ed-4b14-b0d3-1706608a6fcb>. Acesso em 13 nov. 2014.

4 UNITED STATES SENATE. *Special Committee on Aging.* Disponivel em: < http://www.aging.senate.gov>. Acesso em 15 nov. 2014.

5 UNITED STATES SENATE. *Select Committee on Inteligence.* Disponível em: < http://www.intelligence.senate.gov/index.html>. Acesso em 15 nov. 2014.

6 UNITED STATES HOUSE OF REPRESENTATIVES. *Permanent Select Committee on Inteligence.* Disponível em: < http://intelligence.house.gov>. Acesso em 15 nov. 2014.

7 UNITED STATES HOUSE OF REPRESENTATIVES. *Select Committee on Benghazi.* Disponível em: < http://benghazi.house.gov>. Acesso em 15 nov. 2014.

Uma nota que merece ser frisada é que, diversamente do direito pátrio, a essência das Comissões Parlamentares de Inquérito no Reino Unido e dos Estados Unidos está nos poderes que reúnem (intimar testemunhas e ouvi-las sobre compromisso e requisitar documentos). A transitoriedade ou permanência de uma Comissão investigativa é requisito acessório no *Common Law* britânico e americano.

Entre nós, nossa primeira Constituição (1824) em seu artigo 19, § 9º confiava "... uma atribuição que o direito de fazer as leis por certo importa; ele inclui necessariamente o direito de inspecionar, de examinar se elas são ou não fielmente observadas..." (Bueno, 1978, p 106). O texto constitucional não criava expressamente órgãos próprios para o exercício de fiscalização, o que não impedia que internamente a Assembleia Geral, por si ou por qualquer de suas casas, confiasse essa atribuição a "... comissões ou inquéritos que penetrem nos detalhes da gestão administrativa, mormente quanto à administração financeira" (Bueno, 1978, p 107). Efetivamente foram várias as Comissões de Inquérito criadas para investigar repartições públicas. Nenhuma conseguiu, contudo, atingir qualquer autoridade (Baracho, 2001, p 102).

A primeira Constituição Republicana permaneceu silente no que se refere ao tratamento constitucional das Comissões Parlamentares de Inquérito. Durante sua vigência, dentro da compreensão que a fiscalização é atribuição inerente do Legislativo, foram propostas dezenove comissões. Poucas, contudo, reuniram adesão para aprovação. Duas variáveis concorreram para o resultado. Uma variável jurídica consistente na ausência de previsão constitucional e legal e uma política decorrente da ausência de oposição organizada para fazer frente ao regime de ampla maioria de que dispunha o sistema presidencialista da República Velha (Sampaio, 1988, p 22).

A Constituição de 1934 foi a primeira que as mencionou em seu texto. Atribuía sua criação à Câmara dos Deputados – o Senado tinha função acessória e colaborativa (art. 22, caput) – pela adesão de 1/3 de seus membros. Estabelecia com fim a investigação "fatos determinados" e exigia a aplicação das normas do Processo Penal (art. 36 e § único). O exíguo tempo de vigência da Constituição de 1934 fez com que somente seis fossem criadas.

Com o fechamento do Congresso Nacional e a outorga de uma Carta que nunca entrou em vigência, as Comissões Parlamentares de Inquérito seriam retomadas com a redemocratização em 1946. A Constituição de 1946 foi um divisor de águas na institucionalização das Comissões Parlamentares de Inquérito como instrumento de fiscalização empreendido pelo Legislativo. O texto promulgado mantinha a exigência de 1/3 de adesão para sua aprovação e exigia que o fato apurado fosse determinado, mas, inovava ao conferir a atribuição às duas Casas do Congresso Nacional e à exigência de se guardar a proporcionalidade partidária na composição de seus membros (art. 53 e § único cc § único do art. 40). Novidade também foi a promulgação da Lei 1.579/1952, vigente até hoje, que regulamenta a aprovação, instalação e os trabalhos das Comissões Parlamentares de Inquérito. Durante a vigência desta Constituição democrática, inúmeras e importantes Comissões de Inquérito foram instaladas para investigação: da Indústria têxtil; da arrecadação e aplicação das rendas dos Institutos de Previdência; de atos delituosos da Ditadura de Vargas; do Porto de Santos e várias outras (Baracho, 2001, p. 113).

O período de independência do Congresso Nacional e de liberdades dos parlamentares findar-se-ia em março de 1964. O regime de Atos Institucionais ampliou os poderes presidenciais, criou simulacros jurídicos para legitimar a investidura do Presidente da República, cassou mandatos parlamentares, suspendeu e suprimiu direitos políticos, ceifou direitos e garantias individuais.

No período, um Congresso Nacional enfraquecido e intimidado promulgaria uma nova Constituição (1967) para, logo em seguida e fechado pela força, ter o seu texto inteiramente alterado (Emenda nº 1/69). O tratamento normativo confiado foi exclusivamente formal, pois, efetivamente, o Congresso Nacional não tinha independência para o exercício de suas prerrogativas de fiscalização. Elas renasceriam com a redemocratização do Estado brasileiro e a promulgação da Constituição de 1988.

Excertos dogmáticos das Comissões Parlamentos de Inquérito: a Constituição de 1988.

A Constituição de 1988 restaurou um tratamento jurídico adequado às Comissões Parlamentares de Inquérito. Trataram-na em seu artigo 58, § 3º, possibilitando sua criação por ambas as casas do Congresso Nacional, separadas ou conjuntamente, relegando suas especificidades para os regimentos internos. Em verdade, o regramento positivado deu acabamento acertado ao exercício do poder de fiscalização do Congresso Nacional e de suas casas por meio de investigações empreendidas pelas Comissões Parlamentares de Inquérito. Ao menos em três aspectos, consolidou o que a prática e a compreensão dos juristas sedimentaram diante da prática parlamentar: a) os requisitos formais de criação, instalação e desfecho; b) a extensão e a profundidade do objeto a ser investigado; c) as amplitudes dos poderes de investigação.

A criação de uma Comissão Parlamentar de Inquérito exige a assinatura (adesão) de 1/3 de deputados federais, senadores ou deputados e senadores. A fração diz muito, pois se pensado o número total de cadeiras no Senado Federal, bastam 27 assinaturas para a sua criação. É um baixo quórum, mesmo contando o número de assinaturas necessário para a instalação na Câmara dos Deputados. Logo, por excelência, é ferramenta de minorias parlamentares. Obtidas as assinaturas e lido o requerimento de criação em plenário, as Comissões têm-se por criadas. As amplas maiorias não têm como impedir sua criação, pois ela não depende de sua aprovação (votação).[89] Mas, isso não quer dizer que criadas,

---

8 BRASIL. Supremo Tribunal Federal. Acórdão. Mandado de Segurança nº 26.441/DF. Tribunal Pleno. Relator Ministro Celso de Mello. Julgado em 25.04.2007. DJU 18.12.2009.

9 BRASIL. Supremo Tribunal Federal. Acórdão. Mandado de Segurança nº 24.831/DF. Tribunal Pleno. Relator Ministro Celso de Mello. Julgado em 22.06.2005.

obrigatoriamente sejam instaladas. Outros expedientes de obstrução legislativa podem inviabilizar sua instalação.

As Comissões Parlamentares de Inquérito prestam-se à "apuração de fato determinado", o que não quer dizer "fato qualquer", mas fato de interesse público, não somente os criminosos ou ilícitos, "...da vida constitucional do País, para que dele tenham conhecimento, preciso e suficiente, a Câmara dos Deputados ou o Senado Federal; e possam tomar as providências que lhe couberem" (Miranda, 1968, p 46). Como é ferramenta para um fim maior, de exercício parlamentar, deve haver aderência entre o fato investigado e as competências constitucionais federativas da União, sendo inconstitucional, a investigação do que se refere à competência de Estados-membros e Municípios (Schier, 2002, p. 82). Não é despropositado que durante as apurações, novos fatos venham à luz e, em cadeia, insiram-se no âmbito do que está sendo auferido (Zauli, 2011, p. 202).

São criadas por prazo certo, próprio de sua natureza de comissão temporária. O termo de sua conclusão sói estar expresso no requerimento de criação, sendo possível prorrogações. O regimento interno da Câmara dos Deputados fixa um prazo inicial de 120 dias com a possibilidade de prorrogação por mais sessenta, enquanto o do Senado silencia, não sendo incomum mais de duas prorrogações. Nenhuma, contudo, pode suplantar o prazo de uma legislatura, sendo compreensível, se lembrado que o contrário coibiria a discricionariedade de futuros legisladores, a própria independência de casa legislativa a ser instalada com ulteriores eleições (Sproesser, 2008, p. 245).

Para apurar os fatos as Comissões Parlamentares de Inquérito contam com "poderes de investigação próprios das autoridades judiciais", uma inovação do Constitucionalismo brasileiro. Em verdade, são atribuições referidas à produção de provas, colheita de depoimentos, requisição de documentos e realização de perícias (Barroso, 2000, p 12). Nem todas as provas, contudo, estão sob a sua discricionariedade. A própria

DJU 04.08.2006.

Constituição excepciona diligências que exigem a intervenção de uma autoridade judiciária - princípio da reserva constitucional - tendo em vista que diretamente implicam restrição a direitos e garantias fundamentais: inviolabilidade do domicílio, interceptação de comunicação telefônica e decretação de prisão preventiva ou temporária (art. 5º, incisos XI, XII e LXI da CF). Os poderes de investigação também não dispõem de auto executoriedade, força processual própria, daí que a recusa de comparecimento ou de entrega de documentos exigirá também uma intervenção do Estado-juiz (Barroso, 200, p. 27). Os regimentos internos da Câmara dos Deputados (art. 36 e incisos) e do Senado Federal (art. 148 e incisos) esmiúçam e especificam cada uma destas atribuições.

A Lei 1.579/52, que regulamenta as Comissões Parlamentares de Inquérito, foi recepcionada pela Constituição Federal. Ocorre que seu texto emprega indevidamente a expressão "indiciado" (art. 3º). Indiciados são que sofrem o peso de serem suspeitos da prática de ilícitos criminais. Expressão própria dos Inquéritos policiais e do processo penal, não de órgãos parlamentares de apuração de fatos das mais distintas naturezas. Pois, se ao final se encontrar infração penal, a diligência cabível é a provocação da autoridade com atribuição para dar início à persecução penal. A menção não é cerebrina. Enquanto as testemunhas intimadas são compromissadas a dizer a verdade, e sua falta com o que sabem, podem fazê-las incorrer em fato típico; aos eventuais "indiciados" (ou assim chamados) reservam-se o direito de não se auto incriminar e as medidas judiciais cabíveis para se recusarem ao comparecimento ou mesmo responderem o que lhes forem perguntado (Baracho, 2001, p 192).

O desfecho das investigações é formalizado pelo relatório final. Não é peça acusatória, não consiste em decisão condenatória, tão somente descreve o que foi descoberto pela investigação. Geralmente são recomendações de inovação ou reforma legislativa, instauração de processo disciplinar ou de abertura de procedimento criminal (Martinelli, 2008, p. 205). Obrigatoriamente, após a publicação, o relatório é encaminhado à Mesa da Câmara dos Deputados; ao Ministério Público ou à Advocacia-Geral da União; ao Poder Executivo; à Comissão Parlamentar Permanente respectiva; à Comissão Mista de Planos, Orçamentos Públicos e Fiscalização e ao Tribunal de Contas da União (art. 76 do Regimento Interno da Câmara dos Deputados). Ou então, há envio de seu relatório e conclusões à Mesa Diretora do Senado Federal para conhecimento do Plenário e, sendo o caso, ao Ministério Público, para que promova a responsabilidade civil ou criminal de possíveis infratores (arts. 150 e 151 do Regimento Interno do Senado Federal).

Pode trazer a público dados sigilosos nele contidos, desde que justificados e em caráter de excepcionalidade. Há possibilidade, ainda, de a comissão parlamentar de inquérito produzir, antes de findos os trabalhos, relatório parcial sobre as apurações realizadas até o momento, encaminhando às autoridades judiciais competentes para que sejam tomadas, desde já, as devidas providências. Lembrando que não há necessidade de aprovação Plenária do Relatório Final ou dos Parciais. (CARAJELESCOV, 2007, p. 162).

Comissões Parlamentares de Inquérito no Senado Federal (52ª e 53ª legislaturas): uma análise empírica

A abordagem realizada nos capítulos anteriores teve objetivos estritos e de servir ao cerne do problema que será por ora desenvolvido. Primeiro se investiu em uma arqueologia institucional das Comissões Parlamentares Legislativas, quer porque dá suporte para a interpretação do direito atual, quer em virtude de possibilitar um vislumbre sobre a persistência de valores jurídicos, quer, por fim, por desenvolver a sensibilidade para uma dimensão institucional tecida no espaço e no tempo (não só um instituto). Permite, destarte, uma visão crítica, e desfaz uma ingênua, de que as soluções são contingentes e não sistêmicas e provenientes de uma teia que se desenvolve lentamente em eras (Hespanha, 2003, p 15). Segundo se empreendeu um esforço analítico, e *a posteriori* de síntese, de uma perspectiva dogmática. Olhares estáticos sobre um passado e um presente jurídico.

Importantes questionamentos, mas, que são instrumentais do que ora se perquirirá. Prossegue-se, daí, com o objetivo de investigar as comissões parlamentares de inquérito criadas no Senado Federal durante a 52ª e a 53ª legislaturas. A investigação se submete a *dois recortes*.

O primeiro se fecha sobre as Comissões Parlamentares de Inquérito criadas, instaladas e concluídas ou não no Senado Federal. A escolha da Câmara alta – e não da Câmara baixa ou de ambas – tem por pressuposto a hipótese de que nos Sistemas de Governo Presidencialistas, com legislativos bicamerais e nos quais as Câmaras altas representam unidades federativas, o prestígio e a ascendência de seus membros são maiores, o que acaba por conferir maior *independência* a este órgão legislativo como um todo. Se não na função legislativa, ao menos seu papel de refreio e fiscalização é maior se comparado com o da Câmara baixa (Ruffia, 1984, p 265)[10]. Mormente como na ordem constitucional brasileira, em que, tradicionalmente, são eleitos três senadores pelo voto majoritário em cada unidade da federação (representação federativa), o que, de certa forma, dilui as influências ideológicas provenientes de um sistema eleitoral proporcional (próprio de Câmaras baixas). Outras variáveis a dar-lhe ascendência na função de controle estão na senioridade proveniente do requisito da idade mínima de trinta e cinco anos para elegibilidade (art. 14, inciso VI, alínea "a" da CF), de o seu funcionamento ser permanente em virtude da renovação dos mandatos, na proporção de 1/3 e 2/3, a cada oito anos por eleições quadrienais e ser menor o número

10 As competências constitucionais de controle e fiscalização do Senado Federal encontram-se no artigo 52 e incisos da CF e consistem em atribuições jurisdicionais (art. 52, I e II), de ratificação administrativa e política (art. 52, III, IV e XI), de autorização e fiscalização financeiras sobre diversos entes da Federação (art. 52, V à IX) e de revisão jurídica (art. 52, X). Cerca de 80% das atribuições constitucionais privativas do Senado Federal, nos termos da Constituição vigente, são de natureza de controle.

de seus membros, o que facilita a colheita de assinaturas para abertura de Comissões Parlamentares de Inquérito.

O segundo recorte circunscreve a investigação às 52ª e 53ª legislaturas (a vigente é a de número 55). São legislaturas encerradas há algum tempo, o que permite, de um lado, certo distanciamento do investigador. Dá-lhe uma perspectiva isenta do objeto investigado. O afastamento não é demasiado, menos de uma década, o que de outro lado, torna a investigação atual (não se trata de pesquisa histórica). O recorte tem, outrossim, por pressuposto a constatação de que o período pesquisado foi de relativa estabilidade política. Por estabilidade política compreenda-se a situação na qual, ao menos em princípio e a despeito das intempéries, o sistema político evolui de forma autônoma (transforma-se), sem perder suas características, ou seja, "... a capacidade previsível que um sistema tem de se prolongar no tempo" (Morlino, 1992, p 394). As variáveis em sistemas políticos estáveis são de certa maneira de identificáveis e previsíveis. Ocorre que desde 2013 (54ª legislatura) o sistema político ingressou em um torvelinho de crises políticas que tornou arriscado qualquer cálculo ou certeza: as jornadas de junho (2013); uma eleição geral acirrada; grave clivagem ideológica na sociedade; um impeachment de uma Presidente da República; pautas parlamentares paralisadas e erráticas; parlamentares e ex-parlamentares, ministros e ex-ministros investigados, processados e presos; Presidente e ex-Presidentes da República sob suspeita de corrupção, grave crise econômica. Tudo em um período não superior a quatro anos (2013-2017). Neste quadro se mostra impossível, senão incerto, qualquer pesquisa, investigação e vaticínio. As variáveis neste cenário são de ambiguidades quânticas. Por esse motivo, a preferência de investigação por uma paisagem que *ao menos na aparência* era de regularidades.

O método utilizado na empreita a seguir será empírico e indutivo (terceiro capítulo). A pesquisa debruçar-se-á sobre as atas das reuniões das Comissões Parlamentares de Inquérito que foram instaladas e sobre os motivos de sua instalação, desenvolvimento dos trabalhos e conclusão. Obtidos os dados, extraídos de suas atas de trabalho e do Diário Oficial, serão confrontados e esquematizados para descortinar as razões da conclusão de umas e do não resultado de outras.

Dados e análise individual das CPIs criadas e instaladas

CPI dos Transgênicos (2003)

A justificativa do requerimento de criação foi a polêmica envolvendo o contrabando de sementes transgênicas e seu plantio ilegal em território nacional.

O requerimento de criação RQS - 928/2003 foi apresentado em 09/10/2003 pelo Senador João Capibaribe – PSB e trazia prazo determinado (60 dias), assinatura de ao menos 1/3 dos senadores (39), recursos financeiros determinados (R$150.000,00), número de senadores (18). Foi instalada em 11/11/2003.

A seguir, quadro sistematizado da CPI:

CPI DOS TRANGÊNICOS (2003)[11]	
Requerimento	RQS 928/2003
Quantidade de Assinaturas	39
Data do Requerimento	9/10/03
Data da Instalação	11/11/03
Data de Encerramento	15/12/2004
Senadores Titulares (Requerimento)	11
Senadores Suplentes (Requerimento)	7
Recursos Financeiros	R$150.000,00
Autor/Partido	João Capibaribe/PSB
Prazo Inicial (Dias)	60
Quantidade de Prorrogações	1
Duração (Dias)	212
Número de Sessões	6
Presidente/Partido	João Capibaribe/PSB

11 SENADO FEDERAL, online.

Vice-Presidente/Partido	Jonas Pinheiro/PFL
Relator/Partido	Leomar Quintanilha/PMDB
Senadores Titulares (Participantes)	12
Média de Presença	51%
Senadores Suplentes (Participantes)	7
Média de Presença	14%
Média de Tempo das Reuniões (Minutos)	74
Média Entre as Reuniões (Dias)	28
Aprovação do Relatório Final	NÃO

Em uma análise prévia nota-se: a) um número elevado de senadores subscritores do requerimento de criação, 39, número muito superior ao mínimo de 27. Possibilita a compreensão de que o elevado apoio dos senadores subscritores não se refletiu em seu resultado.

Em relação a outras no mesmo período, releva alguns pontos: (a) o prazo inicial no requerimento de criação é incomum na prática parlamentar, a sua média no período é de 130 dias; (b) a duração, em dias, é menor que a média analisada, sendo de 212 e a média 475. A menor duração não pode ser considerada fator determinante da ausência de conclusão dos seus trabalhos, tendo em vista que outras duas CPIs estiveram abaixo desta média, porém concluíram seus trabalhos, sendo elas a CPI do Apagão Aéreo (142 dias) e a CPI da Petrobras (141 dias). Parece que o seu insucesso aconteceu pela pequena quantidade de reuniões. A média do período foi de 42 para a conclusão dos trabalhos, enquanto a dos Transgênicos se reuniu apenas 6 vezes. A CPI da Petrobras, que apresentou menor número, se reuniu 14 vezes, mais do que o dobro que a CPI dos Transgênicos. Outro dado destoante é a pequena duração das poucas reuniões, com a média de 74 minutos por cada, inferior aos 143 minutos de todas do período.

O disparate existente entre as médias dos lapsos temporais das CPIs: as duas CPIs que não aprovaram relatório final são aquelas que possuem maior lapso entre as reuniões, CPI dos Transgênicos, 28 dias, e

CPI das ONGs (2007), 23 dias. A terceira que tem lapso temporal entre as reuniões mais elevado é a CPI da Pedofilia, com 12 dias.

A seguir tabela demonstrativa dos membros da Comissão Parlamentar de Inquérito dos Transgênicos, seus partidos políticos e média de presença:

CPI DOS TRANGÊNICOS (2003)[12]	
Requerimento	RQS 928/2003
Quantidade de Assinaturas	39
Data do Requerimento	9/10/03
Data da Instalação	11/11/03
Data de Encerramento	15/12/2004
Senadores Titulares (Requerimento)	11
Senadores Suplentes (Requerimento)	7
Recursos Financeiros	R$150.000,00
Autor/Partido	João Capibaribe/PSB
Prazo Inicial (Dias)	60
Quantidade de Prorrogações	1
Duração (Dias)	212
Número de Sessões	6
Presidente/Partido	João Capibaribe/PSB
Vice-Presidente/Partido	Jonas Pinheiro/PFL
Relator/Partido	Leomar Quintanilha/PMDB
Senadores Titulares (Participantes)	12
Média de Presença	51%
Senadores Suplentes (Participantes)	7
Média de Presença	14%
Média de Tempo das Reuniões (Minutos)	74
Média Entre as Reuniões (Dias)	28
Aprovação do Relatório Final	NÃO

12 SENADO FEDERAL, online.

A frequência dos personagens-chave (presidente e relator) é alta, sendo do Senador Presidente João Capibaribe de 100% e do Senador Relator Leomar Quintanilha de 83%.

A última atividade que se tem registro oficial da Comissão Parlamentar de Inquérito dos Transgênicos é a 6ª e última reunião da Comissão que ocorreu no dia 09/06/2004. Após, não houve reuniões ou requerimentos. A Comissão foi oficialmente extinta em 15/12/2004, com o Ofício número 43/03 de autoria do Presidente da Comissão, o Senador João Capibaribe. No Ofício não há detalhes sobre os motivos que levaram à extinção da Comissão sem a apresentação de um relatório Final. A única justificativa foi o decurso do prazo inicialmente fixado para seu funcionamento, sabendo-se, contudo, que uma comissão parlamentar de inquérito pode ter seu prazo de funcionamento prorrogado, sendo seu único limite temporal o final da legislatura.

CPI dos Bingos (2004)

A justificativa do requerimento de criação foram as denúncias de práticas de lavagem de dinheiro e ocultação de bens por casas de bingo. Além da ocultação de bens, o requerimento trazia como justificativa a necessidade de investigar a relação das casas de bingos e empresas concessionárias de apostas com o crime organizado.

O requerimento de criação RQS - 245/2004 foi apresentado em 05/03/2004 pelo Senador Magno Malta– PL e trazia prazo determinado (120 dias), assinatura de ao menos 1/3 dos senadores (38), recursos financeiros (R$200.000,00), número determinado de senadores (30), sendo instalada em 29/06/2005. Para melhor análise, segue o quadro sistematizado de informações:

13 SENADO FEDERAL, online.

CPI DOS BINGOS (2004)[13]	
Requerimento	RQS- 245/2004
Quantidade de Assinaturas	38
Data do Requerimento	5/3/04
Data da Instalação	29/6/05
Data de Encerramento	4/7/06
Senadores Titulares (Requerimento)	15
Senadores Suplentes (Requerimento)	15
Recursos Financeiros	R$200.000,00
Autor/Partido	Magno Malta/PL
Prazo Inicial (Dias)	120
Quantidade de Prorrogações	2
Duração (Dias)	705
Número de Sessões	82
Presidente/Partido	Efraim Morais (DEM)
Vice-Presidente/Partido	Mozarildo Cavalcanti (PTB)
Relator/Partido	Garibaldi Alves Filho (PMDB)
Senadores Titulares (Participantes)	27
Média de Presença	69%
Senadores Suplentes (Participantes)	17
Média de Presença	29%
Média de Tempo das Reuniões (Minutos)	201
Média Entre as Reuniões (Dias)	9
Aprovação do Relatório Final	SIM

Análise dos dados: a) elevado lapso temporal entre o requerimento da comissão e sua efetiva instalação. Tal fato pode ser explicado pelas consecutivas questões de ordem formuladas no sentido de tentar impedir o seu funcionamento. A primeira, elaborada pelos Senadores Artur Virgílio – PSDB e Eduardo Siqueira Campos – PTB com o fim de impossibilitar a designação de membros pelo Presidente do Senado diante da omissão das lideranças partidárias. A questão de ordem não foi acatada pelo Senador Presidente, sendo encaminhada à Comissão de Constituição e Justiça sob n. 5/2004. Ainda, a questão de ordem do Senador Eduardo Siqueira Campos – PTB de que não havia "fato determinado" a ser investigado pela comissão, pretendendo-se o arquivamento do requerimento de criação, também rejeitado pelo Presidente da Casa e encaminhado como recurso n. 6/2004 à Comissão de Constituição e Justiça.

Para a indicação dos membros e a instalação da CPI, foram impetrados respectivamente os Mandados de Segurança n. 24945, 24946, 24847, 24848 e 24849, de autoria dos Senadores Efraim Morais (DEM), Jorge Bornhausen (DEM), José Jorge (PFL), Demóstenes Torres (DEM) e José Agripino (DEM). Os mandados de segurança visavam garantir e consolidar a jurisprudência de garantir ao Presidente do Senado Federal a possibilidade de indicar os membros faltantes daqueles partidos que se omitiam em indicar. É considerado *leading case*, pois a partir deste momento não restou dúvida quanto a essa possibilidade por parte do Presidente da Casa, garantindo, assim, a prerrogativa das minorias em procederem com inquéritos parlamentares. Os mandados de segurança foram julgados em conjunto, sob relatoria do Ministro Celso de Mello. Segue ementa do acórdão de julgamento no dia 22/06/2005[14].

---

14 COMISSÃO PARLAMENTAR DE INQUÉRITO - DIREITO DE OPOSIÇÃO - PRERROGATIVA DAS MINORIAS PARLAMENTARES - EXPRESSÃO DO POSTULADO DEMOCRÁTICO - DIREITO IMPREGNADO DE ESTATURA CONSTITUCIONAL - INSTAURAÇÃO DE INQUÉRITO PARLAMENTAR E COMPOSIÇÃO DA RESPECTIV A CPI - TEMA QUE EXTRAVASA OS LIMITES "INTERNA CORPORIS" DAS CASAS LEGISLATIVAS - VIABILIDADE DO CONTROLE JURISDICIONAL - IMPOSSIBILIDADE DE A MAIORIA PARLAMENTAR FRUSTRAR, NO ÂMBITO DO CONGRESSO NACIONAL, O EXERCÍCIO, PELAS MINORIAS LEGISLATIVAS, DO DIREITO CONSTITUCIONAL À INVESTIGAÇÃO PARLAMENTAR (CF, ART. 58, § 3º) - MANDADO DE SEGURANÇA CONCEDIDO. CRIAÇÃO DE COMISSÃO PARLAMENTAR DE INQUÉRITO: REQUISITOS CONSTITUCIONAIS (STF - MS: 24849 DF, Relator: CELSO DE MELLO, Data

Somente após a decisão do STF é que houve a possibilidade de instalação da CPI. Segue tabela constando todos os Senadores que compuseram a CPI, seguido de suas porcentagens de presença:

			Percentual de Frequência[15]
Senadores Titulares	1	Romeu Tuma (PTB)	91%
	2	Antônio Carlos Magalhães (PFL)	93%
	3	Efraim Morais (PFL)	87%
	4	Reginaldo Duarte (PSDB)	80%
	5	Leonel Pavan (PSDB)	66%
	6	Valdir Raupp (PMDB)	82%
	7	Hélio Costa (PMDB)	0
	8	Luiz Otávio (PMDB)	70%
	9	Paulo Paim (PT)	100%
	10	Sibá Machado* (PT)	66%
	11	Fátima Cleide* (PT)	60%
	12	Magno Malta (PR)	68%
	13	Jovêncio da Fonseca* (PSDB)	83%
	14	Mozarildo Cavalcanti (PP)	53%
	15	Augusto Botelho (PDT)	54%
	16	Flávio Arns (PSDB)	79%
	17	Tião Viana* (PT)	94%
	18	Tasso Jereissati (PSDB)	91%
	19	Leomar Quintanilha* (PMDB)	36%
	20	Eduardo Suplicy (PT)	87%
	21	Aelton Freitas (PR)	33%
	22	Gilvam Borges (PMDB)	9%
	23	Álvaro Dias* (PSDB)	56%
	24	Antero Paes de Barros* (PSDB)	62%
	25	José Agripino (PFL)	100%
	26	José Jorge* (PFL)	75%
	27	Garibaldi Alves Filho (PMDB)	95%

de Julgamento: 22/06/2005, Tribunal Pleno, Data de Publicação: DJ 29-09-2006 PP-00035 EMENT VOL-02249-08 PP-01323)

15 SENADO FEREDAL, online.

Senadores Suplentes	28	Geraldo Mesquita (PMDB)	85%
	29	Demóstenes Torres (PFL)	27%
	30	Álvaro Dias* (PSDB)	74%
	31	Alberto Silva (PMDB)	0
	32	Leomar Quintanilha* (PMDB)	0
	33	Antônio Carlos Valadares (PSB)	0
	34	Tião Viana* (PT)	10%
	35	Sérgio Zambiasi (PTB)	10%
	36	Fátima Cleide* (PT)	0
	37	Arthur Virgílio (PSDB)	20%
	38	Herácito Fortes (PFL)	51%
	39	Sibá Machado* (PT)	40%
	40	José Jorge* (PFL)	0
	41	Juvêncio da Fonseca* (PSDB)	65%
	42	Ideli Salvatti (PT)	56%
	43	Wellington Salgado (PMDB)	50%
	44	Antero Paes de Barros* (PSDB)	20%

A CPI dos Bingos apresentou a maior quantidade de Senadores em uma única comissão no período. Houve o encaminhamento de 41 ofícios das lideranças partidárias solicitando a mudança de membros, o que elevou sua composição para 44 senadores.

O prazo fixado de 120 dias esteve longe de ser cumprido, contando a comissão com 705 dias de trabalhos, possibilitados por dois requerimentos de prorrogação. Apresentou o maior número de reuniões, 82, enquanto a média foi de 41 reuniões. A média temporal (em minutos) das reuniões também apresentou valor acima da média, com 201 minutos, enquanto a média se mostrou 143 minutos.

A média de presença dos membros titulares foi a maior apresentada no período (juntamente com a CPI da Petrobras), com 69%, enquanto a média mostrou-se com 57%. Outro dado interessante é o pequeno lapso temporal entre as reuniões, de apenas 9 dias, enquanto a média se mostrou sendo de 14 dias.

Diante do trabalho dos senadores, apresentou e aprovou-se um extenso relatório final com 1130 páginas.

CPI das ONGs (2007)

A justificativa do requerimento de criação foi a apuração das liberações financeiras do Governo Federal para as organizações não governamentais e organizações da sociedade civil de interesse público, além da utilização das referidas verbas pelas entidades no período de 1999 a 2006.

O requerimento de criação RQS- 201/2007 de autoria do Senador Heráclito Fortes (DEM) trazia para a criação o prazo (120 dias), assinatura de ao menos 1/3 dos senadores (78), recursos financeiros determinados (R$200.000,00), número determinado de senadores (18), sendo instalada em 03/10/2007.

Foi apresentado nos primeiros dias da 53ª Legislatura, pois a CPI das ONGs (2006) criada no último mês da legislatura anterior. As duas CPIs das ONGs (2006 e 2007) possuem as mesmas características no requerimento de criação, inclusive o autor e objeto de investigação. A tabela a seguir ilustra as características gerais da comissão:[16]

CPI DAS ONGs (2007)[16]	
Requerimento	RQS 201/2007
Quantidade de Assinaturas	78
Data do Requerimento	15/3/07
Data de Instalação	03/10/07
Data de Encerramento	05/04/10
Senadores Titulares (Requerimento)	11
Senadores Suplentes (Requerimento)	7
Recursos Financeiros	R$200.000,00
Autor/Partido	Heráclito Fortes/DEM
Prazo Inicial (Dias)	120
Quantidade de Prorrogações	6
Duração (Dias)	781

16 SENADO FEDERAL, online.

Número de Sessões	34
Presidente/Partido	Raimundo Colombo e Heráclito Fortes/DEM
Vice-Presidente/Partido	Lúcia Vânia/PSDB
Relator/Partido	Inácio Arruda e Arthur Virgílio/ PCdoB e PSDB
Senadores Titulares (Participantes)	21
Média de Presença	55%
Senadores Suplentes (Participantes)	11
Média de Presença	24%
Média de Tempo das Reuniões (Minutos)	120
Média Entre as Reuniões (Dias)	23
Aprovação do Relatório Final	NÃO

Nota-se o maior número de subscritores para a criação da matéria (78 senadores em um universo de 81 parlamentares). Houve grande apoio dos senadores no desenvolvimento dos trabalhos da CPI, apesar de que existiu lacuna temporal de mais de 6 meses da criação da comissão até sua instalação e efetivo início dos trabalhos.

Quanto ao prazo inicial, mais uma vez longe de ser cumprido, a comissão apresentou o segundo maior tempo de duração de uma comissão desta espécie, de 781 dias, em uma média geral de 475. Além do exposto, apresentou o maior número de requerimento de prorrogação, em um total de 6, tendo em vista a média de 2. Houve o encaminhamento de 27 ofícios das lideranças partidárias solicitando a troca de membros da comissão. Neste quesito, ficou atrás apenas para a CPI dos Bingos.

Já a média de presença se mostrou estável em relação à média das outras CPIs, havendo pouca variação. A seguir a tabela de senadores que atuaram na comissão e seus respectivos percentuais de presença:

			Percentual de Frequência[17]
Senadores Titulares	1	Heráclito Fortes (DEM)	88%
	2	Raimundo Colombo (DEM)	76%
	3	Flexa Ribeiro (PSDB)	70%
	4	Lúcia Vânia (PSDB)	67%
	5	Fátima Cleide (PT)	54%
	6	Inácio Arruda (PCdoB)	100%
	7	Sibá Machado (PT)	38%
	8	Valdir Raupp* (PMDB)	62%
	9	Wellington Salgado Oliveira (PMDB)	29%
	10	Valter Pereira (PMDB)	23%
	11	Jefferson Péres (PDT)	20%
	12	Sérgio Guerra (PSDB)	62%
	13	Antônio Carlos Valadares (PSB)	100%
	14	Flávio Arns (PT)	100%
	15	João Pedro* (PT)	83%
	16	Jefferson Praia (PSDB)	66%
	17	Eduardo Suplicy (PT)	75%
	18	Neuto de Couto (PTB)	42%
	19	Tasso Jereissati (PSDB)	60%
	20	Artur Virgílio (PSDB)	37%
	21	Patrícia Saboya (PDT)	12%
Senadores Suplentes	22	César Borges (PR)	0
	23	Álvaro Dias (PDT)	73%
	24	Mozarildo Cavalcanti (PTB)	100%
	25	Leomar Quintanilha (PMDB)	18%
	26	Romero Jucá (PMDB)	8%
	27	Osmar Dias (PDT)	0
	28	João Pedro* (PT)	12%
	29	Valdir Raupp* (PMDB)	42%
	30	Augusto Botelho (PT)	0
	31	Paulo Paim (PT)	0
	32	Demóstones Torres (DEM)	20%

17 SENADO FEDERAL, online.

A CPI das ONGs (2007) apresentou relatório final de seus trabalhos, porém sem aprovação. Todos os encaminhamentos e sugestões legislativas, inclusive a remessa de documentos para que o Ministério Público procedesse a responsabilização civil e criminal foram obstados.

Apesar de ser a CPI mais longa do período, não houve resultados práticos para justificar o trabalho legislativo. A razão para não se ter um relatório final aprovado, neste caso, é simplesmente o término do prazo estabelecido que, nos termos do art. 76, II do Regimento Interno do Senado Federal, todas as comissões temporárias devem ser arquivadas no término do prazo. O que não se explica, no entanto, é por que não houve o requerimento de prorrogação do prazo mais uma vez. No dia 28/10/2010 houve a apresentação de um relatório final, no entanto recusado pelos membros da comissão. No dia 03/11/2010 ocorreu o encerramento da comissão pelo decurso do prazo. Haveria a possibilidade de mais uma prorrogação deste prazo até o término da 53ª Legislatura, que ocorreria 20 dias mais tarde. Ou seja, os membros preferiram encerrar os trabalhos da presente comissão por entenderem ser impossível a apresentação e aprovação de um novo relatório final em apenas 20 dias.

Alguns apontamentos devem ser feitos. O primeiro diz respeito ao lapso temporal entre uma reunião e outra, a segunda maior dentre as CPIs analisadas – ficando atrás apenas da CPI dos Transgênicos, que também não aprovou relatório final – com a média de 23 dias, enquanto a média global de todas as CPIs em análise foi de 14 dias. Isto explica o fracasso da CPI, uma vez que com lapsos temporais menores haveria a possibilidade da elaboração de novo relatório e sua possível aprovação. O segundo diz respeito à relatoria – considerado juntamente com a presidência como cargo mais importante – em que houve mudança na reunião 25. O cargo era ocupado pelo Senador Inácio Arruda (PCdoB), que contou com 100% de presença nas reuniões em que era membro da comissão. Na reta final da CPI houve a mudança da relatoria para o Senador Artur Virgílio (PSDB), que esteve presente em apenas 37% das reuniões. Estes são os motivos aparentes que levaram a CPI das ONGs (2007) a não aprovar um relatório final dos trabalhos

CPI do Apagão Aéreo (2008)

Esta CPI apresentou como motivo de criação apurar as causas, condições e responsabilidades referentes aos problemas ocorridos no sistema de tráfego aéreo. O acidente ocorrido em 26 de setembro de 2006, envolvendo o Boing 737-800 da companhia Gol e um jato lato *Legacy da American ExcelAire,* acidente que matou mais de 150 pessoas. Em seguida, as manifestações dos controladores de voo em outubro de 2006, que resultou no atraso de 43% dos voos no período. Outro fato trazido dizia respeito às denúncias de irregularidades apresentadas nas obras de reforma dos Aeroportos de Congonhas, Guarulhos, Viracopos, Antônio Carlos Jobim e Juscelino Kubitschek e outros problemas envolvendo a aviação civil brasileira.

O requerimento de criação RQS - 401/2007 foi apresentado em 25/04/2007 pelo Senador José Agripino– DEM. Trazia um prazo determinado (180 dias), assinatura de ao menos 1/3 dos senadores (34), recursos financeiros (R$200.000,00) e número de senadores (23), sendo instalada em 17/05/2007. Segue o quadro sistematizado de informações:[18]

CPI DO APAGÃO AÉREO (2007)[18]	
Requerimento	401/2007
Quantidade de Assinaturas	34
Data do Requerimento	25/04/2007
Data da Instalação	17/05/2007
Data de Encerramento	31/10/2007
Senadores Titulares (Requerimento)	13
Senadores Suplentes (Requerimento)	10
Recursos Financeiros	$200.000,00
Autor/Partido	José Agripino/DEM

18 SENADO FEDERAL, online.

Prazo Inicial (Dias)	180
Quantidade de Prorrogações	0
Duração (Dias)	142
Número de Sessões	34
Presidente/Partido	Tião Viana/ PT
Vice-Presidente/Partido	Renato Casagrande/ PSB
Relator/Partido	Demóstenes Torres/ DEM
Senadores Titulares (Participantes)	15
Média de Presença	54%
Senadores Suplentes (Participantes)	11
Média de Presença	36%
Média de Tempo das Reuniões (Minutos)	222
Média Entre as Reuniões (Dias)	4
Aprovação do Relatório Final	SIM

A CPI do Apagão apresentou resultados positivos. Juntamente com a da Petrobrás, foram as únicas que conseguiram finalizar os trabalhos e aprovar o relatório final antes do prazo estabelecido de 180 dias. Apresentou a menor taxa de lapso temporal entre as reuniões, de apenas 4 dias, muito abaixo da média geral, de 14 dias. A média de duração das reuniões, de 222 minutos – a maior apresentada na análise das CPIs deste trabalho – podem ser os fatores determinantes para sua conclusão de maneira eficaz, com a apresentação de relatório final e sua aprovação em tempo muito inferior ao prazo previsto. A tabela a seguir mostra os Senadores que atuaram na referida CPI e seus percentuais de presença:

			Percentual de Frequência[19]
Senadores Titulares	1	Antônio Carlos Magalhães (DEM)	42%
	2	Demóstenes Torres (DEM)	95%
	3	José Agripino (DEM)	54%
	4	Mário Couto (PSDB)	75%
	5	Sérgio Guerra (PSDB)	46%
	6	Tião Viana (PT)	67%
	7	Sibá Machado* (PT)	29%
	8	Sérgio Zambiasi (PTB)	62%
	9	Renato Casagrande (PSB)	63%
	10	Leomar Quintanilha (PMDB)	58%
	11	Gilvam Borges (PMDB)	33%
	12	Wellington Salgado (PMDB)	50%
	13	Osmar Dias (PDT)	0
	14	Antônio Carlos Magalhães Jr (DEM)	37%
	15	João Pedro* (PT)	100%
Senadores Suplentes	16	Raimundo Colombo (DEM)	50%
	17	Romeu Tuma (PTB)	75%
	18	Ideli Salvati (PT)	70%
	19	Tasso Jereissati (PSDB)	8%
	20	João Pedro* (PT)	58%
	21	Inácio Arruda (PCdoB)	33%
	22	Romero Jucá (PMDB)	29%
	23	Valdir Raupp (PMDB)	25%
	24	João Duarval (PDT)	0
	25	Arthur Virgílio (PSDB)	0
	26	Sibá Machado* (PT)	50

19 SENADO FEDERAL, online.

A CPI do Apagão Aéreo, juntamente com a CPI da Petrobras, pode ser considerada a mais eficaz instalada durante o período. O relatório final desta CPI continha 944 páginas, foi aprovado na última reunião, em 31/10/2007, sendo encaminhado aos órgãos competentes para tomarem as devidas providências, utilizando-se das informações e conclusões da CPI do Apagão Aéreo.

CPI da Pedofilia (2008)

A justificativa do requerimento de criação era investigar e apurar a utilização da Internet para a prática de crimes de pedofilia. O interesse para o seu surgimento se deu pela operação da Polícia Federal, denominada Operação Carrossel. Buscava-se colher novas informações, aprofunda-las e sistematizar dados para fins de aprimoramento legislativo.

O requerimento de criação RQS - 200/2008 foi apresentado em 04/03/2008 pelo Senador Magno Malta- PL. Trazia prazo determinado (120 dias), assinatura de ao menos 1/3 dos senadores (27), recursos financeiros (R$400.000,00), número de senadores (14), sendo instalada em 25/35/2008. Segue o quadro sistematizado de informações:

CPI DA PEDOFILIA (2008)[20]	
Requerimento	RQS 200/2008
Números de Assinaturas	27
Data do Requerimento	04/03/08
Data da Instalação	25/03/08
Data de Encerramento	16/12/2010
Senadores Titulares (Requerimento)	7
Senadores Suplentes (Requerimento)	7
Recursos Financeiros	RS400.000,00
Autor/Partido	Magno Malta/PL
Prazo Inicial (Dias)	120
Número de Prorrogações	5

20 SENADO FEDERAL, online.

Duração (Dias)	873
Número de Sessões	76
Presidente/Partido	Magno Malta/PL
Vice-Presidente/Partido	Romeu Tuma/PTB
Relator/Partido	Demóstenes Torres/DEM
Senadores Titulares (Participantes)	8
Média de Presença	45%
Senadores Suplentes (Participantes)	8
Média de Presença	29%
Duração Média das Reuniões (Minutos)	82
Lapso Temporal Entre as Reuniões (Dias)	12
Aprovação do Relatório Final	SIM

A CPI demandou o maior tempo para a conclusão de seus trabalhos, utilizando-se de 873 dias, distante dos 120 dias inicialmente previstos. Contou com elevado número de reuniões, ficando atrás apenas da CPI dos Bingos (2004), com 76 encontros. Foi a CPI com o menor número de presença média de seus membros (45%).

O lapso temporal entre as reuniões, um aspecto positivo exposto nos tópicos das CPIs dos Transgênicos e das ONGs (2007), é fator fundamental para a aprovação ou não do relatório final. Aqui, o lapso médio foi de 12 dias, e, devido ao elevado número de sessões internas, não haveria tempo suficiente para a conclusão em lapso médio mais elevado.

O percentual de presença dos respectivos Senadores:

			Percentual de Frequência[21]
Senadores Titulares	1	Demóstones Torres (DEM)	55%
	2	Eduardo Azeredo (PSDB)	47%
	3	Marcelo Crivella* (PRB)	0
	4	Magno Malta (PR)	94%
	5	Romeu Tuma (PTB)	71%
	6	Almeida Lima (PMDB)	0
	7	Geraldo Mesquita (PMDB)	53%
	8	Paulo Paim (PT)	46%

21 SENADO FEDERAL, online.

Senadores Suplentes	9	Maria do Carmo Alves (DEM)	0
	10	Cícero Lucena (PSDB)	2%
	11	Sérgio Zambiasi (PTB)	50%
	12	Paulo Paim (PT)	22%
	13	Marcelo Crivella* (PRB)	0
	14	Papaléo Paes (PSDB)	53%
	15	Virgínio de Carvalho (DEM)	28%
	16	José Nery (PSOL)	83%
	17	Geraldo Mesquita (PMDB)	0

Concluída, a data da aprovação do relatório final ocorreu 6 dias antes do final da Legislatura. Não fosse a reduzida média de tempo entre as reuniões, estaria no rol daquelas que não concluíram seus trabalhos. O relatório final contou com 1696 páginas.

CPI da Petrobras (2009)

O requerimento de criação foi a investigação de irregularidades envolvendo a Petrobras e a Agência Nacional de Petróleo, Gás Natural e Biocombustíveis. As irregularidades foram apontadas pela Polícia Federal na Operação conhecida como Águas Profundas e diziam respeito à licitações e contratos de construção de plataformas. Além destas irregularidades apontadas pelo requerimento de criação, buscava-se investigar as denúncias de desvios dos *royalties*, apontadas pela Operação Royalties da Polícia Federal. A Polícia Federal, o Ministério Público Federal e o Tribunal de Contas da União apontaram sucessivas irregularidades. A seguir tabela de informações da Comissão:

CPI DA PETROBRÁS (2009)[22]	
Requerimento	RQS 569/2009
Quantidade de Assinaturas	32
Data do Requerimento	15/05/09
Data da Instalação	14/07/09
Data de Encerramento	17/12/09

22 SENADO FEDERAL, online.

Senadores Titulares (Requerimento)	11
Senadores Suplentes (Requerimento)	7
Recursos Financeiros	R$50.000,00
Autor/Partido	Álvaro Dias/PSDB
Prazo Inicial (Dias)	180
Quantidade de Prorrogações	0
Duração (Dias)	141
Número de Sessões	14
Presidente/Partido	João Pedro/PT
Vice-Presidente/Partido	Marcelo Crivella/PRB
Relator/Partido	Romero Jucá/PMDB
Senadores Titulares (Participantes)	11
Média de Presença	69%
Senadores Suplentes (Participantes)	7
Média de Presença	39%
Média de Tempo das Reuniões (Minutos)	164
Média Entre as Reuniões (Dias)	8
Aprovação do Relatório Final	SIM

Teve curta duração e a aprovação de seu relatório final antes do prazo previsto, hipótese verificada apenas duas vezes durante o período. A frequência dos Senadores, de 69%, foi a maior apresentada no período em tela. Não só os titulares, mas os suplentes apresentaram a maior taxa de presença, de 39%. Outra peculiaridade e exclusividade desta comissão: não houve troca de membros em seus trabalhos, os mesmos 11 senadores que nela iniciaram permaneceram até a sua conclusão. O mesmo pode ser dito dos 7 suplentes que a compuseram. É fato a se noticiar, tendo em vista as 42 mudanças na composição, apresentada pela CPI dos Bingos, por exemplo. Mais uma vez, o lapso temporal médio entre as reuniões mostrou-se item essencial para a conclusão dos trabalhos de uma CPI.

A seguir tabela com os Senadores que compuseram a referida CPI, seguido de seus percentuais de frequência:

			Percentual de Frequência[23]
Senadores Titulares	1	Antônio Carlos Júnior (DEM)	78%
	2	Álvaro Dias (PSDB)	78%
	3	Sérgio Guerra (PSDB)	64%
	4	Ideli Salvatti (PT)	78%
	5	Marcelo Crivella (PRB)	42%
	6	João Pedro (PT)	100%
	7	Paulo Duque (PMDB)	50%
	8	Romero Jucá (PMDB)	92%
	9	Fernando Collor (PTB)	57%
	10	Jefferson Praia (PDT)	78%
	11	Valdir Raupp (PMDB)	50%
Senadores Suplentes	12	Heráclito Fortes (DEM)	14%
	13	Tasso Jereissati (PSDB)	35%
	14	Inácio Arruda (PCdoB)	85%
	15	Delcídio Amaral (PT)	78%
	16	Almeida Lima (PMDB)	7%
	17	Gim Argello (PTB)	57%
	18	Neuto de Couto (PMDB)	0

A título de informação outra CPI com os mesmos objetivos foi criada a partir do Requerimento 302/2014 e foi instalada em 14/05/2014.

Dados e análise individual das CPIs criadas e não instaladas

Serão abordadas as CPIs que tiveram os requisitos regimentais e constitucionais para a criação, porém, sem instalação. O objetivo é demonstrar que, além das 6 CPIs apresentadas e instaladas, mais 8 foram criadas (obtidas as assinaturas necessárias). Como não houve instalação, seus dados são exíguos.

23 SENADO FEDERAL, online.

CPI do Caso Waldomiro Diniz

O requerimento de criação tinha como objeto central investigar as acusações de corrupção ativa e tráfico de influência contra Subchefe da Casa Civil, Waldomiro Diniz. Investigava-se a renovação de um contrato de R$130.000.000,00 entre a Caixa Econômica Federal e a empresa multinacional Gtech. Discutia-se a relação do então Chefe da Casa Civil, José Dirceu, com o esquema. A seguir tabela informativa em relação à comissão:[24]

CPI DO CASO WALDOMIRO DINIZ[24]	
Requerimento	RQS 160/2005
Quantidade de Assinaturas	30
Data do Requerimento	16/03/2005
Data da Instalação	NÃO HOUVE
Data do Arquivamento	22/01/2007
Senadores Titulares (Requerimento)	11
Senadores Suplentes (Requerimento)	6
Recursos Financeiros	R$150.000,00
Autor/Partido	Artur Virgílio/PSDB
Prazo Inicial (Dias)	180

Na data de requerimento de criação da CPI, a Presidência do Senado expediu Ofícios aos líderes dos Blocos Parlamentares para que indicassem os membros que a comporiam, obedecendo-se a proporcionalidade parlamentar. Nenhum dos partidos apresentou os nomes para a composição, nem o proponente, o PSDB.

Como de praxe nas atividades parlamentares, a matéria foi oficialmente arquivada em 22/01/2007, ou seja, no início da Legislatura seguinte, obedecendo-se norma prevista no § 4º do art. 76 do Regimento Interno do Senado Federal. O motivo do insucesso foi a ausência de indicação das lideranças partidárias para a sua composição proporcional.

24 SENADO FEDERAL, online.

CPI das Privatizações

O objetivo foi averiguar as insinuações do então Presidente da República, Luiz Inácio Lula da Silva, e outros integrantes do alto escalão do Governo em relação às privatizações ocorridas de 1990 a 2004. O objeto de investigação eram os critérios adotados pelo Banco Nacional de Desenvolvimento Econômico e Social na concessão de crédito nos processos de privatização. A comissão pretendia investigar, especificamente, as privatizações da Companhia Siderúrgica Nacional (Vale do Rio Doce), o Sistema de Telecomunicações Brasileiro e a privatização do setor elétrico. A seguir informações gerais acerca da CPI

CPI DAS PRIVATIZAÇÕES[25]	
Requerimento	RQS 161/2005
Quantidade de Assinaturas	30
Data do Requerimento	16/03/2005
Data da Instalação	NÃO HOUVE
Data do Arquivamento	22/01/2007
Senadores Titulares (Requerimento)	11
Senadores Suplentes (Requerimento)	6
Recursos Financeiros	R$180.000,00
Autor/Partido	Artur Virgílio/PSDB
Prazo Inicial (Dias)	180

Há grandes semelhanças com a anterior (CPI DO CASO WALDOMIRO DINIZ), sendo protocolizadas no mesmo dia, pelo mesmo autor, com as mesmas características estruturais (número de titulares e suplentes e prazo dos trabalhos). As 30 assinaturas que constam em ambos os requerimentos são as mesmas, inclusive quanto à ordem. Diversamente da CPI de Waldomiro Diniz, ao menos, ocorreram indicações pelas lideranças partidárias:

25 SENADO FEDERAL, online.

COMPOSIÇÃO CPI DAS PRIVATIZAÇÕES[26]	
Titulares	Suplentes
Artur Virgílio (PSDB)	Flexa Ribeiro (PSDB)
Tasso Jereissati (PSDB)	Marco Maciel (PFL)
José Jorge (PFL)	Hélio Costa (PMDB)
Rodolpho Tourinho (PFL)	Mão Santa (PMDB)
Garibaldi Alves Filho (PMDB)	Roberto Saturino (PT)
Amir Lando (PMDB)	Marcelo Crivella (PL)
Pedro Simon (PMDB)	Heloísa Helena (PSOL)
Ana Júlia Carepa (PT)	
Serys Slhessarenko (PT)	
Eduardo Suplicy (PT)	
Jéfferson Péres (PDT)	

Apesar da designação dos membros - ocorrida em 28/06/2005 - a CPI não apresentou qualquer outra atividade até seu arquivamento em 22/01/2007, obedecendo-se norma prevista no § 4º do art. 76 do Regimento Interno do Senado Federal. O autor do requerimento de criação da Comissão - Artur Virgílio -pertencia ao mesmo partido político - PSDB - do Presidente da República investido quando da ocorrência das investigações objeto de aferição.

CPI das ONGs (2006)

O tema de investigação se voltava para a liberação de recursos pelo Governo Federal para organizações não governamentais (ONGs) e organizações da sociedade civil de interesse publico (OSCIP) e a utilização desta verba. O requerimento inicial de criação (RQS 1182/2006) tinha como foco investigativo o período de 2003 a 2006. Porém, uma semana depois de lido em plenário, houve o encaminhamento do reque-

26 SENADO FEDERAL, online.

rimento RQS 1237/2006, aditando a material e prolongando o foco das investigações para o período de 1999 a 2006.

A seguir amostra, de maneira sistematizada, as informações gerais da CPI:

CPI DAS ONGSs (2006)[27]	
Requerimento	RQS 1182/2006
Quantidade de Assinaturas	47
Data do Requerimento	29/11/2006
Data da Instalação	NÃO HOUVE
Data do Arquivamento	12/03/06
Senadores Titulares (Requerimento)	11
Senadores Suplentes (Requerimento)	7
Recursos Financeiros	R$100.000,00
Autor/Partido	Heráclito Fortes/PFL
Prazo Inicial (Dias)	60

No dia seguinte em que houve a protocolização do requerimento de criação, foram emitidos ofícios pela Presidência da Casa aos líderes partidários a fim de prosseguirem as indicações. Em apenas 6 dias, lapso temporal considerado célere, considerando-se o mesmo tempo necessário em outras CPIs, todos os líderes partidários haviam nomeados seus membros, sendo a CPI composta:

COMPOSIÇÃO CPI DAS ONGs (2006)	
Titulares	Suplentes
Efraim Morais (PFL)	Demóstenes Torres (PFL)
Heráclito Fortes (PFL)	Lúcia Vânia (PSDB)
Álvaro Dias (PSDB)	Valdir Raupp (PMDB)
Flexa Ribeiro (PSDB)	Wellington Salgado (PMDB)
Gilvam Borges (PMDB)	Fátima Cleide (PT)
João Alberto Souza(PMDB)	Eduardo Suplicy (PT)
Valter Pereira (PMDB)	

27 SENADO FEDERAL, online.

Sibá Machado (PT)	
Flávio Arns (PT)	
Ideli Salvatti (PT)	
Mozarildo Cavalcanti (PTB)	

Como se sabe, as comissões parlamentares de inquérito se extinguem com o final da Legislatura. O requerimento desta CPI é de 29/11/2006, faltando apenas 23 dias para o fim da 52ª Legislatura, excluído o período do recesso de final de ano. Impossível ser instalada e concluída em 23 dias. O próprio prazo inicial fixado no requerimento de criação foi de 60 dias. Em termos comparativos, importante observar a CPI das ONGs (2007), criada na Legislatura seguinte, com as mesmas características e objetos de investigação que mesmo contando com 781 dias de trabalhos não conseguiu aprovar seu relatório final. A CPI que teve seus trabalhos concluídos em menor lapso temporal – no período em análise – foi a CPI da Petrobras de 2009, que aprovou seu relatório final em 141 dias. Diante do exposto, conclui-se que a CPI das ONGs (2006) foi criada já se sabendo que não prosperaria. O questionamento que fica é: por qual razão e interesse um grupo de 47 parlamentares cria uma CPI que sabem não prosperar?

CPI dos Cartões Corporativos

O que justificou o requerimento de criação desta Comissão Parlamentar de Inquérito foram os escândalos divulgados pela mídia, jornais "Folha de São Paulo" e "O Globo", em que foram divulgados gastos de membros do Governo com cartões de crédito corporativos. Dentre os gastos que constavam do requerimento, estão presentes $1.400,00 com conserto de uma mesa de sinuca do Ministério das Comunicações e gastos que somados atingiam o patamar de R$55.000,00, utilizados por um segurança de Lurian Cordeiro Lula da Silva, filha do então Presidente da República, Luiz Inácio Lula da Silva. Além dos gastos divulgados pelos jornais, o requerimento de criação ainda incluía como foco investigativo a decisão de uma reunião de Ministros (Dilma Rousseff, General Jorge

Felix e Franklin Martins) de restringir a divulgação de gastos de cartões corporativos relacionados à segurança do Presidente e Vice-Presidente da República e suas famílias.

O requerimento, de maneira sistematizada, foi apresentado com as seguintes características:

CPI DOS CARTÕES CORPORATIVOS	
Requerimento	RQS 387/2008
Quantidade de Assinaturas	33
Data do Requerimento	08/04/08
Data da Instalação	NÃO HOUVE
Data do Arquivamento	30/03/2009
Senadores Titulares (Requerimento)	11
Senadores Suplentes (Requerimento)	6
Recursos Financeiros	R$180.000,00
Autor/Partido	Artur Virgílio/PSDB
Prazo Inicial (Dias)	180

Em 09/04/08, um dia após a leitura do requerimento de criação em plenária, foram emitidos os ofícios aos líderes partidários para que prosseguissem às indicações para a composição da CPI. Não houve a resposta a nenhum destes. Tal omissão pode ser explicada pelo surgimento de uma Comissão Parlamentar Mista de Inquérito com o mesmo objeto investigativo no Congresso Nacional. Referida CPMI foi iniciada pelo requerimento RQN 2/2008 do Congresso Nacional, de 21/02/2008, tendo sua instalação ocorrida em 11/03/2008. A instalação da Comissão Parlamentar Mista de Inquérito no Congresso Nacional precede ao próprio requerimento de criação da CPI do Senado Federal. Na data da leitura plenária do requerimento de criação da CPI, a CPMI já realizava sua oitava reunião administrativa.

Não houve qualquer tipo de registros oficiais acerca da CPI dos Cartões Corporativos até 25/03/2009, data esta em que a Presidência do Senado Federal declarou prejudicada a sua instalação, remetendo a matéria ao arquivo. Não é objeto da presente pesquisa as comissões de inquérito criadas no Congresso Nacional, portanto não haverá maiores aprofundamentos quanto à referida CPMI.

O arquivamento do material possui embasamento regimental no o art. 334 do Regimento Interno do Senado Federal dispõe: "O Presidente, de ofício ou mediante consulta de qualquer Senador, declarará prejudicada a matéria dependente de deliberação do Senado: I – por haver perdido a oportunidade;".

Houve um julgamento político quanto à oportunidade e conveniência de prosseguimento.

CPI da Amazônia (2009)

A CPI da Amazônia foi a primeira a ser criada no ano de 2009. Este ano representa um divisor de águas no período analisado 2003 a 2010 – por ser aquele em que houve o maior número de criações no Senado Federal, além da que ora se trata: CPI do DNIT, CPI do INSS, CPI dos Medicamentos e CPI da Petrobras. Das cinco criadas, apenas a da Petrobras foi instalada.

Esta comissão não possui registros oficiais até a data de 22/10/2010, quando houve o arquivamento da matéria pelo fim da Legislatura.

Duas observações. A primeira diz respeito ao objeto a ser investigado. Eram vários objetos de análise. Não parece possível que uma comissão formada de apenas 11 titulares e 6 suplentes conseguiria conduzir investigações voltadas a tantas áreas, tangenciando temáticas como conflitos indígenas, saúde pública, soberania nacional, tráfico de drogas, terrorismo e desmatamento da Floresta Amazônica.

Outro apontamento interessante se refere ao número de assinaturas do requerimento de criação, apresentando o maior número dentre as 14 comissões analisadas. As 55 assinaturas do requerimento representam 67% da Casa Legislativa.

Remanesce uma pergunta a guisa conclusão prévia: existiam urgência e conveniência política para investigar os tópicos elencados no requerimento de criação?

CPI DA AMAZÔNIA[28]	
Requerimento	RQS 572/2009
Quantidade de Assinaturas	33
Data do Requerimento	15/05/2009
Data da Instalação	NÃO HOUVE
Data do Arquivamento	04/02/11
Senadores Titulares (Requerimento)	11
Senadores Suplentes (Requerimento)	6
Recursos Financeiros	R$150.000,00
Autor/Partido	Mozarildo Cavalcanti (PTB)
Prazo Inicial (Dias)	180

Na data de 19/05/2009, um dia após a leitura plenária do requerimento, a Presidência da Casa emitiu ofícios às lideranças partidárias a fim de prosseguirem com as indicações dos membros a comporem a comissão. Até a data de 28/05/2009, nem todas as indicações partidárias foram feitas, portanto a Presidência da casa se encarregou de nomear os Senadores dos partidos faltantes, nos termos da jurisprudência consolidada a partir dos Mandados de Segurança nº 24845, 24847, 24831, 24846, 24849 e 24848, da seguinte maneira:

COMPOSIÇÃO CPI DA AMAZÔNIA	
Titulares	Suplentes
Jayme Campos (DEM)	Adelmir Santana (DEM)
Gilberto Goellner (DEM)	Artur Virgílio (PSDB)
Flexa Ribeiro (PSDB)	Marcelo Crivella (PRB)
Aloízio Mercadante (PT)	Flávio Arns (PT)
João Ribeiro (PR)	Valter Pereira (PMDB)
Renato Casagrande (PSB)	Wellington Salgado (PMDB)
Renan Calheiros (PMDB)	João Vicente Claudino (PTB)
Francisco Dornelles (PP)	
Gilvam Borges (PMDB)	
Mozarildo Cavalcanti (PTB)	
Osmar Dias (PDT)[29]	

28 SENADO FEDERAL, online.

29 SENADO FEDERAL, online.

CPI do DNIT

O requerimento de criação desta CPI se firmava nas denúncias e irregularidades apresentadas pelo Tribunal de Contas da União praticadas pelo Departamento Nacional de Infraestrutura de Transportes (DNIT). Segundo o requerimento, as irregularidades tangenciavam convênios e licitações, quase sempre levando à suspensão física e financeira das obras. A tabela a seguir apresenta as informações gerais presentes no requerimento de criação:

CPI DO DNIT[30]	
Requerimento	RQS 783/2009
Quantidade de Assinaturas	29
Data do Requerimento	24/06/2009
Data da Instalação	NÃO HOUVE
Data do Arquivamento	20/01/2009
Senadores Titulares (Requerimento)	13
Senadores Suplentes (Requerimento)	7
Recursos Financeiros	R$150.000,00
Autor/Partido	Mário Couto (PSDB)
Prazo Inicial (Dias)	180

A Presidência do Senado emitiu ofícios para que as lideranças indicassem os membros a comporem a referida CPI em 04/08/2009. Após, reiterou os pedidos, em 28/09/2009. Houve uma terceira tentativa por parte da Presidência para que os membros fossem indicados, em 25/11/2009. Após esta data não houve mais registros oficiais da Comissão Parlamentar de Inquérito criada, apenas em 20/01/2011, em que a matéria pelo término da legislatura.

Nem a liderança do partido político do autor do requerimento se encarregou das indicações. O presidente da casa, por sua vez, também se omitiu em sua obrigação regimental de suprir a omissão relatada.

30 SENADO FEDERAL, online.

Resta-nos questionar os motivos que levam a intervenção do Presidente da Casa em algumas comissões "encalhadas" - como a da Petrobrás e a CPI dos Bingos - e o que motiva a criação de um requerimento de CPI que, de fato, não se tem interesse em prosseguir com as investigações.

CPI dos Medicamentos

O requerimento de criação da CPI dos Medicamentos se firmava nas notícias, pela mídia nacional, acerca da proliferação de falsificação de medicamentos e equipamentos médicos, fato que levou a ANVISA a intensificar a fiscalização a todos os materiais relacionados à saúde. A máfia que falsificava os itens médicos conseguiu, inclusive, abastecer o Sistema Único de Saúde. O requerimento especificava duas grandes companhias fabricantes de equipamentos médicos do Rio Grande do Sul, a TITANIUM e a EQUIMED. Além destas empresas, foi descoberta a 200 milhas da costa brasileira uma fábrica flutuante de bandeira chinesa, produzindo e abastecendo o mercado interno brasileiro com seringas e agulhas descartáveis. Há, ainda, a denúncia pelo Ministério Público de 154 médicos envolvidos no esquema fraudulento. Segundo o requerimento, a falsificação de medicamentos se transformou em um problema de saúde pública, com status de crime organizado e infiltrado no Estado. A tabela a seguir mostra a estruturação do requerimento de criação da CPI em questão:

CPI DOS MEDICAMENTOS[31]	
Requerimento	1106/2009
Quantidade de Assinaturas	29
Data do Requerimento	04/09/09
Data da Instalação	NÃO HOUVE
Data do Arquivamento	20/01/2009
Senadores Titulares (Requerimento)	11
Senadores Suplentes (Requerimento)	7

31 SENADO FEDERAL, online.

Recursos Financeiros	R$50.000,00
Autor/Partido	Romeu Tuma (PTB)
Prazo Inicial (Dias)	180

Os ofícios para os líderes partidários foram emitidos em 04/09/2009, não havendo nenhuma resposta. Outro ofício reiterando os anteriores foi expedido em 02/12/2009, igualmente sem resposta. O último registro oficial da Comissão Parlamentar de Inquérito dos Medicamentos foi seu arquivamento em virtude do término da 53ª Legislatura Ordinária.

CPI do INSS

O requerimento de criação da Comissão Parlamentar de Inquérito do INSS tinha como objetivo central investigar o déficit do Instituto Nacional do Seguro Social. A intenção do requerimento era esclarecer à população sobre os programas, ações, investimentos, resultados, apurações, cobranças, e procedimentos administrativos e judiciais de competência do Governo Federal quanto ao gerenciamento da previdência social e recuperação da dívida previdenciária. A tabela a seguir mostra, em linhas gerais, as características da comissão parlamentar de inquérito que se visava criar:

CPI DO INSS	
Requerimento	1531/2009
Quantidade de Assinaturas	36
Data do Requerimento	18/11/09
Data da Instalação	NÃO HOUVE
Data do Arquivamento	20/01/2009
Senadores Titulares (Requerimento)	11
Senadores Suplentes (Requerimento)	7
Recursos Financeiros	R$150.000,00
Autor/Partido	Mário Couto (PSDB)
Prazo Inicial (Dias)	180

Seguindo as mesmas características procedimentais de duas CPIs analisadas – CPI dos Medicamentos e CPI do INSS –, logo após sua criação, solicitaram-se indicações às Lideranças partidárias, porém sem resposta. Seguindo os mesmos moldes, a justificativa oficial para o arquivamento da matéria foi o término da legislatura Ordinária.

Conclusão

Ao ocaso de uma investigação exaustiva de todas as comissões parlamentares de inquérito instaladas no período, não se encontrou diferenças marcantes quanto ao seu esquema de funcionamento. Há, evidentemente, diferenças estruturais em virtude da própria matéria objeto da investigação, podendo ser de maior ou menor extensão. A tabela a seguir é síntese de todo o apurado e, por meio dela, podemos traçar os paralelos entre as CPIs e tecer críticas pontuais sobre cada uma:

	COMISSÕES PARLAMENTARES DE INQUÉRITO[21]						
	Transgênicos	Bingos	ONGs	Apagão Aéreo	Petrobras	Pedofilia	Média
erimento Criação	RQS 928/2003	RQS 245/2004	RQS 201/2007	401/2007	RQS 569/2009	RQS 200/2008	–
nero de inaturas	39	38	78	34	32	27	41
ata do erimento	10/09/03	03/05/04	15/3/07	25/04/2007	15/05/09	03/04/08	
ata da talação	11/11/03	29/6/05	03/10/07	17/05/2007	14/07/09	25/03/08	–
ata de rramento	15/12/04	07/04/06	05/04/10	31/10/2007	17/12/09	16/12/10	–
adores lares no erimento	11	15	11	13	11	7	12
adores entes no erimento	7	15	7	10	7	7	9
cursos nceiros n R$)	150.000,00	200.000,00	200.000,00	200.000,00	50.000,00	400.000,00	200.000,00
r/Partido	Jõao Capibaribe/ PSB	Magno Malta/ PL	Heráclito Fortes/ DEM	José Agripino/ DEM	Álvaro Dias/PSDB	Magno Malta/PR	–
o Inicial Dias)	60	120	120	180	180	120	130
nero de rogações	1	2	6	0	0	5	2
ıração Dias)	212	705	781	142	141	873	475
nero de ssões	6	82	34	34	14	76	41
sidente/ rtido	João Capibaribe/ PSB	Efraim Morais/ PFL	Raimundo Colombo e Heráclito Fortes/ DEM	Tião Viana/ PT	João Pedro/ PT	Magno Malta/PR	–
'ice- idente/ rtido	Jonas Pinheiro/PFL	Mozarıldo Cavalcanti /PTB	Lúcia Vânia/ PSDB	Renato Casagrande/ PSB	Marcelo Crivella/ PRB	Romeu Tuma/PTB	–

Relator/ Partido	Leomar Quintanilha/ PMDB	Garibaldi Alves Filho/ PMDB	Inácio Arruda e Arthur Virgílio/ PCdoB e PSDB	Demóstenes Torres/ DEM	Romero Jucá/ PMDB	Demóstenes Torres/DEM	–
Senadores que Exerceram a Titularidade	12	27	21	15	11	8	16
Frequência Média	51%	69%	55%	54%	69%	45%	57%
Senadores que Exerceram a Suplência	8	17	11	11	7	9	10
Frequência Média	14%	29%	24%	36%	39%	29%	28%
Duração Média das Reuniões (Minutos)	74	201	120	222	164	82	143
Lapso Temporal Médio Entre as Reuniões (Dias)	28	9	23	4	8	12	14
Aprovação do Relatório Final	NÃO	SIM	NÃO	SIM	SIM	SIM	–

No período das seis CPIs instaladas, duas não aprovaram um relatório final dos trabalhos (trabalho e esforço parlamentar desperdiçados). Em especial, a CPI das ONGs (2007), que já contava com sua segunda tentativa de conclusão, sendo que a primeira nem ao menos foi instalada – e não se esperava sua instalação, de fato, como analisado no tópico específico. A CPI das ONGs (2007) perdurou por toda a 53ª Legislatura, sendo criada logo em seu início e arquivada apenas em término. O que se apreende do caso foi a falta de planejamento na condução dos trabalhos, razão do fracasso. Não se discute o mérito investigativo. Mas, no início de cada apuração, diante do esforço a ser executado, um plano de trabalho deveria ter sido criado.

Na prática, as comissões parlamentares de inquérito não dispõem de planejamento ou rito. Os trabalhos são conduzidos de maneira desorganizada. O que se verifica, em verdade, é a falta de metodologia, de expertise, de um rito perene e obrigatório e de um amparo técnico na condução das investigações.

Quando do início da pesquisa, levantou-se a hipótese de que a "não conclusão das CPIs" era a desatualização da Lei 1579/1952 e das normas constitucionais sobre o tema. Ou seja, a ausência de poderes determinados – especificação dos "poderes das autoridades judiciais" – e a falta de limites ao seu exercício seria a causa primeira de atrasos e não conclusões. Hipótese que foi infirmada. Não há controvérsia sobre a extensão e limites dos seus poderes, quer na teoria existente, quer nos regimentos internos, quer na jurisprudência do Supremo Tribunal Federal ou mesmo na prática política do Senado e do Congresso Nacional. Há um consenso sobre quais são eles, como se empregam e quando há necessidade e de que forma executá-los pela intervenção de outras autoridades (externas).

Também foi apurado se diferenças regimentais entre o Senado e a Câmara dos Deputados impactariam o seu desenvolvimento. Há, contudo, grande similaridade ou aproximação. Foi hipótese não corroborada. Duas diferenças de nota, entretanto, enquanto o Regimento do Senado Federal é omisso quanto ao número de CPI em exercício concomitante, o da Câmara dos Deputados as limita a cinco. As normas regimentais do Senado não obstaculizam a prorrogação automática de seus trabalhos, sendo suficiente a assinatura de um terço da casa, enquanto as da Câmara dos Deputados fixa um prazo inicial de 120 dias e permite sua prorrogação por outros 60. Ocorre que, acredita-se que a ausência de um termo certo para a conclusão dos trabalhos faça-o ser percebido como acessório, secundário e sem importância para senadores. Como demonstração, a CPI das ONGs (2007), que não aprovou seu relatório final, mesmo sendo a mais extensa CPI do período analisado. A da Pedofilia, de maior duração durante o período (873 dias), quase não teve seus trabalhos encerrados. Em resumo, foram desperdiçados 873 dias, com 76 reuniões de aproximadamente 82 minutos cada. Não só esforço e trabalho parlamentar despendido, mas receita da ordem de R$400.000,00 para o funcionamento.

Alguns fatos, todavia, foram demonstrados. O primeiro é a descoberta do baixo número de reuniões e decurso de tempo exagerado entre cada uma. Ambas as CPIs que não tiveram relatório final aprovado – CPI dos Transgênicos, 14 reuniões; CPI das ONGs (2007), 34 reuniões – tiveram número de reuniões inferiores à média de 41 do período estudado. É variável, por outro lado, que não pode ser considerada de maneira isolada. Outras CPIs no período tiveram número de reuniões abaixo da média, como exemplo CPI do Apagão Aéreo, com 34 reuniões, e a CPI da Petrobrás, com 14 reuniões. Analisada isoladamente, não é determinante no sucesso ou insucesso da apuração, o que justifica o cotejo com outras, em especial, a demora entre uma reunião e outra. O exagerado decurso de tempo entre as reuniões está presente nas CPIs não concluídas. São elas: a CPI dos Transgênicos apresentou 28 dias e a CPI das ONGs (2007) 23 dias, enquanto a média foi de 14 dias. As variáveis lidas em consonância explicitam um claro desinteresse em se levar à frente as investigações das CPIs. Um planejamento prévio, com reuniões marcadas com antecedência e dentro de um lapso temporal certo, talvez as levassem à conclusão.

Instaladas, houve um baixo comparecimento de senadores. A média para os senadores titulares foi de 57%, enquanto os suplentes ostentaram uma de 28%. São números muito baixos em todas estas comissões. Com exceção do Presidente e do relator, com alto comparecimento, a presença foi muito baixa que com muito esforço se atingiu o quórum mínimo de funcionamento.

Na 52ª legislatura as maiores bancadas pertenciam respectivamente: a) PMDB (40 senadores); b) PFL (20 senadores); c) PSDB (19 senadores); d) PT (quinze senadores). Na 53ª legislatura, por sua vez, as maiores bancadas pertenciam: a) PMDB (31 senadores); b) PSDB (21 senadores); c) DEM (19 senadores); d) PT (16 senadores). O baixo comparecimento não foi exclusivo da base parlamentar de apoio do governo. Tendo como pontos de observação a CPI dos Transgênicos e a CPI das ONGs (2007), as menores taxas de presença dos senadores nas reuniões foram de membros do PMDB, PFL e PSDB, para a primeira CPI, e o PMDB e o PDT, na segunda. Se considerado que na legislatura de nº 52 o PMDB podia ser considerado como bloco independente ou não pertencente a coalização governamental, ou parcela dele, a partir do escândalo do Mensalão este partido, com o maior número de representantes, vai cada vez mais integrar a base de apoio governista. E, mesmo com esta ressalva, não pode ser dito que os maiores números de ausência sejam da base de apoio governista.

Quanto aos partidos dos membros-chave (presidente e relator) verificou-se um equilíbrio entre os partidos de apoio e os partidos oposicionistas. O PSB (membro do bloco de apoio ao governo) presidiu uma CPI, o PFL (membro do bloco da minoria, atual DEM) presidiu duas CPIs, o PR (membro do bloco de apoio ao Governo) presidiu uma CPI e o PT (partido governista) presidiu 2 CPIs. Quanto à relatoria, o PMDB relatou três CPIs, o DEM duas e o PSDB uma. Ou seja, a atuação dos partidos ligados ao governo não é tese que pode ser sustentada como insucesso das CPIs não concluídas, umas vez que nas duas CPIs em que não houve aprovação do relatório final, a CPI dos Transgênicos foi presidida por partido do Bloco de Apoio ao Governo e relatada pelo PMDB (membro isolado de blocos partidários), enquanto a CPI das ONGs (2007) foi presidida pelo DEM (partido do Bloco da Minoria) e relatada pelo PSDB (partido do Bloco da Minoria).

Das CPI criadas e instaladas, seis ao total, quatro investigaram assuntos de relevância nacional, às vezes crimes, mas sem indícios de participação direta de órgãos elevados da administração federal (CPI dos Transgênicos-2003, CPI dos Bingos - 2004, CPI do Apagão Aéreo - 2008, CPI da Pedofilia - 2008); duas, ao menos, versavam sobre malversação de recursos públicos ou corrupção propriamente dita (CPI das ONGs - 2007, CPI da Petrobras – 2009).

Existiram, contudo, CPIs que foram criadas, mas não instaladas. estas oito CPIs criadas e não instaladas foram propostas por senadores dos partidos fora do Bloco de Apoio ao Governo: PSDB, PFL e PTB. Nestas oito, o número acima se inverte, cinco delas tocam diretamente assunto de malversação de recursos ou corrupção entre membros da alta administração federal (CPI do Caso Waldomiro Diniz- 2005, CPI das Privatizações-2005, CPI das ONGs-2006, CPI dos Cartões Corporativos-2008, CPI do DNIT-2009), enquanto somente três abordam grandes temáticas de interesse nacional (CPI da Amazônia-2009, CPI dos Medicamentos -2009 e CPI do INSS-2009).

O que se extrai do quadro é que, mesmo em se tratando da Câmara alta do Congresso Nacional, a criação de comissões não tem o propósito de conduzir e concluir as investigações e obter resultados. Muitas receberam grande apoio dos senadores no momento da assinatura do requerimento, para cair no esquecimento no correr de seus trabalhos. Temas polêmicos e de grande repercussão na mídia prestam-se, em muitos casos, só como mecanismo de autopromoção dos seus autores perante a opinião pública.

Este levantamento empírico corrobora tese de que muitas das CPIs criadas não têm real objetivo de serem concluídas (FIGUEIREDO, 2001, p 695). Funcionam como "moeda de troca" para "ganhos" ou "achaques" políticos. Mesmo em sendo Câmara legislativa com ascendência constitucional pertinente às atribuições de controlar (fiscalizar), as CPIs não tem o objetivo fático de investigarem. O que, sem dúvida, coloca em xeque a respeitabilidade do instituto e, em especial, da casa legislativa em que as apurações se desenrolam.

Parece que uma medida legislativa, de aprovação de pouco custo, poderia melhor este quadro. Refere-se à vinculação do senador ou senadores proponentes à CPI criada. No momento em que o requerimento for apresentado por determinado senador, cabe-lhe a responsabilidade de prestar constas sobre o seu andamento e resultado por meio de relatórios, mesmo nas situações de não instalação, de arquivamento por término da legislatura e não aprovação do relatório final. Poderia ser inclusive, responsabilidade a ser compartilhada com outros integrantes da Comissão (presidente ou relator). Daria transparência e evitar-se-ia a personalização de sua propositura (criação e divulgação da proposta como forma de exposição do proponente para fins de ganhos políticos junto ao eleitor).

Em uma visão geral, a disfuncionalidade das Comissões Parlamentares de Inquérito é uma verdade mesmo no Senado Federal. Suas causas estão atreladas a variáveis mais complexas do que aquelas que a teoria jurídica em sua maioria insiste em diagnosticar: fragilidade dos poderes de investigação. O presente trabalho procurou trazer um diagnóstico empírico de ordem institucional: deficiência na metodologia dos trabalhos, ausência de um rito estrito, perene e homogêneo de investigação e falta de ferramentas eficazes de transparência e *accountability*. Insinua-se, talvez, a presença de variáveis sociol ógicas importantes para a anomalia funcional. É pesquisa, contudo, a ser desenvolvida em outra oportunidade.

Referências bibliográficas

ABRÚCIO, Fernando L.; PÓ, Marcos V. *A accountability da burocracia: revisão bibliográfica e algumas lições para o caso brasileiro*. In: ENCONTRO DE ADMINISTRAÇÃO PÚBLICA E GOVERNANÇA, 2004, Rio de Janeiro. *Anais*. Rio de Janeiro: ANPAD, 2004. Ref. APG 236.

ALECRIM, Otacílio. *As Comissões Congressuais de Investigação no Regime Presidencialista*. Revista Forense, Rio de Janeiro, vol. 151, n. 607 e 608, p. 45, 1954.

ARATO, Andrew. *Representação, soberania popular e accountability*. Lua Nova, São Paulo, n. 55-56, p. 85-103, 2002. Disponível em: <http://dx.doi.org/10.1590/S0102-64452002000100004>. Acesso em: 4 jul. 2013.

BARACHO, José Alfredo de Oliveira. *Teoria geral das comissões parlamentares: comissões parlamentares de inquérito*. Rio de Janeiro: Forense, 2001.

BARROSO, Luís Roberto. *Comissões Parlamentares de Inquérito e suas competências: política, direito e devido processo legal*. Revista Forense, Rio de Janeiro, v. 350, p. 87- 104, 2000.

______. *Judicialização, ativismo judicial e legitimidade democrática*. (Syn) Thesis, Rio de Janeiro, v. 5, p. 23-32, 2012.

BEHN, Robert D. *O novo paradigma da gestão pública e a busca da accountability democrática*. Revista do Serviço Público, Brasília, DF, ano 49, n. 4, p. 5-44, out./dez. 1998.

BOBBIO, Norberto. *O futuro da democracia*: uma defesa das regras do jogo. São Paulo: Paz e Terra, 1986.

BONAVIDES, Paulo; ANDRADE, Paes de. *História constitucional do Brasil*. 3ª ed. Rio de Janeiro: Paz e Terra, 1991.

BUENO, José Antônio Pimenta. *Direito Público Brasileiro e Análise da Constituição do Império*. Brasília: Senado Federal, 1978.

BUENO, José Antônio Pimenta. *Direto Público Brasileiro e análise da Constituição do Império*. Rio de Janeiro: Ministério da Justiça e Negócios Interiores, 1958.

BULOS, Uadi L. *Comissões parlamentares de inquérito:* técnica e prática. São Paulo: Saraiva, 2001.

CAMARGO, Heloísa Helena T.; KAIN, Maria de Lourdes M. *O Senado como controlador externo.* Revista de Informação Legislativa, Brasília, DF, ano 32, n. 125, p. 207-234, jan./mar. 1995.

CANOTILHO, J. J. Gomes. *Direito Constitucional e Teoria da Constituição*. 3ª ed. Coimbra: Almedina, 1998.

CARAJELESCOV, Yuri. *Comissões Parlamentares de Inquérito à luz da disciplina constitucional, legal e jurisprudencial luso-portuguesa e brasileira.* Curitiba: Juruá, 2007.

CAMPOS, Anna M. *Accountability: quando poderemos traduzi-lo para o português?* Revista de Administração Pública, Rio de Janeiro, v. 24, n. 2, p. 47-56, 1990.

CLAMMER, John. *Corruption, Development, Chaos and Social Disorganisation: sociological reflections on corruption and its social basis.* In BARCHAM, Manuhuia, HINDESS, Barry et LAMOUR, Peter. *Corruption: expanding the focus.* Camberra: The Australian National University, 2012 [e-book]. pp 113-132.

COMPARATO, Fábio Konder. *Comissão Parlamentar de Inquérito: limites.* Revista Trimestral de Direito Público, São Paulo, n. 5, 66-74, 1994.

DIMOCK, M. E. *Congressional Investigating Committes.* Studies in Historical and Political Science, series 47, nº1. Baltimore: John Hopkins University, 1929.

DUARTE NETO, José. *Rigidez e Estabilidade Constitucional.* Belo Horizonte: Editora Del Rey, 2010.

FERNANDES, André Eduardo da S.; BANDEIRA, Luiz Fernando. *Aspectos jurídicos da escolha e substituição do presidente e do relator em comissões parlamentares de inquérito*. Brasília, DF: Senado Federal, 2005. (Texto para discussão, n. 23).

FERREIRA, Jorge. *Regime Jurídico dos Inquéritos Parlamentares*. Coimbra: Almedina, 1999.

FERREIRA FILHO, Manoel Gonçalves. *Comentários à Constituição Brasileira*. 3ª ed. São Paulo: Saraiva, 1983.

FIGUEIREDO, Argelina Cheibub. *Instituições e política no controle do executivo*. Dados: Revista Brasileira de Ciências Sociais, Rio de Janeiro, v. 44, n.4, p. 689-727, 2001.

______. *Institutional power and the role of Congress as a mechanism of horizontal accountability: lessons from the Brazilian experience*. In: MAINWARINE, Scott; WELMA, Christopher. (Ed.). *Democratic Accountability in Latin America*. Oxford: Ed. Oxford University, 2003.

HESPANHA, António Manuel. *Cultura Jurídica Europeia: síntese de um milénio*. 3ª ed. Portugal: Publicações Europa-América, 2003.

KLEIN, Odacir. *Comissões Parlamentares de Inquérito: a sociedade e o cidadão*. Porto Alegre: Sérgio Antônio Fabris Editor, 1999.

LIMA, Nelia Pamplona C. *O controle externo pelo Poder Legislativo: a eficácia dos instrumentos legais do Congresso Nacional – Análise do período 1984-1993*. Dissertação (Mestrado em Administração) - Universidade de Brasília, Brasília, DF, 1997.

MADISON, James; HAMILTON, Alexander; JAY, John. *O federalismo*. Brasília, DF: Ed. UnB, 1984.

MARTINELLI, Mário Eduardo. *Comissão Parlamentar de Inquérito*. Tese (Mestrado em Direito) – Faculdade de Direito, Universidade São Paulo, São Paulo, SP, 2003.

MENDES, Yolanda. *O Inquérito Parlamentar*. Brasília: Câmara dos Deputados, 1964.

MIRANDA, Jorge. *Manual de Direito Constitucional*. 7. Ed. Coimbra: Coimbra, 2003.

MORLINNO, Leonardo. In BOBBIO, Norberto; MATTEUCCI, Nicola et PASQUINO, Gianfranco. *Dicionário de Política.* 4ª ed. Brasília/DF: Editora Universidade de Brasília, 1992. verbete estabilidade política. p 394-401.

OLIVEIRA, Erival da S. *Comissões parlamentares de inquérito.* São Paulo: Ícone, 1999.

OLIVEIRA, Mauro Maurício. *Comissões Parlamentares de Inquérito no Senado Federal: sua história e desempenho no período de 1946 a 1989.* Brasília: Senado Federal: Centro Gráfico, 1991.

PIÇARRA, Nuno. *O Inquérito Parlamentar e os seus Modelos Constitucionais*: o caso português. Coimbra: Almedina, 2004.

PONTES DE MIRANDA, Francisco Cavalcante. *Comentários à Constituição dos Estados Unidos do Brasil de 1934.* Rio de Janeiro: Guanabara, t. 2, 1937.

RIANI, Frederico Augusto D'Avila. *Comissão Parlamentar de Inquérito: requisitos para criação, objeto e poderes.* Revista de Direito Constitucional e Internacional, São Paulo, v. 36, p. 185-204, 2001.

SANDOVAL, Ovídio Rocha Barros. *CPI ao pé da letra.* São Paulo: Millennium, 2001.

SAMPAIO, Nelson de Souza. *Do Inquérito Parlamentar.* Rio de Janeiro: Fundação Getúlio Vargas, 1964.

SCHIER, Paulo Ricardo. *A comissão parlamentar de inquérito e o âmbito de limitação competencial de sua atuação.* Revista da Academia Brasileira de Direito Constitucional, Curitiba, v. 2, p. 105-116, 2002.

SCHILLING, Flávia. *Corrupção: ilegalidade intolerável? Comissões Parlamentares de inquérito e a luta contra a corrupção no Brasil (1980-1992).* 1997. Tese (Doutorado em Sociologia) – Faculdade de Sociologia, Letras e Ciências Humanas, Universidade de São Paulo, São Paulo, 1997.

SPROESSER, Andyra Klopstock. *A Comissão Parlamentar de Inquérito - CPI no ordenamento jurídico brasileiro.* São Paulo: Assembleia Legislativa do Estado, 2008.

SOUZA, Alexandre Barreto de. *Comissões parlamentares de inquérito como instrumento de* accountability *horizontal: a*nálise do período 1989-2005. 2006. Tese (Mestrado em Administração Pública) – Faculdade de Economia,Administração, Contabilidade e Ciência da Documentação e Informação, Universidade de Brasília, Brasília, DF, 2006.

ZAULI, Eduardo Meira. *Judicialização da Política, Poder Judiciário e Comissões Parlamentares de Inquérito no Brasil.* Revista de Sociologia e Política, Curitiba, v. 19, p. 195-209, 2011.

SAMPAIO, Nelson de Souza. *Do Inquérito Parlamentar.* Rio de Janeiro: Fundação Getúlio Vargas, 1964.

Fundamentos da cidadania para professores e alunos fundamentais: a integração da Pós-graduação com a Graduação, na Política Nacional de Extensão Universitária

Paulo César Corrêa Borges
e Paulo César de Oliveira Borges

Introdução

Em decorrência do conceito contemporâneo de "sala de aula", como todo espaço que propicie uma relação horizontal entre aluno, professor e comunidade, dentro e fora da universidade, a incorporação de professores e estudantes de pós-graduação em ações extensionistas, juntamente com os graduandos, pode e deve ser integrada aos programas de pós-graduação na área do Direito, qualificando tanto aquelas ações extensionistas, como esta forma de produção de conhecimento.

Nesta linha, o Documento de Área do Direito da Diretoria de Avaliação da Coordenação de Aperfeiçoamento de Pessoal de Nível Superior (CAPES, 2013), inclui na avaliação da inserção social dos programas de pós-graduação a realização de atividades de extensão, observando o disposto no artigo 207 da Constituição Federal.

A execução do projeto de extensão universitária, "Fundamentos da cidadania para professores e alunos fundamentais: construindo cidadania e reconhecimento.", em duas escolas do ensino fundamental de Franca/SP (E.E. "Evaristo Fabrício" e E.E. "Dante Guedini"), em 2016, objetivando difundir a concepção pré-violatória de DDHH e fortalecer a formação em direitos humanos, por meio dos aportes teóricos da Teoria Crítica de Direitos Humanos, tendo por referencial teórico autores como Joaquim Herrera Flores, David Sanchez Rubio, Helio Gallardo, Antonio Carlos Wolkmer, Salo de Carvalho, dentre outros, tem proporcionado a integração de alunos da graduação com alunos de pós-graduação da UNESP.

A sensibilização sociocultural, como preconiza a Teoria Crítica de DDHH, está associada à difusão de uma cultura pré-violatória, que vem sendo desenvolvida através do projeto de extensão, em diversas escolas, desde 2010, por meio de oficinas quinzenais, com alunos, alunas, professores e professoras, sobre temas de direitos humanos, para visibilização das diversas formas de intolerância e violações existentes na sociedade e, particularmente, na escola.

Abordam-se temas como racismo, homofobia, gênero, violência doméstica, violência de gênero e violência escolar (bullying), liberdade religiosa, entre outros, ressaltando-se, assim, uma dimensão dialógica da educação e a transversalidade temática nos parâmetros curriculares nacionais, a partir de pesquisas, que estão em andamento, utilizando-se referencial teórico-metodológico dialético, e também está sendo feita uma revisão bibliográfica e legislativa do estado da arte.

Para tanto, a preparação das oficinas, a serem realizadas nas escolas, ocorre por meio de pesquisa bibliográfica e da realização prévia de oficinas na própria universidade com pesquisadores, professores e alunos da pós-graduação e da graduação, que também coordenam as oficinas com os professores e as professoras das escolas, enquanto os alunos da graduação executam as oficinas com os alunos e as alunas do 6º. ano do ensino fundamental.

Neste trabalho, é analisada a integração da graduação e da pós-graduação na execução do referido projeto de extensão universitária, como importante resultado decorrente da implementação da Política Nacional de Extensão Universitária, e para ampliação da sala de aula, para além dos muros da universidade, como espaço privilegiado de ensino e de pesquisa, indissociáveis da extensão. Muito embora seja necessário o protagonismo dos participantes externos, normalmente referidos como beneficiários da extensão, como resultado do projeto de extensão em desenvolvimento, conclui-se que, para os graduandos e pós-graduandos, essas experiências não são apenas para formá-los como "juristas" e pesquisadores, mas, também, cidadãos críticos, mais participativos e comprometidos com as relações horizontais, com um conhecimento que considera as necessidades das pessoas em sociedade, principalmente os mais vulneráveis às violações de direitos fundamentais, efetivamente construindo cidadania e reconhecimento a todos e a todas.

A verificação do grau de interação entre a graduação e a pós-graduação em Direito, tem relevância para a implantação da Política Nacional de Extensão Universitária, porquanto tem por objetivo o estímulo de atividades de extensão que propiciem uma relação interprofissional de setores da Universidade e da sociedade e, por outro lado, estabelece uma perspectiva que reafirma a extensão como um processo acadêmico construído dialeticamente e executado em consonância com a realidade, em decorrência da indissociabilidade de ensino-pesquisa-extensão, que proporciona a formação dos discentes (ensino) e a geração de conhecimento (pesquisa).

Como conclusão, tem-se que a vinculação de estudantes de graduação e de pós-graduação a grupos de extensão universitária lhes proporciona uma visão mais crítica e ampla da sociedade, uma vez que é um dos principais objetivos das extensões a produção acadêmica e a devolução dos seus frutos à sociedade, em uma relação horizontal e de protagonismo mútuo, considerando extensionistas e membros da sociedade como beneficiários.

Material e metodologia: a extensão universitária como ampliação da sala de aula

Conquanto Direitos Humanos e cidadania sejam temas discutidos desde a antiguidade, até os tempos atuais não se logrou obter uma definição concreta de cada termo, que pudesse ser alcançado apenas com a revisão bibliográfica. Entretanto, com a vinculação de graduandos e pós-graduandos em grupos de extensão das universidades, sejam públicos ou não, o aluno passa a ter uma visão mais crítica e ampla da sociedade, o que é um dos principais objetivos das extensões, além de proporcionar a produção acadêmica e a devolução dos frutos à sociedade, através das oficinas realizadas sob a perspectiva da cultura pré-violatória dos direitos humanos, em consonância com a sensibilização sócio-cultural, como etapa da construção dos DDHH.

A extensão universitária, hoje, não pode mais ser vista apenas como parte extracurricular, para o preenchimento de horas exigidas para completar a grade do curso de graduação. Sua função é também permitir o retorno dos investimentos públicos e privados à sociedade, de forma a garantir um acesso ao conhecimento a todos os envolvidos, graduandos, pós-graduandos, e o setor da sociedade vinculado ao projeto. Portanto, é insuficiente que os projetos universitários não consigam um alcance global dos alunos da graduação e da pós-graduação, ainda mais diante do princípio da indissociabilidade de ensino, pesquisa e extensão, que atingem ambos os segmentos universitários.

Através do Núcleo de Estudos da Tutela Penal e Educação em Direitos Humanos (NETPDH), vinculado ao Programa de Pós-graduação em Direito da UNESP, os graduandos participam de oficinas em escolas estaduais com o intuito de contribuir, ao máximo, para suprir as necessidades dos alunos do 6º. ano do ensino fundamental de duas escolas estaduais, no âmbito da formação em direitos humanos, sob uma perspectiva crítica e pré-violatória, ao passo que muitas vezes se surpreendem com as noções que os alunos já possuem e apresentam, favorecendo uma nova visão que demanda um enfoque que enfatize a horizontalidade nas relações sociais.

A partir das oficinas nas escolas, os extensionistas passam a ter mais um espaço de aula e aprendizado, fora da própria universidade, gerando assim, e ao mesmo tempo, um ambiente de empatia, se não de amizades, e de interação entre alunos, alunas, professores, professoras, tanto da universidade como da escola, principalmente pelos métodos lúdicos utilizados, beneficiado pela quebra da rotina formal na escola, para apresentação de algo "diferente" das disciplinas formais, o que torna o aprendizado mais agradável, acessível e fácil em relação aos DDHH. No mesmo ambiente, surgem observações e manifestações de estudantes da escola, sobre situações desagradáveis, vinculadas a experiências vividas que, muitas vezes, não podem ser solucionadas diretamente pelos extensionistas, mas que contam com a coordenação docente do projeto de extensão, com a direção da escola, com os profissionais da mediação da escola, ou mesmo com outras autoridades que possam agir em prol desses estudantes.

Os benefícios que podem propiciar essa interação entre universitários da graduação e da pós-graduação, professores da pós-graduação, e alunos e professores da escola fundamental são inigualáveis, por outras estratégias que prescindam da extensão universitária.

O espaço concreto para as atividades extensionistas traz benefícios na construção do conhecimento, que não fica adstrito ao ensino e à pesquisa formais, da graduação e da pós-graduação, nem à transversalidade dos parâmetros curriculares quanto à relação entre direitos humanos e as disciplinas da escola fundamental.

Estudantes, professores e professoras do ensino fundamental, que participam do projeto, crescem eticamente, reciclam conhecimentos e, muitas vezes, mudam opiniões, ou até mesmo pré-conceitos, que tinham ao iniciarem as atividades extensionistas e que viam como certas, ou como indiferentes. E para os graduandos e pós-graduandos, essas experiências não são para formá-los apenas como "juristas", mas, muito mais que isso, cidadãos participativos e comprometidos com a concepção pré-violatória dos DDHH, para a concretização dos direitos fundamentais e pleno exercício da cidadania, com reconhecimento social de todos os beneficiários, através das atividades preparatórias e concretas, no âmbito da realidade escolar e universitária.

Neste sentido, o art. 207 da Constituição Federal, fixa uma concepção integral da autonomia universitária, com aspectos relevantes que alcançam a autonomia didático-científica (Nascimento, 2008) e, ao mesmo tempo, dentro dos "freios e contrapesos", impede que a universidade quebre o princípio da indissociabilidade (Pinto Ferreira, 2004, pág. 207), o que significa que o ensino, a pesquisa e a extensão devem ser complementares, sem que um prepondere em detrimento do outro, nem devem ficar reclusos a um só meio ou forma (Nascimento, 2008), e deve trazer impactos benéficos à sociedade. Além disso, há estudos que destacam o papel da extensão universitária como ampliação do conceito da sala de aula (Luz; Peres, 1998, pág. 180), ressaltando aquela indissociabilidade:

> Reforça, com isso, a necessária ampliação da sala de aula para os espaços comunitários, na qual o acadêmico em formação pode experienciar saberes teóricos e metodológicos enriquecedores para sua adequada formação, pela reflexão compartilhada com outros acadêmicos e profissionais de distintas áreas do conhecimento.

A compreensão de que o caráter democratizante da extensão, produzindo conhecimento e socializando-o, implica em que "...esta não apenas se articula à pesquisa e ao ensino, mas ela é pesquisa e ensino. Trata-se de pesquisa e ensino com caráter extensionista, expressão aqui cunhada para se contrapor ao ativismo que, muitas vezes, é entendido como extensão" (Michelotto, 1999, pág. 127-128).

A integração da graduação e da pós-graduação, na política nacional de extensão universitária

Tem sido baixa a produção científica a respeito da participação da pós-graduação brasileira na execução de projetos de extensão universitária, embora sejam encontrados documentos fazendo referências sobre a integração da graduação universitária com a pós-graduação, bem como a inserção desta em projetos extensionistas voltados para o ensino fundamental e médio, ou para a graduação.

Na pós-graduação, inegavelmente, destacam-se o ensino e a pesquisa, mas a extensão universitária fica relegada aos cursos de graduação, na grande maioria das áreas do conhecimento, mas, particularmente para este estudo, na Área do Direito, tornando mais relevante a integração da pós-graduação com a graduação, para essa dimensão importantíssima na formação do discente e pesquisador, em nível de pós-graduação, tanto acadêmico como profissional.

No Documento de Área do Direito (2013), da CAPES, consta expressamente que, entre os critérios de avaliação dos Programas de Pós-graduação, a "Inserção e impacto regional e (ou) nacional" verificará: *(3) realização de atividades de extensão, voltadas à concretização de interesses públicos ou sociais.* Nas "Considerações gerais sobre a Avaliação Trienal de 2013", esclarece o Documento de Área do Direito (CAPES, 2013) que a avaliação examinará a qualidade da formação nos programas de pós--graduação stricto sensu, a partir de três eixos, isto é, ensino, pesquisa e extensão, incorporando aquela indissociabilidade já mencionada, mas enfatizando, entretanto, que por extensão deve-se entender aquela:

> c) (...) representada, sobretudo, por intercâmbios interinstitucionais de docência e pesquisa, a solidariedade interinstitucional, além da tradução da produção acadêmica em resultados concretos de solução de problemas jurídicos e sociais.

Este conceito evidencia uma concepção de que a extensão universitária, para a Pós-graduação em Direito, refere-se aos intercâmbios e às formas de solidariedade interinstitucional, envolvendo a docência --- sem qualquer referência a discentes, ainda que aquela pressuponha esta; a pesquisa, à qual docentes e orientandos se vinculam necessariamente através de projetos de pesquisa; e à produção acadêmica. Neste sentido, ainda que não fosse o objetivo declarado, excluiu-se a dimensão da extensão no âmbito da educação cidadã dos pós-graduandos, através da inserção na comunidade em que o programa de pós-graduação tenha a sua nucleação, notadamente em atuação conjunta com a graduação.

Isto reflete a concepção de que a extensão universitária está umbilicalmente vinculada aos cursos de graduação, mantendo-se as raízes da pós-graduação voltadas precipuamente para a pesquisa, enquanto a dimensão do ensino limita-se à formação para a pesquisa e, ocasionalmente, tal pesquisa pode utilizar como objeto investigativo "aspectos relevantes da extensão universitária", gerando produção acadêmica. A ampliação da sala de aula da pós-graduação para a relação docente-discentes-sociedade, durante a formação do pós-graduando, depende de "intercâmbios interinstitucionais de docência e pesquisa", muitas vezes representados pela realização de atividades acadêmicas e de extensão entre os próprios programas de pós-graduação.

A extensão universitária, no âmbito da Política Nacional de Extensão Universitária, é mais ampla, e acreditar que poderá haver produção acadêmica sem a imersão do pós-graduando em projetos de extensão, junto com alunos de graduação, ainda que fora dos intercâmbios interinstitucionais de docência e pesquisa – que também devem ser implementados, seria o mesmo que anular esta mesma característica da pós-graduação, ou seja, a produção acadêmica referente à extensão universitária, na Área do Direito.

Neste sentido, veja-se a observação de Patrícia Elaine Pereira dos Santos (2011), que é da Área de Educação:

> No documento a Política de Extensão Universitária destaca-se essa discussão da formação e publicação acadêmica de forma associada, permeando posições em que seja inserida a pós-graduação nas ações extensionistas. Embora enfatize a participação dos estudantes, a lógica do conhecimento a ser incorporada nos programas de pós-graduação, enfatizando a qualificação tanto da extensão quanto dos mestrados, doutorados e especializações. Outra vertente complementar identificada são as produções a partir de atividades e ações da extensão. (...) Vale destacar que o debate sobre o conhecimento acadêmico é de suma importância para o entendimento do que se propõe a universidade no que se refere ao trabalho de extensão. Todavia, no discurso sobre formação e produção acadêmica não é suficiente

> que seja elevado apenas a participação dos estudantes, mesmo ao incluir a pós-graduação. A busca do processo democrático ocorre em diferentes instâncias e sujeitos, desconstruindo uma perspectiva de hierarquia e poder centralizado.

Nos resumos apresentados por José Augusto Drumond, na seção "Estado da Arte", em relação à tese de doutoramento de Paulo Ernesto Diaz Rocha, defendida em fins de 2001, na Universidade Federal Rural do Rio de Janeiro, discutindo a construção da interdisciplinaridade ambiental, em quatro programas brasileiros de pós-graduação da Área Interdisciplinar, foram ressaltados aspectos importantíssimos para a extensão universitária:

> A função de extensão universitária, junto com as atividades de ensino e pesquisa, tem papel fundamental na busca de participação e democratização do conhecimento, a partir e através de pesquisas interdisciplinares. Embora não tenha sido consensualmente colocada pelos entrevistados, e não tenha sido abordada no questionário, a extensão universitária é apontada como saída para o isolamento de programas de pós-graduação no meio acadêmico. Segundo os depoimentos, a extensão acontece porque orientadores e alunos têm desenvolvido esse trabalho. (...) a função da extensão universitária e do retorno de resultados de pesquisa à sociedade, além de ser feita na forma de ensino e pesquisa (ação), é cumprida também através de ações pontuais, em que ocorre a contribuição para resolução de problemas específicos na comunidade. As iniciativas interdisciplinares na pós-graduação brasileira se mostram um promissor campo de ação junto a associações organizadas da sociedade civil – tanto no setor empresarial quanto no chamado terceiro setor.

O Documento de Área do Direito (2013), reconheceu expressamente a abertura para a interdisciplinariedade e afirmou a integração entre a pós-graduação e a graduação, ao mencionar os deslocamentos para as escolas dos níveis fundamentais e médio, atuando junto às escolas. Neste sentido, os intercâmbios interinstitucionais se ampliaram para outros espaços da sociedade, não se limitando a atividades entre programas de pós-graduação.

A orientação agora é bastante clara, no sentido de que o envolvimento com a graduação destina-se à formação continuada e à riqueza da parceria no âmbito do ensino fundamental e médio, com novas parcerias, em atuação direta no âmbito da extensão universitária, espaço privilegiado que está além dos limites tradicionais da sala de aula e da própria universidade. Esta se abre para a relação ensino, pesquisa e extensão universitária, e é representada no âmbito da pós-graduação nos intercâmbio interinstitucionais e na produção acadêmica, mas também pela inserção na comunidade, embora ainda refira-se à escola fundamental e média, exemplificativamente, porquanto diagnosticou-se este espaço de inserção dos programas de pós-graduação, no Sistema Nacional de Pós-graduação:

> O contato permanente entre graduação e pós-graduação sob a ótica da formação continuada despertou a atenção dos docentes e discentes da pós-graduação para esta enriquecedora possibilidade de observação científica. Para além da atuação como descrita, agora os níveis de graduação e pós-graduação deslocaram-se para as escolas dos níveis fundamentais e médio, na forma de assistência à escola pública e de implantação de disciplinas ou de conteúdos disciplinares pertinentes aos direitos fundamentais e à nova realidade constitucional e democrática brasileira.

No documento de Área do Direito de 2016, foi destacado um item específico em que se explicitou a necessária inserção da Área do Direito no ensino fundamental e médio (CAPES, 2016, pág. 6-7), para a formação cidadã através da participação em projetos de extensão, afirmando que:

> Sobre a formação para a cidadania, é evidente que na formação escolar há um déficit de informações sobre direitos e sobre o fun-

> cionamento das instituições. Os cursos de Direito precisam de uma maior aproximação com as escolas, levando informações e provocando discussões, municiando o cidadão em formação para o exercício consciente da cidadania. A extensão é o instrumento mais eficiente para isso. A participação de docentes de programas de pós-graduação em projetos de extensão com essa finalidade pode indicar um maior impacto social desses programas.

O Fórum de Pró-Reitores de Extensão das Universidades Públicas Brasileiras (2012, pág. 19), analisando a relação entre extensão e pesquisa, destacou que a Política Nacional de Extensão Universitária enfatizou o pleno desenvolvimento de dois processos na vida acadêmica: a) incorporação de estudantes de pós-graduação em ações extensionistas; e, b) a produção acadêmica a partir das atividades de extensão, no formato de teses, dissertações, livros ou capítulos de livros, artigos em periódicos e cartilhas, eventos etc..

O projeto de extensão "Fundamentos da cidadania para professores e alunos fundamentais" tem propiciado aos alunos da pós-graduação em direito a oportunidade de desenvolvimento de atividades do estágio docência, que integra sua formação, além de interagir com os alunos da graduação que participam do projeto, orientando as pesquisas que são realizadas e a produção bibliográfica correlata, com produtos como pôsteres e artigos científicos. A preparação dos graduandos começa, também, na extensão universitária, já que são despertados para a iniciação científica e já começam a se deparar com os parâmetros normativos da pesquisa de qualidade e com as regras da produção científica.

Por outro lado, em paralelismo na execução metodológica das oficinas, na escola do ensino fundamental, os alunos da graduação e da pós-graduação se deparam com demandas teóricas mais complexas, para lidar em um ambiente distinto da sala de aula da universidade, com outros sujeitos da ação extensionista—docentes do ensino fundamental – que, ao mesmo tempo que já possuem experiência até em nível universitário, na Área da Educação, anseiam pela expertise e especificidade da formação na Área do Direito, em direitos humanos, para compreender temáticas transversais às disciplinas que ministram na escola. Isto exige maior preparação e contribui para que o pós-graduando seja iniciado no contexto de desenvolvimento de atividades de alto nível, junto a grupos universitários com formação superior. Esta situação já apresenta similaridade com a docência e as atividades profissionais em nível superior, para as quais os pós-graduandos são preparados.

Da mesma forma, os alunos da graduação realizam atividades lúdicas com estudantes do sexto ano do ensino fundamental, na escola, na presença de professor da escola – aquele cuja disciplina estava programada para o mesmo horário – garantindo o acompanhamento especializado em educação e a supervisão institucional da própria escola, que garante solução rápida e segura, para eventuais intercorrências disciplinares – que até o momento não foram registradas. Conquanto a preparação dos graduandos ocorra nas mesmas oficinas, na universidade, mantendo o mesmo nível de exigência de pesquisa e de formação, o grau de exigência dos sujeitos extensionistas – estudantes da escola – nas suas oficinas, é correspondentes à pré-adolescência e adolescência, que estão em formação de conceitos incipientes acerca de direitos humanos. Isto garante aos graduandos atender plenamente as expectativas da escola, que representa um ambiente distinto da sala de aula universitária, com desafios próprios, e propicia-lhes a ampliação de seus horizontes.

Os discentes da graduação e da pós-graduação estão interagindo e disseminando conhecimento científico, junto com docentes e alunos do ensino fundamental, através da aplicação prática de superação de deficiências que envolvem a rede de ensino, enquanto os beneficiários entram em contato com conteúdos de suma importância para sua formação pessoal e cidadã, rompendo barreiras preconceituosas, assim como promovendo maior reflexão acerca de temas recorrentes em seu contexto, muitas vezes expressos como formas de intolerância.

A formação complementar de todos os envolvidos e a propagação de uma cultura que respeite direitos humanos dentro e fora do ambiente escolar e universitário estão sendo conseqüências decorrentes da interação dos agentes oriundos da Universidade, com estudantes e professores do Ensino Fundamental, além dos colaboradores externos. Todos têm se tornado multiplicadores da cultura pré-violatória e da visibilização de violações de direitos humanos.

A integração dos graduandos e pós-graduandos, também, tem permitido a execução do projeto de extensão em consonância com o Plano Nacional de Educação, estabelecido pela Lei n. 10.172, de 9 de janeiro de 2001 (BRASIL, 2001), por implicar na reciclagem de conteúdos, previstos na Meta/Objetivo n. 12 da Educação Superior, que prevê a inclusão

> (...) nas diretrizes curriculares dos cursos de formação de docentes temas relacionados às problemáticas tratadas nos temas transversais, especialmente no que se refere à abordagem tais como: gênero, educação sexual, ética (justiça, diálogo, respeito mútuo, solidariedade e tolerância), pluralidade cultural, meio ambiente, saúde e temas locais.

Por outro lado, a integração dos graduandos e pós-graduandos tem observado o Plano Nacional de Extensão Universitária, na medida que tem cumprido a função de instrumentalizar o "(...) processo dialético de teoria/prática", e o "trabalho interdisciplinar que favorece a visão integrada do social" (FORPROEX, 2001).

A integração de graduandos e pós-graduandos na Extensão Universitária decorre da própria necessidade de aproximação do Fórum de Pró-Reitores de Extensão Universitária a outros fóruns, dentre os quais, o Fórum de Pró-Reitores de Pós-graduação, para articulação diante da indissociabilidade entre ensino, pesquisa e extensão.

A participação dos estudantes universitários, integrados na consecução da extensão universitária, em sintonia com o Plano Nacional de Extensão Universitária, amplia a dimensão da construção de sua cidadania e do seu reconhecimento, como está indicado pelo FORPROEX na Agenda de Compromissos Institucionais elencados na Carta de Goiania, aprovada por ocasião do XXXVI Encontro Nacional do Forproex, entre 16 e 19 de novembro de 2014, como Compromisso n. 6 (FORPROEX, 2014):

> A Extensão, ação acadêmica contributiva da formação profissional, construção e difusão do conhecimento, que amplia a participação do estudante na implementação das políticas públicas brasileiras, expondo-o ao diálogo com a sociedade diretamente implicada em suas ações, deve ser reconhecida e legitimada como tal...

Confirmando esta participação política, no projeto "Fundamentos da Cidadania para Professores e Alunos Fundamentais", os extensionistas, graduandos e pós-graduandos, também, contribuem para a implementação de ações programáticas do Terceiro Programa Nacional de Direitos Humanos, em cujo Terceiro Objetivo Estratégico da Diretriz n. 19, referente ao "Fortalecimento dos princípios da democracia e dos Direitos Humanos nos sistemas de educação básica, nas instituições de ensino superior e nas instituições formadoras.", em cuja ação prevista na letra "d" expressamente refere-se à extensão universitária (BRASIL, 2010 : pág. 197).

Considerações finais

Ao longo de 2016, foram realizadas oficinas preparatórias com a participação de docentes, pós-graduandos e graduandos da UNESP, no âmbito da execução do projeto de extensão "Fundamentos da Cidadania para Professores e Alunos Fundamentais: Construindo Cidadania e Reconhecimento", desenvolvendo pesquisas sobre temas concernentes a direitos humanos e, principalmente, formas de manifestação de intolerância na universidade e nas escolas do ensino fundamental, objetivando disseminar uma cultura pré-violatória dos direitos fundamentais.

Como conclusões, tem-se que a integração de graduandos e pós-graduandos é fundamental para as respectivas formações e, também, para a implementação da Política Nacional de Extensão Universitária e até mesmo do Terceiro Programa Nacional de Direitos Humanos, com a atuação junto a professores e estudantes de escola do ensino fundamental, com participação que valoriza o papel social da universidade, e amplia o conceito de ensino universitário para além da sala de aula.

O processo dialético teoria-prática, que representa a extensão universitária, estabelece oportunidades de formação dos extensionistas, na graduação e na pós-graduação, como cidadão críticos e conscientes da sua função social e que consideram as necessidades das pessoas em sociedade, comprometidos com a construção e transformação da realidade social, estabelecendo um recorte comprometido com os mais vulneráveis às violações dos direitos humanos, e com a disseminação de uma cultura pré-violatória.

Referências

BORGES, Paulo César Corrêa et. al. *A construção de noções de cidadania e direitos humanos com estudantes do ensino fundamental.* In. FONSECA, G.A; SILVA, M.P; GIOMETTI, A.B.R; COLOMBAROLI, A.C.M. Ensino e práticas pedagógicas na escola pública: experiências do núcleo de ensino, GINGA, NEACE. Franca-SP: UNESP:FCHS, 2013, p.49-57.

______. LEITE, T. S. C. . *Education as protection*: An experience of human rights education in the corners of Brazil. 2012. Disponível em: <http://isaconf.confex.com/isaconf/forum2012/webprogram/Paper27541.html>. Acesso em: março de 2016.

BORGES, Marina Soares Vital. Apreendendo à cidadania: Extensão universitária e direitos humanos. *Revista da Faculdade de Direito da UFPR.* Curitiba, v.43, n.0, 2005. Disponível em: <http://ojs.c3sl.ufpr.br/ ojs/index.php/ direito/ article/ view/ 7035>. Acesso em: abril de 2016. DOI: http:// dx.doi.org/10.5380%2Frfdufpr.v43i0.7035

BRASIL. Câmara dos Deputados. *Projeto de Lei n. 8.035.* Aprova o Plano Nacional de Educação para o decênio 2011-2020 e dá outras providências. Projetos de Leis e Outras Proposições. Disponível em:

<http://www.camara.gov.br/proposicoesWeb/fichadetramitacao?idProposicao=490116> Acesso em: março de 2016.

______. CAPES - Coordenação de Aperfeiçoamento de Pessoal de Nível Superior, Diretoria de Avaliação. *Documento de Área* – 2016.

______. CAPES - Coordenação de Aperfeiçoamento de Pessoal de Nível Superior, Diretoria de Avaliação. *Documento de Área* – 2013. Disponível em: <http://www.capes.gov.br/images/stories/download/avaliacaotrienal/Docs_de_area/Direito_doc_area_e_comissão_16out.pdf>. Acesso em: abril de 2016.

______. Congresso Nacional. *Lei no 9.394, de 20 de dezembro de 1996.* Estabelece as diretrizes e bases da educação nacional. Diário Oficial da União, de 23 de dezembro de 1996, p. 27.833. Disponível em: <http://portal.mec.gov.br/seed/arquivos/pdf/tvescola/leis/lein9394.pdf> Acesso em: março de 2016.

______. Congresso Nacional. *Lei no 10.172, de 9 de janeiro de 2001.* Aprova o Plano Nacional de Educação (PNE) e dá outras providências. Diário Oficial da União, de 10 de janeiro de 2001, p. 128. Disponível em: < http://www.planalto.gov.br/ccivil_03/leis/leis_2001/l10172.htm > Acesso em: março de 2016.

______. Congresso Nacional. *Lei n. 10.861, de 14 de abril de 2004.* Institui o Sistema Nacional de Avaliação da Educação Superior-SINAES e dá outras providências. Diário Oficial da União, de 15 de abril de 2004, p. 3. Disponível em: <http://portal.mec.gov.br/arquivos/pdf/leisinaes.pdf> Acesso em: março de 2016.

______. *Constituição* (1988). Constituição da República Federativa do Brasil. Texto consolidado até a Emenda Constitucional no 70 de 29 de março de 2012. Senado Federal. Disponível em: <http://www.senado.gov.br/legislacao/const/con1988/CON1988_29.03.2012/CON1988.pdf>. Acesso em: março de 2016.

______. Presidência da República. *Decreto n. 7.233, de 19 de julho de 2010.* Dispõe sobre procedimentos orçamentários e financeiros relacionados à autonomia universitária, e dá outras providências. Diário Oficial da União, de 20 de julho de 2010. Disponível em: <http://www.planalto.gov.br/ccivil_03/ Ato2007-2010/2010/Decreto/D7233.htm> Acesso em: março de 2016.

______. Secretaria de Direitos Humanos da Presidência da República. *Programa Nacional de Direitos Humanos* (PNDH-3). ver. e atual. Brasília : SEDH/PR, 2010.

CHAUÍ, Marilena. A Universidade operacional. *Folha de S. Paulo.* Caderno Mais, São Paulo, 09/05/1999.

DRUMOND, José Augusto. Resumo da Tese de Paulo Ernesto Diaz Rocha "Trajetórias e perspectivas da interdiciplinariedade ambiental na pós--ambiental, na pós-graduação brasileira.", *Ambiente & Sociedade*, 6.2 (2003). Disponível em: < http://www.scielo.br/pdf/%0D/asoc/v6n2/a10v06n2.pdf >. Acesso em: abril de 2016.

FORPROEX – Fórum de Pró-Reitores de Extensão das Universidades Públicas brasileiras. *O Plano Nacional de Extensão Universitária.* Ilhéus: Editus, 2001. (Extensão Universitária, v.1). Disponível em: <https://www.ufmg.br/proex/renex/documentos/Colecao-Extensao-Universitaria/01-Plano-Nacional-Extensao/Plano-nacional-de-extensao-universitaria-editado.pdf>. Acesso: abril de 2016.

______. *Avaliação Nacional da Extensão Universitária.* Brasília: MEC/SESu; Paraná: UFPR; Ilhéus, BA: UESC, 2001a. (Extensão Universitária, v.3).

______. *Extensão Universitária:* Organização e Sistematização. Belo Horizonte: COOPMED, 2007. (Coleção Extensão Universitária; v.6).

______. *Política Nacional de Extensão Universitária.* Manaus : FORPROEX, 2012. Disponível em: <http://www.renex.org.br/documentos/2012-07-13-Politica-Nacional-de-Extensao.pdf>. Acesso em: abril de 2016.

______. *Carta de Goiânia.* XXXVI Encontro Nacional do FORPROEX - Fórum de Pró-Reitores de Extensão das Instituições de Educação

Superior Públicas Brasileiras. 2014. Disponível em: <https://www.ufmg.br/proex/renex/index.php?option=com_content&view=article&id=148%3Acarta-de-goiania&Itemid=20>. Acesso em: abril de 2016.

LUZ, Araci Asnelli; PERES, Emerson Luiz. Reflexões sobre a extensão universitária e a participação da psicologia num programa de prevenção ao abuso de álcool e outras drogas. *Interação*, Curitiba, v. 1, p. 179-192, jan./dez. 1997. Disponível em: < http://ojs.c3sl.ufpr.br/ojs/index.php/%EE%80%80psicologia%EE%80%81/article/viewFile/7641/5449>. Acesso em: abril/2016.

MICHELOTTO, Regina Maria. *A Liberação do acesso e a extensão como estratégias de democratização da universidade:* A experiência da Itália e do Brasil. 1999. 194 f. Tese (Doutorado em Educação) – Universidade Federal de São Carlos, São Carlos, 1999. Disponível em: < http://www.nupe.ufpr.br/regina.pdf>. Acesso: Abril de 2016.

NASCIMENTO, Cristiano Santos do. Autonomia Universitária e a Constituição Federal do Brasil. *Universo Jurídico*, Juiz de Fora, ano XI, 20 de fev. de 2008. Disponivel em: <http://uj.novaprolink.com.br/doutrina/4918/Autonomia_Universitaria_e_a_Constituicao_Federal_do_Brasil >. Acesso em: 02 de mai. de 2016.

NOGUEIRA, M. D. P. (Org.) *Extensão Universitária:* diretrizes conceituais e políticas. Belo Horizonte: PROEX/UFMG; O Fórum, 2000.

______. *Políticas de Extensão Universitária Brasileira.* Belo Horizonte: Editora UFMG, 2005.

PINTO FERREIRA. *Comentários à Constituição Brasileira.* Art.s, 193 a 245, ADCT - Art., 1° a 70 - EC.1/92, 2/92, 3/93, 4/93, ECR-1/94, 2/94, 31/94, 41/94, 5/94, 6/94. São Paulo : Editora Saraiva, 1995. 7. Vol.

RENEX. *Plano Nacional de Extensão Universitária.* Coleção Extensão Universitária, n. 1. Disponível em: <http://www.renex.org.br/documentos/Colecao-Extensao-Universitaria/01-Plano-Nacional-

Extensao/Plano-nacional-de-extensao-universitaria-editado. pdf>. Acesso: abril de 2016.

SANTOS, Patrícia Elaine Pereira dos. *Extensão universitária e saberes mobilizados no ensino superior:* Um olhar para os documentos "oficiais". 2011. Disponível em: <http://www.anped11.uerj.br/texto_Patricia. pdf>. Acesso em: abril de 2016.

SANTOS, B. S. *A Universidade no século XXI:* para uma reforma democrática e emancipatória da Universidade. São Paulo: Cortez, 2004. (Coleção Questões da Nossa Época, v. 120).

SANTOS, W. G. *A Trágica Condição da Política Social.* In: ABRANCHES, Sérgio Henrique et. al. (Orgs.). Política Social e Combate à Pobreza. Rio de Janeiro: Jorge Zahar Editora, 1987, p. 33-63. SEN, Amartya. Desenvolvimento como liberdade. São Paulo: Companhia das Letras, 2010.

VIEIRA, G. T. *et al.* A utilização da idéia de "empoderamento"em políticas públicas e ações da sociedade civil. *Cadernos de Gestão Social,* Salvador, v.2, n.1, p.135-148, set.-dez. 2009.

Sobre os autores

Caio Gracco Pinheiro Dias: Professor de Direito Internacional da Faculdade de Direito de Ribeirão Preto da Universidade de São Paulo. Doutor em Direito Internacional pela Faculdade de Direito da Universidade de São Paulo (USP).

Daniel Campos de Carvalho: Professor Adjunto do Curso de Relações Internacionais da Escola Paulista de Política, Economia e Negócios (EPPEN) da Universidade Federal de São Paulo (UNIFESP). Doutor em Direito Internacional pela Faculdade de Direito da Universidade de São Paulo (USP).

David Held: Mestre do University College e Professor de Política e Relações Internacionais da Universidade de Durham, Reino Unido. Doutor em Ciência Política pelo MIT (Massachusetts Institute of Technology) /EUA.

David Succi Júnior: Mestrando em Relações Internacionais no Programa de Pós-Graduação em Relações Internacionais San Tiago Dantas – UNESP-UNICAMP-PUC-SP, pesquisador do Grupo de Estudos em Defesa e Segurança Internacional, GEDES/UNESP. Bolsista CNPq.

Fernanda Mello Sant'Anna: Professora de Relações Internacionais da Universidade Estadual Paulista "Júlio de Mesquita Filho" (UNESP) – Campus de Franca – SP. Doutora em Geografia Humana pela Universidade de São Paulo (USP).

Fernando Adolfo Iglesias: Professor do UCES e da Universidade de Belgrano, Argentina. Presidente del Consejo del World Federalist Movement.

Giovanni Allegretti: Pesquisador Sênior do Centro de Estudos Sociais da Universidade de Coimbra, Portugal. Doutor em Planejamento Urbano, Territorial e Ambiental pela Universidade de Florença, Itália.

Guilherme Pinho Ribeiro: Bacharel e Mestrando em Direito pela Universidade Estadual Paulista "Júlio de Mesquita Filho" (UNESP) – Campus de Franca – SP.

José Carlos de Oliveira: Professor de Direito Administrativo da Universidade Estadual Paulista "Júlio de Mesquita Filho" (UNESP) – Campus de Franca – SP. Doutor em Direito pela Universidade Estadual Paulista "Júlio de Mesquita Filho" (UNESP).

José Duarte Neto: Professor de Direito Constitucional e Direitos Humanos da Universidade Estadual Paulista "Júlio de Mesquita Filho" (UNESP) – Campus de Franca – SP. Doutor em Direito do Estado pela Faculdade de Direito da Universidade de São Paulo (USP).

Júlia Abdalla Lunardi: Graduada em Relações Internacionais pela Universidade Estadual Paulista "Júlio de Mesquita Filho" (UNESP) – Campus de Franca – SP. Foi bolsista pela FAPESP, desenvolvendo a pesquisa "O papel das energias renováveis na geopolítica energética da América do Sul".

Liz Marina Tamião Santana: Discente de Graduação em Direito da Universidade Estadual Paulista "Júlio de Mesquita Filho" (UNESP) - Campus de Franca - SP.

Marcela Benhossi: Bacharel em Relações Internacionais pela Universidade Federal de São Paulo (UNIFESP).

Maria Galleno de Souza Oliveira: Professora, consultora e advogada. Doutora em Sociologia pela Universidade Estadual Paulista "Júlio de Mesquita Filho" (UNESP).

Maria Hylma Salgado Alcaraz: Pesquisadora Colaboradora do Centro Interdisciplinar de Pesquisas sobre Direitos Humanos da Universidade do Minho, Portugal. Doutora em Direito pela Universidade de Vigo, Espanha.

Murilo Gaspardo: Professor de Teoria do Estado e Ciência Política da Universidade Estadual Paulista "Júlio de Mesquita Filho" (UNESP) - Campus de Franca - SP. Doutor em Direito do Estado pela Faculdade de Direito da Universidade de São Paulo (USP).

Paulo César Corrêa Borges: Professor de Direito Penal da Universidade Estadual Paulista "Júlio de Mesquita Filho" (UNESP) - Campus de Franca - SP. Doutor em Direito pela UNESP. Pós-doutor em Direito pela Universidade de Sevilla.

Paulo César de Oliveira Borges: Discente de Graduação do Curso de Direito da Universidade Estadual Paulista "Júlio de Mesquita Filho" (UNESP) - Campus de Franca - SP.

Regina Claudia Laisner: Professora de Teoria Política e Políticas Públicas na Universidade Estadual Paulista "Júlio de Mesquita Filho"

(UNESP) – Campus de Franca – SP. Doutora em Ciência Política pela Universidade de São Paulo (USP).

Samuel Alves Soares: Professor de Relações Internacionais da Universidade Estadual Paulista "Júlio de Mesquita Filho" (UNESP) – Campus de Franca – SP. Doutor em Ciência Política pela Universidade de São Paulo (USP).

Alameda nas redes sociais:
Site: www.alamedaeditorial.com.br
Facebook.com/alamedaeditorial/
Twitter.com/editoraalameda
Instagram.com/editora_alameda/

Esta obra foi impressa em São Paulo no verão de 2017. No texto foi utilizada a fonte Minion Pro em corpo 10,25 e entrelinha de 15 pontos.